AMAZING RACERS

AMAZING RACERS

THE STORY OF AMERICA'S GREATEST RUNNING TEAM

AND ITS REVOLUTIONARY COACH

MARC BLOOM

PEGASUS BOOKS

NEW YORK LONDON

AMAZING RACERS

Pegasus Books Ltd.
148 W 37th Street, 13th Floor
New York, NY 10018

Copyright © 2019 by Marc Bloom

First Pegasus Books edition August 2019

Interior design by Maria Fernandez

Library of Congress Cataloging-in-Publication Data is available.

ISBN: 978-1-64313-079-8

10 9 8 7 6 5 4 3 2 1

Printed in the United States of America
Distributed by W. W. Norton & Company

For the young: the audacious

cross-country runners of

Fayetteville-Manlius, and

my grandchildren—Jordana,

Max, Jade and Levi—

truth seekers all

CONTENTS

PROLOGUE

BROADWAY BOUND

At the camp, we learned a lot about love. That's what brings all of us together as a team, the runners and coaches. Each person has that bond of love. That's what we use to run hard.

—Jared Burdick, Fayetteville-Manlius cross-country runner

I n the fall of 2004, on a pleasant Saturday at Van Cortlandt Park in the Bronx, I learned of some powerful new ideas in the training of young runners. These ideas heralded a new era in the development of high school cross-country teams, the foundation of the sport. The significance of these bold ideas was so deep and far reaching that they would alter the nurturing of children into teenagers and teenagers into young adults. While the ideas grew out of an athletic commitment, they were intended to create a new person first, a new way of looking at the self, the team, the land, the community. With the forming of this new athlete—a new boy, a new girl—a dramatic transformation would occur: indeed, a revolution.

And when these boys and girls ran, when they won again and again, when they were so far superior to all opposition, separating themselves into a realm all their own with a mystique they carry to the present day, they became . . . *revolutionaries.*

The ideas were conveyed to me that October day by the athletes' coach, Bill Aris, after his high school boys team, Fayetteville-Manlius, from the Syracuse area, had achieved a performance never before thought possible in a cross-country competition. Breakthroughs usually have some finely wrought essence to them, a peak built on inner strength and perhaps a touch of daring risk. As I found out that day, Bill had the goods.

Near the finish of the Manhattan Invitational's high school two-and-half mile racecourse, a hilly pathway used by runners since the late nineteenth century, I corralled Aris and two of his boys after the race for an interview. I was putting out my *Harrier* publication on cross-country running and needed to report on how a team that few people knew about could not only defeat but vanquish Christian Brothers Academy (CBA) of New Jersey in the most important regular-season cross-country event in the United States.

At the time, I lived just a few miles down the road from CBA in Monmouth County. I'd seen the Colts run roughshod over state opposition for decades and earn national prominence just about every year for their distance-running prowess in both track and cross-country. The previous fall season, in 2003, CBA, winner of thirteen New Jersey State Meet of Champions cross-country titles, captured the Eastern States Championship, held at Van Cortlandt, by over one hundred points. In my *Harrier* national team rankings at the end of 2003, I had CBA at eleventh in the country. And they promised to be every bit as good, if not better, in 2004.

So how could a bunch of young men who had not done a single thing of note in the previous spring's track season suddenly, a few months later, demolish CBA? Fayetteville's race that day at Van Cortlandt was like a ball club from the cellar rising up and winning the World Series. Or like a marathoner from Liechtenstein winning the Olympics.

There was just no precedent for what F-M, as they would come to be called, did on those Bronx hills. It made no sense. Running was a science. Training was progressive. Racing was logical. Boys were boys.

Something new had to be responsible. But what?

We—the running community, from name-brand coaches and exercise physiologists on down—thought we knew everything there was to know about running. This was the twenty-first century, after all. We had every technological convenience. We could size up runners in the lab and come up with acute subtleties on how they should run every mile for optimal performance. We attended clinics by specialists using PowerPoint displays to show how much oxygen was consumed at every running pace and how slight variations in arm swing or hip tilt meant seconds faster or slower in competition.

We knew that the necessities of racing the two-and-a-half mile cross-country race on the undulating Van Cortlandt Park course—a near sprint on the opening flats for a quarter-mile or so, good rhythm on the bouncy Cowpath, unrelenting toughness on the steep Back Hills, freewheeling fearlessness around Roller Derby Turn on the downhills, and a final, furious kick on the long home straight—depended on this:

You did your summer base work, putting hundreds of miles in your legs. As fall approached, you added long tempo runs, like hard six-milers, and long repeat work, like six times a thousand meters. You did a weekly long run of ten to fifteen miles at a steady pace, building your aerobic reserves. Once racing began, you added some shorter, quicker work to the mix. And all along you did hills, every hill you could find, while your quadriceps muscles strengthened with the hardness of a fully inflated bicycle tire. These were the staples. Every good coach knew them. Every good team did them. CBA did them. The CBA head coach, Tom Heath, lived by them.

The Colts had made the most of their close proximity to Holmdel Park, the New Jersey state meet site with its abundantly hilly trails, most notably the feared "Bowl," and all manner of terrain for every type of workout. Over the years, Heath had devised training that had become legendary for its rigor, and any young Colt who could handle it was, almost by divine providence, a candidate for the school's vaunted varsity cross-country lineup.

∽

Cross-country was not for the weak of heart or muscle or spirit. It was—and is—a consuming endeavor. In the high school ranks, wiry, freckle-faced boys with the small, innocent features of a Norman Rockwell painting would become ferocious competitors, astounding parents who never dreamed their sons had that kind of capacity, waiting to rise up with volcanic force, waiting for a coach—the seer who knew how to bring it out. Whether his style was humorous or full of bluster, whether he was a true-blue runner himself or had a spreading girth, the coach would be the one to push that boy into manhood and up to the heavens.

At CBA—an all-boys private school with no football team to get in the way of cross-country recruitment—Heath fashioned a commanding character all his own. A boy did not dare let him down. A boy did not dare fail to keep up. It was not by happenstance that by 2004, CBA had surpassed three hundred straight dual-meet victories (one team versus another) in a national-record streak that has continued to build, unbroken, to the present day.

On this Saturday at "Vannie," when Fayetteville lined up with CBA in the Manhattan Varsity C race, CBA was like Goldman Sachs and Fayetteville a feisty entrepreneurial start-up trying to establish credibility in a mergers-and-acquisitions fight with the big boys. The previous week, Fayetteville had set a team time record at the McQuaid Invitational, New York's largest upstate meet, in Rochester. The course, Genesee Valley Park, had no hills to speak of. CBA was coming off a victory in a statewide event in New Jersey, the Shore Track Coaches Association meet, at Holmdel Park. While the Colts were as well known as Yankees sluggers stepping up to the plate, Fayetteville brought an element of mystery to Van Cortlandt. The F-M runners were from the boonies, or so many thought. Manlius, where the school was located, was one of those upstate towns you heard about only when some dark crime was committed, as in a Joyce Carol Oates novel. Could these boys handle the "showtime" factor of the big city (something that would come back knocking on Fayetteville's door at the end of the season)? Rochester was off-off-Broadway. Van Cortlandt *was* Broadway. Many cross-country fans were just hoping the upstate boys would not embarrass themselves.

I waited on the sidelines near the finish for the Varsity C boys to come flying down the long home straight and into the finish chute. The Manhattan event, begun in 1974, featured thirty-six high school races that went off every twelve minutes—varsity, JV, and freshmen races for boys and girls—with more than ten thousand participants from upward of fifteen states including, almost every year, a team or two from California. At the time, the seven boys varsity races were set up more or less equally, with the top teams spread out. But in 2004, Heath, hearing about Fayetteville, asked officials to place CBA in its race to teach the upstate boys a lesson.

In high school cross-country, the Manhattan meet had become a must-do midseason event for top-level teams from the Northeast and beyond. Van Cortlandt Park was to cross-country what Boston was to the marathon. Even though the meet offered few creature comforts—parking was terrible, visiting teams had to find a hotel miles away—the park did lay out the New York City urban running habitat for all it was worth.

City kids from the outer boroughs hauling their backpacks from Brighton Beach or Forest Hills stepped off the number 1 subway line at the New York transit system's last stop, 242nd Street and Broadway, at the foot of the park's grounds. It was as far north as you could get in the city before dipping into suburban Westchester County. Runners from places like Palos Verdes, California, looking every bit the young Beach Boys, must have had some stories to tell back home after seeing the Riverdale-Fieldston North Bronx mix of Irish rugby players, muddy calves bulging, and pious Jews, dressed in top hats and their Saturday finest, strolling down Broadway.

The Manhattan course finish at the time, hugging the periphery of the park's woods across from Broadway, presented a theatrical set piece with every race bursting with drama. With a final six hundred yards to cover, athletes had to time their kicks in stages, holding their most explosive reserves till the last strides. At the same time, the runners had to gauge their opposition, using tactical cunning to inch ahead, break a man, and gain valuable points across the line.

The drama was amplified by the curvature of the homestretch, concealing runners to the finish-area crowd until the end, the last breathless breaths. The first runner would usually come across in about twelve-and-a-half minutes, but for twelve minutes there could be no calculation of team victory. In the last few, overwhelming seconds, runners could move back and forth, their last energies spent, and scores could change. Prior to the advent of chip timing and video recording, finish officials managing the procession of heaving bodies into the chute had to be alert to prevent a runner from inadvertently collapsing in front of an opponent who'd crossed the line ahead of him.

In all its simplicity, its honesty, its accountability, it was beautiful: the cinder path, the roped chutes, the mundane finish tape, devoured orange slices from the coach's bag. And Van Cortlandt itself: this was the place—unadorned, horse crap in the hills—where running reputations were made.

In 2004, the Manhattan results, as a measure of excellence, would be felt well beyond the Bronx. That season, the Nike Cross Nationals* high school championships began in Portland, Oregon. Leading teams, looking to meet top-ranked opposition, did all they could to be considered for selection to the all-expenses-paid event, which would invite the top two boys teams and top two girls teams in eight geographical regions, plus at-large teams, to a 5k

---

* Nike's championship event was called Nike Team Nationals (or NTN) until 2008, when the name changed to Nike Cross Nationals (NXN) after individual qualifiers were added. For consistency, I refer to it as Nike Cross Nationals, or NXN, throughout the book.

championship at the end of the fall season. Each of the boys and girls fields would have twenty teams from across the nation that first year. I headed up the event's rankings committee of cross-country veterans and meet officials to determine the selections. While the emphasis was placed on late-season results, especially state championships, the Manhattan standings would be factored into the mix.

∾

The advent of NXN was a Disneyland for elite running teams like CBA or York of Illinois or Mead of Washington state or The Woodlands of Texas. Schools searched for the best competition they could find beyond their state borders, looking for a high national ranking. With my *Harrier* publication putting a spotlight on high school cross-country, a national community had been built, and top teams could choose from a growing number of events set up to draw competitive race fields.

In the fall of 2004, my preseason rankings had York and The Woodlands one-two in the country. In my regional rankings, I had CBA first in the Northeast with Fayetteville fifth. In New York, I had Lockport, from the Buffalo area, first, and Fayetteville second. The Manhattan meet looked to give CBA a nice opportunity to stretch its legs before hunkering down for nationals.

And then they came, with spikes flying and arms pumping: the Varsity C boys hauling down the ribbon of cinder. Spectators looked for the midnight blue of CBA. Instead they saw the forest green of Fayetteville-Manlius. One, two, three, four, five. All F-M. All in a row, close together, as one. First, second, third, fourth, fifth. A perfect score in cross-country: fifteen points. Tommy Gruenewald, Owen Kimple, Jared Burdick, John Heron, Andrew McCann. They had achieved running's version of a perfect game.

Every cross-country coach falls asleep with this dreamy image of perfection. All five scorers in unison—a reflection of more than just a team and a race, but a goosebumps feeling that speaks to community, sacrifice, and, to some, a kind of love. After all, do you know what it took to get here?

It was a sight to behold, an ideal to be cherished. Right then and there, in those few seconds of green flashing to the finish in a collective wh-o-o-o-sh, it was evident something new and fresh had been discovered. I absorbed it as a spiritual endowment. Van Cortlandt had done it again.

That spot had been my finish too. Oh, the relief that chute offered when I tumbled into it as a New York City high school runner in the early 1960s. While struggling to achieve "scrub" status in cross-country—I had a great excuse, our team barely trained fifteen miles a week—somehow I found honor in it, a whiff of nobility. The extremes of effort struck me as our little secret, "our" being the family of runners tough enough to try hard at something barely known to the outside world. I'm sure the kids at my high school, Sheepshead Bay of Brooklyn, knew more about chess than they did about cross-country. To be honest, I kind of liked that. I always felt comfortable as an outsider.

When, soon after at the age of eighteen, I broke into the *New York Times* and started covering cross-country for the sports pages, I was usually the only reporter present for the fall season at Van Cortlandt. At Vannie, from the midsixties to the late seventies, I *was* the press section. I would set my Olivetti Lettera 32 manual typewriter on a picnic bench near the finish area. Parks department barriers cordoned off my little private space. If it rained, I worked in my car. I had a special parking pass.

The more I took ownership of cross-country, the more I could share in its sublime spectacle and be a part of some heroic and communal mission while attempting to climb the journalistic ladder. I looked around and saw no cross-country publication, so I started *Harrier*. It became running's indie.

∽

When the Manhattan excitement ebbed, I found Aris and spoke with him briefly. He said something about "Stotan" ideals. My heart thumped because what I thought I heard related to ideals of my own that I tried to follow but that seemed, at times, all too elusive. I asked him to have a couple of his runners join us for an interview.

A boys time under thirteen minutes at Van Cortlandt was considered the elite level. The F-M times[*]: 12:41.90 for Gruenewald, 12:48.40 for Kimple, 12:49.50 for Burdick, 12:50.70 for Heron, 12:53.20 for McCann. The compression—the time from the first to fifth runner—was 11.3 seconds. This "spread" was the gold standard of team excellence. A team could have one or two good runners, or even four, but if all five scorers were not in tight formation, nothing big could be achieved.

---

[*]   Cross-country race times are typically rounded "up." A 15:24.07, for example, becomes 15:25 officially. In some instances, because of records or meet custom, I refer to performances in tenths or hundredths.

Who were these guys—these revolutionaries? For one thing, they were young. Gruenewald was a sophomore. Kimple, Heron, and McCann were juniors. Burdick was the only senior. For another, not one of them had qualified for the New York State track and field championships four months earlier.

Yet, their aggregate times at Van Cortlandt produced a scoring average of 12:48.74, breaking a record that had stood for thirty-three years. I had seen the former record set back in 1971. It was 12:53.56 by St. Joseph's of Buffalo. I could recall the St. Joe's team. It was not the tight pack of F-M but paced by two front-runners, twins named Trammell, with a bit of a gap to the next three scorers. With all the great runners who'd raced Van Cortlandt in the three decades since, there was still not a single team that had gotten close to the St. Joe's record.

Even CBA, to that point, had never broken thirteen minutes for a team average. Following Fayetteville on that 2004 day, CBA placed second with an average time of 13:20.64. That degree of separation from the rest of the field—thirty-two seconds per man—would become an F-M hallmark in the years to come, not just among the boys but even more so among the girls.

∽

As I sat on a bench with Aris and the two boys, cocaptains Kimple and Burdick, we were a few strides from where the opening flats fed into the Cowpath that linked to the first of the hills. When I ran Vannie, my coach would yell at me, "C'mon Bloom, blossom . . . !" but the ensuing ascent was like a fraternity hazing that wouldn't stop. Still, I had acquired some strange sense that the "pain" of running did me some good, and that running would be my only truth.

∽

Seated, Kimple and McCann wore T-shirts signifying their story. On the front, the shirts were adorned with STOTAN and an image of the great Australian miler, Herb Elliott. The back read, PAIN IS THE PURIFIER.

Aris went into more detail on the Stotan concept, originated in the 1950s and '60s by Elliott's coach, Percy Cerutty. Aris said he was intrigued by Cerutty's approach, which Aris interpreted as a natural but rigorous value system that stressed a pure and healthy lifestyle. The term *Stotan* combined "Stoic" and "Spartan." The T-shirt's bold claim about pain—a philosophy, really—had come from Cerutty, the coaching rebel of his time.

Aris told me then, "Stotan refers to the unflinching, dedicated pursuit of excellence, the stoic belief married with a spartan existence, of taking on all challenges and desiring excellence. That's what our team embodies."

Aris spoke of an F-M training camp that summer in the Adirondacks attended by the boys as a pivotal team bonding and Stotan learning experience. Kimple added, "Now we refer back to camp and apply it to everything we do. It taught us a lot about focusing on what we want as a team." Burdick agreed: "At the camp, we learned a lot about love. That's what brings all of us together as a team, the runners and the coaches. Each person has that bond of love. That's what we use to race hard."

When a teenage boy could talk proudly about his love for his teammates, and with someone he's just met, well, I was won over right away and convinced that something special was going on at Fayetteville-Manlius. As F-M broke away for the trip home, Aris left me with this: "I learned that anything is possible if you have your heart and mind and soul in it. I'd felt that. And it was affirmed today."

ℰℴ

I vowed to find out more. I was filled with questions. I'd met Aris. I'd met the boys. They'd run an historic team performance. I would make F-M number one in the next week's national rankings.

But this was one race. Could they do it again? I thought about Stotan—stoic and spartan, love and pain. Team. Excellence. Academically, it all made sense. On an emotional level, I wondered if these ideas, at least what I'd heard that day, could really explain the dramatic breakthrough witnessed at Van Cortlandt Park. There had to be more to it, didn't there? I felt like a student in Stotan 101 who had homework to do. I kept pondering the word *discovery*, the idea that Bill Aris and his boys had made a discovery.

What could that discovery be? Did Aris find a new energy source—something deep in the human cell or soul—for running? A new motivational strategy? New ways to teach running and spur young runners on? Could it be a training method—a new way to take the body, and mind, to the limit? Didn't we already know every conceivable training method? Discovering a new training method would be like discovering a new way to learn how to read, or write, or sing, or bring up a child. It would be experienced so broadly it would be like a new way to *live*.

I'd never met Cerutty or knew much about him. But in an ironic twist of fate—and how fateful the F-M saga seemed to be at every turn—a few months earlier I'd spoken with Herb Elliott in a phone interview from Australia. I was writing a series of pre-Olympic articles for *Runner's World* in advance of that summer's Athens Games, and Elliott was quite willing to give Cerutty full credit for his 1960 Olympic 1500-meter victory in Rome in world record time.

Elliott, sixty-six when we spoke, gave me the skinny on Cerutty's insistence on excellence and his idiosyncratic personality. Elliott spoke of the need to think beyond one's horizons, and, as an athlete, to explore mind, body, and spirit, just as Bill Aris had said at Van Cortlandt Park. Soon I began to appreciate the qualities of the Stotan ideals and see how those ideals could resonate with the young runners at Fayetteville-Manlius.

When I did, I arrived at the view that Aris's breakthrough was as much a belief system as a training system.

∞

After 2004 my relationship with Aris grew. We did more interviews for *Harrier*. We spent quality time at Nike Cross Nationals every December. I was keen to observe his athletes and saw in them, both on and off the racecourse, an aura. They radiated qualities of awareness and maturity rare in high school students. They were not kids trying to be adults. They were kids trying to be the best they could be.

From that year on, the F-M boys accumulated the best overall showing at Nationals of any school in the country. When the F-M girls learned the Stotan ways and demonstrated superiority over their opposition at a level never before seen in the sport, I knew I had to embark on something more comprehensive in my accounts of the team. After the girls' 2010 victory by almost sixty seconds per girl over the next two teams in the field—a performance worthy of young runners from Kenya or Ethiopia—I wrote a long feature in *Harrier*, trying to shed light on the phenomenon. No matter what the conditions—mud, snow, freezing rain—after each race the girls stripped off their spikes and socks and did a set of fast strides in their bare feet.

At once cleansing and audacious, the ritual was an affirmation of Stotan teamwork and a pledge to stand united against all challenges. Back on the Nike campus, these athletes, in the center of attention, admired by many, envied by some, carried themselves with poise and humility. Running royalty, yes, but also role models for any young person seeking higher ground.

The F-M girls also represented Aris's commitment to gender equity. As Aris says, he coaches *one* team of athletes, not separate boys and girls squads. From the outset, dismissing what he saw around him, Aris would not let his girls be thought of as "ornaments." Every F-M girl I've spoken with over the years has linked that equality to her success.

The girls' success also was a triumph over female development conflicts found in running and other sports. Teenage runners, growing from girls into young women while training at peak levels, must overcome a complex web of physical, emotional, social, and cultural issues that can all too often lead to a youngster's demise. At Fayetteville-Manlius, the team's decade-long supremacy—with girls from thirteen to eighteen years old—yielded questions on how Aris tried to keep girls healthy and whole while they were in the throes of body image conflicts, sexual awakening, and, as the author Paul Auster put it, "the never-ending torment of being young."

I would soon see how those girls, eager for spirit and toughness when first in Aris's grasp, would find a new way to live through running—how they embraced a new pathway to excellence. Sports scientists claim that even the world's best runners rarely put forth an effort equal to what their bodies can truly achieve. Coaches urge their athletes: "You always have 20 percent more to give." Few runners really believe that; fewer still act on it.

But at Fayetteville-Manlius High School, as four-time national championship team member Jenna Farrell told me one day at the team's Syracuse-area training site, "We live in that 20 percent."

In my half century as a journalist in the running field, I had never seen anything like it: not the supremacy or mentoring style, the training approach; not the enriching wholeness or transformative impact. I had traveled the country and the world, been privileged to see runners in all their glory, kept a close eye on girls' development, and been credited with helping to elevate high school cross-country to its rightful place in the running landscape. I don't think I had ever been more intrigued by a coach, a team, and its athletes.

In December 2014, after the F-M boys won their first NXN championship to go along with the girls' eighth victory, in a sweep of the national events, the time had come to tell the F-M story. Meeting with Aris and speaking with his athletes, I set out to try and answer the question that had been asked for more than a decade:

How do they *do* it?

AMAZING RACERS

1

SHARED SUFFERING

When you're in pain and breathing hard, you know your teammates are suffering just as much as you are. If I wasn't running with my teammates, I would not enjoy the feeling I get from hard distance running nearly as much.

—*Jenna Farrell, Fayetteville-Manlius cross-country runner*

2014 Starting Line

For Bill Aris, the drama had been building for weeks and months, even years. Never lacking confidence as an outsider, Aris walked around the lustrous, indoor Athletes' Village at the 2014 national high school cross-country championships—Nike Cross Nationals, in Portland, Oregon—not knowing what to do. It was race day, December 5, and Aris was not one to mingle with other coaches, especially before competition. With his familiar stick in his hand, a rod—a few of his runners said he gave off the aura of God—Aris paced the carpeted facility that Nike had fashioned with team dressing rooms and stretching mats and massage benches on which athletes could seek repose for brief rest or contemplation. Aris took note of the benches.

Aris, fifty-nine, had left the Fayetteville runners to themselves to warm up on the grounds of the race site, Glendoveer Golf Course, a new course from the event's first ten years. The girls race would be run first, at 10:05; the boys would run at 11:35. Both races were five thousand meters.

With his emotions wild and discordant with the opportunity his teenagers had for an unprecedented sweep of the national team championships, Aris tuned in to himself and the million-and-one thoughts pouring through his mind: what he'd told the kids in their shake-out run in the darkness that morning, what he forgot to tell them, some quote from Aristotle maybe, or a line from Pink Floyd, or that point about nature from Percy Cerutty. Or did he need to repeat his lecture about selflessness or humility, or about conquering race pain—your best friend, actually, something to covet and embrace, deny and destroy all at once. There were too many ideas, each a paradox, each a pathway to transforming the teenager—boy or girl—on how to run, how to live.

"It seems crazy to anyone outside the program, how coach Aris talks about pain," said Jenna Farrell, a junior who followed her two older brothers onto the team and was competing in her fourth straight national championship in 2014. "How pain is so detrimental to others but a positive thing to us. It's just amazing. He calls pain your 'constant companion as a distance runner.' If you're not feeling pain, you're not working hard enough."

Jenna took those messages as a spiritual commandment. "The biggest thing I get out of it," she said, "is when you're in pain and breathing hard, you know your teammates are suffering just as much as you are. If I wasn't running with my teammates, I would not enjoy the feeling I get from hard distance running nearly as much. We share in the suffering."

With her brothers' influence and family's immersion in the team's Stotan lifestyle of purity, selflessness, and healthful living—embracing old-hat values and disdaining modernity and its flaws—Jenna felt the team's touchstones from her first strides. As a freshman in the fall of 2012, she spent up to four and a half hours a day for two months at a YMCA doing cross-training—swimming, bicycling, and using an elliptical machine—while stress fractures in the first and second metatarsal bones in her left foot healed. "I never lost sight of what I was working for," she told me.

The next season, as a sophomore, her friendship with an older teammate, Alana Pearl, then a senior, grew into a sisterly reliance. They shared the same ideas on hard work and meeting the obligation of holding teammates accountable and being accountable themselves. Accountability was a big F-M commandment. Together the girls overcame their fears of submitting to pain, marshaling a strength they would come to realize stood for life and its grandeur, wonder, promise.

Jenna and Alana were not great runners by nature. They did not stand out for their pure speed or graceful stride. They did not have lithe bodies that seemed ordained for distance running but rather a fuller, more long-lasting athleticism forged by healthy eating and patient progress that Aris insisted on.

At Fayetteville-Manlius, the young athletes saw something attainable through a communion that was new and fresh and had a culture unto itself. "Our team is full of average runners," said Jenna, "but when we run together, we can be great. We run *for* each other. That's what makes us different than other teams. Running can seem like an individual sport, but we channel it into team success. Having goals of personal glory is looked down upon."

For the past decade, since he began to adapt seemingly primitive training ideas and a philosophy unearthed from the sands of southeastern Australia, challenging high school runners, and himself, to live in a world of nobility all their own, Bill Aris has tried to wipe away and bury teenage glorification—enablement, entitlement—perhaps never to be seen again on the foot paths at Fayetteville-Manlius.

"Entitlement leads to enablement, which is crippling and ultimately produces dependence," Aris says with a Bernie Sanders growl, "whereas empowerment leads to enrichment, which leads to independence and freedom. You can stand on your own two feet by working hard and being held accountable, and make something of your life."

While the villages of Fayetteville and Manlius that make up the suburban Syracuse school district of Fayetteville-Manlius are not wealthy enclaves (the hamlet of Manlius and the Village of Manlius are within the larger Town of Manlius), they have elements of privilege that, in Aris's view, often undermine teenage well-being and productiveness. "We have a lot of kids who are very comfortable living on the silver spoon, not having to lift a finger. Dabbling, playing, or, as I like to say, participating. I don't want participants. I want contributors."

In running lore, it is understood that a tough, threadbare upbringing can breed distance runners, who need only running shoes and some coaching to bring them out of subsistence and into the sunlight. Hence, one reason for the success of the East Africans; or, as we've seen across the American west, Native American runners, many living in the throes of the reservation, and Latinos, one generation away from the flight of parents across the southern border.

At Fayetteville-Manlius, Aris has undertaken a different mission. He has attempted to save white suburban kids with money in their pockets from emotional ennui, from the pernicious technoentertainment teenage culture, and give them instead what he believes they already possess deep within: a wholesome beauty and sense of rightness that can be distilled by, and for, running. Bill Aris is Holden Caulfield on the cross-country meadow with his crane-like arms reaching out in desperation. But instead of trying to shelter fifth graders from the "fuck you" graffiti of postwar America, Aris has been armed to the gills trying to help guard kids who might find it hard to wage their own fight against the impact of the twenty-first-century Kardashian windstorm.

Aris's ammunition: "Pain is the purifier." Was that *it*?

After ten years, after all the preaching and the lectures, the hollering for more and more callousing teamwork on the Serengeti Plain at the Green Lakes State Park training site with a stick in his hand—a stick he could turn into a cobra; don't think he couldn't—Bill Aris was in Portland contemplating the idea of F-M cross-country perfection, or, in a vernacular more suited to the Aris blueprint: mastery.

In the era of Nike Cross Nationals, Fayetteville-Manlius boys teams had come teasingly close to mastery. But, like Olympic gymnasts making minor but costly missteps on the balance beam, the boys had experienced lost opportunities. The most difficult to bear occurred at the first NXN championship in 2004.

That year, F-M lost a chance to win with a couple of sluggish performances and by wasting energy in the weekend's high-pitched pre-race activities designed, that first year, for maximum hoopla by Nike organizers. The Fayetteville boys had come to Portland as the national cofavorite after a record-breaking season in New York. But their young squad with its small-town orientation did not have the verve to handle this tumultuous event with the necessary élan. Aris vowed to instill sharper prime-time readiness in the future, insuring that the boys' emotional agility was commensurate with their fitness level.

∞

When the 2014 fall cross-country season took shape, the Fayetteville boys affirmed their potential with tight team bonding. The boys grew so close they could almost coach themselves. For the first time ever, the boys' unity and sense of brotherhood was something the F-M girls could only envy.

In 2013, the girls, undercutting seamless values built over time, had fallen apart. The reason was emotional discord, rare in the Fayetteville camp. The girls simply did not get along. Aris, frustrated all season, tried everything he could to bring the girls together. Nothing worked. Still, even with that crucial void, the girls were well up in the national standings. But well down in Stotan gravitas.

After that, enforcing year-long damage control with, as Aris put it, "attitude correction seminars," the Fayetteville girls regrouped in 2014. By the time of the national event, the girls were in position to compete for top honors. The national polls rated a team from Southern California, Great Oak, as the favorite. Great Oak was a worthy opponent but, in line with the times, seemed to enjoy the spotlight. As motivation for his girls, Aris would stress the higher ground of F-M humility compared with what he considered the self-indulgent demeanor of others.

To Molly Malone, who competed at NXN all four years of high school, the team's authenticity and grace were as important as their athletic virtuosity. "We know how to show ourselves maturely to the rest of the teams that are new to this," she maintained one year at nationals. "Not in a giddy way, not in a way that other teams would look at you, like, 'You're just here for the ride.' We act how we would want to see ourselves."

At nationals, Fayetteville girls were scrutinized like a loupe on a lightbox. Their style had competitive impact. Corbin Talley, the former coach at Davis High in Kaysville, Utah, whose teams made nationals seven times, said, "When we first came to NXN, we watched F-M. Our girls were afraid of them even before the race. They walked around with such confidence."

Taking the Aris crusade to heart, the Fayetteville girls spoke a language all their own. It was not just a departure from the teenage idiom but a manner imbued with a greater enlightenment, as though that, in itself, was the goal.

After a decade of progress while preferring to look inward rather than deliver finish-line gestures for the video cameras—and often pilloried for it—Fayetteville-Manlius in 2014 had a chance to capture both the boys and girls Nike Cross Nationals team championships.

A team sweep at nationals?

It was impossible enough for one school, both boys and girls, to be the best in the country in a sport that was starting to grow in popularity from coast to coast. But cross-country also had its no-wiggle-room scoring system that swallowed up any team with the slightest lapse by a single runner. If just one athlete woke up on race day with a stomach virus or stumbled on a pivotal hill or lost his or her composure in the crowded field—one kid with a bad hair day—points could pile up in competition and your team would be history.

In cross-country, a team's top seven runners take the line. The first five runners across the finish score. Points are tallied based on place. Tenth place, ten points. Low score wins. It's a beautiful system actually, wonderfully egalitarian. A team's fifth man, or woman, is just as important—at times, *more* important—than a team's first runner. A fifth man with a bad hair day stands to lose many more points back in the pack than a first man positioned among the pacesetters. Every year at Nike Cross Nationals, the top-finishing fifth runner from any school in the field receives the coveted Golden Anchor Award.

In central New York, where F-M lives, one would think the school's success would be regarded with local pride. There were plenty of good teams in the area collecting their share of trophies. But all too often it was envy talking after a Fayetteville victory, and after a rare loss or some absurd disqualification—anything that subdued Fayetteville and brought them down to size—the grandstanders erupted with boisterous cheer.

Aris shrugged off the enmity to his teams as something to be expected. It was the same with the old Yankees teams that won the World Series year after year, he reasoned. Winners had to accept a little loathing here and there.

But perhaps there was another dynamic at work—the suspicion that Fayetteville in its professed purity, honor, and beyond-category work ethic had discovered something too good to be true; there had to be something wrong with it. The coach, with his subversive ingenuity, had ideas that could not easily be adopted by others, and therefore he, and the athletes, had to be suspect. They had to be resented. And when the F-M runners closed ranks and kept to themselves, that posture could be misconstrued as arrogance. By the same token, when the coach seemed aloof, immersed in a kaleidoscope of thought, that posture could be misconstrued as self-righteousness.

Those misconceptions have traveled far, from central New York to Portland, where at nationals, coaches could be heard whispering about Fayetteville. It's not just envy but bewilderment as one coach or another wondered, "What's this business about Aris and his mind-body approach? What does he know that we don't?" The answer could not be reduced to a sound bite in the corridors of the Nike campus. It could not be expressed in a particular "secret" workout but within a belief system, in the fine cloth of Aris's words, that allowed for everything else of a surpassing nature to take place.

Fayetteville's physical presence in itself did not suggest superiority. One New Jersey girl of national standing that I knew once looked at the F-M girls standing nearby at a meet, and then turned to me, exclaiming, "They're just *regular* girls."

If, with stimulating ideas of the mind, these regular girls could be groomed to win Nike Cross Nationals by fifty-nine seconds per runner—let's call it a minute—as they did one year over the second-best team in the country, it must be deduced that the mind is much more powerful than we'd thought, and that girls are much more powerful than we'd thought. In my view, these two notions are undisputable.

They are also humbling. Could it be that the experts have been shortsighted all along—that they, and therefore, we, still know very little about the mind's effect on athletic performance? Could it also be that four decades after federal Title IX legislation opened the door for girls in sports, we, in the postfeminist era, still sell girls short on the playing field?

Perhaps we also sell short the power of the word. In our shortcut, text-and-tweet world, words lose meaning, and we forget our own power in shaping the young. A word, a lecture, the whole oratorical Greek schmear—that's what Bill Aris had going for him every time he spoke to his runners and could tell, in a second, one kid's crying need at that moment, one kid's fears or doubts or facility for conquest.

Aris was up against some heady science. In 2014, just as Fayetteville's summer training was getting started, an article by the psychiatrist Richard A. Friedman appeared in the *New York Times* opinion pages with the headline, WHY TEEN-AGERS ACT CRAZY. Dr. Friedman, professor of clinical psychology at Cornell Weill Medical College, explained that because the brain's prefrontal cortex, the seat of calm reasoning, does not mature until the midtwenties, "adolescents, on average, experience more anxiety and fear and have a harder time learning not to be afraid than either children or adults."

This was not the accessory of grace Aris was looking for. However, soon after, I attended a lecture by the neuroscientist Frances Jensen, who said that while teenagers' brains were still in development, recent research showed that when the brain's pathways, or synapses, were stimulated, learning could occur. "Teens are learning machines," asserted Dr. Jensen, author, with Amy Ellis Hutt, of *The Teenage Brain*. Jensen said that while the teenage brain could function like "a Ferrari with bad breaks," there was also a "sweet spot" when, in the proper environment, the teenage brain could be enriched. "It's a window of opportunity," she said.

Aris tries to capitalize on that. He wants to see the human cell without a microscope. When Aris pulls a boy or girl aside, grabs him or her by the shoulders, and says, no punches pulled, that he or she needed to better keep pace with teammates on a run, and says it in a way that draws upon the entire context of what he had said for weeks and months, change becomes possible in the complex pathways of this young mind. Emotional vulnerability could be transformed into emotional power. You just need the right mentor. And the right words.

∞

One fall afternoon, the team was at Green Lakes State Park in Manlius, a short drive from the high school. This was where the team did its best training, not just on the hilly pathways but beforehand, when Aris would deliver his passionate lectures on Stotan staples: selflessness, teamwork, "the process is the goal," whatever flew into his mind at that moment.

Aris's daily practice sessions were really two practices in one. First, the mind was tackled; then the body. When the body was at work, lessons of the mind were inextricably woven into the effort, like the patterns of a quilt. At Green Lakes, Aris never stopped working the mind.

Upon arrival, the team members gathered at sheltered picnic tables where they unloaded their backpacks and grouped tightly as one. They were silent, waiting for Aris to speak. Their faces held expressions of brightness and longing, a sense that something new and vital would soon be handed to them. Their fertile minds needed only do their work, summoning strength they once never knew they had and thinking, in their own way, the hell with the outside world.

It was late in the season and the junior varsity events were over. The squad of about forty was scaled back to nine boys and nine girls, the varsity lineups plus alternates. From behind the picnic area, Green Lake's emerald-blue waters glistened with the sun's reflection. The beech, white cedar, and sugar maples were mesmerizing with their fiery late-fall bounty of yellows and oranges.

Aris was on fire himself. Standing in front of the team, he embarked on an exercise he'd done before. Referring to crowd reaction after Fayetteville victories, Aris said forcefully, "What's the sound of F-M running great?" The team remained silent. "What's the sound of F-M doing okay?" Light clapping. "What's the sound of F-M having a mediocre day?" More vigorous clapping. "What's the sound of F-M running lousy?" Raucous applause. "Think about that and what it means,"

Aris told his runners. "It means we are resented because we are so successful. It means we are among ourselves."

It was a moment of power—eerie and magnificent. Aris said that the previous year one boy told him that his motivation for winning was this: "I want to hear silence at the finish line."

The Fayetteville requirement of squelching the teenage ego, seemingly a denial of human nature, was put to a test at every Nike Cross Nationals event. With the 398 athletes, 199 boys and 199 girls, celebrated at every turn on the sprawling Nike campus, and cross-country running taking its place as a major enterprise in the sporting orbit, the runners in Portland were bathed in glory and self-absorption. Each year, the F-M athletes tried to remain below the celebratory radar. Their pre-race posture, diffident and gallant, was in contrast with many of their opponents' selfie seducements and entranced consumption of cool Nike gear.

One year, as the F-M runners stood apart from the hoopla at the Tiger Woods Center on the Nike campus, Alana Pearl discussed her development as an athlete. She said, "We train with our boys' team. Our philosophy is, we're not boys or girls. We're athletes. No difference."

Pearl's imposing physique, gaining credence in some sectors of girls distance running, led to questions about her food choices. Aris was a stickler for good nutrition. Every "team family" that abided by Aris's program changed its eating habits. That was always the first big family transformation. Alana was five feet five and 110 pounds. Since joining the team, she ate an iron-rich diet, what she called "clean" protein. She ate more fish and red meat than in the past. At Aris's suggestion, Alana took iron supplements to assure that the oxygen-carrying particles in her blood would remain at healthy levels. Her mother looked into the iron content of various foods. "Instead of steak," said Alana, who went on to run for the University of Connecticut, "I occasionally eat bison because it's more iron-enriched."

When Nick Ryan, the first of the team's four Ryan kids, started running for Aris in 2009, the family "cleaned everything up," said Peter Ryan, a junior on the 2014 team with two sisters, Olivia, a senior, and Sophia, a freshman, also on the 2014 squad. The Ryans cut out sweets, limiting desserts to Saturday. The timing was ideal. On Saturdays, Fayetteville either had a meet or, if not, a long run, up to two hours, was always scheduled. Afterward, Peter said, he would satisfy his sweet tooth, and exhaustion, by diving into a "ton" of ice cream.

After the challenging Saturday runs, best friends Jenna Farrell and Alana Pearl would satisfy their cravings in a different way. Fayetteville did not do "easy" runs or what teams typically called "recovery" runs. While balancing the "hard" and "easy" in running was taken as gospel—its patron saint was Nike's own Bill Bowerman, the University of Oregon coach who practically invented the concept—Aris didn't buy it. To Aris, easy, jog-along running was fine as exercise, but it was not training. To excel in cross-country, in the 5,000 meters, Aris insisted that his athletes always run at a pace that would elevate their heart rates to a training intensity of least 75 percent of maximum. "Training," he would say. "Not exercise." To Aris, "exercise," to the aspiring competitor, was almost as demeaning as being "normal."

Thus, in a midseason Saturday long run of two hours, the leading F-M girls would be required to sustain a pace of a little more than seven minutes per mile (the boys ran about a minute per mile faster), covering at least sixteen miles. Like virtually all runs, it would be done on hilly terrain, with an emphasis on sticking close to teammates, so close you could touch the girl in front of you or brush shoulders with the girl to your side, working the mind as well as the body. This ambitious effort, culminating a week of boot camp intensity, was calibrated to burnish an athlete's total being and fill out a training mix that would escalate in demands as the championship events neared.

There would always be a point in the second hour when one or two girls would feel a particular zeal and run faster than required, and the rising doubts of others would have to be quelled. Jenna Farrell would tell herself: "You can do it. You can do it." And she would repeat a team mantra: "Run hard, be strong . . . think big."

Jenna would always think big, and so would Alana Pearl, and after the two-hour run, after a big team brunch at Dave's Diner in Manlius, after the team members devoured their pancakes, dispersed and went their separate ways, Jenna and Alana would go to Alana's house and into her bedroom. They would each lie down, face the ceiling, and let the effort drain out of them, their fitness secure. They would take some deep breaths, fall into a woozy bliss. Each girl knew how the run made the other feel. Each girl knew why the other did it. They would lie in silence. They would not speak. Not a word. Their shared suffering was now emboldened into shared silence. They were at peace.

2

KILLER EYES

Bill would walk around at Green Lakes up above us on a hill carrying a big stick, like a staff, as tall as him. With his bald head
shining in the sun, he looked like God walking around.
        —*Heather Martin, Fayetteville-Manlius cross-country runner*

Early 2000s

The roots of the Fayetteville-Manlius cross-country dynasty—and new
concepts like "self-governance" and "pain is the purifier" that would
redefine the capacity of teenage runners—go back to the worst of
America's sedentary excesses at the dawn of the new millennium.

Around 2000, the American way of life seemed to be getting softer. Obesity
rates were going through the roof. The sedentary life had settled over the nation
like some sort of poisonous cloud. Two-thirds of the adult populace was overweight, and similar statistics of sloth applied to children and teenagers. While
many in the health professions sounded alarms, at the time there seemed little
that could be done about Americans' ever-deepening plunge into the unfit abyss.
High-fat, processed food was everywhere, marketed effectively and with plenty
of political muscle by corporate interests. Technology continued its bullet-train

pace, providing handy gadgets guaranteed to captivate our short attention spans while keeping us secure in one place, no need to move a muscle. Our weakness of body and mind was mocked on magazine covers like the one from *Newsweek* that showed an overweight child clutching a huge ice cream cone with the headline, FAT FOR LIFE?

As a high school track and cross-country coach, Bill Aris could see evidence of this lack of will and work ethic at Fayetteville-Manlius. While he had some dedicated runners, he had others who would come to practice and react to the coach's planned workout with the comment, "We have to do *that*?" In addition, most of the athletes maintained very poor diets. It was clear to Aris that team members were not living very healthy lifestyles. How could they if they were not pointed in that direction at home or, for that matter, in school?

The scope of poor nutrition could not be overstated. As Molly Malone would recall about her first season on the squad, "I was eating Halloween candy before races like an idiot."

As a runner himself, and a veteran of a dozen marathons, Aris knew that his team would never achieve true excellence on a consistent basis without a commitment to nutritious eating and a healthy lifestyle. Aris labored with a high school cross-country coach's lament: What were the athletes doing all day long when they were not in his grasp? What were their habits when under the influence of unknowing parents and siblings, and a mass culture that did everything it could to undermine the development of a healthy body, mind, and spirit?

He wondered if there was anything he could do about this. Could he change the thinking, the attitudes, and the actions, of teenage athletes? What values of running—of living—that he held dear could he try and impart to the team? And how would he do this given the limitations he saw around him? The town of Manlius was typical of suburbs everywhere. The people were comfortable. The living was easy. The kids were not looking to be challenged. As Aris liked to say, "Mediocrity was the new excellence."

These shortcomings were equally true within the running community itself. At the time, American distance running was going through a protracted period of weakness in the international arena. The successes of the previous generation in world and Olympic events were not being sustained as the twentieth century drew to a close. As a society, it seemed we no longer had the get-up-and-go and communal striving that had once led to historic US running exceptionalism.

It got so bad that, at the 1996 Summer Olympics, on home soil in Atlanta, the brightest US distance result, male or female, was a sixth place in the men's 5,000 meters. The 2000 Summer Games in Sydney, Australia, would prove to be even worse. With Kenyan men sweeping all the distance-event medals, the lone US men's marathoner placed sixty-ninth among the eighty-one finishers, twenty minutes behind the winner.

For runners, the marathon, at the world-class level, was emblematic of a nation's strength and character. In 1972, when Frank Shorter won Olympic gold in Munich, with Kenny Moore fourth and Jack Bachelor ninth, the best showing by any nation, it said something about American drive coming out of the turbulent sixties and our ability to bolster initiatives in human rights—even the "right" to run—and in the realm of human potential. Before long, the federal Title IX legislation would pave the way for girls' and women's sports, and a decade later it was Joan Samuelson of Maine who would win the first Olympic marathon for women, in 1984 in Los Angeles.

But the twenty-first century landed with a thud. As a coach, Aris had to emerge from the locker room every day and try to inspire self-satisfied teenagers. A malaise permeated the landscape, and Aris struggled to find ways to overcome it.

How did we arrive at a point in 2003 in which hospitals were doing gastric bypass surgery—"stomach stapling" so that the body could no longer take in normal amounts of food—on kids? How did we arrive at the point, that same year, in which half of New York City's 1.1 million schoolchildren were deemed overweight?

While poverty, lack of athletic facilities, and a dearth of healthy food choices in minority neighborhoods probably made such findings inevitable, a different mosaic of suburban privilege could also pose challenges at a place like Fayetteville-Manlius. The school, with about 1,350 students, was reputed for its academic standards. But as Aris patrolled the building sizing up potential cross-country recruits, he saw students overwhelmed by one AP class after another, immersed in the college sweepstakes, while in need of a good meal and a night's sleep. If some did choose cross-country as their sport, all too often it was to pad their resume. Ironically, some students came out for the team because they knew there was a no-cut policy and assumed cross-country was a haven of last resort for those who wanted to coast through a varsity season.

Aris feared he was becoming part of the problem. With a decade of coaching under his belt, he was getting bored with the sameness of each year and the mundane rituals, the training sessions that seemed to lack spark. Even though he had coached some good teams and individual stars through the 1990s—Fayetteville's 1997 boys team had been ranked number two in the nation—Aris worried that he wasn't giving kids his best. He felt restless, in need of a blueprint to reinvigorate his passion. Something bold.

∞

Growing up in New York City in the borough of Queens, and on Long Island, in Floral Park, Aris had never been bold, not outwardly so. Still, he nurtured a certain inner boldness to survive, as his grandparents had when they left Greece, and as his father had in carving out a career in a postwar New York business world that was not hospitable to those of Greek ancestry.

All four of Aris's grandparents had been born in Greece. They and other relatives were farmers living hardscrabble lives in all parts of the country at a time of great strife. The Balkan wars, hostility between Greece and neighboring Turkey, and the effects of World War I had brought about severe schisms in Greek society in the period before and after 1920, when Aris's ancestors fled for better opportunity in America. Aris owns a prized family photograph of relatives on their Greek farm brandishing shotguns to defend themselves against marauders.

Typical of the immigrant culture, Bill's family sought to adopt American ways while still holding close to its Greek roots. Aris's paternal grandparents settled in the Bronx, where his father, John, grew up. After getting a high school education, John Aris had been drafted into the army for service in World War II. In 1945, he was all set for combat in the Pacific theater when the atomic bombs were dropped. He finished his tour on the West Coast, and then went to college in New York, at Pace University, on the GI Bill. Bill's father majored in accounting and attended night school to earn an MBA.

"My family took what came, had a strong sense of right and wrong, valued education," Aris said. "It was a clean and honest life, and I think I took from that the belief that you had to make your own way, be true to yourself, and embrace all challenges and opportunities."

Aris's heritage endeared him with other virtues—the pursuit of new ideas, an avid interest in philosophy, and inquiry into the intersection of a healthy body with an eager mind. The ancient Greeks were great philosophers and teachers, as well as the originators of sporting contests and the Olympic Games. Greek athletics was also endowed with the legend of the ancient runner Phidippides, whose heroic running during the Persian War of 490 B.C.E. was said to contribute to the Greek victory in the Battle of Marathon.

From his earliest running days, young Bill had a restless bent. He always craved a more joyful and well-rounded experience. At Floral Park High School, he went out for track as a freshman and ran the 800 meters. He ran okay but did not like the coaches' training methods. In the late 1960s, interval training—fast laps around the track with brief recovery jogs—was all the rage. Bill considered intervals a mind-numbing system that took the fun out of running. While some runners liked the repetitive work for its immediate feedback and testing baseline, Bill needed to branch out and just run on his own. He completed his freshman season of track but, despite prodding from teammates, refused to go out for cross-country the next fall.

At the time, Aris thought he'd given up cross-country running forever.

Aris proceeded to run by himself through the streets and byways of Floral Park, situated just across the Queens border in Nassau County. His running was informal, spontaneous, made up as he went along. His stamina was solid; he could run without getting winded. Aris recalled, "I was the neighborhood Forrest Gump, innocent and bouncing along like I owned the place."

Aris played, at various times, on the high school football, basketball, and lacrosse teams. He had already grown to his full height, six feet two. In local parks and on the streets, Aris played roller hockey and ice hockey. He would run, play hockey, run some more. He was always itching for the next run.

It was around this time when the Aris family acquired a touch of notoriety. Bill had an uncle who owned a restaurant in Manhattan, and somehow the establishment was recruited for a scene in the 1971 Academy Award–winning film *The French Connection*. The movie's stars, Gene Hackman (Oscar winner for Best Actor) and Roy Scheider (nominated for Best Supporting Actor), were seen entering the place, where Bill's Uncle Peter, a bon vivant with jet black hair who once played Canadian football, seated them at the bar. Bill's cousin, Lenny, the bartender, served them. Another part of the Aris heritage—the movies.

✑

In 1973, Aris graduated from Floral Park High School and went on to Le Moyne College in Syracuse. He studied business and economics and let his running go for a year. When he resumed, he decided to train for a local marathon, in the spring of 1978, his senior year. "I can't remember the name of the event," he said, "but, from my standpoint, it could have been the Seat of the Pants Marathon." On a bare minimum of thirty miles' training a week, Aris ran about three and a half hours. The next spring Aris ran another marathon, also in 3:30.

By then he was married and with his first child, to be named John, after his father, on the way. Aris was twenty-four, a college graduate, and starting his first job at a bank. He had to put the marathon on hold. Two years later, after feeling more secure, he trained for his third marathon, New York City, finding the time to log fifty miles a week. He ran it in 3:01. In 1982, his second child, Andrea, was born.

Aris was now entrenched in the business world as a real estate manager with a company called United Technologies Corporation, a military-industrial giant that owned Carrier air-conditioning, Otis elevators, Pratt and Whitney engines, and Sikorsky helicopters.

Aris's marathons had continued and improved. In 1990, he ran the first of three straight Boston Marathons, in 2:47. In 1991, he posted his lifetime best of 2:43:12. For the next year's Boston, Aris built up to seventy to eighty miles a week but went out too fast and struggled to the finish in 2:49. That was his twelfth, and last, marathon.

That same year, United Tech downsized and Aris was let go. What would he do with his life? He had two kids, college expenses on the horizon, and no job. (Aris's wife, Christine, was a nurse.) His runner's instinct coupled with that dash of Greek boldness told him to quit the business world and take the opportunity to become a teacher's aide and volunteer coach at Fayetteville-Manlius. At F-M, he wouldn't make real money, but he might be happier and more fulfilled at this point in midlife. So, like some Wall Street titan who gives it all up to run a B&B in Vermont, Aris (minus the titan bank account) stepped into the high school arena cold. He'd never coached or worked with kids. He had no teaching experience whatsoever.

Aris considered his aide position to be temporary, and the F-M principal was fine with that. As things turned out, Aris would remain an F-M aide for fifteen years. His duties were mundane: hallway supervision, cafeteria duty, and the like. The main reason for Aris's longevity was that being in the building gave him access to potential cross-country and track prospects.

After one season as a coaching volunteer, Aris became a paid assistant coach in 1993. Mike Guzman, head coach of both boys and girls, retired after 1997, and Aris became girls head coach. Jerry Smith, another assistant, was named boys head coach. Smith left after a year, and another assistant, Jim Nixdorf, was moved up to boys coach, with Aris helping. In 2004, Aris was named head coach of the boys program, and from then on Aris was head coach of track and cross-country for both boys and girls in all three seasons. Actually, it was four seasons, year-around, since the team trained over the summer—a must for cross-country.

To narrow his search for potential runners, Aris would approach younger siblings of current team members, or athletes in other sports who struck him as cross-country material. It was more about personality than body type or any noticeable physical attributes. Aris looked into the students' faces. From his business experience, he knew how to look into someone's eyes and size them up.

One of the exceptional things about cross-country is that it requires a menu of qualities different from that of most other sports. Someone who is just getting by in another sport might have the inner richness that makes him or her ideal for distance running. This submerged desire presents a wonderful opportunity for the coach, who develops ways to bring out that richness, which all too often lays dormant.

"When I saw Kathryn Buchan, a basketball player, in the Fayetteville hall-ways," said Aris, "I approached her about cross-country. Buchan had never done any running and was not involved in a fall sport. I could see intensity in her eyes. I called them 'killer eyes.' Her eyes told me she had the desire to express herself as a competitor and that running could be the perfect platform for her."

Aris told Kathryn straight out, "I've heard you're a good athlete. I can see in your eyes that you'd be a hell of a runner. Would you consider running in our summer program and coming out for cross-country?" Kathryn appeared stunned by Aris's invitation. Maybe her reaction had to do with his reputation. As an aide, Aris was often involved in disciplinary measures and walked around as an intimidating authority figure. That bothered him, he said, because he couldn't be his jolly self. Add to that the misguided student chatter that had character-ized Aris as a tyrannical coach forcing kids to run; and his inclination to take greasy food off runners' plates in the cafeteria (not entirely true).

Aris told Kathryn and others he approached, "Don't see me for what I am here during the day or what you may have heard about me. See me for what I am when I work with you."

Buchan took Aris's sales job to heart, joined the squad, and, over time, became a member of three national championship teams.

Many of the F-M girls and boys shared Buchan's star quality. Even a quiet type could exemplify it. Perhaps the best example was Courtney Chapman, another basketball player, with an older sister on the team. Courtney's mom was shocked when Aris did his sales pitch on her younger daughter. Her mom said, "What kind of runner could Courtney be if she got winded after a few minutes on the basketball court?" But Aris knew Courtney had something—those eyes. She joined the squad in eighth grade, which is permitted in New York State, and went on to run on five national championship teams.

"I have to admit," said Aris, "that I'm pretty effective at convincing someone that something—well, running—is their calling. Maybe I have killer eyes myself, but only when driven by my passion for excellence. I can be unrelenting. To me, a runner is a terrible thing to waste."

Though the athletes didn't know it at the time, and maybe Aris didn't either, these brief encounters in school served as the first inkling of a strong belief system he was able to create. Over time, the belief system bred a new culture, and the new culture transformed teenagers. In turn, they, too, became new.

Chapman, later on in college, recalled joining the team and feeling intimidated by Aris's stump speeches filled with wild tales, unusual training methods, and impossible standards of achievement. "Having an innocent, naive young mind made it easier for me to believe what coach was telling us," she said. "Bill has a certain magic to him. He manages to convince you that you are capable of anything, whether it is athletics, your career, your life, but you must make the change and put forth all of yourself to achieve whatever it is."

Magic? Aris believed that kids' authentic selves were being upended by screwed-up, nonsensical American ways, and he wouldn't stand for it. His mind leaped ahead with crazy ideas about running domination, boys and girls, all doing the same hard work together. All on the same page. Aris and his runners: a perfect world.

3

THE STOTAN CHALLENGE

Go out and run until you'd rather be dead. Go home and eat the
entirety of your fridge. Fall asleep by nine. Wake up the next day
and repeat. Try not to cry.

—*Molly Malone, Fayetteville-Manlius cross-country runner*

2004 Season I

Preparing to take charge of all Fayetteville-Manlius runners in 2004,
Bill Aris dove into an exploration of every training method, motivational technique, and athletic philosophy he could get his hands on. He
tried to come up with new methods that a teenager might respond to within a
framework of higher standards and values of team running. Cross-country was
first and foremost a team sport, and Aris wanted to overcome the "me first"
sports ethos that had America in its grasp.

All of distance running owed a tribute to Arthur Lydiard, the wondrous New
Zealand coach of Olympic champions who a half-century ago created a template
for success from the mile to the marathon. Many coaches today, high school
and otherwise, say they "use Lydiard" when asked about their training methods.
Lydiard, who coached the three-time Olympic champion Peter Snell and other

all-time greats, emphasized high mileage and hill training as a strength-building foundation. He structured a "periodization" system to set up a different focus for each phase of a training year. Aris liked Lydiard's methods, some of which, such as hill work, are so fundamental they can't help but be instrumental in any runner's success, especially in cross-country.

While the Lydiard approach lacked the well-roundedness and spiritual ardor Aris was looking for—and by the early 2000s seemed a little too "common" and regimented for his taste—some elements of Lydiard's long-distance program would make their way into Aris's grand plan. But on the whole, Aris felt he had to get away from regimentation and traditional dogma. There was nothing in the American training canon that spoke to him. It was all too clinical and laboratory based. Science had its place but not as a defining emphasis for Aris. The training schedules generated by US coaches and exercise scientists seemed to him dry, generic, and restrictive. This day you do that, the next day you do this. Run X, run Y. This pace, that distance. Aris found the exactitude stifling.

Aris hunted for freedom, spontaneity, something imaginative that he could put his stamp on. He wanted a program that would make a statement—a lightning rod. To be a pathfinder and completely reeducate the masses, at least in his modest corner of upstate New York. He kept thinking of terms to help guide his search: *audacious, bold, cutting edge, outside the box, collaborative . . . revolutionary.*

Aris's research led him to Percy Cerutty, a Down Under coaching "cousin" of Lydiard's from Australia. Like Lydiard, Cerutty came to prominence in the 1950s and '60s. He struck out on his own and was despised by the Australian running establishment. The feeling was mutual.

While Lydiard's most noted protégé was Snell, Cerutty's marquee athlete was the miler Herb Elliott, Snell's predecessor as Olympic 1500-meter champion in 1960. Both Cerutty and Lydiard were eccentric trailblazers who disdained convention and challenged not only their coaching fraternities but their nations' cultures of complacency.

The genesis of each man's program was different. Lydiard learned from his own running as a marathoner, testing the effects of long mileage. An undistinguished teenage runner, Cerutty was a sickly child who'd been rejected from the military and suffered a physical and emotional breakdown in his early forties that required hospitalization. He found he could not trust doctors or conventional methods of medical care and set out to heal himself through holistic methods. Cerutty studied food, psychology, and philosophy, all in the context of total fitness and a harmony with nature. He lost weight, resumed running, and won many races while breaking Australian records for ultramarathon distances like fifty miles.

There's a classic, arresting photograph of Cerutty running. He looks to be about sixty. In the photo, he is in full-out racing posture, arms churning, face grimacing. What stands out is Cerutty's torso. It has the sinewy leanness of a teenager. From the neck down, Cerutty looks like an underwear model. Not an ounce of body fat. Cerutty's rib cage, abdominals, and chest muscles are all visible, each bone a branch on the Cerutty tree of a life properly lived. That image was the embodiment of the athletic worldview Cerutty fashioned for himself and his runners. It was an outlook that embraced the naturalness present in all of us in a holy way.

Aris said, "I had found my man. And I had found my program." Cerutty called it "Stotan," a marriage of "stoic" and "spartan." Cerutty had developed a "Stotan Creed." It was a manifesto of running and living. This became Aris's new coaching foundation. It was bold and audacious, to say the least. Cerutty used Stotan ideas to nurture Elliott and other Olympic greats. Impressed, Aris took the essence of the creed and adapted it to his high school team.

The "stoic" component of Stotan included standing up to all challenges, developing strength of mind and body, training in a robust way, persevering in the face of adversity, applying athletic values and healthy practices like good nutrition in one's daily existence, having a strong work ethic, appreciating the beauty of life, and showing modesty and humility while seeking new levels of excellence. The "spartan" component included being satisfied with basic comforts, seeking harmony with nature, eschewing material gains, and living a pure and honest life that running helps engender.

In Cerutty's view, and in Aris's, running and life were intertwined. There was no halfway. To run and live as a Stotan, you were either in or out.

Would the Fayetteville runners buy into it? Aris knew many would not. But he hoped that some would, enough to change the team culture. As he thought about these new attitudes he hoped to develop, Aris kept repeating to himself, "What if?"

Within the Stotan framework, there were many novel training and lifestyle specifics to employ. They were bound to shock the Fayetteville runners, maybe scare them away. Aris said, "I was willing to take that risk. I'd learned in business that a new idea, if inspiring, if driven by excellence, not pretense, could become infectious."

The athletes confronted the risk and took it. "We weren't living the normal life of a high school kid," recalled Heather Martin, a converted sprinter who would run cross-country on three national championship teams. "We were training like elite athletes. One of Bill's favorite quotes was, 'Normal has nothing to do with excellence.' What we were doing at Fayetteville was not normal. But it's also not normal for one team of girls to have a chance to win the national championship every year."

Aris did Cerutty one better. Cerutty had never coached a team; he'd only worked with individuals. While some of those individuals did a bit of training together, Cerutty had no reason to shape a group of runners with different abilities, ideas, and backgrounds into a unified team for competition. Aris faced the added challenge of revamping his program not only for individual success but also for team success. For that he was on his own. It's one thing to nurture a boy or girl with new ideas. To try that with an entire team required reengineering many layers of imbedded psychological assumptions. Aris was not reinventing the wheel. He was reinventing the automobile.

Aris felt that no one had ever tested what teenage athletes were capable of. Could he develop a unique kind of team that would learn, train, and race as no other? Would the whole thing be rejected by, well, "normal" kids who just couldn't accept it?

And would Aris come off as a self-righteous, Berkeley-style protester when he preached that when "team" was spoken of people really meant the glorification of individuals? Would he be shipped off to some commune in the mountains when he gave his narcissism speech: that narcissism was corrupting us as a people; that, for the high school kid, running was the antidote, the inoculation, against narcissism; and that he sought to create a team culture of selflessness and egolessness. Are you in or out?

∞

Divining the remarkable success of the Fayetteville-Manlius runners inevitably leads to the enigma of the young runner, boy or girl, and the enigma of Aris himself. At practice sessions and competitions near and far, at premeet dinners and postmeet celebrations, during the furious racing and in the afterglow of victory, the young runner appears as a hybrid. The child growing seamlessly into something greater—not an adult, but something better, something clean and pure—something full of life. The postchild: the runner young enough to extinguish fear and old enough to welcome the pain of transcendent effort and strive to overcome it. Even the teenage mind of an early team member, Andrew

McCann, a handsome devil chasing girls and golf balls, could elucidate an insight that would change his young life: "Pain and fatigue vastly differ."

Aris saw that this well-worn conflict of maturation—the cri de coeur in our society of "What am I going to do with these crazy kids?"—was not a conflict at all if we could only stop and see what *they* saw, feel what, deep inside, they really wanted. Aris would strike out into new territory and take that youthful "craziness" not to fix but empower it. He took their energy, their innocence, and their need for connection. (He also took their burgers and cheese fries.) At the same time, Aris took stock of who he was, what he, too, needed, and formulated an audacious plan for communion unearthed from the sand dunes of Australia.

Stotan—the word itself sounded alien—seemed perfect for Aris. As a teacher, Aris would have had the go-it-alone daring inspired by the Robin Williams character, John Keating, in *Dead Poets Society*. Rip out the first page of the dusty poetry text. Start anew.

Like Williams's Keating, Aris would have never lasted in a conventional classroom. Maybe he could have found comfort in one of those 1960s "schools without walls," but not in a traditional school. He wanted to find ways to meet the teens where they lived emotionally. With their sense of invincibility, the young runners were equipped to take risks. Who better than the restless Aris to feed teenagers' need for rebellion? Who better than Aris to convince teenagers to eat healthy for a teammate?

"Experimental behavior is actually important for adolescents to engage in because it helps them establish their autonomy, Jensen and Hutt state in *The Teenage Brain*. In addition, the authors explain, in adolescents the greater release of the substance dopamine in the "nucleus accumbens" section of the brain makes them hypersensitive to positive feelings, with an emotional reliance on immediate gratification. In another words, as every parent knows, a teenager lives in the "right now."

Cross-country running is everything but right now. It is built on delayed gratification. It is not: take a basketball, drill it through the hoop, and be happy. On the contrary, it is: train hard today and every day for weeks and months, and after that you might run a good race and you *might* be happy.

Confronting this conflict, borne in our genes, Aris found another way. He encouraged the young runners to find so much delight and satisfaction every day in hard work and teamwork so that, while experimenting to establish their autonomy, they could feel reward in the *right now*. At Fayetteville-Manlius, there was no such thing as immediate gratification or delayed gratification . . . just gratification.

High school cross-country had come far since Aris began coaching in 1992. Increasing media exposure showed that some of the most formidable athletes in any sport were cross-country runners and that year-round running along with weight training and other supportive exercises were required to compete with the best. Cross-country was getting some overdue respect. Why mess with it? Because, Aris said, it could be even better.

After reading Cerutty and other texts on group dynamics and sport psychology, Aris felt an opportunity to create a new athlete, transformed from good to great, from normal to extraordinary, who would become the template at Fayetteville-Manlius for a redefinition of the runner. The teenage runner, with enhanced physical, emotional, and spiritual powers, would now stand as the model athlete, the athlete supreme.

That was his goal. Aris would start by throwing away the coach's favorite tool, the stopwatch, and train the runners with spontaneity, creating workouts as he went along. He would write nothing down, have no preconceived notions, no schedule, no system, as it were, only his instincts to tell him, as he sized up the boys and girls, what would stimulate their hearts and minds and muscles on that day, at that moment.

A typical summer practice at Green Lakes State Park, preparing for the fall cross-country season, was a three-hour event, starting in the heat of the day at three P.M. (because many an early-season meet had hot weather). Molly Malone recalled how she experienced it:

- Arrive in mandatory sweatpants to keep warm even though it was eighty-five degrees.
- Gather at the oak tree at the corner of the Frisbee golf course and wait for Bill to start talking.
- Listen to him talk.
- Keep listening.
- Oh my God, we're going to be here forever.
- Holy shit, is this over yet, it's gonna get dark.
- Wait . . . actually . . . keep talking . . . if it gets dark I won't have to run.
- Ugh, Bill's stopped talking, time to do five minutes of barefoot drills.
- After barefoot drills, ten minutes (which felt like an hour) of rigorous core work.

- **WOW, WE HAVE TO RUN AFTER ALL THAT?!**
- Go out and run until you'd rather be dead.
- Go home and eat the entirety of your fridge.
- Fall asleep by nine.
- Wake up the next day and repeat. Try not to cry.

Whether purposeful or not, Aris took on the aura of a prophet. In his speech and carriage and body language, he could convey an idea that, among the F-M runners, would acquire Talmudic weight. Let it be spoken, let it be done.

"Bill would walk around at Green Lakes up above us on a hill carrying a big stick, like a staff, as tall as him," said Heather Martin. "With his bald head shining in the sun, he looked like God walking around."

From Cerutty, Aris learned to decry "schedule addicts," insisting that running should be "play," a view advocated by running philosopher Dr. George Sheehan, the cardiologist and best-selling author who excelled in competition well into his sixties. Cerutty said that when the athletic endeavor—running—is fashioned in a "routine, scheduled" way, "we depart from the natural, the joyous, the exhilarating."

Aris felt, the harder the run, the more exhilarating. As the F-M runner Owen Kimple would say later, "Coach had a specific workout style that I'd never seen or heard of anywhere else. He would never tell us how long the total workout would be. We would never know if the end was near till Bill gave us the signal by calling 'finisher,' always the most difficult and grueling part of the workout."

That little bit of Cerutty mischief alone would have profound effects. Not knowing when the training was over, athletes ran each segment hard—harder than what they were capable of—instead of backing off to save something for the end or bowing to fears of not finishing. Suddenly, the boys and girls were running at a new level, with confidence that accrued each day and a zest for more.

Every workout would have elements of surprise. Aris was the chef cooking up a new dish, with new ingredients, but not based on a traditional recipe—all to serve the human need, and certainly the teenage need, for newness, variation, excitement. No runner would be limited by what they thought they were capable of. Aris would never limit an athlete by yesterday's workout, yesterday's definition of success.

As one of Aris's more precocious young ladies, Katie Sischo, told me after one of Fayetteville's national championship victories: "I'm never going to say that I've fulfilled my potential because I'll never know if that's the case."

Sischo could have been speaking about her coach as well. Once Aris stepped away from conventional coaching, he began to redefine not only his runners but also himself and who he was as artist, scientist, and philosopher-guru. Aris's canvas of ideas, of instructional strategy, of motivation and inspiration, had no end point. There was no way to stop. All day long, Aris thought: How could I make it even better?

Imagine getting up every morning and meeting eager young runners who, in time, felt everything you felt, who wanted to run as hard as you could ask them to, who made one breakthrough after another, not to garner some trophy but for inner peace, same as you, and a sense of giving to others in the spirit of selflessness, just as you taught them. You would never stop thinking about those moments of grace when the whole world seemed right.

∽

Cerutty had published six books, all cult classics, and Aris devoured them. "I studied the training, psychology, philosophy, nutrition," said Aris. "I hung on every idea ascribing each one a kind of biblical significance. I treasured not only the ideas themselves but the fact that Cerutty threw them in the faces of the establishment—running and otherwise—as though blessing a new way of life with holy water from the sea outside his training camp in Portsea, near Melbourne."

Cerutty was years ahead of his time. In the 1960s, he had the courage to say that white flour was a poison and that, for his runners, only whole-wheat bread was acceptable. Considering Australia's white-bread society—literally and figuratively—Cerutty could have gotten arrested for espousing such radical views. Aris noted, "They were still somewhat radical in the Syracuse area a half century later."

Cerutty pined for nature, for forest trails, broad meadows, the sea. It was not just to have soft ground underfoot and to be inspired to run faster by the beauty of the habitat. It was to feel the land as the perfect, primitive tool for excellence. It was to give back to the land out of respect and humility, and to consider running "in the wilds" as a sacred endeavor of enhancement. It was also to recognize that, as Cerutty wrote, "Nature is in us and can measure out time to a fraction of a second, when we learn to trust her without equivocation, absolutely and finally."

In Cerutty's philosophy, nature was, thus, a teacher, too. He said that Elliott, considered by many to be the greatest miler ever, never used a stopwatch in training. "He learned to trust himself."

"In Manlius," said Aris, "we were privileged to have the ideal training environment in which to nurture every new idea, every type of run, every team-bonding effort, every link with nature. An immaculate Stotan landscape was available to us for the taking at our very own training site—Green Lakes State Park—situated minutes from the high school."

Green Lakes, about two thousand acres, had a vast trail system, endless hills, pristine lakeside pathways, and a menu of delicious expanses for any configuration of looped repeats, hill circuits, tempo runs, and distance efforts that Aris could dream up. Aris would take to naming various workout sections of Green Lakes after hallowed grounds from Africa and elsewhere, like the Serengeti Plains. "The kids loved that," he said.

By comparison, Cerutty's Portsea camp outside Melbourne was serviceable but not spectacular. Cerutty made it spectacular. Using whatever the landscape had to offer, Cerutty's training runs were on undulating cliff-top trails and ocean beaches, over sand dunes (in particular an eighty-foot-high dune), dirt roads, grass fields, and golf courses. Cerutty's long sand hill became iconic.

Aris sat himself down and contemplated the Stotan ideas and the life before him. His corporate work was over and done with. He had little money coming in, but it was enough. He continued his running but had given up marathons. He had few things to grasp in the American way that excited him. He was a kid from Floral Park doing his own thing, a kid on the verge of a discovery that no one in running could imagine.

When Bill Aris said, "What if?" again and again, he could not know what pearls he would find in the young runners and how his discovery would lead to a quest for something thought to be unattainable: a boys-and-girls sweep of the national high school cross-country championships.

Aris decided that the first step in the Fayetteville-Manlius cross-country transformation would, as an experiment, take place at a secluded summer-camp site similar to what Cerutty fashioned at Portsea. It would be a Stotan camp in every way from start to finish.

4

THE MACHINE IS BORN

This was one of the scariest and most difficult things I've ever had to do in my life. The exercise forced a vulnerability that allowed us to address things we were too afraid to confront before.

—*Owen Kimple, Fayetteville-Manlius cross-country runner*

2004 Season II

As Bill Aris planned for the Stotan camp in 2004, he made copies of the following Cerutty "Stotan Creed," taken from the Graem Sims biography of Cerutty, *Why Die?*, to present to the campers:

Stotan Creed

A Stotan is one who hardens, strengthens, toughens and beautifies the body by consistent habits and regular exercises, which are consciously and irrevocably made part of the life plan of the individual, as well as consciously determining that the mind will be cultivated upon such abstractions as purity, beauty and logic. Erudition, in as complete a degree is possible, shall be the lifelong aim: Truth, in relation to all aspects of life, the unending search.

Stotans will, by virtue of their philosophy, be nature lovers, with a respect and appreciation of all evolved or created things. They will appreciate the sanctity of creative effort both in themselves and in others. They will strive to understand the significance implied by reality, will be able to discern the real from the spurious, and see no anomaly in nudity, either in body or mind. But neither will they cast pearls before swine.

Stotans, for all the reasons that their philosophy stands for (hardness, toughness, unswerving devotion to an ideal), would look upon the sea (or mountains) as their pristine element and endeavor to associate themselves with their primeval source by immersing themselves at least once per month in all seasons of the year. No practice is disposed to toughen, both the body and the morale, more than this.

Stotans believe that neither the body nor the mind can be maintained at a high pitch of efficiency unless sufficient and regular rest is obtained, and aim at a daily average of eight hours of sleep. Stotans, also, will not be found in social places after midnight. Stotans shall so regulate their lives that at the end of the period, varying with the intensity of effort, each shall realize that they have attained, without conscious striving, to a state of knowledge, and a position of leadership within the community. It is axiomatic that only the pure can understand purity, only the cultivated appreciate beauty, and only the strong truly measure their strength. Therefore, only the self-disciplined can command genuine respect. A program shall be aimed at which shall be designed to (train each Stotan):

- To withstand physical hardship, to accomplish feats of strength and endurance, to understand orderliness, and the true meaning of intelligence.
- To know himself [and herself] as an organism and a personality.
- To emerge, eventually emancipated, from all dogmas, creeds and beliefs, as well as worldly and unworldly hopes and fears.
- To habitually function upon the highest planes of thought and physical effort.

- To place the objective of an alert informed intelligence, and a perfected body, as primary in Life. And to arrive at the conclusion that all else will follow on.
- To learn that on this basis, the whole world, and all that it has to offer, opens out as a vision, splendid, normal and realizable.
- To understand that Past, Futures, Fears, Death, Selfishness, Egoism, Pride, Envy, Hate and Prejudice can be replaced by Intelligence that controls emotion, dominates destiny, manifests completeness and exults in Life.
- To understand that in actuality, evolved man is a King, but without the trappings. That Kingship is his right and his destiny. That we can make ourselves, in time, all that we would. That we honor real men but are subservient to none.

In addition, Stotans shall train themselves to withstand, stoically, personal criticism, also skepticism as the necessity or wisdom of such a Way of Life. In this regard, Stotans soon learn that they command knowledge, experience and ability not available to the prejudiced, the ignorant or the slothful.

Also, to have embarked upon the Stotan Way of Life, like the Spartans, one must go through with it to the end. There is no giving up throughout life. The first prerequisite for a Stotan is tenacity. The next is to understand that his loyalties are towards making the most of the material that it is, to the expansion, or at least the manifestation of the Life Force, and a constant identification of himself with his Life Force through his Way of Life.

To live this Way of Life is hard. It is not for weaklings. It is the Way that is traveled by all the truly great ones. It requires strenuous effort of body and mind.

It was formidable. It was intimidating. The creed was not something to take in full, but, for Aris and his Fayetteville team, to take *from*. In group discussions, Aris would filet the text to its essentials: endurance in all its forms, nature's gifts, excellence in mind and body, submerging of ego, and the transcendence acquired through hard work, but "Truth" in particular would always stand out.

Cerutty was extremely well read—from Plato and Aristotle, to Buddha and Einstein, to George Hackenschmidt, an early-twentieth-century wrestling champion and legendary body builder who was "without peer," wrote Cerutty, as a thinker and athletic proponent of fitness and nutrition. In his later years, Hackenschmidt—who was born in Estonia to German and Swedish parents and lived most of his life in London—consumed huge quantities of nuts, fruit, and raw vegetables and, in his eighties, could outrun most men half his age. Cerutty came to the view that for an athlete to do his best, he needed to become "a complete man," as Hackenschmidt had advocated, "and not merely a physical exponent of some prowess he may have been gifted with in the first place."

Aris's experiment was ready to get underway. He set out to try and build complete men out of tentative teenage boys. If his experiment worked with the boys, the girls would follow.

The year before, in 2003, the F-M girls team had not qualified for the cross-country state finals, and the returning runners for '04 did not, at that time, seem to Aris like they might have the emotional fortitude to take on Stotan values. It would have been too risky to demand such dramatic changes of this particular group of girls, especially without first seeing how it worked with the more seasoned boys lineup.

Fayetteville's 2003 boys team had placed second in the state Class 2A race, returned most of the scorers, and some of them, while young, had shown small signals of Stotan potential. "I could tell they were looking for a greater feeling of community," said Aris. He would invite the top eight boys to the summer of 2004 Stotan camp.

First Aris had to enlist the support of the boys' parents. After throwing out hints to the athletes all spring, he had a two-hour team meeting with the boys and their parents as the 2004 track season ended in June. Aris told the parents his vision for the future. "Some of what I'm going to share with you might seem outlandish. It's a complete departure from everything that's taken place up to now." Aris told them about Cerutty and the Stotan concepts. He discussed psychology, philosophy, nutrition, and lifestyle. He said, "What I want to do is change the entire culture of the operation. It's gone along well, but I think we can do better. For that, we need a radical transformation. Your child could be the beginning of something great."

Parents' heads nodded in agreement.

Aris went on, explaining that the camp was optional, and your son does not have to participate. But the effect has to be all or nothing, not halfway.

He explained that with the camp scheduled for early August, the boys would have a rigorous July training plan so they could arrive at camp with sufficient fitness to handle the workload planned for that week. "I told them that everything we did would be collaborative," said Aris. "The boys would be asked to contribute their own ideas and viewpoints and share in the responsibility for their success."

More parents nodded. Some were positively excited.

Aris told them that the camp week was free of charge. He said, "I don't want a dime. My payment will be in the boys' pursuit of excellence."

The only requirement was that the parents would have to buy the food based on a shopping list of healthy items Aris would provide. And they would have to drive their sons to and from the camp site. Aris told the group that his son, John, then twenty-five, would join him in organizing the week. With his experience as a part-time chef during his college years, John would prepare the camp meals. The exact site had yet to be determined, but Bill and John were hoping it would be in the mountains somewhere.

At that point, many parents stood up to cheer, and one father, Jim Kimple, prompted by his son, Owen, offered his family's summer cottage on Lake Bonaparte in the Adirondacks as the camp base. It was a one-hour forty-five-minute drive from Manlius. Every family was on board. The camp would run from Sunday, August 8, through Saturday, August 14. It would be the eight boys and Bill and John. The Stotan camp that Bill Aris hoped would change the Fayetteville-Manlius world was born.

∽

Father and son began to map out the camp itinerary. The schedule would feature two or three runs per day plus clinics on various Stotan concepts. "We would run sand hills as Cerutty had done at Portsea," said Bill. "After running, we would dive from the cliffs into the lake, which adjoined the Kimple home, as Cerutty's athletes had done into the Pacific. We would eat only nutritious food, and, by the way, no snacking."

Aris set up the six-week precamp training at home, to start on June 28 and conclude the day before camp. For that, the boys were on their own. They were told to run every day, sometimes twice a day, for forty-one days straight, while also doing weight training and core exercises three times a week. The longest runs grew from 75 to 110 minutes (about seventeen miles). The workouts included an array of faster-paced tempo runs and repeated short sprint-type runs at various distances.

Aris also gave the boys a homework assignment for camp. He had introduced them to a book, *Thinking Body, Dancing Mind*, by the sports psychologist Jerry Lynch. The book's subtitle was *Tao Sports for Extraordinary Performance in Athletics, Business, and Life*. (Lynch's coauthor was Chungliang Al Huang.) Aris told the boys to read the book from cover to cover twice and choose at least one chapter in particular to discuss in a group talk at camp. He also told them not to dare show up late on August 8. One P.M. sharp. Punctuality was important in showing sincerity for the enterprise. The boys would also need plenty of gear and multiple pairs of running shoes. Oh, and one more thing: a supply of 100 percent DEET bug spray.

August 8 arrived, and the Aris saga into the unknown—his journey into the center of the teenage human—was ready to begin. Up at Lake Bonaparte, he waited for the eight boys: Jared Burdick, Tommy Gruenewald, John Heron, Owen Kimple, Geoff King, Danny Marnell, Andrew McCann, and Tim Page.

Aris was a little concerned about McCann, who had spent his summers as a golf caddy in Rhode Island. McCann was a bit of a political schmoozer, as Aris put it. He had caddied for the actor Mark Wahlberg and it was possible that some of Wahlberg's rough-hewn celebrity had impressed him. McCann had called Aris the day before and said, "I'm still in Rhode Island ready to make a lot of money this weekend caddying for Mark. He told me I could make . . . bank," McCann said. "Mark told me I could make some good bank, that's what he called it." Aris said to him, "Andrew, let me make this simple for you. You'd better be here tomorrow, and on time. I don't give a rat's ass about . . . "

In Rhode Island, McCann's family had a summer place in Westerly, down by the beach, an inheritance on his mother's side. He grew up playing golf and caddying at the nearby country club, Misquamicut, down the road in exclusive Watch Hill, overlooking Block Island Sound, on the state's southwestern tip.

Caddying for the area's upper crust was hardly a cross-country runner's typical summer. McCann said that when he went out for the Fayetteville-Manlius squad, he looked for the cohesion of the team and its support system after leaving friends who played lacrosse, the Syracuse area's most popular sport. McCann felt he had the drive that could make him a good runner. McCann described Wahlberg with his streetwise background as "super-relatable" to the teenage caddies. Wahlberg had let McCann and his buddy take his car, a

Mercedes SL 500, out on the town for an evening. "Sixteen-year-old kids going to the hot spots impressing the girls," was how McCann described his dreamy summer of '04.

In midsummer the dream changed. The phone conversation with Aris rankled McCann. "There was a back and forth," said McCann. "Something Bill and I had over the years." There was no two ways about it. McCann had to step out of the Mercedes and put the golf clubs away.

McCann's father drove him to the Adirondacks, and when McCann, the last boy to show up, finally made it, everyone breathed relief. To start the camp, Aris had a 115-minute run, about seventeen miles, planned to get the boys going. Everyone was growing testy, anxious to run. Aris had sworn to get back in his car and go home if just one boy did not show up.

McCann hopped out of the car wearing pink pastel chinos and a yellow shirt. He had a designer belt right out of Lilly Pulitzer around his waist. A bag of green bananas stuck out from his gear. Thank God for that. Bananas were on the shopping list. Green ones so they could ripen during the week.

But would McCann be able to run? He was covered in poison ivy, as bad a case as anyone had seen. The itch was so bad that McCann would take to covering his welts with Scotch tape. McCann was able to run, all right, but with a chip on his shoulder. He was further peeved when Owen Kimple was named one of the two team captains, a spot McCann felt he deserved. "That didn't go down well," said McCann. But he admitted, "I had some growing up to do."

With it all, McCann did everything asked of him, showing Stotan flair and courage, earning his nickname "Bulldog." His poison ivy was so bad it forced one eye shut. When McCann would remove the tape, his screams could be heard all the way to Watch Hill.

Of the eight boys, two, Page and Burdick, were headed into their senior year. Burdick, the other captain, brought up summer reading assignments for an English course to gain college credit. There were four juniors: Heron, Kimple, McCann, and Marnell. Gruenewald and King were sophomores.

"I was mortified," King recalled. "I was very much the youngster rebelling against any identity as a runner. I refused to wear regulation running shorts and was embarrassed to be judged as part of the running subculture."

On the other hand, Kimple recalled that in his previous season as a sophomore, "I had ridden an exhilarating curve of improvement and found myself desperately craving more." Kimple's introduction to Cerutty at spring meetings had made an impression. As Kimple recounted, "I remember a story about

Cerutty proving to his athletes that warm-up exercises were unnecessary by dumping a bucket of water on a lounging cat, upon which the cat leapt in the air and bolted away at full speed. I was both skeptical and intrigued."

This was the week's schedule:

Sunday: 1:00 Arrival, move in, set up. 2:30 Team meeting. 3:00 115-minute aerobic run. 6:00 Dinner. 7:30 Clinic. 10:30 Lights out.

Monday: 7:00 thirty-minute warm-up run and thirty minutes strength/core work. 8:30 Breakfast. 10:00 Clinic. 10:30 forty-five-minute training run. 12:00 Lunch. 2:00 Clinic. 3:00 sixty-minute training run. 6:00 Dinner. 10:30 Lights out.

Tuesday: Same as Monday.

Wednesday: 7:00 thirty-minute warm-up run and thirty minutes strength/core work. 8:30 breakfast. 10:00 Drive two hours to Otter Creek trail system. 12:00 fifty-minute relaxed run. 1:00 sixty-minute fartlek run plus sand hill repeats. 2:15 Lunch at Otter Creek, swimming, relax. 3:00 thirty-minute cool-down run. 4:00 Drive back to Kamp Kimple. 6:00 Dinner. 8:00 Clinic. 10:30 Lights out.

Thursday: Same as Monday.

Friday: Same as Monday except at 3:00 it's a one-hour hike instead of running.

Saturday: 9:00 two-hour run to end camp training. 11:30 Brunch, awarding of Stotan T-shirts. 1:00 Clean up and departure.

This was the week's meal plan:

Breakfast choices: egg whites, cereal with milk, peanut butter-and-jelly sandwich, fruit, orange juice.

Lunch choices: turkey, tuna fish, cheese, peanut butter-and-jelly sandwiches (whole-wheat bread, of course), and fruit.

Dinner: *Sunday* Steak with rice and vegetable. *Monday* Spanish rice.
Tuesday Mahi mahi steak with brown rice and vegetable. *Wednesday*
Pasta with chicken and vegetables. *Thursday* Steak with potato and
vegetables. *Friday* Salmon with brown rice and vegetables.

Aris was inspired to see how boys accustomed to junk food devoured John's
meals. They spoke of the food in the following terms: "incredible," "fantastic,"
"best I've ever eaten," and, as another compliment, "seriously healthy." Kimple's
favorite was the mahi mahi, which, after camp, he tried in vain to find prepared
the way John had. Gruenewald's favorite was the salmon, which he described
as "those beautiful raw, red salmon filets." Burdick favored the Spanish rice.
McCann said that no one prepared a better tuna-fish sandwich than John.
Everyone asked for more bowls of fruit salad. Back home, after camp was over,
it was common to get word that the boys would plead to their moms, "Why
can't you cook like John Aris?"

The revolution had begun. The culture had shifted. A new lifestyle was
taking hold.

When the boys ran their hearts out two and three times a day, arriving at
the table famished, they could see the direct link between healthy, nutritious
eating and running performance. Aris did his preaching to be sure, spurning
old-hat running sound bites like, "Get the furnace hot enough and anything will
burn." And endorsing others like, "You don't put conventional-grade gasoline
in a Ferrari."

But the boys learned for themselves. They did so while bonding over meals,
sharing in the spent relief of replenishment and camaraderie, reinforcing, bite by
bite, a brotherhood in which any one of them would be turned off by unhealthy
food choices and embarrassed to even consider them. Most importantly, they
knew, from that point on, a Big Mac attack meal would do them harm, abuse
the Stotan ideas they'd begun to cherish, and let teammates down.

Aris and his boys were now on the same page. When they gathered that
week for meals in the Kimple kitchen, the scene was right out of Cerutty, as he
described it in his rundown of the Portsea camp in *How to Become a Champion*:
"Large plates are piled high, since we enjoy, possibly, as large and beautiful
vegetables as are to be found anywhere in the world. Cauliflowers . . . cabbage
. . . carrots . . . and potatoes . . . baked in their jackets in the oven. . . . Fish and
poultry prevail, or minced steak cooked as hamburgers with onion. . . . Animal
fats are never used in our cooking. . . . The dessert is invariably fruit salad."

At Portsea, the Australian runners turned in for the night at ten thirty. Just like the F-M boys did at Lake Bonaparte.

∞

Lake Bonaparte, on the western edge of the Adirondacks, was a remote, idyllic spot far from everywhere and most everyone. The lake itself, about thirteen hundred acres, was a pristine postcard setting with the Kimple cottage backing onto a bay. Granite cliffs rose from its shore. Loons, blue heron, ducks, and osprey were common on its cobalt-blue waters. Occasional hunters' firearms could be heard in the distance. So too could war maneuvers from nearby Fort Drum. Spider jets would thunder overhead, grazing treetops. The boys were some six miles from the nearest village Harrisville, population about six hundred.

This was the North Country. Harrisville had a few scrubby-looking shops—movie rentals, anyone?—bowling lanes with manual scoring, a fish-and-gun club, rod-and-gun club, American flags on sentry, and the Oswegatchie River cutting through town.

"Our own perfect little running paradise," said Kimple.

Temperatures all week were in the sixties with a mix of sun and clouds. The humidity was tolerable, the wind soft. Logging roads, single-track paths, and power-line trails were at the runners' disposal. On workouts, the F-M team was flanked by cedar trees, red pine, hemlock, birch, and maple, with cooling breezes to temper the strain of hard faces and beating hearts.

Each day presented new and delectable terrain, hills everywhere. The boys were bare-chested, sinewy, all skin and bones, running up one hill and down another, accompanied by one almost-fifty-year-old man, wearing a FORECAST PAIN T-shirt, racing alone from one checkpoint to the next to supervise the workout. The boys ran harder than ever but felt uncommonly serene. Like settlers in the New World, they may have been the first to run at Lake Bonaparte—certainly the first high school cross-country team to train there as a group.

At six A.M., Bill's cowbell would sound reveille. The boys would dress and hustle up the staircase, sixty-six steps, from the cabin to the road and embark on a four-mile shake-out run. It was almost a workout unto itself with three "category" climbs topped by one referred to as "Sleeping Beauty." Upon completion, Bill would instruct, "Okay, boys, get your bricks."

Jim Kimple worked for a masonry firm and supplied makeshift weight-training tools. Each boy had four bricks totaling eighteen pounds. After the muscle-building regimen, there were bounding drills (like skips and leaps) on Wigwam Road; then the boys would repair to the Kimple deck for core work while looking out onto the lake. After that, breakfast.

Owen had come up on weekends in July for reconnaissance work. He scouted for trails, like the eighteen-mile dirt-and-gravel route out of Harrisville where the boys would see road signs riddled with bullet holes. The path was wide enough for the group to run eight abreast. Aris called it the Deliverance Trail, from the 1972 film set in rural Georgia.

"Sacred ground," said Kimple. "All of us would be feeling it." Owen, Tommy, and Jared, the three strongest, would tear away at some point, leading the pack for the better part of two hours, sending a message of unspoken greatness to one another.

Bill would run to checkpoints, stop, and count the boys' strides: 180, or 90 per leg, were considered optimal running efficiency. "Keep everything in line," Bill would say, referring to head, shoulders, arms, hips. John would come along on his bike.

The rustic Kimple cottage, on the lake's south shore, centered around one big sitting area, roughly twenty-by-thirty feet, with two couches, two beds, a large eating table, and warming wood stove. Off the main room was a six-by-eight-feet kitchen, two small bedrooms with double beds that were a tight squeeze, and a large master bedroom at the back. Six of the eight boys slept in the bedrooms. Bill and John took the beds in the sitting area next to windows facing the lake. Two other boys crashed on the couches.

The place sat about twenty feet above the water's edge. A staircase led to the lower deck and dock. The upper porch, a perfect spot to relax, was lined with more than twenty-five pairs of running shoes. Cabinets in the boathouse were stocked with food like supermarket shelves. The group had ninety gallons of water on hand. For the ten of them, this worked out to more than a gallon of water per day. At camp's end, the water was gone.

Even though the Kimples had gladly donated the family place, Jim Kimple harbored reservations at what would come of it. While Owen was expected to set a good tone, Jim worried whether the teens could be trusted at the water's edge, even with the Arises' supervision. Jim's wife, Emily, held hope that neighbors would guard against lakeside sins.

The Kimples' parting words to the boys were, "Nobody jumps off the cliffs!"

When the week was over, Jim and Emily were treated to pictures of the boys jumping with abandon off the cliffs including one of Owen doing a backflip.

The Kimples' shoreline friends reported how entertained they were by the boys' "antics" in the water. And some days later, a boatful of local girls, who'd apparently noticed the bare-chested contingent, pulled up to the Kimples' dock, asking, "Is this where the track boys are?"

Quarters at the cottage were close enough for the boys to engage in quiet conversation, but not too close to spoil anyone's need for privacy. In the limited downtime, when they weren't leaping from cliffs, the boys took out the Kimples' boat, played cards, napped, read, or gave each other buzz cuts with an electric razor. Some looked to John as an older brother to confide in. John was not too old to have abandoned his teenage side. The boys trusted him and were able to express their fears and frustrations in a personal way that might have been too difficult to reveal to someone older.

If in the close quarters the boys' personalities clashed, John would exit the room, leaving the boys to settle their own affairs. Burdick was the quiet leader, the Aris surrogate. He said little, but when he spoke, the others listened. "We learned about strength," he told me. "Strength in every aspect of your life." At times Burdick needed to tame Heron, the jokester trying to lighten the mood, when a more sobering air was needed. McCann's emotional wound was still festering. The hard runs could repair a lot of damage, but at the end of the day, the Stotan-living experience still needed to foment a seamless unit.

Since John was the cook, he and the boys forged an intimacy at mealtime. If a boy wanted more food, he asked John. Sometimes, John would give him the food off his own plate. As a father-and-son duo, John and Bill were an efficient team, and after camp ended Bill asked John to join him as an assistant coach during the fall season.

John Aris had captained the Fayetteville cross-country team in 1997 and been raised, he said, "to focus on what was essential in life and try to perfect it." In addition to running, John had been a concert violinist who'd won many honors in music competitions. The instrument he played had historical significance. It was made in 1917 in Italy by the world-famous violin maker Lucio Leonardi.

John had a fine touch and could accomplish a lot with little. To prepare meals in the tiny kitchen, John worked with a stove-top oven circa 1950 that he cleaned spotless. Windows and doors were kept open for ventilation. The menu was planned to the smallest detail. For hydration, in addition to water, the boys drank Endurox R4 for nutrition replacement.

Bill conducted daily clinics based on the reading matter he'd given the boys. The "classwork" was intended to enrich the boys' thought process and fortify their understanding of the mind-body relationship, through a kind of cleansing or purification. Once clean, once their self-limiting emotions were out of the way, the boys could learn and accept and even rely on key ideas that related to what Aris called "shared suffering" and what Cerutty had asserted as a central message: "Pain is the purifier."

It was evident that all of the eight boys had read the Lynch sports-psychology book. Maybe not twice, but they'd read it. Gruenewald was said to have read it three times. Who would doubt it? Tommy was a run-through-walls type who was seeking a touchstone after losing his mother to cancer a couple of years before. While only a sophomore, and with a baby face, Tommy embraced every Stotan concept, referring to the camp as "a place of rebirth" in which "I knew something revolutionary was happening in my personal life."

McCann, his sores oozing, was a work in progress. After McCann fell asleep during the first clinics, Bill made him stand the next time.

Aris constantly searched for ideas, developing a personal library of relevant resources: all of the Cerutty books, with emphasis on *Why Die?* and *How to Become a Champion*; the Peter Snell autobiography, *No Bugles, No Drums*, featuring much about Lydiard; Jim Collins's business and team-building books, especially *Good to Great*; *Brain Training for Runners*, by the sports scientist and trainer Matt Fitzgerald; *Speed with Endurance Process* by the noted Boston-area coaches Bill Squires and Bruce Lehane; and the Lynch sports-psychology text.

Aris had no idea how Lynch's advanced, broad-based ideas would impact the boys, or whether they would even understand them. Kimple was onto the coach from the outset. Kimple said later on, "Bill took a big risk trying to introduce that kind of 'spirituality' to a group of high school kids, a concept that most would reject as 'not cool' or 'too intense.' But it paid off."

When asked to discuss a chapter of *Thinking Body, Dancing Mind*, each boy spoke with conviction, whether it was about "Integrity," "Confidence," "Fear of Success," or "Perfectionism." Aris did what he could to embellish the learning process, trying not to take over the conversation while seeking as much input and analysis from the boys. It was hard not to leave one of those sessions feeling uplifted, said Aris.

This demonstrated to Aris that young people had a greater capacity for learning than we often give them credit for; that deep inside they really wanted to grow and explore and seek right-minded ideas, and that with supportive group dynamics the results could be extraordinary. The boys became students of the sport, expanding their investment in the Stotan process, and living a team mantra, "The process is the goal."

The two Lynch chapters that Aris stressed were "Egolessness" and "Selflessness," both central to the F-M mission. The runner who is consumed with himself and immersed in the self-centered illusions of his ego, Lynch wrote, creates anxiety and tension, within himself and others, and wastes a lot of energy doing so. "Whereas egolessness is a passive process of holding back, of not forcing yourself on others," explains Lynch, "selflessness is an active process of devotion to others' welfare and interests—even sometimes at the expense of your own." Aris said, "I would add that by being selfless, you free yourself of the constraints and stresses of having to perform only for yourself by thinking of performing for others, your teammates."

This intellectual exercise, applied successfully, helped the team grow. Could teenage boys be selfless, consumed by the process of running and racing for others? Yes. Could teenage boys take their "ego identity" crisis—the age-twelve-to-eighteen realm of Erik Erickson's eight stages of psychosocial development—and subordinate their sometimes uncontrollable egos in order to serve the team's greater good? Yes, they could. By doing this, the runners would learn over time to hold one another accountable and accept being held accountable themselves.

The paradox of selflessness was apparent to Kimple, as sharp an athlete as Aris has coached. Kimple understood that while being selfless the runner still retains his individual identity and does not lose sight of who he is; and at the same time each teammate strives for the other. It may be a subtle distinction, but Kimple explained it perhaps better than even Aris could.

"Instead of being afraid of blowing up," he said, using running vernacular for a poor race or workout, "you were excited to see how far you could go. Who cares if you failed? Who cares if you took a chance and came up short? You knew that all the other guys had one thing on their minds: running for you. It almost sounds paradoxical, to not care [about yourself] and care at the same time. But that's what made the relationships we shared so successful. We completely bought into the idea of total selflessness."

Kimple took his insight further by recounting the boys' training dynamic in the Adirondacks. "Camp was the first time our top five guys trained together at this whole new level, and it was exciting. We had never run workouts before where any one of five or six different guys could theoretically dominate the day if he was feeling really good. It was this very organic, profound mental shift in what we were running for. We learned to take shots *for* each other rather than *at* each other."

With camp soon to end and the boys diving back into the norms of suburban Syracuse, Aris wanted to give them a heavy dose of Stotan armor to combat the discordant milieu they would soon find at home. Aris would challenge the boys to use their "privilege of birth" as an asset—not as a crutch but as a foundational point "to become something greater."

Plush living does not tend to create strong cross-country runners and, according to a number of studies, does not produce healthy young people. Paul Tough's 2013 book, *How Children Succeed*, cites disturbing findings in the research by Suniyar Luthar, a psychology professor at Columbia University Teachers College. Luthar, who is an expert on the impact of affluence on adolescents, found a higher percentage of drug and alcohol use and depression in affluent teenagers than in those from low-income families. Another psychologist, Madeline Levine of California, author of *The Price of Privilege*, says in *How Children Succeed* that child-rearing practices in well-off homes result in high rates of emotional problems with kids as they enter the teen years.

Aris had taken on this fight and vowed to keep at it. He felt the boys needed the fortitude to stand on their own against the ills of their environment, on and off the running course.

∽

The day that epitomized the camp week was the Wednesday when the boys trained at Otter Creek, a two-hour drive east of the Kimple house deeper into the interior of the Adirondacks. Otter Creek had a utopian network of secluded trails, dense woods, creeks to ford, and, the main reason the group came, long sand hills like the ones Cerutty's men had run at Portsea.

The day began with a five A.M. wake-up. The boys did their morning shake-out run followed by core work and weight training. A soft breeze rustled the trees. The air smelled of lilac. After breakfast, Bill and John filled their van with food and water for the trip, and off they went.

At Otter Creek, Bill led the boys on their first run of fifty minutes. At forty-nine, he could still run with the boys, as long as the pace was not too fast or the distance too far. After that, the boys on their own did a one-hour "fartlek" workout—a mix of fast-paced runs—on rolling hills, ending with sand hill running on a massive earthy bowl that stretched about 275 feet. The bowl was about one hundred feet wide and one hundred feet deep. The boys proceeded to run up and down the heavy, dense hill, one repeat after another, each effort delivering new levels of strength and emotional resolve.

Then, for their "finisher," said Aris, "I took the boys to another sand hill, about one hundred meters from the bowl, for a final, grueling sprint. The team had already put in about two and a half hours of running that day, a good twenty miles, counting the morning shakeout. They were as tired as they'd been all week."

In the scientific literature, the longstanding belief that running fatigue results from a "mechanical" breakdown—limits on oxygen transport that compromise the muscles—has been replaced by a more nuanced view. This theory claims that fatigue is a balance between effort and motivation and that, as Alex Hutchinson wrote in *The New Yorker*, "The decision to stop is a conscious choice rather than a mechanical failure." Aris had seen considerable proof of the latter assessment. He believed that runners could always give more.

With one more sand hill left, Aris's boys were ready to reach for that "more." The density and looseness of the sand required more of everything: strength, power, balance, toughness, and precise form, no wasted motion, with high knee action and sweeping arms, elbows close in, and an intense mental focus.

A University of Michigan study found that the energy cost of running on sand was 10 to 100 percent greater than that of running on a hard surface—and that was on flat sand, not the steep sand hill on the Fayetteville bill of fare. This advanced effort was the whole point of the Cerutty sand-hill method—make it tougher and bring out each runner's best.

Aris grouped the eight boys in pairs, as though in military-drill formation. The hill, about 150 feet long, was almost twice what Elliott had run in Australia. It was as steep as a double-diamond ski slope and narrow, all of six feet wide. The boys had to remain in pairs, each half of the duo drawing strength from the other—and from the group overall. As Aris jogged to the top of the dune to give the starting signal, Burdick called the group into a huddle and said, "We're all going to finish this one *together*."

"Did they ever whip up that hill to the pinnacle," Aris recounted. "That was a prized moment of shared suffering, pain purifying . . . freedom." As the boys said later, "The machine was born." They would always think back to that sand hill. They would recall the image, the formation, the effort, that made them feel as one, as a well-engineered machine.

Kimple, looking back, said, "It marked the first time we looked at one another with the feeling, *this* was the 2004 team, and we were going to be dominant. Doubters became believers, and followers became leaders. It was a truly magical moment."

Afterward, as the boys had been doing all week, they leapt from cliffside rocks and bluffs into the water below. They could finally cool off and relax. Bill and John joined them.

After lunch, the boys went for a thirty-minute cool-down run. Disoriented from exhaustion and the unfamiliar trail network, the boys got lost, and thirty minutes became eighty-five minutes, about eleven miles, giving them over thirty miles of running for the day. Crazy, but a good crazy. It was nap time on the drive back to Lake Bonaparte.

∽

Before the week was out, the boys would take one final test, the toughest of the camp. Without advance notice, Aris gathered everyone in the main sitting area of the Kimple cabin. He had the boys sit in a circle and said, "Each of you, I want you to look at each other and tell me something you admire about the person, and something they could improve upon. This includes John and me. What you like and don't like about me. No worries, you can rip John and me to threads, that's fine. Don't you dare tell me what you think I want to hear."

The boys had learned to love salmon, and they'd run through sand dunes and they'd memorized complex mind-body ideas—but this? An adult-style encounter group? Bill Aris had some nerve.

In one last attempt to break down barriers and fears and open up pathways of unshakeable team bonding, Aris—without warning—asked the eight boys to marshal the courage to confront their emotions, to challenge their friends, their peers, with honesty and insight, while also doing the same with their coach, their authority figure—God himself.

In all his pontifical Greekness, his marathoner's idiosyncratic alienation, his Cerutty worship, had Bill Aris gone nuts? Could the boys be mature enough, and close enough, to confront one another in this most intimate, and open, setting? Could these kids find a clarity and understanding of emotion, a power within that few adults could marshal, and deliver a cogent assessment of a teammate, and the coach too, right then and there with no place to hide? Or would they be so overwhelmed by the pressure they might turn on the camp experience and suffer a lingering hurt?

"This was one of the scariest and most difficult things I've ever had to do in my life," recalled Kimple. "We were only fifteen or sixteen and had to look our best friends in the eye and say, 'This is what I don't like about you.'" Kimple himself was chided for being a Goody Two-shoes, for trying to be "some golden boy." John Heron, the jokester, was taken to task for not knowing when to turn off the levity. Andrew McCann, Mr. Cool, was given a dressing down for his outsized ego and socialite's air, hardly commensurate with cross-country.

Some feelings may have been hurt, but amid the honest intent and closeness fortified all week, the daring encounter worked. As a result, Kimple and his teammates overcame their fears, got closer, and came out stronger. "The exercise," said Kimple, "forced a vulnerability that allowed us to address things we were too afraid to confront before, and how to conquer the demons that running can oftentimes amplify."

Aris said, "The boys bared their souls. They walked out of that room as trusted friends and teammates. The week was complete. One hundred and eleven miles' worth, and much, much more."

On the final day of camp, the boys took a concluding, valedictory, two-hour run. Aris was so awed by them that he joined in for the entire effort. This was followed by a Stotan graduation ceremony in which Stotan T-shirts, designed by John, were awarded as symbols of achievement and a commitment to a Stotan way of running and life. On the front, the shirts had STOTAN and an image of Herb Elliott. The back was inscribed with PAIN IS THE PURIFIER. Purposely, the shirts were not pretty. The design and lettering were rough to represent the ethos of the camp, and of cross-country running.

As a personal tribute, Danny Marnell, an artist, painted a collage depicting the Stotan shirt, F-M uniform, and racing spikes and presented it to the other seven boys as gifts later in the season. Marnell, despite hearing loss, went on to earn a PhD in bioengineering from the University of Rochester.

When Aris returned home, he experienced a satisfaction he had not felt in years. He gave the boys a couple of days off to get some rest. After that, these boys, and their coach, would challenge conformity and running assumptions like never before.

But Aris still had a restless feeling in his gut. He thought about the girls team. The Stotan experiment was far from over. Would the boys' week away in a vacation setting have staying power back home? Could he convince a new group of teenagers—the girls, this time—of this new way to run, live, and find communion with teammates? He had to.

But it was one thing to believe in gender equity and another to see in the girls' faces not just killer eyes but an underlying vulnerability. How would Aris deal with the girls' differing expectations, cultural imperatives, psychosocial dispositions, and more complex physical maturation process? Was Aris inviting a perfect storm, something that could upend what he had thus far achieved with the boys? And when you came right down to it, were girls really "equal" to boys in running?

"As an eighth grader," recalled Courtney Chapman, "I was scared out of my mind that we would have to do the same amount of training as the boys and put so much time into such a simple sport."

Chapman could not have known at the time, but she and her teammates would be asked to change their lives while confronting the assault of puberty and the impact of heavy-duty running on menstruation, body fat, body image, social orientation, and just who they were as they walked the halls at Fayetteville-Manlius High School. How would Aris talk to girls about their monthly cycles and emerging sexuality? How would he calm fears about bodies and minds taken to the limit by exhaustive workouts?

Aris had not only athletes to transform. "My parents weren't ready for it," said Molly Malone. "They would say things like, 'You kids do too much.' When I would fall asleep at the dinner table, they would say, 'That guy's a slave driver!'"

As Aris devised ways of introducing the Stotan gospel to the girls, he had a more immediate challenge: how to achieve perfection with the boys when the Bulldog with the golf clubs and Lilly Pulitzer belt fell behind.

5

PAIN IS THE PURIFIER

To make a point—that was my mentality. As a unifying act, I wanted to suffer, too.

—*Jared Burdick, Fayetteville-Manlius cross-country runner*

2004 Season III

In late August of 2004, two weeks after the Fayetteville-Manlius boys returned home from the Stotan camp, the annual New York State Fair was held in Syracuse. The more than thirty performing acts during the ten-day festival included the Temptations and Shangri-Las, Cyndi Lauper and Crystal Gayle, Dion, Mary Wilson, and, fatefully for the F-M squad, the Allman Brothers Band.

One of the Stotans, Andrew McCann, was an Allman Brothers fan. On the day of their appearance, a Friday, Fayetteville had its usual afternoon practice scheduled for Green Lakes State Park. McCann told friends to pick him up after practice so he could attend the concert.

Since the pivotal camp experience in the Adirondacks, Bill Aris continued the process of teaching the tenets of a runner's pain tolerance—not mere acceptance but welcoming pain, embracing pain, defeating pain. For his sermons before practice, in the stillness of a picnic area, Aris bellowed with command-ments of selflessness and shared suffering. He summoned his patron saint, Percy Cerutty, with his Stotan gospel and eccentricity, in pleas to the boys to remember what they'd learned in the wilderness, running three times a day, bonding in the climactic sand-hill workout, and in the final awarding of the treasured camp shirts.

McCann felt his transformation was magical. "It was surreal," he said. "Like we were floating on air. To execute beyond pain, you always knew it was shared with your teammates. Each of us felt indestructible."

The boys craved higher levels of training, and Aris gave it to them. A week before the state fair opened, the boys, in the morning, did a forty-minute run along with weight training and core work. In the afternoon, they did a 10k time trial—all-out running, a virtual race—on the hilly trails of Green Lakes. This was twice the standard high school cross-country 5k race distance.

Tommy Gruenewald, the fifteen-year-old sophomore, led the Stotan pack that day in 35:45. Given the slow-footed terrain, that was a college-level effort. The previous year, in the state cross-country meet Class A division, Gruenewald, as a freshman, was the fifth Fayetteville scorer, almost a minute behind the first man. Gruenewald had embraced the team's new ideas, saying, "I knew I was becoming something better than I had ever been before."

After the time trial, the boys ran another forty-five minutes that afternoon, giving them two hours of running for the day. Two days later, in a ninety-minute session, the boys did sixty minutes of running in five-minute "fartlek" segments on hilly loops at 80 to 90 percent of maximum effort. They took short recovery breathers between each run. This amounted to running about a mile nine times on wickedly tough terrain at close to all-out effort.

No problem. Pain was the purifier. "Cookie bakes and sleepovers don't build team unity," said Aris, mocking what is sometimes done in cross-country. "Suf-fering together does."

Aris sucked up suffering like a spent man taking his first drink. At camp, still a daily runner, Aris had logged almost all 111 miles with the team, at his own pace. He ran and exhorted the boys and ran some more and gesticulated while running and exhorting like some crazy soul lost in the woods beseeching the elements for succor.

However, the new program was barely a month old since that first day of camp. Back in the real world—the self-satisfied suburbs—would the Fayetteville runners' new normal hold up? Aris held his breath.

Indeed, Aris detected some "mouthy, braggy" comments and off-kilter body language on the team, which flew in the face of Stotan humility. Aris was waiting for the right moment to do something about it. But was Aris overreacting? After all, McCann spoke of a "new serenity," the otherworldly confidence that Aris had tried to instill. John Aris could feel it himself, too. "We knew something special was about to happen," he said. "And nobody knew our secret."

On the Friday of the Allman Brothers concert, the boys had run thirty minutes in the morning. They also did barefoot drills to strengthen their feet. Trainers, while supportive, were sometimes "too much shoe," mediating the need for the feet to do the work in facilitating a strong forefoot lift off the ground.

Aris scheduled a ten-mile run for Green Lakes that Friday afternoon. Even the newly empowered Stotans needed an occasional "easy" run. Aris told them today's ten-mile pace should be about seven minutes per mile, no faster. McCann fretted. Could he run the seventy minutes and make it from the interior of the park to meet his buddies and get over to the fairgrounds in time for the concert?

Andrew—never call him Andy, he hated it—seemed a contradiction. He was the one who'd first told Bill Aris about the sports-psychology text that became a hallmark of the Stotan camp and much F-M running thereafter. But McCann was also the last of the boys to finish the book and the one who fell asleep during team discussions.

This day, McCann proceeded to run a much faster pace than Aris had instructed, dragging the rest of the boys with him, in order to leave the park early. Was McCann satisfying the immediate-gratification part of his teenage brain, or was his return to the real world too much enticement to remain faithful to the squelching of the teenage ego?

Either way, Aris was livid. To Aris, this transgression was unforgivable. It was like a soldier leaving his battalion to go out on his own during a combat mission. It was desertion.

All training had a broad calculation. Every application, whether fast or faster, hills or distance; every extension of the body to near maximal effort was a piece of work that had to fit in—not based on regimentation, which Aris despised, but on a canvas with a touch of blue here, a spot of red there, a mosaic based on science, instinct, and a petri dish of poetic inspiration. Mess that up and everything went kaput.

McCann went out on the Green Lakes trails and ran six minutes per mile for an hour on the perimeter loop. "It was completely stupid, teenage, idiotic," said Owen Kimple, who, along with the other top runners had no choice but to follow. Senior cocaptain, Jared Burdick, who could have put a stop to it, was away on a college visit. McCann had told no one of his plan. He just flew. Then he went to see the Allman Brothers.

John Aris was seething. "You don't change the program by running faster than you're told to," he said. "You don't put your teammates in a state of compromise, affecting the next workout or race. By doing this, you confuse the coaching staff. It's dishonest."

The Allman Brothers set included a cover of the blues artist Elmore James's "Done Somebody Wrong." The lyric in part:

> *It's all my fault*
> *I must have done something wrong, oh yeah*

Bill Aris kept his feelings to himself. He would wait for the next day, Saturday morning, to unleash his formidable teaching moment. Morning came to Green Lakes. It was sunny, temperatures in the eighties, humid, with a light breeze. The broad trails beckoned.

∽

Aris's Greek pontification was ready to burst. But instead of using a philosophical weapon from, say, Homer, Aris turned to the most unlikely of moral guideposts—Bear Bryant and Texas football.

Aris had read the 2001 book *The Junction Boys: How Ten Days in Hell with Bear Bryant Forged a Championship Team*, written by Jim Dent. The book told the story of Bryant's summer of 1954 preseason Texas A&M summer camp in 110-degree weather on the edge of Texas Hill Country. It was Bryant's first season with A&M, and he was determined to make men out of boys. As Dent told it, Bryant did not allow water during practice, which lasted from morning to night. Bryant relied on a doctor, who'd told him, "You don't pour cold water on a hot engine. So why would you pour cold water on a hot boy?" About half the players left the camp in exhaustion. Those who stuck it out were called "survivors."

Aris certainly had no truck for Bryant's style of abuse, and he cared nothing about Texas football. But in thinking of a way to test the boys' commitment after McCann's act, which threatened everything the team had worked for and achieved, Aris felt he needed something dramatic and memorable. He called it "the Junction Boys workout."

The entire team, boys and girls, gathered at the park without any notion of what was to come. Certainly McCann was in the dark, suckered by naivete. "I thought I'd gotten away with it," he said.

Aris proceeded to single out the eight boys who'd attended the Stotan camp. He wanted every team member to know that this elite corps would never be treated with kid gloves, never be given any concession. Aris had no problem throwing it into McCann's face, saying that he'd ditched the team to do his own thing.

"I knew I was to blame pretty quickly," McCann recalled. "Bill getting mad at me was not a rarity."

Aris told them, "Some of you have forgotten what we learned at camp," and he then read the "Stotan Creed," word for word, adding with disgust, "Does that ring a bell?"

Aris went on. "You embraced it and loved it. Guys, today we're going to find out if you still want to be 'normal.'" Aris told them the tale of the Junction Boys. "Fellas," he said, "today you're going to do a Junction Boys workout. After we're done, you're going to think back to the Stotan camp and tell me what you learned that week."

For two hours, the eight boys were instructed to run just about every loop, circuit, hill, and pathway on the Green Lakes trails, nonstop, hill after hill, brutal hills, full-out pace, each segment designed to test toughness and will and a commitment to shared suffering.

"It's the only punitive workout I've ever given," said Aris years later. "If they rebelled, if they said, 'the hell with it,' it would mean the whole experiment had failed."

Burdick would not let that happen. Saying nothing, he set the pace, pushing relentlessly as Aris wanted, and Burdick was not even present for the prior day's misdeed. "To make a point—that was my mentality," Burdick said. "As a unifying act, I wanted to suffer, too."

Kimple recalled the suffering with clarity. "There were three-minute hills. There was a short, steep hill, done repeatedly, waiting for Bill's whistle for us to move on. Then, a twelve-minute loop; then, one-minute hills. We had no idea what was coming next, no idea when it would be over."

Checking his stopwatch, Aris could see the Stotan armor as never before. Like fighters taking punches in the ring, the boys' body language and countenance called to Aris, "We can take it; give us what you've got."

One measure of the blistering session was the timing of John Heron's stomach problem. "I would puke in every workout, every run, every race," said Heron, who'd run track and come into the cross-country season after playing soccer in the fall. Later on, in college, said Heron, tests showed that exercise caused him to produce extra bile in his gall bladder. This condition caused vomiting under physical stress. At F-M, all Heron could do was run through it, not even stopping, as teammates or stunned opponents darted away from the surprise assault. For his part, Aris ignored it.

In the Junction Boys workout, the effort was so rich from the start that it took little time for Heron to unload his breakfast. "The harder the run, the sooner I'd puke," he said. "That day I was puking all over the place."

Heron had been an easy Stotan convert. His older sister, Lauren, had been a nationally ranked track runner for Fayetteville who went on to college running at William & Mary. In fall 2002, Lauren's college-freshman year, she made the Tribe's varsity squad that qualified for the NCAA cross-country championships held at Indiana State University in Terre Haute.

John, his dad, and Bill Aris piled into a car, drove eleven hours out to Terre Haute, and shared a hotel room to see Lauren compete. John, then fourteen, had yet to come out for track and had just met Bill for the first time. "He was just some guy to me," he noted. "My sister's former coach."

But in observing Bill's mannerisms, quirkiness, speech, and persona on the long drives, over meals, and at the hotel and racecourse, young John was thoroughly impressed, deciding he wanted Bill as his coach, too, and thinking of him with awe as "the hairiest man I have ever met."

A little puking was a small price to pay for the privilege of joining Aris's alien escapades. When the Junction Boys workout was over, after the eight young bodies had been taken to the limit, a strange thing happened: the boys were proud of it, reveling in yet more mind-body synergy—everybody in a new realm, perhaps beyond anything ever seen in a team of high school cross-country runners.

"It was thinking on a different plane," said Aris.

Punishment had bled into affirmation. "It was a major inflection point early in the season, a source of enlightenment," said Kimple. "The Junction Boys workout was a rock to fall back on."

McCann, who ran every minute knowing his Stotan loyalty was at stake, said the experience gave him a new definition of himself, his motives, what that season could turn out to be. A great way to spin it, he offered, was, after the accountability, after the anger, "We just accomplished *this* workout! We ran *that.*"

∞

In the first meet of the 2004 fall season, it was McCann who led an F-M sweep of the first five places in the Vernon-Verona-Sherrill (VVS) Invitational, held in Fayetteville's central New York region. There were three boys' varsity races with about four hundred runners from fifty-six teams, and Fayetteville had five of the six fastest times across all divisions. More importantly, the tight pack that had been fashioned in the Adirondacks and nurtured at Green Lakes materialized with a twelve-second spread in the 5k from McCann's 16:31 to Burdick, the team's fifth scorer that day, in 16:43.

Twelve seconds was a razor-thin compression, hardly ever seen in a big meet. Even twenty or thirty seconds was considered excellent. A team of good runners with a thirty-second compression would likely win a state championship and rank among the nation's best.

Aris's ultimate goal was "zero compression." No separation. All five scorers crossing the finish line as one in a major competition. Just the idea of it, the image, could make a cross-country coach weep. It was cross-country's impossible dream. Zero compression was the equal of a perfect game in the World Series, maybe one with twenty-seven strikeouts.

While the VVS meet was large in size, the competition level was modest, and F-M dominance did not make any sort of national splash. After the sweep, the respected tullyrunners.com assessment was that F-M was now "one of the best teams in New York."

The Fayetteville girls, third that day, were in the development stage as a team unit. Lacrosse star Kristen Taylor, a junior, was the individual winner for Fayetteville, running a snappy 19:51, and Fayetteville put two more girls in the top ten. But their five-girl compression was a slowpokey four minutes. The girls were young with one senior in their varsity seven.

Taylor's mother, Kathy, was the coach of Fayetteville's state championship girls lacrosse team. Kathy had encouraged her players to run track for Aris to gain fitness. Kristen did winter track, training through Syracuse snowstorms, and, with her athleticism, gravitated to cross-country in the fall. In her first cross-country workout as a sophomore, she could run nine miles comfortably.

Aris was feeding the 2004 girls bits and pieces of Stotan lore like seeds for a fall harvest—the next fall perhaps, or maybe the one after. Taylor and other girls were a little miffed that they hadn't been invited to the summer camp. When the boys returned, the ideas tossed around gave Taylor the impression that the camp was something "mystical." She said, "It had a trickle-down effect on us. What rubbed in most was a shift in mindset from individual to team."

Jessica Hauser felt the shift when she needed it most. She'd left soccer to join cross-country as a sophomore in 2004. However, in an early Green Lakes 5k time trial, she suffered a severe injury, a torn hip flexor, and had to be carried off the course to the parking lot by John Aris. She could not run for months but spoke repeatedly with Bill about nutrition, attended practices and meets, and tried to find out more about the mysticism of the boys' camp.

One day at Green Lakes when Hauser was feeling down, Owen Kimple came up to her and put his arm around her for support. Hauser recalled, "He was an older boy who I didn't know very well, and he was handsome, and I remember as a young high school girl being a bit embarrassed."

Kimple gave Hauser the *Thinking Body, Dancing Mind* book. "He told me to read the chapters about overcoming failure and the one about injury. He told me that everything would be okay and I just needed to change my perspective. If I could control how my mind approached this setback, then I would be stronger when my recovery was over. It was my first exposure to the Stotan realm."

I asked Jerry Lynch, the book's coauthor, what he thought about the powerful effect his sophisticated ideas had had on the young Fayetteville runners. He told me that the book's core values of "selflessness," "suffering," and "community" were fundamental and called to the youngsters' native impulses and cravings. "These runners may not know how to express it," said Lynch, "but they were starving for such a deep connection." At Fayetteville, they embraced the incandescent truths that running bestowed.

Kimple won the next race, the East Syracuse-Minoa Invitational, close to home on a muddy course. The five Fayetteville scorers finished fourteen seconds apart. The girls took second, their compression now under three minutes.

Burdick won the race after that, the McQuaid Invitational in Rochester, in 15:12 for the three-mile course through Genesee Park. On a rainy day, F-M forged a near-sweep of its Varsity AAA division, taking five of the top seven places for nineteen points and setting a new course record for five-man team average time: 15:20. The compression: fifteen seconds.

Three meets, three different F-M winners. It was something new to cross-country. "Any one of the five of us could be top man," said Burdick. That's what happened in training. Every runner challenged the others to run harder, carried along by Aris's pronouncements about conquering pain. Whoever was strongest took charge, leading a conjoined pack fazed only by the hydraulics of John Heron's vomit.

"Keep in mind," said Kimple. "We were sixteen. A lot of us did not have the ability to think deeply about things." Aris's greatest skill may have been his ability to convey complex ideas—like "the search for truth"—in ways that teenagers could grasp, appreciate, and ultimately long for.

In every workout it was always there: sixteen-year-olds devouring community, purity, and sacrifice in their own ways. Learning never stopped. It defined workouts like six repeated one-mile loops around Green Lake's exquisite Round Lake—each loop faster than the one before—at close to race pace with three minute jogging breaks in between. The boys ran too fast to notice the hissing of owls, who would announce their proprietary presence.

"It was like boom, boom, boom, boom," Kimple recalled of the training. "Everyone was accountable to everyone else. You truly believed that. You'd rather die than fall off the back of the pack."

While the first two meets were small potatoes, McQuaid had twenty-four races with six thousand runners. In the F-M race, there was a team from Georgia and a team from Canada. They probably did know what hit them. The team that meant the most to Fayetteville was Lockport, from the Buffalo area, considered a 2004 state rival. After placing sixth in a poor showing at the 2003 State Federation Championship, Fayetteville vowed to come back and win in 2004. At McQuaid, F-M's fifth scorer, Heron, was thirteen seconds ahead of the first Lockport man. "We made Lockport completely irrelevant," said Kimple.

After McQuaid, F-M allowed itself a touch of macho pride, and the boys' idea of calling themselves The Machine crystallized. Maybe it wasn't the best example of Stotan humility. Aris had introduced the boys to Pink Floyd, his favorite band, and their 1975 hit "Welcome to the Machine." The team played it on rides to Green Lakes. "A badass song," said Kimple. "The lyrics spoke to us."

To the boys, the meaning and relevance were elliptical. The tune, written by Pink Floyd front man Roger Waters, started off, *"Welcome my son, welcome to the machine/Where have you been?"* It describes the band's disillusionment with the music industry. The Fayetteville boys framed it as a Stotan-style challenge to convention, with a little sarcasm thrown in. But mostly The Machine—from the title itself—became an F-M calling card, rallying closeness, toughness, and the emergence of a new definition of running excellence.

Teenage boys could make purity and badass go together.

The week later, leading into the Manhattan Invitational at Van Cortlandt Park in the Bronx, running people were starting to compare Fayetteville-Manlius with top teams from around the country like York, from the Chicago area, and The Woodlands of Texas. In its regional rankings, *Harrier* magazine had Fayetteville ranked number one in the Northeast. But F-M was still cloaked in mystery. Not one of its boys was known to be a credible runner.

The statewide talk that season, especially in Fayetteville's central New York backyard, had been the dazzling track performances of two "Lost Boys of Sudan" at Tully High who'd been taken in by local families. Lopez Lomong and Dominic Luka fled from murderous militias, came to the United States through humanitarian organizations, and proceeded to win state championships in the 1600 and 800 meters, respectively, with national-class times. Lomong ran 4:10.12 and Luka 1:50.33. The Fayetteville boys could not imagine such running. (Lomong became a US citizen in 2007 and, four years out of high school, was the American flag-bearer at the 2008 Olympic Games in Beijing.)

The 2004 state track meet had been held in late May with no Fayetteville scorers. The question was asked: What could have happened to the unheralded Fayetteville boys over the summer to put them within reach of the nation's best runners come fall? It was now October, and the word *Stotan* had never been uttered in public by the F-M contingent. Percy Cerutty, who died in 1975, was long forgotten. "Pain is the purifier" was best kept quiet. Who would dare to express it in early-twenty-first-century America?

F-M prepared for Manhattan with its menu of mile circuits, hill repeats, short, fast runs; long, aerobic runs; and power sprints. After their final workout two days before the meet, Aris gathered the boys to a quiet spot in the back of the school grounds to discuss the race plan.

The Manhattan meet was the largest one-day high school event in the country with upward of ten thousand runners. Times in the various varsity divisions would be compared and an overall "winning" team would receive wristwatches as special prizes. The overwhelming boys favorite, Christian Brothers Academy of New Jersey, would race Fayetteville in the Varsity C race. CBA had been the dominant distance-running school in the Northeast for twenty-five years. With the inaugural Nike Cross Nationals to be held in Portland, Oregon, in December, teams from around the country were seeking the best competition to prove themselves to Nike selectors assessing performances in all fifty states.

CBA hoped to make short work of Fayetteville, establish its credentials, and then coast to Portland. CBA coach Tom Heath did not take F-M's upstate record seriously. Fayetteville had competed in Verona, Manlius, and Rochester. This was New York City, baby, the Bronx. Van Cortlandt Park, the cradle of cross-country civilization. The Van Cortlandts themselves, wealthy Dutch settlers, had their family burial plot in the vicinity of the most badass hill of all—Cemetery Hill—located on the college five-mile course.

A death of a certain kind would occur on Saturday, prompted by Heath himself. Website stories before the meet highlighted comments by Heath on the impending race. They quoted him as saying, "We're itching to get 'em." This statement went viral in running circles. Again and again, story after story: we're itching to get 'em.

Aris was no internet hound, but he got the message and it made him furious. "We weren't even thinking about CBA," Aris said. "But this egocentric posture was completely anathema to our whole value system."

At the F-M team meeting, Aris possessed the fury of Macbeth. "I'll never forget it," said Kimple. "Bill started talking about the race and CBA. He told us, 'We're going to keep the pressure on, keep the pressure on, keep the pressure on.' . . . Everything was building in his voice."

"I can still picture it," said Heron. "Veins were popping out of his head. None of us had seen him like this before."

Aris took a pencil from his pocket. He held it with both hands so it was visible to the boys. As he spoke, he slowly bent the pencil. He mocked the cocky quotes from the CBA coach. He said CBA had disrespected them and that they were going to relentlessly hammer them at Van Cortlandt Park. Then, to finish his point, Aris bent the pencil in half and said, "We're going to snap the freaking pencil."

The boys, at once startled and inspired, were like, "Fuck, yeah, we're going to snap the pencil."

The next day, Friday, the team, boys and girls, bussed to New York. For a relaxed workout, the boys ran the two-and-a-half-mile racecourse twice, finishing with sprints on the home straight. On Saturday morning of the race, after a twenty-minute shake-out run, the boys had a meeting of their own in a wooded area behind their hotel. It was still dark. The seven varsity runners sat in a circle to meditate. They needed to contemplate their aggressive marching orders while also finding a certain peace. To set the mood, Heron brought Indian flute music to play, as well as the soundtrack from the film *Endurance*,

about the great Ethiopian Olympic champion, Haile Gebrselassie. They closed
their eyes, talked, settled in.

∾

The day was beautiful for running. Springlike. No wind. The race trails were dry.
A fast day. The two-and-a-half-mile course had been run virtually unchanged
for almost a hundred years. Every so often, however, Parks Department renova-
tions would impact the racing. In 1997, trails were spruced and debris removed
with railroad ties added as safety markers. Some complained that the smoother
ride took away some prized Bronx grit and resulted in faster times. In 2002 and
2003, the park's lake was dredged, which caused the race start to be moved. It
was, frankly, disorienting.

But in 2004, everything was back to normal for a run at history. It was still
treacherous in the downhill section of the Back Hills. There were rocks, tree
roots, sharp turns, narrow paths. Catch a spike and you'd go flying. It was
not for the timid. CBA had never been timid. Fayetteville-Manlius? Time to
scratch the itch.

Bill and John Aris had reviewed every inch of the course. The broad opening
flats funneled into the bumpy, narrow Cowpath after about a quarter-mile,
creating a bottleneck. The seven F-M boys were instructed to start out fast in
a 2-3-2 formation, a phalanx up front, for clear running room, then drop the
hammer. "CBA is nothing more than a part of the play," Bill Aris told them.

The meet had a festival atmosphere. Hundreds of team tents with picnic
paraphernalia added color to the bland grounds. The view from high up, from
the subway platform or the bluffs above the course, revealed Bronx emblems
like the posh Fieldston School, Manhattan College, New York Botanical
Garden, and now-touristy Italian sections where Dion and the Belmonts once
sang a cappella on the street corner.

Aris waited at the Cowpath. Heath took his usual position a half-mile out
where the field exited the Cowpath, climbed the short Freshman Hill, and angled
over a bridge and into the hills. Other than coaching zeal, Aris and Heath had
little in common. Aris was the lean marathoner with big ideas who started from
scratch every year. Heath was no runner, learned on the job, and counted on
school running traditions for empowerment.

Anxious crowds lined the course from the start to the bridge. They'd read
the stories. They knew what was at stake. They knew that CBA had a great

race the week before at the New Jersey state meet site, Holmdel Park. They dismissed Fayetteville. To them, to Heath, upstate New York was like Canada. Everyone expected a CBA coronation.

Kimple, usually confident, was edgy. "I remember feeling nervous during our warm-up," he recalled. "CBA was this big, bad team, the best we'd ever faced."

In their pre-race huddle, the F-M boys, eyeing CBA doing its final strides off the chalked line, agreed: "Let's snap the pencil."

Four F-M boys—Jared Burdick, Tommy Gruenewald, John Heron, and Owen Kimple—went out in a dead sprint and into the lead as one. Andrew McCann was a few strides back with the first CBA runner, Chris Horel. "It was not an easy pace," said Horel when we spoke years later. "I felt it." The rest of the CBA boys trailed from behind.

Heath waited. He couldn't believe his eyes. After little more than two minutes of running, the Fayetteville runners whizzed by in their prescribed formation. Heath's CBA Colts were in another race. A tornado might as well have battered Heath into submission. "The gun went off," he said, "and it was over."

The CBA fans and alumni that turned out were less sanguine. Runners go out too fast all the time and die at the end. The CBA boys would catch up, wouldn't they? Beyond a half-mile no one could see the race. The Back Woods were too remote. It was just runners and trees and a canopy of shade.

Up the hills, as steep as a staircase in a Costa Rican rainforest, Kimple glanced around, saw only teammates, took in the solitary quiet, and thought, "Holy shit, it's just us. Where *is* everyone else?"

Heron nominally led the foursome. He said the spirited pace felt no different than training at Green Lakes. Heron just wanted to get through the uphills before throwing up. He just about made it.

The front four did not see McCann. "We had no clue where he was," said Kimple. "I was almost going to turn around and look for him."

McCann's position was paramount. It was not about a possible five-man Fayetteville sweep—not yet. ("That was preposterous," said John Aris.) It was about the quirky beauty, and logic, of cross-country scoring. In a field of over two hundred runners, a team taking the first four places could lose if its fifth and final scorer was far back while the second-place team bunched all of its scorers in the first twenty or so.

With the twists and turns of the wooded trails, vision was obscured. Like the Bronx itself, nothing back there was neat. Hiking trails intersected the running path. One trail led to the park stables. Horseback riders were known to leave the bridle paths and trespass on running turf, where they'd leave behind quite a mess. In competition, patience was not a virtue. The layout, with its lived-in surprises, valued quick feet and quick instincts. It was more "go get 'em" than "pace yourself."

The F-M front four had to rely on faith that McCann had not twisted an ankle, or that the Bulldog had not undermined his reputation and surrendered to lack of will. "I could see *them*," said McCann. "I'd yielded too much early on. I was gritting to make up ground." Horel, a future navy lieutenant, was ahead by thirty yards. They were fifth and sixth as the field crested the last ascent and bounded into free-fall downhills.

F-M assistant coach Dave Davis was right there at the apex as Horel passed first. Davis, spurring McCann on, launched into "singing sweet lullabies," his primal scream of unmentionables.

Burdick pulled ahead of Heron and led the foursome. Each of the four felt he could win, perhaps Gruenewald most. The night before, at the hotel, Bill Aris had taken Tommy aside for a private meeting. "He told me he thought I was fit enough to win," said Gruenewald. "That race carried deep meaning for me."

The F-M leaders flew out of the woods and back over the bridge to a final, steep downhill leading to the long home straight. Spectators also flew to get to the finish area and witness history. At this point, rousing cheers went to quiet like lights turned off. Where was CBA?

"We were strung out," said Horel. "Getting crushed."

Off the downhill, young Gruenewald, fueled by his boost from Aris, asserted himself for the first time in a race—like "the prodigal son," he would say—and took the lead. Burdick and Kimple were a stride back with another stride to Heron. McCann? Where was McCann?

He and Horel, the CBA first man, tumbled desperately off the downhill together and into the sweeping openness of the closing straight in the race for home. McCann, five feet eight, ran low to the ground. Horel, five feet eleven and a feathery 125 pounds, used his long strides to gain five yards, then ten, as the cinder path sprayed up dust in the runners' faces.

McCann could see that his four teammates had the finish to themselves. The sweep depended on him. "There was only one thing on my mind," said McCann. "I can't be the guy who blows it. That scared the shit out of me."

Even with his golf clubs and Lilly Pulitzer belt, McCann took his bulldog stature with pride. Of the top five, Burdick was the intellectual, dragging schoolbooks to the summer camp. Gruenewald was the young pup with the most talent. McCann, Kimple, and Heron were all juniors who would compete against one other. Kimple and Heron had more basic foot speed, so McCann usually had to work the hardest to keep up.

"You could see Andrew's frustration," said Heron. "He was a runner before the rest of us. And he had that 'fucking' attitude, which sometimes got him in trouble."

"I perceived myself as gritty," said McCann. "That's how I managed to get the most out of myself."

Horel, who would shoulder two Middle East tours, had his own reputation for honor, even in high school. "Chris was the one you'd want in your foxhole," said Heath.

McCann drew even with Horel as the pair reached Aris, practically standing on the racecourse, with about 250 yards left. Spectator fencing extended about a hundred yards from the finish chute, and there were no officials beyond that point to prevent a coach from screaming into the ear of a runner on wobbly legs praying for the agony to stop.

CBA? Fayetteville? "It's all green! All green!" an F-M parent, Jay Marnell, Danny's father, shouted, referring to the team's turquoise uniforms.

Amid the tumult of the finish area, that was the only voice heard: the one parent. "It was quiet," Heron recalled. Spectators were speechless.

Heron tried not to throw up in front of the crowd. He also realized he was wearing a ring. At the time, jewelry of any kind was disallowed in high school cross-country. The rules varied by state. You could get disqualified, and some runners did. Heron wiggled the ring off and secured it in his fist.

The Fayetteville first four, led by Gruenewald, approached the finish in close order. The same closeness as camp. The same closeness as Green Lakes. Taking it all in, from the summer sand hills to the salmon dinners, Aris got emotional. "I still choke up to this day," he said. "Everyone together, with McCann a little farther back."

With tears on his cheeks, Aris ran up to McCann, as close as he could get, and hollered, "You need to make this *hurt!*"

Bulldog surged ahead with 150 yards to go. It wasn't over yet. "It was terrifying," said McCann. "Trying to hold on."

But Horel had nothing left and McCann swept across the finish in fifth. His teammates embraced him, and the sport of cross-country, whose origins were evident in every tendon of the course, tried to figure out how the greatest team performance ever by these boys from upstate Manlius just happened.

For a moment, Aris's Stotan purity took a hit. As McCann rushed home with room to spare, and the sweep was tied up, Aris ran around yelling, "They're itching to get us! They're itching to get us!" The boys themselves were reserved, humble. "Bill needed a release," said Heron.

It was Heron's father, Larry, seeing the unbecoming spectacle, who saved Aris from himself, telling him, "That's not Stotan." Aris agreed and apologized. "That was my dark side," Aris admitted.

Remember the scene in the 1967 Oscar-winning film *In the Heat of the Night*, when the scrupulous Sidney Poitier character, in an unguarded moment, tells costar Rod Steiger, the beleaguered Mississippi sheriff, "I can pull that fat cat down"? Poitier, playing a homicide expert, was referring to the town's racist landowner. "I can bring him right off this hill," Poitier adds, his cool grace leavened with fighting anger.

Detecting Poitier's vulnerability, Steiger takes his shot. "Man," he says, "you're just like the rest of us. *(pause)* Ain't ya?"

That was Bill Aris in the kaleidoscope of Van Cortlandt Park. The "itching" thing had riled him because he didn't like to play by those rules. When Aris felt compelled to address the taunts, it undercut what he'd tried to stand for.

The CBA PR machine had shaken the F-M architecture. Beforehand, Aris needed to apply what he called an extrinsic accelerator as a flag to boost his team. He'd picked up the concept from management expert Jim Collins, author of *Good to Great*. Based on years of research, Collins had identified intrinsic or extrinsic "accelerators" to build positive corporate momentum. F-M held to the intrinsic—"being better for our own sake," said Aris—but this urban-orbit putdown required something different. This was not the last time an opposing coach would challenge F-M authenticity before a big race.

Ironically, without realizing it, Aris, in his untoward revelry, taught another lesson. "We realized we're all human," said John Heron. "Bill showed us that this is what 'normal' looks like if we behave that way."

Heath would chalk up his premeet remarks to shortsightedness. "We were a very good team," he told me. "I thought Fayetteville was good, but not that good." Afterward, the mood was awkward in the CBA camp. "We were embarrassed," said Horel. "Our parents didn't know what to say to us." Heath tried to ease his runners' despair. "We just got beat by the best team ever at Van

Cortlandt," he told them. For some closure, CBA had to do something. They decided to find the F-M guys, along with Aris, and congratulate them.

Aris sent the F-M boys on their cool-down run before meeting the media. While flush with success, they were still, in their own way, babes in the woods. "We didn't understand what we just did," said Kimple. "That would take weeks."

∽

This is what the Fayetteville-Manlius boys had just done:

- Recorded what may have been the first boys one-through-five perfect sweep for fifteen points in any major competition against a top-ten nationally ranked team, high school or college. By comparison, at the 1981 NCAA men's cross-country championship at Wichita State, a team comprised of African record holders, causing a recruiting uproar, led the University of Texas–El Paso to take five of the first eight places for seventeen team points. The individual UTEP winner, from Kenya, would go on to set the world record for 10,000 meters on the track. The runner-up, also from Kenya, would set the world record for 10,000 meters on the road. The team's fourth scorer, from Tanzania, Suleiman Nyambui, was the previous year's Olympic silver medalist in the 5,000 meters at Moscow.

- Broken the Van Cortlandt Park all-time boys' team time record with a 12:48.82 five-man average for the two-and-a-half-mile course. The previous record, 12:53.56, was set in 1971 by a team from Buffalo. Any boy who could run the course in under thirteen minutes was considered elite. The F-M times were 12:42.0 (Gruenewald), 12:48.5 (Kimple), 12:49.6 (Burdick), 12:50.7 (Heron), and 12:53.3 (McCann).

- Raced to a five-runner compression of 11.3 seconds, as close to zero as any high school boys team had come in a multistate race of such caliber.

- Defeated the runner-up team, CBA, by a margin of thirty-two seconds per man. (McCann wound up thirty yards ahead of Horel and only twenty yards behind Heron, the teammate ahead of him.)

As a varsity individual champion, Gruenewald received a second wristwatch as an award. It was John Aris's twenty-fifth birthday that day, and, as gift for all he had done as a big brother for Gruenewald after his mother passed away, Tommy presented John with his watch.

For his Stotan dedication, Tommy received another "award"—a nickname. Bill gave Gruenewald the moniker, "Manchild." "I had a small torso but long arms and legs that I used to win the Manhattan race," said Gruenewald. "Bill took something that could have been seen as negative and awkward and made my prepubescent characteristics into a badge of honor."

Gruenewald and his team returned to the Syracuse area with the first Nike Cross Nationals less than two months away. When the new rankings came out, F-M was number one in the country, with York of Illinois second and The Woodlands of Texas third. But Fayetteville did not yet look to Portland in December as the promised land. First, they had important business to take care of in New York.

The Fayetteville runners were still small-town boys at heart. The State Fair was as big as it got in town. The Allman Brothers fiasco was history, and McCann had showed his better side in keeping the Stotan belief system close. For his part, Bill Aris was not dwelling on the top ranking but just trying to savor "the richness of the experience."

Aris could not know—no one could—that the new Nike Cross Nationals would test the great teams off the course as well as in competition. That every team's competitors, with little preparation, would have to come up on stage and perform for an audience of their peers. That their stage presence and wit would be judged by elite runners. That they would be expected to mix in tight quarters with some three hundred of their own, male and female, in a boisterous forty-eight-hour social whirlwind prior to race day.

The only thing Fayetteville-Manlius was trained to do was run.

6

THE WHITE MOMENT

When people saw how close we were, what we ate, they would say, "You guys are weird, a cult."

—*Andrew McCann, Fayetteville-Manlius cross-country runner*

2004 Season IV

Two days after the Manhattan meet, Fayetteville-Manlius coach Bill Aris sat in Drumlins Country Club, a Syracuse landmark, with Mark Parker, a Nike top executive in line to become CEO in two years, and Mark's wife Kathy, a former world-class runner who grew up in Syracuse. The fortuitous union, with the first Nike Cross Nationals less than two months hence, was one of the many elements of deliverance aligning the Fayetteville-Manlius path that 2004 season. Kathy Parker, the former Kathy Mills, was being inducted into the Greater Syracuse Sports Hall of Fame and had invited Aris to attend the induction dinner.

Aris was awed to meet Mark Parker, fast becoming one of the most important executives in sports and counted on to enhance the Nike brand while remaining faithful to its running origins. Aris was just in his first year as head coach, and, though he might have a beatific presence for his athletes, he was only human. Nike was a big deal.

It was said time and again that even with the Air Jordan shoes, World Cup soccer, fancy ad campaigns, sexy women's tennis outfits, and beyond, Nike was at heart "a running company." Nike started in the early seventies with the iconic racer Steve Prefontaine, probably as much a "Stotan" as any American runner, and could be counted on to sponsor distance running, including cross-country. It was probably impossible to find any professional distance runner who did not start out on the high school cross-country team, and thus Aris was hoping to help Nike recall that tradition.

Parker, who grew up in Connecticut, had been a runner himself, competing in track and cross-country in high school and then at Penn State. That's where he and Kathy met. Kathy had started running for a club, Syracuse Chargers, in the midseventies, when opportunities for girls and women were limited. At the same time, Kathy ran for her high school team, which happened to be Fayetteville-Manlius. How's that for good karma? Soon, when the Title IX women's rights legislation became law, Kathy had more chances to compete, and many young girls followed her lead.

At F-M, some two decades before Bill Aris would arrive, Kathy won the first New York State high school girls cross-country title. At Penn State, Kathy won national titles in track and cross-country and set a world record for 5,000 meters. She went on to twice represent the United States in the world cross-country championships.

Though never coached by Aris, Kathy Parker kept a keen interest in F-M running, continued running for fitness, and would eventually get into high school coaching herself in the Portland area. She was especially delighted when an F-M girl would rise up, as Laurel Burdick, Jared's older sister, had as a three-time national finalist, 1999 through 2001, in the Foot Locker high school cross-country championships. (The Foot Locker program, begun in 1979, was an event for individual qualifiers, not teams.)

By the time of the induction dinner, Kathy and Mark knew all the details of the Fayetteville Manhattan event sweep, and when Bill Aris shook Mark Parker's hand, flushed to meet the man holding Nike running in his lap, it was Parker making a fuss about Aris and what his team had just accomplished.

Running royalty had met running royalty. The Fayetteville-Manlius boys were running's new rock stars.

Thus did Bill Aris have to confront a new challenge, and it had nothing to do with which hills to attack at Green Lakes. How would he keep his teenage boys from being sucked into celebrity, which ran counter to everything he had tried to teach them. To the Stotans, celebrity was even more despised than "normal." Aris and his team faced the eternal conflict of the clean and spiritual versus modernity and hype, but, after all, wasn't that what Stotan persistence—*Stoic and Spartan*—was all about: learning to deflect the impure, the superficial, the profane?

"Stoic implies a sense of peace," said Aris. "A great deal is going on beneath the surface. One doesn't need to express it outwardly. The Stoics were calm, introspective, strong, active, humble." As Cerutty asserted in the "Stotan Creed": only the pure could understand purity.

Stoics held to this doctrine more than two thousand years ago. In a *New Yorker* piece, "How to Be a Stoic," the writer Elif Batuman told of the Stoic philosopher Epictetus, born a slave, around 55 c.e., in the Greco-Roman town of Hierapolis. Epictetus, wrote Batuman, postulated that "the only thing we can control, and therefore the only thing we should ever worry about, is our own judgement about what is good."

Take food. Every day in the Fayetteville-Manlius cafeteria, Andrew McCann's lunch—in keeping with the team's clean-food mandate—was two bananas and two peanut butter–and-jelly sandwiches on whole-wheat bread brought from home. He would sit with Kimple and Heron, his junior-class compadres, using the moment as "bonding time."

Students and others, wary of the cross-country runners and their wild ways—"they never stop running"—would become more forceful in their criticism of the team. They questioned why the team referred to themselves as Stotans and not Hornets, the school-sports nickname. Since their critics could not take issue with specific training practices (who knew anything about Green Lakes hills?), they latched onto the athletes' unusual food choices and seemed threatened by them. "Diet was what people harped on," said McCann. "There were no magic beans. We just ate good, clean food. When people saw how close we were, what we ate, they would say, 'You guys are weird, a cult.'"

It didn't help when a columnist for the *Syracuse Post-Standard*, Bud Poliquin, writing about the team, included this quip: "These guys would rather shove a squirrel down their shorts than a Whopper down their throats."

To the outside world, Bill Aris himself—an adult, mind you—was the weirdest of all. The word in the F-M school corridors was that Aris would drift into the cafeteria with a surprise assault on any of his runners eating unclean food, like cheese fries, and snatch the food off their plates. "My answer to that," said Aris, "was that I had never done that but wish I had."

The more the team was cast as a society apart, the more they took pride in their differences and dug in their heels as an act of defiance. Bananas, yes; fries, no.

Teenagers and defiance went together like, well, peanut butter and jelly. A 2016 study in the *Proceedings of the National Academy of Sciences* found that teenagers would make wiser food choices if they could view their decisions as acts of defiance. Looking at almost five hundred eighth graders in a Texas middle school, the researchers found that when informed about indifferent food-company executives producing junk food for kids, the youngsters rebelled, choosing fruit and trail mix over Oreos and Doritos, and drinking water instead of Coke.

"What I like about this study," wrote Amanda Ripley in the *New York Times*, was that "it depicts teenage rebellion as a potential asset to be cultivated, rather than a threat to be squashed."

The study led Ripley to further her inquiry into teenage potential by looking into the work of Dr. Ronald E. Dahl, director of the Center on the Developing Adolescent at the University of California, Berkeley. She wrote, "Dr. Dahl's own brain-imaging research suggests that adolescent brains are not inferior to adult brains, as is sometimes assumed; to the contrary, they may have special advantages in navigating social hierarchies and adapting to rapid change." She quoted Dahl: "If they are motivated, you can change their behavior profoundly."

∽

The dramatic changes evident in the Fayetteville boys were starting to occur with the girls. At the 2004 Manhattan meet, Kristen Taylor, the lacrosse star—she continued playing lacrosse while running—had raced to a varsity-level victory by twenty seconds in 15:29 for the two-and-a-half-mile course. Another F-M girl, Hilary Hooley, placed eighth. The girls took third place in the team standings.

"What the boys accomplished was infectious and inspired us," said Taylor. "Being exposed to what was out there on a national scale, seeing the boys go further. We were feeling, 'How do *we* get there?'"

It was hard to imagine that in two years some of these same F-M girls with their zeal stirred would be able to challenge Saratoga Springs, the New York school also up near the Adirondacks that had ruled girls cross-country nationally for fifteen years. At Manhattan in '04, Saratoga, like F-M, set a Van Cortlandt team time record and had the individual champion, Nicole Blood, who set the girls course record of 13:57.0. It was Saratoga's fifth straight girls Easterns team title and ninth overall.

The day after Manhattan, the boys ran one hundred minutes, about fifteen miles, on their own. On Monday they were back at Green Lakes for various "hill sets," on the Campground Hills, God's Country Hill, and Cloverleaf Loops. On Tuesday they made a rare fall appearance on the school track for five-hundred-meter repeats. On Saturday, Aris used the high school grounds for the Woods Loop, access road speed hills, mixed fartlek, mile reps. Training was freewheeling, spontaneous, by feel, instinct, pulled from Cerutty, with a dash of Arthur Lydiard, something thrown in from the Kenyans—whatever Aris could apply as work, work, work, team, team, team. The top boys together—no one off the back.

The next week, on the Serengeti, Aris christened a new Green Lakes trail the "Cerutty Loop," and the boys poured over it, up and down, in each direction, till spent. For its end-to-end length of two miles, scabrous footing, and repeat ascents, the Cerutty was Green Lake's prize.

Training-ground designations featured every high concept in the Aris theatre. The broad Serengeti itself (which means "endless plains" in the Maasai language) spanned a vast area from northern Tanzania to southwestern Kenya. "It was arguably the most famous terrestrial wildland ecosystem in the world," states Sean B. Carroll, author of *The Serengeti Rules*. Serengeti was how Fayetteville runners spoke, thought, and imagined.

Serengeti was the spirit driving a two-mile time trial with Gruenewald leading in 9:36. "Outstanding," Aris declared. The boys finished the day with eight fast one-minute runs.

Aris called this five-week period, after Manhattan and before the state championships, block three in a four-block system starting in early summer. Here, the greatest volume of mileage was done, as well as the highest quality of fast work and hill training. Every conditioning element was enhanced before a final block four, which Aris deemed, "sharpening the sword."

Overall, Aris focused on addressing several pathways of energy production. Racing the 5k, said Jeffrey I. Messer, PhD, chairman of the Mesa Community College exercise-science department in Arizona, demanded primarily aerobic energy, and F-M training centered on aerobic development and improving the maximal rate of oxygen consumption, known as VO2 max. Messer said the 5k also benefitted from anaerobic power in which carbohydrate is more rapidly metabolized, and explosive speed, supported by the metabolism of phospho-creatine as a fuel for energy production. That's why F-M distance runs were complemented by shorter, faster runs, along with sprint training.

With the introduction of Nike Cross Nationals, there was a certain ambi-guity thrown into the F-M endgame. The State Federation Championship in mid-November always capped the New York State season. How long should a high school cross-country season last? The NXN date, in December, was seen by some as too much of a good thing. Most serious runners had started training in early July if not before. A five-month season? When the Nike event was announced back in March, it was greeted with tentative excitement in the high school running community.

The idea for the championship event was conceived on the run by a pair of Nike employees, Josh Rowe and John Truax, as they logged their miles together on the Nike campus. At the time, Rowe was the company's High School Running Manager, and Truax, a longstanding shoe designer. Seeing the vibe created by *Harrier* and its national team cross-country rankings since the 1980s, and with that vibe further enhanced by the advent of the internet and running websites, Rowe and Truax felt the time was ripe for Nike to jump in and settle the argu-ment as to which teams were best in the country. The two recruited a number of national cross-country experts to serve on a committee to fine-tune the event's concept and selection process, which, at the start (until regional qualifying was adopted in 2008), would be based on my regional rankings vetted by the working committee.

From the start, NXN faced various roadblocks in clearing the way for high school teams to be allowed to compete in a postseason event sponsored by a major corporation. Nike would pay the expenses of eight runners per team (twenty boys teams, twenty girls teams, based on two teams from each of eight regions, plus at-large selections) plus two adult "chaperones" per team, and once on the Nike-world-headquarters campus in Beaverton, outside Portland, the athletes would receive a basketful of free Nike gear.

This type of thing never sat well with state and national high school sports officials, who spent sleepless nights attempting to control the abuses in shoe company–sponsored basketball tournaments. Compared to sports like basketball and football, with their professional infiltration, cross-country was squeaky clean. But the National Federation of State High School Athletic Associations, and their state affiliates, took a one-size-fits-all approach. If you didn't play ball with them, various sanctions like being declared ineligible for future competition were threatened.

Nike was accustomed to working with the National Federation and, when all was said and done, on this defining issue, all parties agreed that teams at NXN would not compete as "high school" teams but as "club" teams, registering with the national governing body, USA Track & Field, and using club names, not the names of the schools. This was awkward and everyone saw through it. But, for the most part, it worked.

So it would be that a boys team like York of Illinois decided to compete in 2004 as "Kroy," York spelled backward. Fayetteville would compete as—what else?—Stotan. The Saratoga Springs girls would use "Kinetic."

All of that was last-minute stuff as Nike organizers rushed to smooth out a million rough edges—precisely what you'd expect for the ambitious undertaking of flying out 320 teenagers, putting them in hotel rooms, and devising a four-day weekend schedule designed to keep them occupied and inspired from morning till night (ten P.M. curfew).

As the racing season moved along, no one knew what to expect in Portland. Would all the invited teams even show up? Would the event truly be a national championship? "We weren't even sure NXN would happen," said Burdick.

Underpinning the new event was the egalitarian ideal that gave cross-country its stunning uniqueness and led Nike to come up with annual slogans like "Every Teammate Counts." Every teammate *did* count. Since a team's fifth runner was as important as its first—and the sixth and seventh runners, if strong enough, could "push back" runners from opposing teams—just about all of the 140 athletes in each race had a role to play. There was no "bench."

∽

Continuing to shock upstate cross-country fans during the 2004 season, the F-M boys swept the first five places in both the Onondaga League meet and Section 3 state qualifier, Manhattan style, with Gruenewald first both times. A parochial cynicism was starting to emerge. Not all locals took kindly to their kids being run into the ground by—who were these guys anyway, and what were they doing, training a million miles a week?

Fayetteville came down to earth the following week in the State Public Schools Championship. The boys ran a sloppy race, their only letdown of the regular season, while still winning by twenty-two points. Burdick led the team in seventh place. Gruenewald was the team's fourth scorer in fifteenth. With the tepid showing, McCann spoke up and said, no donning of their PAIN IS THE PURIFIER T-shirts, a ritual after a good race; we don't deserve it.

The State Federation meet followed a week later. Since the public schools meet did not include schools from New York City or various private-schools groups, the "Feds" was established in 1973 as, technically, a postseason event with invited teams of merit from Brooklyn to Buffalo.

The Feds started at Van Cortlandt and rotated sites, twice running at Fayetteville-Manlius, on the high school grounds in the early years. In the 1987 meet at F-M, officials learned a hard lesson in the merciless Syracuse-area weather in November. A sudden snowstorm with fifteen-degree temperatures and near-zero windchill caught everyone by surprise. The meet was called off midway, and dozens of runners were treated by EMS workers for frostbite and hypothermia in the school gym or by doctors at the hospital—until they ran out of ambulances.

In 1989, the Feds settled on its permanent site, Bowdoin Park in Wappingers Falls, about a ninety-minute drive north of Manhattan. (One exception: the twenty-fifth running was held at Van Cortlandt.) With its succession of steep hills, heavy ground, and sharp turns, Bowdoin was considered one of the more rigorous courses anywhere. At most 5k courses, the top high school boys would run under fifteen minutes. At Bowdoin, few boys ran under sixteen minutes.

In the weeks since their Manhattan breakthrough, the boys had accrued more and more strength on the hilly Green Lakes trails, raising their aerobic capacity to outlandish levels, acquiring the fitness to sustain near race pace without letup day in and day out. They seemed to deny science itself and challenge the fundamental concept of lactate threshold. This is known as the fastest pace you can run without generating more lactic acid than your body can utilize and reconvert back into energy. The higher your threshold, the more you could run close to your supposed limits without a deadening effect in your legs.

It's not the acid itself, but a product of it that diminishes power, said Messer, the exercise physiologist. Messer said the lactic acid produced in the muscle immediately dissociated into two products—lactate and hydrogen ion. "The ion, in particular, is what will impair the ability of skeletal muscle to generate force and velocity," noted Messer, former coach of two Phoenix girls teams, Xavier Prep and Desert Vista, both Nike nationals qualifiers. "When the hydrogen ion accumulates, it will bind to muscle proteins, and then diminish their capacity to generate both force and velocity." Then you slow down.

But the F-M runners did not slow down much, if at all. They ran and ran, and ran some more, and so something else, not scientific limits, must have been at work. That's where selflessness entered and wielded its incantatory power.

Indeed, no less a thinker than the celebrated Norwegian novelist Karl Ove Knausgaard, author of the six-volume *My Struggle*, referred to the feeling of selflessness as a kind of "religious ecstasy." In a *Paris Review* interview with the critic James Wood, Knausgaard said that in selflessness "you yourself disappear," as when experiencing great literature or art.

Knausgaard asked, "And what *is* that? Is it just emotions? And why should emotions be important, a little movement in your soul?" I can't contend with the intellect of Knausgaard, but I would suggest that the Fayetteville runners, in seeking selflessness, were beholden to their true selves, to emotions that may have been hard to pin down but found clarity on the cross-country course.

These teenage boys did find movement in their souls. *That* was their power. Bill Aris gave them the opportunity, as Marilynne Robinson wrote with poetic grace in *Gilead*, "to be stripped of the accretion of smugness and pretense and frivolity."

Fayetteville's mid-November training leading up to the Feds lurched into the darkness. Snow fell on Green Lakes. Frigid air arrived. Winds whipped the Serengeti. As the boys did their last tune-ups, sweat crunched to their bony frames and they sped up their cooldowns to get to the parking lot, where parents waited with motors running and lights on, a spooky ring of blinding glare on the edge of wilderness. Oh, the comfort of a heated car and healthy snack.

On Feds weekend in Wappingers Falls—the race they'd waited a year to run—Aris counseled the boys on "pushing through that wall of pain to another threshold they did not even know existed, to another dimension"—a kind of runner's twilight zone. Aris felt he'd come close to attaining it himself. The genesis of his pain inquiry went back to his Boston Marathon days when, he said, "I beat people with more talent than me on sheer will." Aris said that at six feet two he was big for a runner and possessed of average talent. "My abilities came in pain threshold. I could drive myself beyond and learned that many people are a lot tougher than they realize."

In that sense, Aris was a lot like the young Stotan who would get under his skin: Bulldog McCann, who had to make up for lack of pure "talent" with will.

For a final dose of inspiration, before the boys took the Bowdoin Park starting line, Aris referred them to The Doors' 1967 hit "Break on Through (To the Other Side)," written by lead singer Jim Morrison. As Aris understood the piece, it told of breaking through the doors of perception to the "other side," to find one's own version of truth in life.

Jared Burdick, cocaptain, found his truth in sacrifice. As he'd done many times before—in the sand-hill workout at camp, in the Junction Boys workout, at Manhattan—he shot out to the lead in the Federation meet to set the tone, push the pace, make sure the team would perform at its best. The week before, in the state public schools meet, Burdick had been the first of the Stotans across the finish, and at Feds he stood to contend for a podium position.

Dispensing with potential individual glory, Burdick attacked the hills at the front of the field of 252 runners. With temperatures in the low forties, a bit of drizzle, and a surprisingly still wind off the nearby Hudson River, conditions were excellent. After an opening flat section of about a quarter mile, the course funneled to a skimpy path leading to the testing ascent. Gruenewald, McCann, Kimple, and Heron followed Burdick as the five boys linked into what was, midway, virtually zero compression.

The pressure of running over his head for the sake of others finally overcame Burdick, who slipped to fifth in the F-M pack a little after two miles as the downhills fed to the flat last kilometer to the finish. The five runners were still close to "zero" until the flatness of the final stretch allowed for latent speed to emerge and produce a marginal separation in the race for home.

A boy from Long Island led the field and would go on to win by seventy-five yards in 15:44. Then came Gruenewald, the first Stotan, in sixth. Seconds later, rushing home in close order, were the remaining four Fayetteville scorers within the next ten finishers. It was McCann seventh, Kimple fourteenth, Heron fifteenth, and a gallant Burdick sixteenth. Their times in succession: 16:10, 16:13, 16:17, 16:18, 16:19. It was a sight to behold: the turquoise uniforms blending across the line, the boys' bodies flecked in mud. As Kimple liked to describe it: boom, boom, boom, boom . . .

Fayetteville set an all-time course record for average time: 16:15.2. Only nine boys in the entire race other than the F-M runners themselves ran faster than the F-M *average*. It was another Manhattan, only better. Manhattan had been two and a half miles, equivalent to 4k. The Feds were 5k. Bowdoin Park was much tougher than Van Cortlandt Park. The Feds' field was much deeper. "It was as perfect a race as we could run," said McCann.

How much had the Fayetteville boys improved from the previous year? In 2003, only one boy, Burdick, had placed in the top twenty, at seventeenth. The other four scorers finished between 69th and 105th. The team's scoring average was 17:20, more than a minute slower than in 2004.

The team worked with a selflessness that touched new ground. "Jared gave us everything. He left everything out there," said McCann. "Coach always said, 'Use your teammates as beacon points.' To know we were executing—it felt serene. It felt like the 'White Moment.'"

Aris agreed. In that championship race, with a nine-second compression at Bowdoin Park, Fayetteville-Manlius had achieved the elusive, transcendent White Moment—"a state of bliss beyond pain," said Aris.

In his readings on history and philosophy, Aris had found a perfect meditation to bolster what he'd taught the team. At Green Lakes, he'd told the boys about the ideas of Yury Vlasov, a Russian 1960 Olympic-champion weightlifter, poet, and philosopher. This, from Vlasov, is what Aris distilled as the White Moment:

> At the peak of tremendous and victorious effort, while the blood is pounding in your head, all suddenly becomes quiet within you. Everything seems clearer and whiter than before, as if great spotlights had been turned on. At that moment you have the conviction that you contain all the power in the world, that you are capable of everything, that you have wings. There is no more precious moment in life than this, the White Moment, and you will work very hard for years just to taste it again.

The Fayetteville boys had two weeks.

7

PARTY TIME IN PORTLAND

I figured we were ranked number one. People would want to know
what we were about. But we were laughed off the stage.
—*Tommy Gruenewald, Fayetteville-Manlius cross-country runner*

2004 Season V

With the first Nike nationals coming up in Portland, meet officials
had everything covered: the myriad travel details, hotel setup,
idiosyncratic race site, innovative technology to track team
scoring, Athletes' Village team tents on course, meals at the hotel and on the
sprawling Nike campus, world-class runners to meet and greet, a minute-by-
minute athletes' agenda with barely a moment's respite, and first-night opening
ceremonies to break the ice, introduce the teams, and bask in Nike cool.

After their White Moment performance in New York, various polls, websites, and analytical computations had proclaimed Fayetteville-Manlius the
boys NXN favorite. It made sense. If F-M could repeat the audaciousness of
its Bowdoin Park run, no team could touch them.

York of Illinois was rated the toughest challenger. It had a team that had
defined cross-country running with its twenty-four state championships and

highest overall national rankings of any boys team since the rankings began fifteen years before. It had a coach, Joe Newton, a charismatic figure known as Mr. Motivator, who could charm you as an after-dinner speaker, teach you as clinic lecturer, and astound you with bold declarations like, "A cross-country course would be a good place to die."

Newton, who only coached boys, wrote a book about his early success, *The Long Green Line*, self-published in 1969, with Karl Schindl as coauthor. It became a cult classic. Eventually, a former athlete of his made a film about Newton, also called *The Long Green Line*. Newton also coauthored other instructional books, like *Coaching Cross Country Successfully* and *Running to the Top of the Mountain*. All were timeless, prescriptive works that held up years later.

When Newton started out, he was a Knute Rockne type out of central casting who insisted on clean-cut athletes with a soldier-straight attitude, no funny business. Tough love was Newton's calling card. As times changed, so did Newton, a softie at heart. He would give his boys a longer leash while still demanding unyielding devotion to long, hard runs and "thousand-mile summers."

Newton's stature went beyond the high school ranks. In 1984, he was contacted by Peter Coe, father and coach of the great British runner Sebastian Coe, prior to that year's summer Olympics in Los Angeles. Before the Games, Seb stayed with the Newtons, doing his final sharpening in Illinois under Joe's tutelage, and in LA won his second-straight Olympic gold medal in the 1500 meters. In 1988, Newton was named to the US summer Olympics coaching staff for Seoul, serving as a manager with the American marathoners.

By 2004, despite racing undefeated en route to Portland and winning the state title by ninety-three points with a 1-2-3 individual finish, the York Dukes were thought to be at a distinct disadvantage on race weekend. Newton was not even in Portland. Age had caught up with him, and he was convalescing from back surgery. This from a man who at one point had run every single day—in the four A.M. darkness before school—for more than twenty years.

Since the Illinois state meet, held a month before NXN, York could not be coached by Newton or any coach on the staff because of Illinois rules prohibiting coach contact with team members once the fall season was officially over. These rules were on the books in a majority of states, which is why Nike did not pay expenses for team coaches but for "chaperones," usually designated parents of team members. In Illinois, if Newton—revered by most, envied by some—tried to get around the restriction in some clandestine way, rival coaches on the lookout would be more than willing to spill the beans.

So it would be that for the month prior to NXN, a York runner, state champion, and senior Sean McNamara coached the team. "I tried to," he told me. "But I was just a goofy seventeen-year-old kid like everyone else."

Even in Portland, many coaches who made the trip on their own, like York assistant coach Charlie Kern, steered clear of their athletes for fear of being "turned in." The York chaperone was ultimately a chiropractor, Mike Calcagno, who'd treated the team. "The boys will get adjustments throughout the weekend, especially after the long plane ride," Calcagno said at the time.

Imagine coaching your athletes every day for months, embracing them, wiping their sweat, convincing them to believe in themselves, weeping with them at their finest moments. And then, when the team earns its greatest prize, a nationals invitation—something you made possible—you are disallowed from coaching the team or even being in the athletes' midst at a practice session or (except in disguise) at the groundbreaking championship event itself.

Aris had no such worries in New York. Rules, schmules; he did what he wanted. After the Feds, with snow blanketing Green Lakes, the F-M boys were back on the school track for signature workouts like running three minutes at two-mile race pace eight times with a mere ninety-second recovery jog between each run. To handle that, the boys had to be so fit and strong that their heart rates, even under such intense stress, would return to a relaxed 60 percent of maximum during each brief respite. "Outstanding Stotan workout," Aris declared. The sword had been sharpened.

Most other boys trying that workout, even those formidable enough to be running in Portland, would likely be vomiting more than John Heron on a bad day. What about York and *The Long Green Line*? Only two weeks before Portland, York didn't even know the precise lineup of its nationals squad. A few of the key guys were sick or hurt. The team hadn't raced in weeks, and no one knew where things stood.

McNamara decided to hold a three-mile time trial twelve days before nationals to determine the seven-man varsity. As in New York, there was snow on the ground. Instead of going to a soaked cross-country site, McNamara used the track at nearby Elmhurst College. But first the boys had to shovel snow off the two inside lanes for a clean surface. The results were unspectacular, not at the level of a similar time trial earlier in the season. One of York's top men, Eric Dettman, was sick with bronchitis. He tried to run the time trial but had to drop out after a mile. He would compete in Portland while, he said, at 60 percent of capacity, and still taking antibiotics.

"We were questionable," said McNamara. "There was concern about our depth."

York had no such F-M–style tight pack. They had a powerful first three in McNamara and junior twins Eric and Matt, but then there was a sizable gap to its last two scorers. The Dukes' fifth runner was an erratic sophomore, Nick Kuczwara, who'd come into nationals with a few good races but poor state meet. The Illinois state meet was run on a flat and fast course with no challenging hills, not the best background for the leg-sucking mud expected in rainy Portland.

For hill training, McNamara took the York boys to the University of Wisconsin–Parkside grounds an hour away in Kenosha. They got the work they needed, but Kuczwara injured a quadriceps muscle on the hills and had to take a week off with physical therapy. What good would he be in Portland?

If the York boys did not bring their best game to nationals, and came without their coach, they did bring something that could prove essential: three-piece suits to wear on the awards rostrum. How's that for gall?

Newton had a longstanding tradition in Illinois in which the boys would wear suits to all meets and bring tuxedos on the school bus to the state championships; if victorious, they would wear the tuxes when receiving their awards. The tradition was not only classy but a keen motivational tactic. Newton reasoned that all boys were tickled to put on a tux, and that the idea of it could spur them on. In fact, over the years the York boys would fuss over white or black tuxes, top hats, and walking canes. Imagine—this was high school cross-country.

For Portland, the York boys opted for suits. That was their way of being understated for the first national championship. With their suits, they brought along attitude. There was no great philosophy backing them, no practiced humility. They had forty years of York aura to live up to, and it was no time for hiding.

"We felt an obligation to live up to York royalty," said McNamara. "NXN was the first objective way of crowning a national champion."

∾

When the curtain was raised on the weekend, with the urgency of something new and transformative, some four hundred teens and adults pressed into a social hall in the Tiger Woods Center on the Nike campus, and then into a theater for the opening ceremonies. When it was York's turn to come up on stage and introduce itself, supposedly with a little skit that reflected on team identity, McNamara stepped from the group of seven boys, took the microphone, and said sternly: "We came here to win." Then York sat down.

"We were surprised by that," said Aris. "We would never act that way." Aris cut the York kids some slack, figuring "they had a rightful chip on their shoulders that we had overtaken them for the number-one ranking, and they wanted to make things right."

Struggling to find a way to entertain the young assemblage and set a tone of corporate engagement for the weekend, Nike had created a talent show and enlisted one of its sponsored runners, Alan Webb, to help out. Webb, only three years out of high school at the time, was idolized by many in the crowd for his high-school-record mile of 3:53.46 in 2001, breaking a Jim Ryun standard that had stood for thirty-six years. The performance got Webb on the *Late Show with David Letterman*. He'd attended college for a year, and then left school to turn pro. Nike had awarded Webb a six-year contract.

Nike had Webb sit in the wings with a gong to bang when teams were, inevitably, shouted off the stage for their skits by the teenage crowd—which, naturally, lusted to vociferously boo the nerdiest presentations of all. It was Nike's Gong Show.

When Fayetteville came up, the boys were tentative, out of place. "It threw us for a loop," said Heron. "To go from a whole season with our stoic ways, and then have to be in the spotlight."

To Cerutty, the spotlight was enemy territory. "Those who have fame thrust upon them," he wrote in *How to Become a Champion*, "are in a most invidious position since it is almost impossible to envisage the conditions of growth that make for collaterally developed character. . . . Nothing can be bestowed."

Gruenewald, the youngest of the bunch, volunteered to take on the role of F-M front man. "I wasn't stage shy," said Gruenewald. "I had done some theatre." Not for a crowd like this. The F-M boys had no skit, no attitude, nothing. The only thing they had, the only thing they knew was . . . Stotan.

Gruenewald decided to use that. "I figured, we were ranked number one. People would want to know what we were all about."

As soon as Gruenewald opened his mouth and began talking about the team's Stotan approach, boos rained from the young audience. Gruenewald kept talking, stone-faced. The booing got louder and turned to laughter. "They laughed us off the stage," said Gruenewald. As F-M retreated, Alan Webb supplied the mocking gongs. "That set the tone for the weekend," said Kimple.

Aris was irritated. He understood Nike's desire to make a big splash for the inaugural event but was frustrated by the weekend's high-pitched counterpoint to the team's subdued lives at home. "The energy vortex in Portland sucked the life out of you," he said. The team concluded: "The hell with them. Let's just leave it all out on the course."

It wasn't a pretty course by any means. The nationals teams had come from beautiful grounds in the Rockies and sun-splashed trails in Southern California, from spiffy golf courses in the Midwest to New York's own biting terrain through the woods and up every type of demanding hill. Portland Meadows, the chosen site, however, had little to inspire a high school runner expecting a peak experience. "It was manmade," said Burdick dismissively. "Not authentic."

When Rowe and Truax went scouting for a Portland-area site, they brought in Jim Spier and Paul Limmer of the National Scholastic Athletics Foundation, the organization that conducted the national indoor and outdoor high school track-and-field championships, as well as the Great American Cross Country Festival, in Cary, North Carolina. The group looked at several potential sites including the Fort Vancouver National Historic Reserve, which had a respected course used for various national events and was situated just across the Columbia River in Vancouver, Washington. However, the site lacked enclosed stadium seating, considered critical.

Thus, NXN landed at Portland Meadows, a horse-racing track with a large, protected viewing stand. "When I looked up at the grandstand," said Limmer, who in his coaching career on Long Island had produced an array of national stars, "and imagined every athlete's parents and grandparents sitting in controlled comfort and watching the race on monitors, I felt it could be something special for cross-country."

"Spectator friendly" was a major concern in cross-country. Merely seeing the race start and/or finish was not sufficient to build interest. Many European cross-country events were held at horse-racing tracks for their indoor seating. In 1984, the first of only two times that the world cross-country had been held in the United States (the other time was Boston in 1992), it was staged at the Meadowlands Race Track in New Jersey.

When Portland Meadows opened in 1946, it was heralded for its lighting system, making it the nation's first track to offer night-time horse racing. However, the facility apparently paid little attention to drainage. When it rained, the site flooded. The athletes often ran in ankle-deep mud and standing water.

Depending on your orientation, such conditions were either made for cross-country or an affront. For the most part, teams from wintry climes were fine with it. Those from dry, warm, fair weather regions: not so much.

Without steep hills to challenge the runners, the rain and slop added a key testing element, said Limmer. "Soft footing was the 'equalizer,'" he said. If the mud got too bad from a week of rain, officials could use water pumps to help with drainage.

The horse racetrack itself was off-limits to two-legged competition. In fact, because of horse racing at that time of year, including the day before NXN, Nike was not allowed on site to start marking the running course and making it championship ready until ten P.M. In darkness, rain, and bone-chilling cold, dozens of staff—mostly from the NSAF, hired by Nike to run the meet—worked through the night.

The course was fashioned on a smallish par-three golf course within the track's interior—kind of a big infield. The racing was laid out in loops around the flat fairways, punctuated by some Euro-style hay bales to hurdle and, primarily, a series of hills constructed of fifty loads of trucked-in dirt, to become known as the whoop-de-doos. This grouping of four small roller-coaster hills did not demand any great degree of strength from the runners but rather good rhythm and balance.

On race morning, the event that would change the course of running—cross-country's moon landing—drew many old Nike hands to witness what was being ballyhooed in its corporate corridors. With Rowe and company looking for every touch of distinction, the first-ever Nike employee, Jeff Johnson, who'd devised the name Nike in 1971, had been enlisted to deliver a keynote address to the assemblage the night before.

However, with the boom of a cannon rather than a starter's pistol ready to send the runners off, the proceedings almost fizzed out like a defective firecracker. The first race, an "open" run to test the course and timing setup, was scheduled for 7:00 A.M. Course workers completed their all-night duty at 5:00 A.M. When the exhausted crew gathered for breakfast, Rowe realized he'd forgotten to bring the timing clock, which remained at his Nike office. After Rowe, in panic, hustled back and forth to the Nike campus to retrieve it, the clock was finally hoisted and set into place at the course finish line at 6:45 A.M.—only to come crashing to the ground after a sleepless staffer dropped it.

Could this thing two years in the making—and some ten years as a dream in some people's minds—actually get off the ground? The clock, bruised but not broken, was put back up, and it was finally time to see which high school teams were best in the country.

With rain all week, runners would have to tackle marshlike mud that could suck a spiked shoe off your foot, and did. The grim conditions were a tribute to the sport's origins. By all accounts, cross-country running began in England in the nineteenth century, and perhaps earlier than originally thought. A February, 2019, "heritage" report from the International Association of Athletics Federations, the worldwide track-and-field and cross-country governing body, claimed "harrier" roots as early as 1819 with races sponsored by the Shrewsbury School in the Shropshire countryside.

A 1908 *New York Times* account of a high school cross-country race referred to "real cross-country," "uneven patches of ground," "tangled masses of shrubbery," and a "cold penetrating wind . . . that chilled many of the runners and stiffened their limbs."

Mud, cold, wind . . . real cross-country—*bring it on!* As the Hyman Roth character told Michael Corleone in *Godfather II*, "This is the business we've chosen." Certainly York's de facto coach, the goofy seventeen-year-old who'd brought the team to its apex, was unfazed by any notion of course wilds. "We're on a business trip," Sean McNamara said with Pacino panache.

Aris, the former businessman, felt his boys were the superior team but did not know whether they could "hold their peak" from their surpassing Federation race two weeks earlier. There was scientific consensus that the running body, whether teenagers or Olympians, could not perform at peak effort beyond a period of about two weeks. The Stotans were on the edge. As race time approached and the circus atmosphere, as Aris termed it, quieted down, Aris was able to find comfort, thinking, "They're at peace. I just want to stand back and behold them."

∽

When the boys 5k race got underway, and some 147 runners from twenty-one teams in sixteen states (an extra boys team was added based on last-minute eligibility issues) tore down the opening straightaway, the heavy turf held some in the field back. "I was buried around sixtieth," said Kimple. "I freaked out a little." Running close by was McNamara, also feeling out of sorts. "I'd never been that far back in a race," he said.

Both Kimple and McNamara would move up, and at 2k, a little past a mile, it was Fayetteville first, The Woodlands of Texas second, and York third in the team scoring. New, high-tech schema enabled team standings to be compiled at each kilometer and shown on huge screens for all to see. This first year the runners had to wear an ankle device, like a penal tracking bracelet, to record positions. When the system, which had many bugs to smooth out, actually worked, Josh Rowe was so thrilled he jumped into Jim Spier's arms.

At that point, midway, both Fayetteville and York had their scorers spread out as McNamara made a move with authority. "When I caught up with the leaders," said McNamara, "it felt like we were walking, so I just took off."

"Sean was on a mission," Newton would tell me later that day from home. "He was the coach."

Self-sufficiency and resourcefulness: qualities of a certain team from New York. When McNamara bolted away, his teammate, Matt Dettman, seeing his twin, Eric, struggling, came alive. "I cannot let this team down. I have to go for it," Matt told himself.

Newton called McNamara "Big Mac." After giving up basketball and golf, McNamara had found a home in running. He ran in the mornings before school and led the Dukes in workouts after school. His mother worried that her son pushed too hard. Big Mac fussed over healthy meals and had something in common with Bulldog McCann of Fayetteville—two peanut butter–and-jelly sandwiches on whole wheat for lunch.

At 3k, with McNamara leading and Matt Dettman gaining ground, York moved to a six-point lead over Fayetteville, led by Gruenewald. As a group, F-M had none of the dazzle that had marked their season in New York. Their White Moment was turning gray. F-M barreled through the mud while McNamara, having a career day, seemed to run above it. But the York boys were spread out, and no matter what Big Mac was doing, a weak fifth man could kill them.

After covering the second of two tours of the whoop-de-doos, at 4k, or two and a half miles, Fayetteville had inched up two points and the scores read: York 99, Fayetteville 103. At this point, the personality of the historic weekend could be seen on the boys' faces. York conveyed an attitude that said, "Victory is ours; you'll have to take it away from us." Fayetteville, while not running "atrociously," as Kimple would put it, was bogged down in damage control.

"We weren't able to drown out everything around us going into the race, and that was exhibited in our performance," said McCann.

But even an imperfect Fayetteville could still win the national title. Kimple, Heron, and Burdick ran as a tight trio within a stride or two of the ailing Eric Dettman. McCann had worked his way into the top twenty, and Gruenewald was in the top ten. After McNamara, headed for victory, and Matt Dettman, well into the top five, the remaining York scorers were vulnerable. Eric Dettman was sick—could he, as number-three man, really marshal enough strength in the last kilometer?

F-M's Heron was having his own problems. It was not just his vomiting, which splattered Burdick at one point, but everything: the mud, ankle-deep water, freezing temperatures. "With 1k to go, past the hay bales and around the final turn," Heron recalled, "I was in a daze. My fingers were frozen, my toes numb. I was just trying to get through it. I'd never felt that way in a race before."

Neither had York sophomore Nick Kuczwara, but for him the setting was a release. He'd barely made the York top seven for nationals. He was a sprinter type, a 400 and 800 specialist in track, not a pure distance runner. He was recovering from the quadriceps tweak in hill training. And Kuczwara always seemed a little unfocused, like, nationals, really, is that what we came for? Before the race, on the bus ride to Portland Meadows, Kuczwara's York teammates had told him point blank, "Don't think, just run."

Suddenly, there was Kuczwara flying from well back in the field in the last half mile—that, he knew how to do. He passed Kimple, then Heron, then Burdick. Then Kuczwara caught the ailing Eric Dettman, gave him a tap on the rear and told him, "You gotta go." Dettman replied, "I can't, you do it." Kuczwara put his head down and drove with all he had, passing McCann. After the race, Kuczwara would say, "My teammates told me, 'Get the maroon guys,'" referring to Fayetteville's Nike-produced uniforms. "'That's Stotan.'"

Practically diving across the finish, Kuczwara placed sixteenth, the third York runner. How did this wet-behind-the-ears sophomore half-miler do it? How did a guy who wasn't even assured of an NXN spot—who placed thirty-seventh in the Illinois state meet—rise up to place sixteenth in the nationals field?

"No one knows," said McNamara, who took the individual victory by seventy-five meters in 15:44, after the race.

"He's a mystery," said Matt Dettman, fourth in 16:09.

"Kuczwara was the dagger in our hearts," said Aris.

Kuczwara's surge stretched York's superficial two-point lead at 4k to thirty-five points at the finish. The scores were York 92 points and Fayetteville-Manlius 127, with third going to Mead High of Spokane, 146. York's triumph—like that of Saratoga Springs for girls—gave the whole of the cross-country enterprise a stamp of historic validity. These were the teams that had been heralded for decades. Their affirmation was like a DiMaggio or Sinatra nailing it for all time.

Likewise for Mead, second only to York in all-time boys rankings, and with a fiery coach of its own, Pat Tyson, who'd roomed with Steve Prefontaine at the University of Oregon in the early seventies.

In the final tally, Tommy Gruenewald placed ninth, Andrew McCann eighteenth, Jared Burdick thirty-first, John Heron thirty-fourth, and Owen Kimple thirty-fifth. Their respective times: 16:17, 16:34, 16:47, 16:48, 16:48. The boys fashioned a thirty-one-second compression, their widest of the season. At the hotel after the race, Heron sat in the bathtub with his feet under hot water to reconstitute his toes.

Kimple, F-M fifth man for the only time all season, blamed himself. "I had a poor day and felt hugely responsible for the outcome," he recalled. "I was angry about the crap we had to deal with that weekend. We may have let the environment get the best of us."

York had a fat sixty-six-second spread but raced first, fourth, and sixteenth, with Kuczwara ahead of all Fayetteville scorers save Gruenewald. While Kuczwara was assessed a mystery to everyone including his teammates, in fact he had quite some armor amassed when he took the starting line. He'd placed well in his regional and sectional meets, done some extra training with McNamara that have him confidence, and said the layoff for the quadriceps injury provided much-needed rest. "It gave me more energy for NXN," Kuczwara said. "I felt great."

The real York mystery, said Eric Dettman years later, was the team's fifth scorer in Portland, senior John Schroeder. *He* was the dagger in Aris's heart. With York's usual fourth man, Mike Arnold, ending up a disastrous ninety-eighth at NXN, it was left to someone—but who?—to make up for it. Schroeder had run well as a freshman but had not run a single good race since—that's three years—because of injury. Schroeder hadn't raced at all that fall of 2004 but somehow resurrected himself for the York time trial that chose its lineup for Portland. He placed fifth, and his NXN slot was assured.

In the championship, Schroeder, in his only race of the fall season, managed to place forty-second as York's fifth and final scorer to seal the victory. He was only a few seconds behind the F-M trio of Burdick, Heron, and Kimple. With Kuczwara and Schroeder coming through, McNamara winning, and the Dettmans overcoming illness, York deserved to wear its three-piece suits at the awards ceremony.

Joe Newton had told the York boys, "Dress good, feel good, run good." Business trip over.

Fayetteville had been an invading force of outsiders, a team born, in effect, only four months before, on the porch of the Kimple cottage in the Adirondacks—born in Cerutty lore, with mind-altering challenges and a coach in search of enlightenment for his athletes and himself. It had been a season of breakthroughs, of new ways to live and train and succeed, of selflessness and purity.

Who knows if Fayetteville could have done anything differently to pull out a victory? In a telling remark, McNamara said, "I remember Fayetteville being more serious than we were. Nice guys, but serious."

Perhaps it was the counterintuitive genius of the seventeen-year-old to do the old master, Mr. Newton, one better by lightening the mood at the time of greatest pressure. Not because of some coaching strategy but because that's just who teenagers were.

In the hours after, F-M moped, disappointed in themselves. Aris would have none of it. He told them, "Fellas, if you are down about not winning, something alien to us this season, you miss the point of what we're about. Look at the season you've had. You finished second in the country and did not have a good day. And you ran against the team that was the benchmark of excellence in the history of high school cross-country. Am I going to glorify second compared to winning? No. You can hang your heads about this, but I'm proud of you. You have to be men. Isn't that what a Stotan is to begin with?"

When York got back home to the Chicago area, there was no celebration at school or anywhere in Elmhurst. Pinned to the wall by state rules, the boys could still not be officially recognized, even with their national championship, for competing as a team in a postseason event. "Kroy" won in Portland, not York. Joe Newton had to keep his mouth shut.

Still, the York boys, their suits at the cleaners, could take comfort in their ghostly covenant among the local Elmhurst citizenry. Fayetteville could take comfort in having four of its top five boys returning for next year with master's degrees in Stotan learning and PhDs in the hazards of teenage normalcy.

The two schools would meet again in 2005, when York was upended by a shocking criminal act and Fayetteville was upended by discord.

8

EARTH, WIND, AND FIRE

It's getting cold, but you've been working so hard you're continuously shedding layers. You're still sprinting. It's getting dark. It feels like it's pitch-black out, and you're running hard into the night.
—*Geoff King, Fayetteville–Manlius cross-country runner*

2005 Season I

When the Fayetteville-Manlius boys gathered at their training mecca, Green Lakes State Park, for the 2005 cross-country season, they sought to rely on the nurturing earth as a salve. The land with its profound lessons of summoning strength, denying pain, and forging spiritual bonds possessed a thundering power, like a coach, like coach Bill Aris himself. Green Lakes had a majesty, and when you ran there and took it all in, ran the loops and the circuits and the hills, ran Round Lake, ran the golf course, ran for two hours without crossing the same path twice, your senses came alive, beholden to a higher power you could not, as a teenager, truly understand.

The 2004 season had been "magical," as Owen Kimple put it. "Everything seemed to happen naturally. It was fun, easy. And it changed our lives." When we spoke, Kimple paused and added wistfully, "We were sixteen. We wanted to hold on to that, but it was hard to sustain."

Kimple and his key returning teammates, Tommy Gruenewald, John Heron, and Andrew McCann, four of the 2004 top five, had the disappointment of the Nike Cross Nationals defeat still festering nine months later. They'd done all they could: learned the "Stotan Creed" of Percy Cerutty's yesteryear, tried to live the pure life, trained till spent and then trained some more, committed to selflessness, fought pain and then laughed at it, followed Aris's commandments point for point and mile by mile through the famous Manhattan meet sweep in the Bronx and State Federation Championship White Moment to—what?

After Portland, the FM runners carried a lingering hurt. Aris did his best to try and heal the wounds. But the boys felt stuck, jilted by impurity, and confused by their own letdown. What did Nike pageantry and an embarrassing Gong Show have in common with a cross-country race? What happened to *just* running?

What about the boys' own failures? Gruenewald and McCann had run well in Portland, but, laboring back in the field, Jared Burdick, Heron, and Kimple, positioned in lockstep, had allowed a runner from victorious York of Illinois, who'd gotten out of bed with bronchitis, to hold them off. What had gone awry with team unity and no one off the back, an F-M hallmark?

"Coach had prepared us to peak at the right time," said Gruenewald. "But after the race, we were devastated."

As summer arrived at Green Lakes, and you could taste the sugar maples in the humid air, Aris gathered four of the boys at the park's Gravel Pit Hill below the Serengeti to make plans for the season. Gruenewald, Kimple, and Heron were present, along with Geoff King, a junior who'd been the team's sixth man at NXN and was being groomed to move up into the top five. Burdick had graduated, and a potential fifth scorer was desperately needed. Also needed was some of Burdick's uncompromising leadership.

"The plan was simple," Aris told the boys. "It was more and better of everything from the year before."

As hard as the boys had trained in 2004, their overall weekly mileage had room to grow, and Aris now outlined a summer base–building training volume of eighty-five to one hundred miles a week for several weeks on end. It was rare for a high school team as a whole to take on that much work. "By this time," said Aris, "they were now hardened and prepared to up the ante."

McCann was not, at least not yet. Instead of remaining in the Syracuse area and training with the team, McCann returned to the country club in Rhode Island for another summer of caddying. McCann was coming back from a case of shin splints in spring track and wanted a more deliberate start to cross-country. McCann said he ran regularly while caddying and checked in with Aris every so often. But his absence and need to be with other friends in a Gatsby-like milieu was an early fissure that would start to imperil the team's prized cohesiveness of the previous year.

Ever on the fence between Stotan ideals and teenage normalcy, McCann sensed a new tension that, to him, was hard to reconcile. "In 2004, it was all positive, all about love," he said. After Nike nationals, he said, the boys, a little older and less wide eyed, were forced to look at themselves and one another through a critical lens. "In 2005," he said, "there was more at stake. And we had to figure out how to be led without Jared."

Burdick's rock-hard leadership had been a stabilizing force, a complement to Aris's need for "constant reinforcement." Mess up and you had not only Aris to answer to but Burdick as well. Get too full of yourself and John Aris might glare at you; Burdick would not have to glare, but just be there, the Burdick who "would habitually function upon the highest planes of thought and physical effort," as Cerutty prophesied, the Burdick who would break down with tears of joy after the toughest workouts.

No one counted on King to be a leader, but in time he showed some of Burdick's loyalty to the Stotan ideas. "I hated the world around me," King said of his early high school years. "I was looking for an identity, a way to fit in. I accepted the kind of counterculture that Bill pitched. What he referred to as bullshit resonated with me."

When King started running as a freshman, convinced by Aris to give up lacrosse, he was noticed for being the sort of runner who didn't try hard but still got results. That summer of 2003, he'd trained at Green Lakes with team members who were running to get in shape for other sports—the scrap heap. King managed to look good doing it, and one day Bill came running by, tapped him on the shoulder, pointed, and said, "Run with *this* group," meaning the top guys. King hung on for an hour. During the 2003 fall season, King was selected for the varsity, competing as the team's seventh man in the state championships.

While King had not been close to the top five, he was treated with respect in what he called the team's "insular, iconoclastic community." As something of an apprentice, however, he was intimidated by the hard training and found it impossible to keep up.

At first, King had trouble living up to the Stotan archetype. "I was still maturing," he said. Friday-night football was a big thing in town, but there was a meet to run the next morning. "Part of me wanted to be the cool kid," he said. "But I still wanted to rebel against the culture I'd left behind."

When King was chosen as one of the eight boys for the 2004 Stotan camp, he found a clarity that nudged him ever so tentatively away from coolness and into the arms of his Stotan teammates. "The camp was unlike anything I'd ever experienced," King recalled. "There were brutal times to be sure, but they were absent of the dread before an impending hard effort, the letdown of an off day, the misery of recovering from a prior effort, or other complications in running."

At camp, King, holding to Aris's faith in his future, dug into the Lynch psychology text, saying "Fear of Success" was his chapter. In that section, Lynch posits that of those "breaking away from stereotypical roles, many feel guilty for achieving beyond the limits society has conveniently ordained." Running 111 miles in a week in the Adirondacks while eating fresh salmon and communing with nature would probably not have impressed King's football friends on a Friday night.

The peer pressures that Aris had feared and confronted like a bulldozer—cracking the hard shell of petrified thought—had proved to be as unrelenting as York's Sean McNamara in the Portland Meadows mud. After Aris gave the boys their marching orders at the start of 2005, King was still "half in, half out," and had to be dragged from the house by Kimple to run. Feeling King could help the team contend for the 2005 national title, Kimple expressed everyone's view when he said, "If Geoff ever gets his shit together . . . "

Once he did, once King knew who his real friends were, he could inhale the aromas of Green Lakes like incense. "Bill morphed Green Lakes onto us," he said. "He curated the identity with a visceral impression." Green Lakes was where the team's insular society celebrated its Stotan purity: the country clubs and football games were left behind. "Bill named all the trails," said King, still prideful years later. "We knew what a Cloverleaf workout was. We knew what a God's Country workout was."

∞

Green Lakes *was* God's country. Straddling the towns of Fayetteville and Manlius a few miles east of Syracuse, the park sat on 1,955 acres, almost half of it old-growth forest. The deep gorge surrounding the lakes and trails was formed toward the end of the last Ice Age, about fifteen thousand years ago. The two lakes, Green Lake and Round Lake, shimmered with emerald beauty from "whitings" that left suspended mineral solids in the water.

The site started to gain currency in the 1920s with construction of roads, trails, and a golf course designed by Robert Trent Jones. In 1945, after World War II, the park housed the Fayetteville Camp for German prisoners of war.

While Green Lakes today is a full-service park with eight hundred thousand visitors annually for hiking, camping, fishing, boating, and the like, the F-M runners typically had the park to themselves. They worked the rich, remote landscape inaccessible to all but the fittest and most adventurous of pleasure-seekers who were willing to climb one hill after another to find it. "Green Lakes was our greatest asset," said Kimple. "That's where you made the transition from a hobby runner, to 'I am becoming a *real* runner here.'"

Remember it was Cerutty who said that "nature is in us," and those who respect it will "appreciate the sanctity of creative effort." Fed up with the afflictions of affluence and sloth he saw around him, Cerutty saw nature as Thoreau did, as the only answer. "Be vibrant in nature," said Aris. "But just don't exist in it, contribute to it."

The team's running was built in layer after layer of new thought and new experience, a merging of everything Aris could think of to impact the boys, hoping small notions would stick and grow. Humility? Aris never stopped. He was so proud after team victories when, he said, "the boys were happy but contained it."

At Green Lakes, in 2005, Aris started to free himself from even token structure. He would write nothing down, devise training in his mind, tinker with it to the moment he assembled the runners and sized them up, letting his thoughts tumble out without, yet, giving the whole thing away. The land and the man and the immediacy joined in an artful commitment to selflessness.

Would we take on the Valley of the Hills today? Or a loop of Round Lake (1,553 meters to be exact) plus a loop of Green Lake (about 1.9 miles), and the connecting link, for a 5k time trial? How about the short, steep Gravel Pit Hill, where Aris used the bleached-out bones of a deer carcass picked clean as markers?

The teamness of modern-day cross-country had no better antecedent than a narrow boat of men moving swiftly on the water. "Where is the spiritual value of rowing?" asked George Yeoman Pocock, a designer of racing shells in Daniel James Brown's *The Boys in the Boat*. The 1930s rowers were akin to the runners Aris attempted to mold in the twenty-first century. Pocock answered, "The losing of self entirely to the cooperative effort of the crew as a whole."

Fayetteville's Saturday-morning run, with an upstate chill in the air and, said King, "a cross-country smell," was unforgettable. It was the smell of earth and flower, muted sun, a mineral breeze off the lake. The tulip trees and hemlock blew with the seductive colors of Gauguin. After a hard finish, the boys would go down into Round Lake to unwind, bask in the perfect mirror reflection, and soak in the cold water up to their thighs. "Even if the air got cool," said McCann, "I remember being at peace in those moments."

King found a separate peace on days after school when Aris kept the boys running well into dusk. "You're doing endless repeats of Round Lake," he recalled. "It's getting cold, but you've been working so hard you're continuously shedding layers. You're still sprinting. It's getting dark. It feels like it's pitch-black out, and you're running hard into the night."

That nature has healing powers is commonly accepted. Nature was also enhancing in more subtle ways, to calm, to simulate, to enrich. Studies done by University of Chicago psychology professor Marc Berman indicate that a natural environment, as reported by Alex Hutchinson in *The New Yorker*, provides "softly fascinating stimulation." As Hutchinson wrote, "Your eye is captured by the shape of a branch, a ripple in the water; your mind follows."

In reaching back to Cerutty, Aris had not so much happened upon a discovery as found something old that had been upended by cultural surrender. Pain, even "pain as the purifier," had been welcomed by generations of runners seeking excellence as an acceptable part of the toughening process. From Emil Zátopek to Herb Elliott to Steve "Pre" Prefontaine to the latter-day Kenyans, the more pain the better; and those runners coming up behind them knew that was their métier, a certain necessary and enhancing "punishment."

Pre had a lot in common with Elliott when he said, "A lot of people run a race to see who is the fastest. I run to see who has the most guts, who can punish himself into an exhausting pace, and then at the end, push himself even more."

But somewhere in the early stages of the American running movement, in the 1970s, the accepted training concept of "no pain, no gain" started to take a beating. It could not hold up to "jogging" and withered under running's new-found political correctness. Coaches were demonized at the mere mention of "pain"; and "run for fun" replaced "no pain, no gain." The two ideas were framed as mutually exclusive.

As a practice, for high school runners, pain became anathema, old school, unenlightened. Avoiding pain, going easy, became a culture unto itself—a symbol of a nation gone soft. Even Joe Newton in Illinois had to back off on some of his favorite York training methods because, as he once told me, "Kids changed."

Aris saw the trends crystal clear in central New York. When he latched on to Cerutty and the Stotan ways, he saw what Cerutty had done with Herb Elliott and realized that so much of it was about a clean slate of thinking—100 percent pure.

When I spoke with Elliott in 2004, he told me that when, at seventeen, he first met Cerutty, he said to him, "Your sport is a device by which you grow into a fuller, more compassionate, stronger, more self-reliant, self-respecting person. To do that, you must be outside your comfort zone." Elliott continued, "That was the guiding for all that I had done in track and field. My training was exceptionally intense. I felt training was wasted if I wasn't at the absolute limit of my ability. That was the secret."

Fayetteville-Manlius had emerged in 2004 with the same secret and attempted to expand on it in 2005. Elliott told me that in the late 1950s, barely out of his teens, he trained six days a week and ran at his limits four of those days prior to winning the 1960 Olympic gold medal in the 1500 meters in world-record time.

That was the template for F-M. Aris refuted the long-held view that top runners could not train with intensity more than once or twice a week. Some tried three. Four? Not unless you were Elliott with Cerutty in his ear at Portsea.

But who wanted that? Who wanted to emulate those crazy Aussies? Didn't Cerutty run around track stadiums waving a towel like some madman urging Elliott on? Aris picked up on the idea. He found his long stick and waved it looking for miracles.

Here were these suburban kids investing in a secret: letting all their senses dwell in the Green Lakes earth, not knowing how far they'd run or what their times were, only that they could blast the earth for one hour, and two, seeking more and more of what they came to love, of what Bill Aris asked for, a small price to pay for excellence.

The boys ran every inch of the park, every little subsection, like a half-mile stretch of the perimeter run, "so beautiful," said Kimple, "so serene, so calm."

Kimple recalled the middle of the run, "the way the morning sun would cut through the trees. It felt like you were deep in nature, a hobbit in the shire."

Or another day it was the pristine ground of the Vista Loop, with the pearls of Round Lake in view, finishing up the huge climb to God's Country Hill with, Heron said, "nothing left." Or perhaps it was the Valley of the Hills, four or five steep ascents, up one, down another, up one face, back down the other side, all connected, for sixty minutes, no relief except in the dull afterglow of a merciful pain finally letting go.

The only thing missing at Green Lakes—what the world-leading Kenyans famously possessed in the Rift Valley—was eight thousand feet of altitude. At this elevation, in the "thinner" air, the hormone erythropoietin (EPO) triggered an increase in red blood cells, which then transported greater amounts of oxygen to the working muscles. This superannuated training effect was the Kenyans' calling card. But here's the thing: Fayetteville-Manlius didn't need it. They had their own "altitude," or, rather, the same dizzying effect of it.

Whatever additional racing benefit altitude provided—no one could know for sure—the Fayetteville runners seemed to have acquired it. They could take every Stotan idea at their disposal, from selflessness to team bonding to "pain as the purifier" to humility and a higher plane of thought, and with that psychic empowerment deliver themselves into the same realm of beyond, within the high school universe, as the mighty Kenyans.

∽

In seeking this new ground, Aris knew what he was up against: the brain's potent distress signals. "It's a built-in mechanism from the brain that while you still have the capacity to run harder, increases in the acidity of the blood cause your body to send the message, 'Be careful, you're starting to get near the line and could hurt yourself,'" he said. But, added Aris, there's still room for greater effort; you have to learn not to fear it. As long ago as 1980, science writer Jonathan Tucker wrote in *The Runner*, "Conquering the fear of pain is half the battle since anxiety heightens the pain experience."

Herb Elliott, honed by the Cerutty lessons, used to say, "When we think we're at 100 percent, we're really at eighty. What you do after eighty determines your success."

A growing scientific consensus on a runner's ability to accept the turmoil of "beyond eighty" now rests with a "psychobiological model." A 2014 study by

Samuele Marcora and colleagues at the University of Kent, in England, as well as a large body of work by the revered sports scientist Tim Noakes, in South Africa, suggest that it's not just the body, but also the mind, that prevents optimal effort.

One nifty Aris trick in tackling this is his "finisher," designed to arrest those fears. Just when the runners think their session is over, when they've trained at about 80 percent of capacity, sipping their water and giving one another high fives, Aris gives them one more intense run from out of the blue: the finisher. Take the body, and mind, to one hundred.

Finishers were usually a few minutes in duration. In 2005, Aris, as per his more-and-better design, started to lengthen them. That summer one finisher was a mile-and-a-half flat and downhill run from the top of Green Lakes, at the Serengeti, down to the parking lot where parents waited. "The first time I heard it," said Kimple, "it came at the end of a ball-buster workout and I said to Bill, 'You must be joking, aren't you?'" It was no joke: ten minutes of all-out strength and speed to waiting moms and dads with their motors running.

That summer Kimple took Aris's prescription for more and did his best training ever. After a two-week buildup, he ran 105 miles a week for six weeks. He ran twice a day every day. Whether with teammates or on his own, at Green Lakes or on weekends at his family's lake house in the Adirondacks, Kimple did short runs, long runs, sprints, tempo, fartlek, barefoot, and a Sunday run that grew to two hours twenty minutes, a good twenty miles. "I had a massive base," he said. "I thought I could be one of the best guys in the country."

In August, Kimple was joined at his cottage by Gruenewald, Heron, and King, along with Bill and John Aris, for a weekend minicamp. The boys were back on the sacred ground where the team's Stotan life had taken root. King, who'd looked up to his older teammates—"staring at them for the past twenty-six months," as he put it—now seemed all in after a two-hour run in close quarters with the other three. Before that, he said, on every run he was dropped. "I was relegated to a different group, plan, or pace," he said. Then, unexpectedly, in the idyllic mountain forest, with Lake Bonaparte casting its spell, here he was keeping up. "I never really belonged until that day," said King.

With McCann still in Rhode Island, the pack of five was a pack of four, and, from a leadership standpoint, really three, since the younger King could not be assertive. For his part, Heron had his own weaknesses stirring, and so when Aris left the boys alone in the cottage to discuss the goals for fall, Gruenewald and Kimple rose up to challenge one another. "It got hostile," said Gruenewald.

Gruenewald, last year's Manchild, was referred to as the greatest Stotan of all for his devotion to every detail of the "Stotan Creed" and lifestyle. He said he experienced a kind of life conversion as a freshman in 2003, even before the Stotan changes, when Bill caught him in a lie about a workout he was supposed to have done with the team. Aris lit into Tommy in front of the other boys, took him out of a meet, and made him do an extra workout by himself to set things straight.

"It was six in the morning, cold, windy, raining," Gruenewald said. After running interval sprints on the school track as a bus waited to ferry the rest of the squad to the meet, he waited for resolution. "Bill came up to me, shook my hand, and told me, 'We're okay now,'" said Gruenewald. "It was all about honesty. From that moment on, I did everything exactly right."

Gruenewald took comfort in "separating myself from the world" and into the world of his teammates, attempting to serve them like a choir boy at the Green Lakes altar. Aris told the boys that by helping teammates improve you show your love for them. Gruenewald, desperate to show that love, used his every run as a demonstration of grace. There was the time at Green Lakes on a section from Overlook Bench to the other side of the Serengeti when he trailed Kimple, who set a hot pace. "I remember thinking, 'I'm going to do this for Owen,'" Gruenewald said. "When I had that thought, I forgot about the pain and ran so hard I ended up passing him."

"Tommy didn't know what pain was," said Aris.

"The team was everything," said Gruenewald. "I could never let my brothers down."

As a purist, Gruenewald could not tolerate anything he considered impure. He would call out teammates, even in training, whenever they diverted from the Stotan ideals, like running harder than required "to look good." In that way, Gruenewald showed leadership, but he didn't really want to be a leader; it was too ego-driven for his taste. He wanted everyone equal, love all the way around. It irked him then when at the camp, Kimple, as Gruenewald saw it, came off as "suave" in assuming leadership based on goals that included individual stardom.

Kimple likely wanted both: team success and his own. The seniors, after all, had the realities of college and possible scholarships to think about. Gruenewald, clinging dearly to the new love he'd found, could not truck any threat to that life. He said, "The effects of the world could always pull us away. The desires of men. If someone wanted to go to a concert and not get enough sleep, that was evil to us. If you made that decision, you were sinning."

With ideas like that swimming in Gruenewald's impressionable mind, it was not a stretch to learn that he'd absorbed what seemed like a throwaway incident with alarm and confusion the year before, on the eve of the 2004 Nike Cross Nationals. From the get-go, Aris had presented Stotan as a secular ideal. At its most penetrating, it could engender spiritual feelings, but it had nothing to do with religion per se. In fact, Cerutty despised religion; he had faith, Aris believed, but was angry at "the government of religion."

Aris was a religious man who practiced his Catholic faith. That was kept to himself, though. Even if he felt an urge to share any religious ideas, Aris would never do so as coach of a public school. Once the regular fall sports season was over, in the postseason leading up to NXN, a coach was on his own, unbound by school policy, and all athletic participation was considered voluntary.

In 2004, with the jarring emotion of the first national event hard to contain, the F-M team had a final pre-race meeting in Aris's hotel room. Seeking to put a final, heartfelt touch on the boys' commitment and deliver one last rally around the purity of their effort, Aris, said Gruenewald, "opened us up to his Christian faith and belief in God." This same sort of message was probably echoing in hotel rooms on every floor.

Even though Gruenewald had modeled his belief system on rejecting sin, evil, and desire, standard church teachings, and even though the godly seeds that Aris planted would lead a thankful Gruenewald, three years later, to change his life even more and join the Mormon church, in that place at that time he was jarred by it.

"We were just Stotans," said Gruenewald. "It was a cool thing that we did. Bill's comment about religion made me suspect." Why the big deal? I believe emotions were raw because of the theatricality of the Nike event and its impact on boys who'd counted on intrinsic satisfaction; screw the fanfare, it's just us in a lovefest at Green Lakes. "We were not in New York anymore," said Gruenewald. "We were on the other side of the country. Everything was unfamiliar. Everything was new. And then coach lands this on us. He wanted to bring us together, but for me it changed things a bit."

Gruenewald, admitting the episode had a role in eventually "leading me to God," said the meeting had no effect on his 2004 race. But Gruenewald kept his discomfort in his craw. And going into the 2005 season, seeing McCann in Rhode Island over the summer and irked over Kimple's grand plan, he felt a pattern of disunity that, with racing soon to start, struck him as "dissonance."

❧

Aris had his hands full. Was there still a chance of achieving the seamless bonding of 2004, or was the task now more about containment? When McCann returned to the fold, the mood picked up. With his freer training style, Aris tried to give the boys more of a way to define themselves and see their efforts as new, not an attempt to replicate the previous year. There was a lot of randomness to the running, like, go do this hill, go do this circuit. Aris wanted freedom and he wanted feedback. Without a true leader in the Burdick mold, the boys needed to renew their passions while respecting differences. Could you be 99 percent pure Stotan, 1 percent "normal," and still achieve the White Moment?

To stimulate greater unity, along with ownership of every workout, Aris had the runners rate their practices. "Gimme a number," he would ask after a last hill. The idea was one to ten, with ten being "your eyeballs come out." First the team had to be honest in assessing their efforts; then they had to find agreement; then they would announce, seven or eight or eight and a half, or maybe a nine. If the number was high, it affirmed toughness. If the number was not high, it also showed toughness because it meant that all the hills Aris asked of them were not auspicious after all. They could do even more.

The exercise was invaluable to Aris as he formulated training. With most work based on a sustained level of effort, Aris could come to practice, say to himself, "Today's an eight," and see if the team felt the same when the running was over. "Nines take more time to recover from," he said. "That's why they're done sparingly."

McCann liked the idea of performing in practice, if the workout allowed for that. He could never shake the lament that on talent alone, in both track and cross-country, Kimple and Heron were his superiors. Ironically, McCann thrived on one Green Lakes element that Aris had introduced the year before during the infamous Junction Boys workout, which had been brought on by McCann's indiscretion. It was known as the Three-Minute Hill.

The segment required repeated sets of a hilly loop that took three minutes to negotiate, and it was done in the middle of a workout, with transitions into other grueling segments like God's Country. This effort was a "nine" for sure, and it brought out the boys' competitive instincts. "I never lost a Three-Minute Hill," said McCann. "I was undefeated."

After the minicamp at Lake Bonaparte, team fitness was on display at a local half marathon, Tromptown. Soon-to-be college freshman Jared Burdick joined his former teammates and came out the winner in 1:14:53. Kimple (1:15:15), Gruenewald (1:15:42), and Heron (1:17:24) took second, third, and fourth. McCann (1:18:38) placed sixth. The most encouraging performance came from King, at 1:22:36 showing a dash of Stotan solidarity in his growing strength.

However, a couple of weeks later, toward the end of summer, Fayetteville's national hopes received a jolt. It was King. In a routine run on a Green Lakes plateau, he suffered pain in his left foot and was diagnosed with a stress fracture in a metatarsal bone. King could not run for six weeks and convalesced with up to ninety minutes of stationary bicycling a day. There was shock: Who would be the team's fifth scorer if King could not regain full strength by December?

The crucial role was turned over to a high-jump specialist, Luke FitzGibbons, one of three brothers who would run for F-M. FitzGibbons, a junior, had a strapping physique and competed in the state meet in the pentathlon. In 2004, in the sectional cross-country meet, in which up to ten runners (as opposed to the usual seven) were allowed to run varsity, FitzGibbons was the team's ninth man, only a few seconds behind King.

But a high jumper counted on by a cross-country team with national aspirations? A high jumper attempting to be the fifth-scoring boy alongside teammates who'd trained ten to fifteen miles a day? Percy Cerutty never coached a high jumper. This would be a Stotan first.

9

SATURDAY NIGHT LIGHTS

I don't know what made me snap that night. I was a teenager. I
guess my hormones were raging.

—John Heron, Fayetteville-Manlius cross-country runner

2005 Season II

When the 2005 racing season began, the Fayetteville seven-man
varsity lineup had four cross-country runners, a high jumper, a
boy in rehab with a broken foot, and one who was deaf and wore
a cochlea implant. It was two months before the state championships, three
months before Nike Cross Nationals.

Right away, Kimple's thousand-mile summer started paying dividends. He
picked up decisive victories in the South Jefferson and McQuaid meets. It was
too soon to talk about a tight F-M compression. At South Jeff, the fifth-scoring
FitzGibbons was, as expected, almost a full minute behind Kimple, who'd led
F-M in every workout. In one session of sub-5:00 mile repeats on the school
track, Kimple did his last mile in a blazing 4:32, well ahead of teammates.

At the midseason Manhattan extravaganza, Fayetteville renewed its rivalry
with Christian Brothers of New Jersey. The historic 2004 sweep was in the

books, and this time a routine victory would be enough. A hurricane had swept through the area, it was still raining, and the two-and-a-half-mile course was a mess. Cross-country meets were rarely cancelled for weather.

F-M defeated CBA, 34 to 67. Hoping to launch his national standing with an individual victory, Kimple raced out hard to try and break the opposition in the Back Hills. A runner from Florida, Justin Harbor of Palm Coast, new to Van Cortlandt, wouldn't let go. Kimple "threw the kitchen sink" at Harbor but couldn't shake him. Harbor won in 12:34.5 with Kimple second in 12:39.7. "That shook me," said Kimple. "I lost some confidence after that."

On the whole, Fayetteville ran remarkably well on the miserable day. The first four runners were separated by twenty seconds, and the five-man scoring team average of 12:56 was somewhat comparable to its 2004 record of 12:48 run in good conditions. The best news for F-M may have come in a junior varsity race. King had returned from the sidelines to resume running, and Aris put him in a JV division to test his foot. King competed in training shoes and felt fine.

It was hard to imagine, but these same grounds that enabled modern-day runners to break free was once part of tragic history. Park historians have reported that the Van Cortlandts owned slaves who worked the family planta-tion at the site; some slaves may even be buried there. The park's use as a burial ground is prominent. There's a "Memorial Grove" near the race start with graves of local men lost in World War II.

It was always a jarring juxtaposition. Steps away from the stones, which are engraved with battle heroics, runners done for the day feasted on lavish spreads before the sleepy bus ride home.

At Manhattan, a potential state and national rival to F-M, Saratoga Springs, also of upstate New York, emerged in another of the meet's varsity divisions. Saratoga, known for its girls teams, had won the 2004 NXN girls champion-ship, and the Blue Streaks were considered contenders again in 2005. In its boys race at Van Cortlandt, Saratoga went 1-2-7-12-14 with a fifty-two-second compression. There was something there.

This time at Manhattan, McCann, and his 2004 CBA "sweep" rival, Chris Horel, had nothing to fight for. Horel wound up in third place, close behind Kimple and well ahead of McCann. McCann was stumbling through his season, caught in "underlying friction" among himself, Kimple, and Heron. "Owen and I were always butting heads," he said. "Outside stressors bled into the team. I probably faltered as a teammate at that time."

It was not forgotten that about four months earlier, at the school's junior prom, McCann had a few beers and, said Aris, "got wrecked." Aris found out about it that same night, and the next morning, a Sunday, bolted unannounced to the McCanns' home to confront Andrew. When Aris arrived, he first sat down in the living room with McCann's father, who shared Aris's outrage.

When Andrew entered the room, after sleeping it off, Aris told him, "This is how you show respect? Have I been wasting my time? This is an insult to me, to everyone. We could be a laughingstock . . . "

McCann knew he had it coming. He also knew he had to find a way to come to terms with his emotions, which had him tilting between the Stotan siren of self-discipline and the temptations of teenaged life and peer pressure. There was training to do and races to run. At that moment Aris rescinded McCann's cocaptain honorific, restoring it in the fall after McCann demonstrated good character.

Could this episode, like McCann's Allman Brothers violation of 2004, again work to provide tighter knitting to the season? Who bought in? Who was astray?

Character was tested as never before a few days after Manhattan on Yom Kippur, the holiest day in Judaism. None of the team members was Jewish, but the "day of atonement," as the sacred time was known, was in the wind that evening at Fayetteville-Manlius High School.

∽

F-M schools were closed for the holiday, and teams were not allowed to practice until nightfall. Without lights at Green Lakes, Aris always took the team to run at the high school track, which had beams for late practices. The workout was a set of four repeat miles at race pace or faster, with a lap jog in between for recovery. The team called the holiday ritual Saturday Night Lights, as Yom Kippur sometimes fell on a Saturday.

With the giddy feeling of a late-night workout on the track with no hills to tackle, and the seductive glare of the lights, the F-M boys liked to let all their speed loose, come what may. It was their version of revving a convertible down Main Street when the shops were closed. Aris let it happen. He knew the boys needed it.

Heron loved running at night. "Cool, crisp, perfect," he said. "Times would get ridiculous." Like the last eight hundred of the closing mile, a la Elliott, in under two minutes.

But this night, Heron grew weary with each repetition. Kimple and Gru-enewald, in particular, were flooring it, well under five minutes. Heron got slower with each mile: 5:08, 5:15, 5:20 . . . With the fourth and last mile to go, he cried to Aris, "I'm done. I've got nothing left." Aris ignored him and said, "Jog a lap and get ready."

When the team took the line for the final repetition, Heron pleaded, "I know my body. I can't do it." Aris wouldn't budge. "You better finish," he said. "Remember, selflessness, team. Unless you're injured, you're completing the workout."

Just then, Heron, muttering "screw this" under his breath, ran off, jumped the fence, and headed over a hill and into the darkness, where he sat in a fetal position in an alcove near the tennis courts. The other boys were aghast. Fuming, Aris told them, "You go find John and bring him back. If he doesn't finish the workout, you're going to do his part after you finish yours."

Saturday Night Lights was becoming the Saturday Night Massacre.

The boys looked, but Heron was in hiding. He sat alone for fifteen minutes, seeing glimpses of his teammates running through a sliver of light. On his own, Heron finally returned to the track. When he did, all Aris said was, "Okay, let's go." It was well past nine o'clock, and Heron ran his mile. He didn't dog it, but he didn't run to the max, either. He didn't want Aris to think that all along he had more to give and was looking for excuses. Aris was pleased. He didn't care about Heron's time. He just wanted him to finish.

Heron's pride was hurt, but he got over it. "I don't know what made me snap that night," said Heron. "I was a teenager. I guess my hormones were raging."

Something good—even great—would come of such turmoil. Heron won the next race, the Section 3 championship, for his first major cross-country victory. On the hilly South Jefferson course, Heron put his raging hormones to use.

After running second man to Kimple at the prior McQuaid and Manhattan meets, Heron made the move of his life at South Jeff when he surged to the lead in a wooded section and never looked back. He came out into the clearing with a big lead, prompting Aris to shout with alarm, "You better know what you're doing!"

Heron did. He stole the race by forty meters in 16:07 as F-M grabbed five of the top seven places. He outran not only all his teammates but also some hefty opposition from local rival Liverpool. FitzGibbons, the fifth scorer, was only a couple of strides behind McCann, giving the team a thirty-second compression, its best of the season.

The Fayetteville girls also won the section title with their best showing in years. Led by Kristen Taylor in second and promising Mackenzie Carter, a scrawny eighth grader, in third, F-M took four of the top ten positions to qualify for the State Public Schools Championship the next week at Queensbury.

Carter had run in seventh grade the previous year like a duckling following the flock. She had a ball sharing in the cachet of the older girls she looked up to. She knew her place: in training, don't pass the veterans and subvert the pecking order. But in her first meet of 2005, with Taylor not racing to satisfy a lacrosse obligation, Carter overcame her timidity and surged ahead of her teammates to place third as first F-M girl in the race. "That's when I truly got the bug," she said.

It was a propitious time for Carter to assert herself and fall in behind Taylor in the lineup. Taylor's mingling of lacrosse and running lightened the girls' emotional load, making their efforts seem more "casual," as Carter saw it. It was nothing like the high-minded blueprint of the boys camp.

In the state Class 2A race, Fayetteville boys were a slight favorite in their showdown with much-improved Saratoga Springs. The two squads were unalike. Saratoga typically had three men well up front. F-M had its tight pack of four, and now it appeared, perhaps five. For Fayetteville to prevail, to set the right tone for nationals, it had to run a rich Stotan race, no one off the back.

F-M blinked. Saratoga ran 2-3-13 for its top three; Fayetteville was close with Kimple, Gruenewald, and Heron placing 4-7-10. Saratoga's last two guys were far back. But McCann had a dismal race, finishing as fifth man, even behind FitzGibbons, who was starting to grasp Thoreau's notion that "Heaven is under our feet as well as over our heads." The score: Saratoga 39, Fayetteville 43. As sixth man, King, still coming back from his injury, placed fifty-seventh, but at least he was pain free.

In a team meeting afterward, McCann took the blame. He told me he had missed some training time at a college visit, where on a run he got "dinged up," and had to go to a chiropractor once home. He could not untangle himself, and told everyone at the meeting that he lacked confidence. "Just admitting that made me feel better," he said. But John Aris could not tolerate McCann's fractious role, and tempers flared.

McCann showed marginal improvement in the next week's Federation Championship at Bowdoin Park. This time, there was no White Moment to aspire to, only the satisfaction of defeating Saratoga, a team F-M did not think was that imposing, and having a positive result going into NXN. Kimple, Gruenewald, and Heron did their jobs up front, running 5-6-8. McCann was back at fourth man, in thirty-fourth place, but that was still enough to enable F-M to win, 66–83, as runner-up Saratoga had a sixty spread for its top five. FitzGibbons had another excellent showing as fifth man within eleven seconds of McCann to seal the victory. King, while still way back, was getting closer, finishing in the top third of the large field.

Fayetteville's girls competed with sparks of strength, placing sixth in state public Class 2A and twelfth at Feds among twenty-seven teams. At Bowdoin Park, Carter was the only F-M girl in the top twenty, taking nineteenth. The other Fayetteville girls were spread out in the field of 253 runners, giving no indication of their promise to come.

The girls were still of such modest development that coach Davis, then in his early forties, could run with them. Davis had previously coached at his alma mater, Onondaga Central, and run in college. "I would tell the girls, 'If you can't beat my fat old ass up this hill . . .'" The girls would laugh and run faster.

The Cerutty lifestyle was quietly taking root with the girls. "Stotanism was such a transcendental way of living that really resonated with me at that point in life," said Jessica Hauser, a junior who was third F-M scorer in both state events. "I loved that it required self-mastery, yet it was about being selfless. My inner well was full when I could help others excel."

Two of the top girls teams in the country were 2004 NXN defending champion Saratoga Springs, which had a chance to sweep 2005 national team titles, and Hilton of the Rochester area. In state Class 2A, Saratoga edged Hilton, 46–47. The Hilton coach caused a local uproar when he chose not to run his team in the ensuing Federation meet, saying too many major meets did not allow for proper recovery. Coaches with their heads in the sand took issue. But Bill Aris heard something he liked.

Restoration was in order, and the F-M boys retreated to Green Lakes, their Walden Pond, to see if they could mobilize a unified effort before getting on a plane to Portland. "We'd do a ten-mile loop," said Gruenewald. "Go around the whole park, past the golf course, on a series of trails, up a steep hill to the Serengeti . . ." In the bucolic setting, with hearts pumping 160 beats per minute, differences were forgotten, and the boys blended: no worries, not even about nationals, just keep the pace, and inhale what few could at that level of exertion.

"I remember feeling very connected to the universe," said Gruenewald. "You could feel the air and taste it. You could feel everything."

What were the Fayetteville boys feeling as they boarded the plane? They were undefeated and ranked second in the country to York of Illinois, the defending NXN champion that had outmaneuvered—some would say outsmarted—F-M the year before. Statistics aside, was Fayetteville whole? Was this team that was soon to complete the second year of its reinvention ready to win the championship that eluded it twelve months earlier? Was this group of boys, elevated with fitness never seen in young American runners, propelled by the elixirs of Green Lakes, pushed by a coach beyond "eighty" and fueled by antique ideas long forgotten, able to come together and forget they were still teenagers who'd tried to quit on a workout, drink at a party, and gotten overcome by an unexpected expression of God?

This was no time for encounter groups. Bill Aris knew that. It was a time to narrow the focus, bring the boys in, closer, to the running, what they did best. How to race like "ruthless savages," a term Cerutty applied to Elliott. Pain, always. "Pain is good," Aris told the boys. "It lets you know you're alive."

All season long, the York boys of the Chicago area had endured pain of their own. In July, as summer training unfolded, two York runners—both members of Joe Newton's elite varsity troupe—committed arson. The two seventeen-year-old seniors, the team's number-three and number-five runners, set fire to a one-million-dollar home under construction in Elmhurst. The home was consumed by flames, and other nearby homes sustained damage. The boys drove away and told no one. They also set fire to a school bus some days later.

When arrested and charged, the boys pleaded guilty and chalked up their actions to a "prank." To say the least, the two were dropped from the team and expelled from school. A little over a year later, in September 2006, the two boys were sentenced to a year in the county jail—nine months of work release plus a ninety-day sentence—according to the *Chicago Tribune*. They were also ordered to pay restitution of $1.3 million.

"Holy shit!" was the reaction on cross-country courses nationwide when news of the crime first spread. The image of cross-country runners, who were known to get some of the best academic grades of any athletes and lead the straightest, even "nerdiest," of lives, was hit hard. And these were Joe Newton's kids no less, the boys who wore tuxes to state meets. Who could explain it?

Even the DuPage County judge who'd handed down the sentence was dumbfounded. "Before this," said Judge George Bakalis, as quoted in the *Tribune*, "these were model teenagers and both came from good families. But neither can explain their actions."

On the York squad, the senior twins, Matt and Eric Dettman, team leaders in 2005, were best friends with one of the arsonists. "It was crushing," said Eric when we spoke years later. "We'd spent all our time together, going to the pool after summer practice, everything."

The York team was battered, and the Dettman twins, in a vicious guilt-by-association assault, were hounded. "Matt and I were actually accused of being part of it," Eric said. "People thought York was trying to 'protect' us. We were attacked in the middle of races, with people literally shouting at us. It got to the point where we had to get lawyers involved."

Prior to the crime, in early summer, the twins had done their best training ever. In one workout, they ran a set of five 1200s, four averaging 3:30, with the last one, by Matt, in 3:07. That degree of excellence had Stotan written all over it.

During the fall season, with Newton doing a masterful job of containing the emotional damage, York collected its twenty-fifth Illinois state title with a tight compression—again, very much in the Fayetteville mold. However, the Dettmans were sick on and off because of the stress, and at one point, late in the season with Nike nationals coming up, Eric suffered a severe panic attack and had to be hospitalized.

When the more than three hundred high school cross-country runners gathered in Portland, York was still the favorite, Fayetteville the primary challenger, and the weeklong cut-to-the-bone weather still miserable. The event's draining social hubbub was old news—no Gong Show this time around—and the talk of the weekend was the mud, cold, and freezing rain. "It was a day designed for us," declared Aris then. In upstate New York, the Stotans had seen it all. Portland's misery, F-M thought, would be a piece of cake.

In his final instructions on the eve of the race, Aris, summoning his best da Vinci, delivered nuggets of art and science, pain and privilege, psychology and philosophy—the entire Green Lakes iconography distilled for this one intrepid moment when all would be right.

Aris likened "pain as the purifier" to the ancient Greek word for competition, *agon*, from which we get agony, both a cleansing and a test. Suffering was longed for. In antiquity, the athletes lived and trained in sacred sanctuaries before the big events. There, they would become free from the "bestial life," as Nicolaos Yalouris wrote in *The Eternal Olympics*.

And so it was with the Fayetteville Stotans as the bugle (no cannon this time) sounded at Portland Meadows, fireworks lit up the grey sky, and the 2005 boys-championship 5,000-meter race was underway.

In the piercing conditions—frozen puddles, ankle-deep ice water, arctic drizzle—team strategy was a tough act, and there was an every-man-for-himself complexion to the race. Gruenewald took it upon himself to run out hard with the leaders. "The cold favored me," he said. Tommy ran "on effort," as Aris had trained the boys, using the eighty-and-above model. "I found myself toward the front. The pace felt easy," he said.

Gruenewald flew. He was not thinking about himself but the honor of trying to score one point—his personal White Moment—for the team. With bull-like strides over the heavy turf, he chased down Saratoga's top man, Steve Murdock, also a junior, and a committed front-runner, who led the field. The 1k scores came up with Fayetteville ahead with 110 points, York fourth with 163, and Saratoga seventh with 195.

Gruenewald's superiority was assumed, but it was McCann of all people running the race of his season that put F-M ahead. In the team's last work-outs at home, McCann led the squad in a series of five-hundred-meter rep-etitions on the track on Thanksgiving morning, and then, at Green Lakes, he powered the turf with an aggressiveness not seen in months. In Portland, McCann, seeing Gruenewald ahead, waited patiently in the mud to make his move. Heron followed McCann but was disoriented in the cold, crunching off frozen puddles. Kimple, wearing a hat, gloves, and long-sleeved shirt under his Manlius XC Club singlet (Nike changed the goofy team names from the prior year), was far back, miserable, panic stricken. "My feet were numb before the race even started," he said. "The entire course was a swamp of forty-degree water."

King was operating with the confidence Aris had given him the night before when he told him: "You're getting fitter every day. You have the talent to surprise yourself. You have nothing to lose. Go for it." As Aris framed it, King was "insur-ance policy," a potential key fifth scorer if the high jumper FitzGibbons faltered. Midway, King could tell he was fifth man, spurring him to run even harder.

At two thousand meters, York led Fayetteville by two points with Saratoga fourth. Murdock and Gruenewald paced the race. They ran side by side, taking the three sets of hay bales in unison. Both Dettmans were in the top ten. The event announcer described the conditions variously as a "lake," "river of mud," "bog," and "the slop."

Soon it was a three-team race among the favorites—what fans longed for when the national event was conceived. At 3,000 meters, York and Saratoga were tied with F-M third four points back. Where did lagging Saratoga come from?

There were two thousand meters left, about a mile and a quarter. Gruenewald, leading the field, was starting to lose ground, while McCann found the heart to surge in the mud and into the top twenty. The individual lead changed hands, and now it was local favorite, Kenny Klotz of Portland, ahead. Murdock tripped in the mud and fell back. The Fayetteville fifth man, FitzGibbons, also fell back, losing precious points. He went from forty-second at 2k to seventy-fifth at 4k.

With 1k to go, Saratoga had stormed into first by a remarkable thirty-two points. Fayetteville and York were in a duel for second. These three teams, in the field of twenty from sixteen states, would decide the championship.

Saratoga (an at-large selection) had snuck up on the two favorites. It seemed almost inconceivable that all Saratoga scorers—except for the risk-taking Murdock—would somehow find reserves in their well and rally together when others struggled. But all season Saratoga's master plan was that they had none. They took each race, victory or defeat, without urgency, and were smart enough to learn a lesson when their know-it-all teenage minds took a midseason hit.

With the Saratoga head coaches, the married couple Art and Linda Kranick, working with the school's preeminent girls team, it fell to an assistant coach, Don Kearns, to handle the boys. The boys respected Kearns, but at the Brown University Invitational in Providence, Rhode Island, in October, the Saratoga boys ignored Kearns' race instructions and wound up losing to Christian Brothers of New Jersey by sixty-two points. "Okay," said Murdock then, reflecting on the team reaction, "maybe these adults *do* know what they're talking about."

After splitting the two state championships with Fayetteville, Saratoga boys looked at the results man for man and saw, in their view, multiple openings for their runners to gain advantage in Portland. They had no great philosophy behind them, only the stock mission: work together, every man counts, especially the fifth man. "Coach Kearns always valued the fifth man," said Murdock.

Saratoga unity was not assumed. The gregarious Murdock was, as he put it, a "goofball." The team's number-two runner, Greg Kelsey, was the serious one. Third man Greg Kiley was the rebel. Kiley said he wanted to play football, but at five feet five and 111 pounds that was a problem. His second choice: jockey. Kiley also had a smart mouth, which got him into trouble with the coaches. He was almost left at home.

Coach Kearns *was* left at home, and in his place the Kranicks chose another adult who the boys did not know to serve as "chaperone." With the Saratoga girls getting most of the coaches' attention, the boys had to look to Andrew Bangert, the number-four runner, for leadership. "Andy was the mediator," said Murdock. "He was the one who made sure we all got along."

They did get along—famously. While Kiley gobbled up opposing runners after a conservative start that positioned him eighty-first at the initial kilometer, Kelsey running steadily, and Bangert making a startling surge to within sight of the weakening Murdock, Saratoga was cashing in, unconcerned about York or Fayetteville or anyone.

As the race took its final form, various runners, seasoned though they were, were overcome by the cold and rendered ineffectual. For Kimple, it was a long way from shirtless summer runs in the Adirondacks. "I could run in ninety degrees all day long," he said. "Not this." Kimple would go on to finish twenty-seventh as the F-M fourth man. The first four Saratoga runners, including the remarkably clutch Bangert, placed ahead of him.

Gruenewald got swallowed up by a trio of charging runners and wound up fourth, the first junior in the field, in 16:48. "I felt I'd done all I could for the team," he said. The conditions caused boys' times to be about a minute slower than usual. The individual title went to Klotz, who ran 16:26 and broke the finish tape held by special guest Paul Tergat, the Kenyan immortal who a month earlier won the New York City Marathon.

McCann, spurred by seeing his parents brave the conditions to cheer him on at close range, picked off several opponents for key points in the final kilometer to place fourteenth in the country. When he saw Heron follow him about fifty meters back in twentieth, McCann thought, "We have three guys in the top twenty, we must have won." But with the frozen Kimple in arrears and then King—late of his broken foot—doing all he could as fifth man but buried in midfield, the scores did not favor Fayetteville.

Not with the kind of race Bangert ran. After placing fortieth back home in the State Federation meet, Bangert took twenty-third in the nation, outrunning a number of state champions. With Kelsey, Gregory, and Murdock running ninth, eleventh, and sixteenth, and key fifth man Chris Allen in fifty-second, Saratoga scored 111 points for a decisive victory.

"It was a guts race," Saratoga's Linda Kranick said in a postrace interview. "We had the guts."

Bangert's out-of-nowhere performance was similar to what York's Nick Kuczwara had inflicted on Fayetteville the year before. In fact, Kuczwara achieved something similar again. York, competing as Elmhurst XC, tied for second with Fayetteville, as both teams scored 134 points. The Dukes, with the arson incident as closeted as it could be, were led by the Dettmans—Eric eighth, Matt twelfth—both in the throes of illness. Kuczwara, coming all the way back from stress fractures in both tibias over the summer, was York's fifth man, securing the tie with Fayetteville by outrunning his F-M fifth-man counterpart, King, by seventeen seconds.

Kuczwara's effort set up the tiebreaker, in which the higher-finishing sixth runners determined the outcome. York's sixth man placed sixty-fifth. Fayetteville's sixth, FitzGibbons, placed seventy-ninth. York was awarded second place and Fayetteville third. FitzGibbons could hardly be faulted. He had come through for a team that desperately needed him. He'd finished in midpack—and certainly as the first high jumper—in horrible conditions in a national field.

Danny Marnell deserved his own salute after completing four years of cross-country without normal hearing. Marnell trained and raced with his cochlea implant, wearing a headband to try and limit sweat dripping into the device and shorting it out. The implant enabled Marnell to talk with teammates on runs. In heavy rain or snow he would take it off, focusing on the pattern of his breathing or foot strikes to guide him along. "I don't think I ever felt like it was an advantage or disadvantage either way," he told me. For his two years on the nationals squad, Marnell achieved almost identical performances as seventh man: 118th in 2004 and 119th in 2005.

As in 2004, Fayetteville didn't have a bad race in Portland. But it didn't have a great race. In 2004, victorious York had a great race. It was the same for Saratoga in '05. Fayetteville's top three were solid. The rest of the unit was not. You could say that if King, a future state 1600 champion, had not broken his foot and been able to run about twenty-five seconds faster, the outcome would have been different. But that was hardly a Stotan way of thinking.

When Kimple crossed the finish, he could barely stand on his own. John Aris held him up and walked him out of the cold and into a bathroom in the grandstand, where, on other Saturdays, horse-racing fans made their bets and watched the sulkies. Kimple was shaking and concerned about frostbite. Aris ran Kimple's feet under warm water and then wrapped him in dry clothing.

The other Fayetteville runners ducked in from the field and sat in a stairwell outside the bathroom as Kimple joined them. They huddled together, shivering. "We were almost too cold to feel sorry for ourselves," said Heron. The boys had to bundle up and go back out into the cold for the awards. "That was the last place on earth I wanted to be," said Kimple.

∽

Two years: What did *you* do during the revolution? Something new had happened in running, but it was not yet complete. It had its abundant highs and a couple of devastating lows. Bill Aris had created a fresh and vital landscape for his runners to build on. He had energized teenagers with purpose and humility and empowered them with spiritual grounding—to learn, said Cerutty, "that the whole world, and all that it has to offer, opens out as a vision, splendid, normal and realizable."

Where could Aris go with this; what imperative was there yet to learn? He turned to his "great uncle" Aristotle. At school, on his office wall, Aris had an Aristotle quote for his runners to see when they stopped by. It read, WE ARE WHAT WE REPEATEDLY DO. EXCELLENCE, THEN, IS A HABIT, NOT AN ACT. Aris concluded, "That goes to the heart of everything we do here."

Of all the boys, Kimple took the result the hardest. His first half of the season was of national standing. Was his over-the-top summer of 105 miles a week a reckless conceit? Did he leave too much of himself on the Van Cortlandt Park trails in his brutal Manhattan-meet duel? Perhaps in the denouement of conflicting loyalties Kimple abused his own power. Kimple would get one more shot, in track, to get it right—in a championship mile race he would never forget.

Departing Portland Meadows, Kimple felt renewal was not beyond his grasp. "At that moment," he said of being tended to in the bathroom after the race, "I remember thinking, 'I just want to throw this over the fence and move on.'"

No one ever assumed, least of all Bill Aris, that teenagers would be easy. They could be just and wicked, innocent and savage, within seconds. And isn't that what made the whole Stotan enterprise worthwhile? It was the opportunity to try and change kids and change the world. The newness was still there. The ideas were still there. Cross-country was still there.

Seconds . . . points. So little could mean so much.

Fayetteville-Manlius boys packed for home pondering: What did they have to do to win a national championship? Before long, the F-M girls would provide some answers.

10

LITTLE GIRLS GROW UP

He talked about the magnitude of our united potential. I'd eaten candy before races, and now you're telling me I could contribute to a national powerhouse?

—*Molly Malone, Fayetteville-Manlius cross-country runner*

2006 Season I

It was a late-summer morning, 2006. In the Syracuse area, the taste of fall was in the air. The colors at Green Lakes were already turning into a Thomas Cole painting. The park's dew was heavy with life. The blend of breezy warmth with a tincture of chill was a heady mix, presenting a sense of place like no other to the Fayetteville-Manlius runners building up for the fall season.

But this day, a Sunday, Green Lakes would have to wait. One of the Fayetteville boys, Tommy Gruenewald, the senior team leader, had a personal agenda that he'd been nurturing for months. He stepped out of his home in Manlius, took a deep breath, and settled his mind for the longest run of his life, a three-hour run that reflected his new, autonomous role and what the season could have in store for him.

"I was competing against myself," said Gruenewald. "It was always, how hard could I run. How far could I push?"

Four of the core athletes in the F-M running revolution—Jared Burdick, Owen Kimple, John Heron, and Andrew "Bulldog" McCann—had taken their transformative Stotan views on pain and suffering, bonding and teamwork, and existence on the highest planes of thought, to college. Burdick had gone on to the Rochester Institute of Technology and some years later would race the Western States Endurance Run one hundred–miler, a pain-and-suffering event if ever there was one. Heron went south to Coastal Carolina in Conway, South Carolina; McCann went north to the University of Massachusetts–Amherst. Kimple ran at Cornell, taking a semester abroad in Australia where he would eventually follow the Fayetteville running trail to its mecca, the seaside spot near Melbourne known as Portsea.

These four boys, now young men, had left behind a precious legacy. The two original Stotans still competing in 2006, Gruenewald and fellow senior Geoff King, felt an urgency to uphold their standards as guardians of the world that Aris had created for them. "What Tommy and I inherited," said King, "we told one another, 'We can't let the program go into disarray.'"

But what would become of the program, of the team-based concepts that Aris had used as the foundation for every punishing run at Green Lakes, every lesson on being of nature with your footfalls and exuding humility after triumph? Other than Gruenewald, running in the stratosphere, and King, an able lieutenant, what did Bill Aris have? Not much.

For the first time since he dared to alter the fabric of high school running, Aris had to face "mediocrity as the new excellence" right at home. "I had to reconstitute the formula," he said.

The emerging boys that Aris had to work with presented him with his greatest challenge yet. None showed any particular toughness or the ability to understand Stotan ideas let alone master them in the short time frame the originals had done. This season there would be no collective "machine."

"They were nice kids," said Aris, "but awkward. It was the Land of the Misfit Boys."

As Gruenewald embarked on his run, the village of Manlius was still asleep, except for the kitchen staff at Dave's Diner and two guys in a Ford Taurus trailing him: Bill Aris and his son John. It was the Arises' job to provide Tommy with drinks to prevent dehydration.

For Bill Aris, the 2004 and '05 Nike Cross Nationals near misses no longer stung. While he thought, "It would be nice to win one some time," Aris considered the disappointments a competitive reality, like his athletes had, the bruise you might get from taking a risk. As Massimo Pigliucci, a City University of New York philosophy professor, wrote in his book *How to Be a Stoic*: "Everything has a cause and unfolds in a natural process . . . "

Aris did not have the luxury of pondering the big picture, or even looking hard at himself and whether his personal approach might need a touch-up. He had too much to do every day: accruing each practice, each Stotan lesson, one on top of the other, to feed the process, not the goal. "Finding new ways to innovate" was what drove Aris as he considered the strengths, weaknesses, and personalities of the 2006 F-M runners with summer base building underway.

Gruenewald, one of the best distance runners in the nation, had been training harder than ever. With his long legs and narrow frame, and covering more miles than his father's pickup, Gruenewald had built deep aerobic reserves. Gruenewald had learned to run through pain with a degree of power and cleanness beyond even what Aris had imagined when he'd gotten his first inkling of what Cerutty had achieved with Herb Elliott in 1950s Australia.

Gruenewald had demonstrated this again and again in track his junior year.

There was the indoor meet last February in Manley Field House at Syracuse University. In the 3200 meters, the last event late at night in a near-empty arena, Gruenewald, racing the clock, lapped the field twice, running 9:06.27 to break a thirty-year-old record. At the finish, in a rare concession, Gruenewald fell to the track spent.

There were the Penn Relays at the University of Pennsylvania's Franklin Field in April when, on the anchor 1600 meters of the distance medley, Gruenewald came from far behind in second to overtake the lead runner, from local favorite Wissahickon, and deliver the victory. On the second of four laps, when Gruenewald drew up to his opponent's shadow, the boy glanced, in shock, to see Gruenewald coming, reminiscent of the historic John Landy–Roger Bannister British Empire and Commonwealth Games "miracle mile" in 1954 in Vancouver.

That spring Gruenewald was training daily with Owen Kimple. "I would push Owen on long runs, and he would kick my butt in speed work on the track," said Gruenewald. "It was poetic."

A week after the Penn Relays, Gruenewald and Kimple ran one-two in a local meet at New Hartford in the 3200, with Gruenewald's nationally ranked 8:59.32 setting a Section 3 record.

And there were the New York State outdoor championships in June at St. Lawrence University near the Canadian border when, in a driving rain,

Gruenewald sprinted the first lap in a suicidal sixty-one seconds—"I wanted to tackle him to slow him down," said Aris—and went on to crush the field by ten seconds in 9:01.75. A week before the race, on a run in the woods near his home, Gruenewald had scraped his chest on a vine and broken out in welts all over his torso. For the race, as ritual, Aris convinced Gruenewald to shave his head like a marine. "It was like a scene out of *The Walking Dead*," Tommy recalled.

Leaving his home that summer Sunday of 2006, Gruenewald took off through those same nearby woods, ran the hills on Sweet Road, and then made the long drag toward Pratt's Falls Park, a remote site known for its waterfall and archery programs. Hopefully, the archers were asleep too.

The three-hour idea came about months earlier during the Syracuse winter doldrums. It was almost whimsical at first. Tommy had read up on distance legend Gerry Lindgren, who'd made the 1964 Olympic team at eighteen and was known for his impossibly long runs, some done in the middle of the night. One day when Tommy and John Aris were in the weight room, it just came out: What about a three-hour run to finish off the summer? After the notion got serious, John mapped out a route on Google Earth.

Running through Pratt's Falls, Gruenewald let his thoughts wander toward anticipated duels with the nation's top performers, like Steve Murdock, practically an upstate neighbor in Saratoga Springs, and the races they would run at familiar haunts like Van Cortlandt Park and Bowdoin Park.

Gruenewald also thought about the Fayetteville girls since, that summer, he was dating one of them—Jessica Hauser, also a senior. Hauser had been the team's number-three girl in 2005. Like Gruenewald, Hauser was at home with Stotan beliefs. She'd watched the boys rise up with them. "To meld the intrinsic to what we were doing physically was intriguing to me," Hauser said.

The two youngsters had something else in common: the Mormon church. While Gruenewald would join the church in college, Hauser was already a Mormon, and her father was a local leader, serving as "stake" president of the Syracuse area. Because of her devout following, Jessica would not run on Sundays. To make up for that, after doing the team's Saturday-morning workout, Jessica would do another run on Saturday night. It was often Hauser's longest run of the week, and often as darkness fell.

As Gruenewald witnessed Hauser's development, he was invigorated by how well the girls seemed to be training, even with the loss of the team's top performer of 2005, Kristen Taylor, now playing lacrosse in college. "We had the makings of something," said Aris, "but we were not sure what."

In Pratt's Falls, Gruenewald ran for ninety minutes, covering just about every inch of the park's three hundred acres, as Bill and John fed him drinks as needed. "I felt controlled, within myself," Tommy recalled. At one point, the coaches timed Tommy's pace at a snappy 6:14 per mile.

While even the most ambitious Fayetteville boys had not trained longer than two hours twenty minutes in any one run the past two years, Gruenewald could not be contained. His weekly long run over the summer began at ninety minutes, eventually hit two hours, and then extended to 2:20 and 2:40 with one more to go. "We always liked to finish the summer with a big, culminating workout," he said.

Departing Pratt's Falls, with two hours in his legs, Gruenewald was barely breathing on the flat run home. "The *son of a gun* averaged 6:10 per mile for three hours," marveled Aris years later. Gruenewald felt the pace was closer to 6:20. In any case, Gruenewald had run at least twenty-eight miles, longer than a marathon, and was barely winded.

Why, Gruenewald had almost matched Herb Elliott, who told an interviewer that he'd once run thirty-three miles in training. But Elliott cautioned, "These very long runs should be the exception rather than the rule."

With his spiritual yearning, the young Gruenewald brought to mind a memorable passage from *The Loneliness of the Long-Distance Runner*, as author Alan Sillitoe told of his protagonist's awakening during a formative cross-country race:

> Then he turned into a tongue of trees and bushes where I couldn't see him anymore, and I couldn't see anybody, and I knew what the loneliness of the long distance runner running across country felt like, realizing that as far as I was concerned this feeling was the only honesty and realness there was in the world and I knowing it would be no different ever, no what I felt at odd times, and no matter what anybody else tried to tell me.

After the run, Bill, John, and Tommy repaired to Dave's Diner. What did Gruenewald eat after his twenty-eight miles on the road? Gruenewald could not recall. Aris could. "Everything," he said.

Gruenewald savored the experience. His coaches were awestruck. They felt Tommy's effort perhaps signified something new for the team. Maybe the boys no longer had their "machine," but in taking the Stotan ethos to yet another realm, Gruenewald had affirmed that teenagers' yearning for realness still had legs, and perhaps fresh imaginings waited.

The three men looked at one another as though bearing witness to an unveiling, like eyeing the treasure at Portsea, with the feeling, "What *can't* we do?"

∞

The next week at Green Lakes, after the team's training, Bill Aris assembled the top seven girls at a lower field and had them sit in front of a baseball backstop like hitters waiting their turn at bat. They were Mackenzie Carter, Kathryn Buchan, Jessica Hauser, Hilary Hooley, Molly Malone, Courtney Chapman, and Catie Caputo. All were recent converts to running from other sports.

Aris's convincing nature—"He could convince a hobo he was a millionaire," said Malone—had drawn the girls in. Chapman, an eighth grader whose older sister, Alexandra, was on the team, fancied basketball, though she could barely run down the court without getting winded. After Courtney started summer training in the squad's junior-varsity group, Aris sized her up and told her, "I've been watching you. You could be pretty good at this. Why not speak with your parents about moving up to varsity?" The next day Courtney said yes. "I was young," she told me. "My mind was wide open."

Other girls had been turned off by the sexism they'd experienced elsewhere. Hauser's freshman soccer coach, she said, insinuated that the girls did not work as hard as boys and demeaned girls when they lost a match. "That was one reason I quit," she said. At F-M, in 2006, Hauser would be named cross-country captain.

Carter grew up trying to emulate her brothers. In second grade, she won a mile race in PE class, defeating all the boys. "I always knew I was strong and athletic," she said. She was feisty too. In the summer, Mackenzie saw her brothers shooting hoops on the driveway shirtless. She wanted to do the same. When her parents insisted she wear a top, Mackenzie threatened to run away from home. She went on to play middle school lacrosse before turning to running at F-M.

Of the other girls, there were two seniors: Hooley, previously a swimmer, and Caputo, who had played lacrosse. Buchan was a sophomore who'd played basketball—the girl with "killer eyes." Black daggers, said Aris. "The killers will tear your head off in competition. Their eyes reveal their souls."

Malone had recently moved to the Syracuse area from southern Vermont. Her family chose the town of Manlius in part because of the reputation of the boys cross-country team. Malone, a freshman in 2006, had played sports and wanted a piece of that. She would soon regret it.

"*Voluntary* summer training?" she said. "That was some bullshit if ever I've heard it." Malone said while every day the athletes were told summer running was optional, missing a day or just coming late was a stigma. The fourteen-year-old had enjoyed a more languid school vacation in pastoral Shaftsbury, Vermont, attending school in nearby Bennington. "Even thinking about working out in hot and sticky weather made me squirm," Malone vented years later.

The seven girls sat quietly waiting for Aris to speak. The sun was setting. One girl said Aris faced them with a "twinkle in his eye." The parents were lining up in the parking lot to ferry their daughters back home. The parents would wait. And wait.

Chapman, the eighth grader, looked away. While she'd let Aris talk her onto the varsity unit, Chapman was still shy and fearful—"scared out of my mind," she would say—about training at a higher level, meeting standards set by the boys, and being roped into the mythic stories she'd already heard from Aris "about mere mortals defeating the great demons of the underworld with their bare hands."

At that moment, in late summer, Chapman recalled, she likened the cross-country team to her first year of French class. "I knew the ideas were real. I knew they were good for me. But it took a while for me to truly learn and comprehend them," she said.

Who could blame Chapman, unfurling into the bloom of adolescence, for struggling to wrench free of convention? The year before, a *Time* magazine special section on "Being 13" described a "mystifying age" of overscheduling, emotional turmoil, and growing alarm over popular culture. *Time*'s female cover model wore a pouty look and a T-shirt inscribed with, I'M A VERY COMPLICATED CHILD.

Aris, drawing a breath, made eye contact with each of the seven girls. Inspired by the girls' efforts he had seen that summer, he told them they were now ready to fully take on the mission embraced by the boys since 2004: the Stotan commitment to excellence. He presented the task as a decision for the girls to make. "You've seen and admired what the boys have done. You can do the same. The question is, do you *want* to?"

As the girls let Aris's words sink in, he unloaded his principal commandment on gender equity. "I want to treat you as athletes," he said. "Not as girls and boys. If you see yourselves as little girls, to be enabled and have your hands held rather than athletes to be empowered and held accountable, then no matter what I say, things will never change. But if you take a step across the water, bridge the gap, and back up what you are truly impressed with—what the boys have accomplished—then in your hearts you are capable of anything."

"He talked about the magnitude of our united potential," said Malone. "I'd eaten candy before races, and now you're telling me I could contribute to a national powerhouse? We were sitting there looking at each other, like, 'This guy's gone mad.'"

Aris kept at it. He pulled out the girls' previous race results and showed them in black and white what he saw and what he believed. After an hour, dusk turned to darkness. The parents, growing more and more impatient—dinner was on the table—flashed their lights, signaling, enough is enough.

"My parents weren't ready for it," said Malone. "They wanted me to have fun in high school. This dedicated thing was not what they had in mind." More experienced girls, like Hooley and Hauser, who'd watched the boys succeed with longing, felt ready for something greater, saying almost out loud, "Why not *us*?"

Finally, Aris shooed the girls to their waiting moms and dads. He felt complete. The school term and competition would soon get underway. The girls had trained and listened. Aris had them in his thrall. He could not be certain of total commitment but sensed a stirring, something daring, maybe something even better than before: the young female runner finally unleashed with all her power.

Aris did not consider himself a feminist. Even then, it was too loaded a term, too fraught with politics. "I would classify myself as an 'equalist,'" he said. His compulsion in converting "little girls" was one of fairness. In the conservative precincts of upstate New York, Aris had seen girls teams treated as adjuncts to the boys; he had seen girls' programs watered down, cultural stereotypes about girls reinforced, their potential untapped.

On moral grounds alone, Aris wouldn't stand for that. He would not allow himself to perpetuate such inequality. He told the girls, "If you see yourself as the ornaments and not the Christmas tree—the boys being the tree, girls the ornaments—you're not going to be successful. You have to see yourselves as the tree, just like the boys do. I see you potentially as the Rockefeller Center Christmas tree. If you agree, then the whole sociodynamic bias of what boys are supposed to be and girls are supposed to be will be transformed."

At the time, high school girls still lacked parity in cross-country. While an Olympic marathon for women, begun in 1984, was old news, twelve states in 2006 still had shorter distances for girls than for boys, whose standard racing distance was the 5k. But Texas, Kansas, Minnesota, Connecticut, Oklahoma, and others still limited girls' distances to two miles or

4k (two and a half miles). When questioned about the inequity, state officials would say that the longer 5k distance would intimidate girls, resulting in fewer participants. Girls couldn't handle it, they said.

Some officials also pointed to girls' high injury risk in cross-country. On that score, they were not entirely incorrect. Some years before, in 1993, I had a front-page story in the *New York Times* on the largest study ever done on high school sports injuries. Looking into sixty thousand athletes in the Seattle area, Dr. Stephen G. Rice, then of the University of Washington, found girls cross-country runners to have the highest rate of injuries per one hundred athletes surveyed in eighteen boys and girls sports—higher than football, wrestling, girls soccer, and boys cross-country.

Ironically, the article was published on the first Saturday in December, the same day on which Nike Cross Nationals would be held. After seeing my piece, running people were aghast, especially if they focused mainly on the story's headline, constructed by a *Times* editor, GIRLS CROSS COUNTRY TAKING A HEAVY TOLL.

The toll, as I explained, resulted not from running per se but from ignorance among all concerned—athletes, coaches, parents, and even medical people—regarding the intersection of girls' uneven physical development and an ambitious running program, especially with college-track scholarship opportunities for women on the rise. Running over your head to qualify for an athletic scholarship, then worth about two hundred grand for four years, was hard to restrain. A "free ride" was practically there for the taking.

Consequently, in a nutshell, prepubescent girls were doing too much running because no one told them not to, and it was easy for them—their light frames and enhanced cardiovascular systems carried them far. But girls' thinness along with pounding their musculoskeletal systems for mile after mile proved to be a toxic combination. With a lack of bone-building estrogen because of a delay in the onset of menstruation—amenorrhea—girls suffered an epidemic of stress fractures.

In time, this trend would be arrested with better nutrition and more widespread knowledge of how to properly develop young female distance runners. However, even today, many ill-informed parents are unfazed when their athletic daughters experience irregular menstruation, according to Dr. Kate Berg, a child and teenage sports-medicine physician at Cincinnati Children's Hospital with a specialty in amenorrhea. After a girl's regular menstrual pattern is established in her first year or two of puberty, Dr. Berg told me, even one missed period is a red flag that could signal various health concerns. Simply eating more—taking in more calories—usually corrects the problem, she said.

At Fayetteville, Aris was aware of these issues from the start. His insistence on good nutrition—"clean" food and plenty of it—played a role in team health. That season, John Aris compiled nutritional guidelines for the entire team, based on the menu at the 2004 Stotan camp, and the athletes, boys and girls alike, held to them. Another factor in the F-M girls' sustenance was their running for intrinsic needs and one another, not for the limelight or a scholarship. In addition, with the girls' trust in Aris, they were comfortable speaking with him about issues like menstruation or adolescent weight gain, so that problems were addressed and not hidden.

As psychologist Lisa Damour, PhD, pointed out in her book, *Untangled: Guiding Teenage Girls Through the Seven Transitions into Adulthood*, girls who are uncomfortable discussing puberty with their mothers "may welcome the support of a neutral third party."

Both Bill and John provided that counsel. "They were attuned to every aspect of our bodies," said Hauser. "If I had a race and it was not a good time of the month, I was never embarrassed talking about it."

When Hauser slimmed down from big mileage and healthy eating, her father was taken aback. "He said I was too skinny," Jessica recalled. "He made me bring two bag lunches to school." Two of everything: two turkey sandwiches, two apples, two energy bars, two cheese sticks with hummus. No matter. Jessica maintained her leanness. She was appropriately running-thin.

∽

On a recent trip to Italy, I came upon some bold historical rectitude that could be taken as philosophical underpinning to what Bill Aris dared to try, five centuries hence, at Fayetteville-Manlius. In a visit to the Uffizi museum in Florence, I viewed Michelangelo's breathtaking painting *Holy Family (Doni Tondo)*, an early-sixteenth-century work considered one of the masterpieces of Italian art. Studying the figures of Mary, Joseph, and the child Jesus, one could be drawn to the iridescent colors and seamless embrace, but also to the physical presence of the Madonna, positioned front and center, with muscles. Provocative, her bulging biceps and Michelle Obama forearms called out beguilingly without pretense. The work was believed to be the first major artistic rendering of a women's strength. This was 1506, but Michelangelo could get away with it.

In 2006, Bill Aris had a touch of the Michelangelo in him, and his brush sweep offered its own lasting impression. Aris had a keen sense of when to tease out the girls' hunger for more formidable training, letting it build, and when to be in their faces with Stotan urgency. "We accepted the challenge of being treated as equals," said Carter, who devoured the Lynch sports-psychology book, focusing on the "Fear of Success" chapter after she started the season leading the team as a freshman. "Success breeds expectation," she said warily.

Carter and Malone could mull over these ideas on summer weekends when, after a Saturday-morning workout, they would pile into Carter's car and her mother, Marnie, would drive them to the family's lake house at Henderson Harbor, on Lake Ontario in Canada. One stipulation: Malone had to agree *not* to remove her shoes on the drive up. At the lake, Marnie would fill up a garbage can with ice, and the girls would take an ice bath to stimulate recovery before dinner. The girls would go jet skiing, swim, bounce on a water trampoline, do some running.

Carter's runner-up performance at the fall's opening Central Square Invitational led Fayetteville to the team victory. But the second F-M girl was forty-five seconds behind her, and the seventh F-M girl, senior Hilary Hooley, was almost two minutes behind, punctuating a weak group showing. Shared suffering? Where did it go?

Hooley had suffered a stress fracture in the growth plate of her hip toward the end of the 2005 season. Typically, a girl's biggest growth spurt, said Dr. Berg, occurred before the onset of puberty. And during puberty, a girl's muscle development was not always in sync with her bone growth, throwing her body out of whack. Hooley swam for cross-training and was treated with physical therapy. In 2006, she felt fine but, she said, lacked confidence. New, young talent on the team gave her pause.

Aris wouldn't hear of it. He used Hooley's poor race at Central Square to let the team know that the days of little girls hand-holding was over. Instead of boarding the bus for home, Aris told the driver to wait. He assembled the girls, as it happened, next to a garbage dumpster. He said, "Hilary, you ran badly. You're walking around feeling sorry for yourself, saying you're ashamed and don't deserve to be on this team. Do you think your teammates have confidence in you when you say things like that? You sit here crying after our first invitational. You better grow up."

Harsh? Maybe. But that's what Aris would have said to a boy in the same situation. Boys and girls: same workouts, same hugs, same calling out. "Brutal honesty," said Aris. For Aris, adherence always returned to Stotan tenets of selflessness. "If you're consumed with yourself, you're not behaving for the good of the team," he said. "You're not holding yourself accountable."

Carter, who nailed another second-place in the next meet, the McQuaid Invitational in Rochester, again leading the team, said Aris's unyielding language was a shock the first few times the girls heard it. Look who Aris was talking to: of the seven varsity girls, Carter and Malone were freshmen, Chapman was an eighth grader, and Buchan was a sophomore who'd skipped cross-country as a freshman.

Buchan's killer eyes started paying off as she was the second F-M girl at McQuaid, fifty-five seconds behind Carter. Hooley still struggled at the rear. Hilton, the defending girls national champion from the Rochester area, had the best showing. Fayetteville would see more of them.

In training, the girls applied their Stotan enrichment, taking on the Green Lakes hills with fervor. Carter and Buchan ran together, each pushing the other. Hauser, less talented, tried to keep their pace. "Green Lakes taught me how to run," she said. One hill the team tackled was so steep, Hauser recalled, "that I literally felt I had to crawl up."

The girls did the Pumphouse Hill workout, seventy minutes of hill circuits and, one particular day, an additional, fast two-mile "finisher" at a point of dizzying fatigue. "I was so tired I almost cried," said Malone. "I came close to faking an injury."

But, another day, that same Malone, on a freezing Saturday morning, could triumph on the Eagle Hill run, outfinessing Carter in a breakthrough workout. "I was elated," said Malone. Molly went home and told her mom that she could finally run with Mackenzie. "When you are surrounded by people who push you," said Malone, "you will be lifted to greatness."

Malone's mother still needed some convincing. When Molly started eating healthy, taking peanut butter-and-jelly sandwiches on whole-wheat bread for school lunch, family members feared she had an eating disorder.

Eating PB&J was one thing, but, for Malone, giving up ice cream, mac 'n' cheese, Friday-night football, and "boys" did not come easily. She was also in some turmoil over the idea of not running for herself but for the team. Was that really possible? Carter would have that same lapse in confidence. "I had the fear of not being able to hold up to the promises I made to my teammates," she said. While leading the team, some days at practice, Carter said, "I felt like absolute garbage."

Oftentimes, John Aris was assigned to run at the rear of the girls' training pack, to try and inspire the trailing runners to gain tighter knitting. He could see how Hauser or Hooley fought their doubts to keep up. He saw the young Chapman's gainliness as her developing body coursed the hills and, at times, how she looked back to check on her older sister. John's calls for "faster, faster" spurred the girls on and he witnessed dramatic improvement in the girls' average daily training pace. This factor—known to coaches as ADTP—played a critical role, said John, when the girls "became world beaters later on."

John's presence was not always welcome, however. "Ugh" was a common response, said Malone. "We weren't cakewalking," she said, "but when John joined us, it became more serious. He would say, 'If you're able to talk, you're not running fast enough.'"

John took some pride when the girls held nothing back and, like the boys, felt free to spit as runners do, and shoot "snot rockets," as runners will also do. On one road run that began at the high school, Malone, always game for anarchy, spit a wad that found its way right into John's mouth. Molly and John were personally close enough that John had been her confirmation sponsor in church.

"I was shocked," said John, of the spit missile. "I expected Molly to say, 'Oh, no, I'm so sorry . . . '"

Instead Malone said, "You've been blessed."

At times, the girls' covenant could seem bathed in contradiction. Pain, hills, body changes, no more little girls, out-front humiliation, new strengths, old weaknesses, seemingly impossible challenges, emerging sexuality, and coaches demanding separation from the norm with messages of love and suffering—these young female runners existed in a kaleidoscope of conflict, one day up, another day down, nothing like the mostly steady-ship boys they were trying to emulate.

On the other hand, the girls' fresh mind-set, lacking any macho upbringing gave them an emotional nakedness to soak up new ideas and perhaps eventually become even better team players than the boys. Girls were also tougher, or so it was believed. There was a common view in running that girls were better than boys in pushing through pain. Some said this notion was based on biology and girls' reproductive function. A leading high school coach in New Jersey once told me, "Girls can suffer more than boys. They're not afraid."

One fall day at the F-M school track, Jessica Hauser personified that fearlessness. Aris dished out three repeat mile runs at 5:30 pace with a four-hundred-meter lap jog for recovery. This was a bread-and-butter cross-country workout.

The hard effort added up to three miles, basically the 5k race distance. The tempo was faster than race pace, hard enough to drive the girls' heart rates to about 180 beats per minute, close to max.

Hauser, as captain, paced the team. Toward the end of the second mile, she felt her lunch coming up, cut to the infield, and threw up everything she'd eaten that day. Then she knelt on the ground, a wreck. From the other side of the track, Aris yelled, "Get up and finish!" Hauser rushed to the start and led the girls through the third mile "as hard as I could to be an example for the team." She concluded, "Despite obstacles, we can do hard things."

∞

Should the girls need any Stotan reinforcement, they could look to Manchild for stimulus. In Fayetteville's annual midseason trip to Van Cortlandt Park in the Bronx for the Manhattan Invitational, Gruenewald's rival, Steve Murdock, hooked up in a duel with New Jersey's Craig Forys of Colts Neck High. Forys won in course-record time, 12:10.7, for the two-and-a-half-mile route. In the very next boys varsity race, Gruenewald, running by himself with no one to push him and no idea what Forys had run, sought to achieve a dominant victory in his senior year.

To prepare for Manhattan and its precipitous downhills, Gruenewald had worked on his weakness—moving his long legs at breakneck speed. At Green Lakes, Aris gave Gruenewald downhill sprints, no holding back. In addition, three mornings a week before school, Gruenewald mounted a stationary bike at home and pedaled as fast as he could at low resistance.

At Van Cortlandt, Gruenewald, feeling faster than ever, attacked the pitched descents, leaning forward, he said, "letting my body catch up with itself." Gruenewald's speed was complemented by his feathery five-ounce shoes, used by steeplechasers in track for their water drainage as well as by cross-country runners in case of rain.

On the home straight, with about a quarter mile to go, Aris yelled to him, "Forys just ran 12:10!" Gruenewald sprang off his toes like a sprinter. He saw the time clock showing 11:40 with about two hundred meters left. Gruenewald eyed the clock as he raced home. Closer . . . closer. . . . As Gruenewald swept across the finish, the clock read 12:10.6, a new record by a hair. Considering the drama and Van Cortlandt's century-old cross-country history—previous course-record holders included greats like Marty Liquori and Alberto Salazar—Gruenewald's performance was like a "high school world record."

For his part, Geoff King took second in 12:39.4, his best Van Cortlandt time and one of the fastest of the meet. The previous week, at the McQuaid meet in Rochester, King said he'd experienced "an existential crisis," being overtaken by his progress from 2005 understudy to 2006 featured player. It had been a long and tumultuous journey for King, from running-culture holdout to Stotan company man, and he marveled at his transformation.

The F-M girls could find reason to marvel. Placed in the selective Eastern States race for the first time, the girls took sixth with Carter continuing her team leadership in sixteenth and Buchan next in twenty-ninth. Keeping the naive eighth grader Chapman under wraps—and kicking himself later for being an "enabler"—Aris put her in a junior-varsity race, which Chapman won in record time. "Right then and there," Aris said, "Courtney came out of her shell."

It was with a mile to go and a big lead when Chapman's shell cracked open. An adult man in running togs jumped out of the woods and joined her on the race paths. He pulled ahead, said nothing, but kept looking back at her. "I was shocked," said Chapman. As a young girl, she had every reason to be. "What's happening?" she thought. Fortunately, the incident was benign. The man ran that way until close to the finish when spectators yelled, "Get off the course!" He was not seen again.

The Eastern States girls team champion, Midlothian of Virginia, was quite a surprise. With its decisive victory over national contenders like Saratoga Springs and Hilton, Midlothian was installed as the nation's number-one team in the next *Harrier* rankings. If Bill Aris was the rare cross-country coach who'd come from the business world, the Midlothian coach, Stan Morgan, was still rarer—he'd come out of pro football. In the early sixties, Morgan played for an old NFL team once known as the Brooklyn Dodgers, which went through various iterations before forming the skeleton of what would eventually become the Baltimore Colts.

Another girls power that season was Forys's school, Colts Neck, led by the Eastern States runner-up, Ashley Higginson, a senior, whose 14:16 time put her thirty-five seconds ahead of F-M's Carter. Higginson was a national threat who didn't look the part: she had a thick physique, carrying more weight than her lithe opponents, and struggled with body image and diet.

With female runners of his own who would face the trauma of adolescent weight gain—maturing out of a little boy's body, as he put it—Aris called this the "I Suck Syndrome" for those who pitied themselves and gave in to it. "This is the body God gave you," Aris would tell the girls. "Now, how will you address it?"

It was not uncommon for a female runner to gain as much as fifteen or twenty pounds as her body matured from, say, sophomore to junior year. She could fall from one of the team's top runners to one left behind. Her race times could plummet a minute or more. Eating habits, training load, and menstrual cycle along with genetics (coaches say, look at a girl's mother) all impacted weight gain and could deliver a devastating verdict.

Aris would lay out three options: accept the development and the prospect of running slower; accept it and try and rise above it; or give up, which probably meant you'd give up on tough things later in life. "If you accept it and try to keep working hard, striving to become an even better runner than before if possible, I applaud you. And, accepting the ups and downs, I will do everything I can to help you," was Aris's rallying cry to the maturing girls.

The F-M girls emerged from Manhattan with much to applaud, but they were still a work in progress. There was no talk of state meets, let alone nationals, only intensified training and racing refinement. In their next event, the Onondaga League meet, Fayetteville girls scored their first major victory with a 40–85 triumph over Cicero-North Syracuse in a field of thirty-one teams. For strategy, Aris had the girls run with the same style employed to perfection by the F-M boys in 2004: a hard-charging 2-3-2 "V" formation to control the race, which had 242 runners. Carter and Buchan attacked out front; the trio of Hauser, holding the middle spot, flanked by Chapman and Malone, followed; then it was Hooley and Caputo, the lacrosse player, at the rear. Carter wound up second with Buchan third and Chapman sixth.

In the boys-league race, Gruenewald and King placed one-two with the high jumper and pentathlete Luke FitzGibbons, now a senior ("built like a brick shit house," said Aris), running a strong fourth in his best showing to date. F-M drubbed Liverpool, 40 to 101, and was favored to dominate the Section 3 state qualifier. However, at the sectional, on Liverpool's home course, Liverpool managed to weave some F-M magic and upset Fayetteville, 39–42, with a brilliant eighteen-second spread for its top five. Gruenewald and King again were well ahead in first and second, but it was not enough. As a result, Liverpool boys would represent Section 3 in Class 2A of the State Public Schools Championship. F-M would stay home—except for Gruenewald and King, who would compete as individuals.

Aris grew frustrated with the second-string boys. He had to water down their Green Lakes workouts. Drilling the team with Stotan lessons, there were always three or four boys who *heard* the spiel but, said Aris, did not *listen*. Thinking on a higher plane? Not when normal was so much easier.

But at least the boys were an easy read. The girls continued to present emotional complexity at every turn. As females, they were designed for complexity, in the view of the Norwegian novelist Karl Ove Knausgaard, who grappled with gender issues in his writing.

"Complexity is feminine," Knausgaard posited in one interview. "The masculine role is supposed to be simple." He meant without feelings, perhaps the most common of all male stereotypes. Growing up, Knausgaard himself felt overcome with "feelings," which he regarded as incongruent with the male nature. This troubled him. He did not know how to behave. He wanted the feelings to go away. Knausgaard would rather have been "cold and effective" in order to "have a much easier relationship to the world and other people."

Aris said that in their desired simplicity, the boys left personal issues off the playing field. Complain at practice if you must; race clean. But the girls' social framework could wreak havoc on team synergy if grievances, as they sometimes did, boiled over into competition. Any hint of discord, Aris felt, had to be addressed openly and settled, emotions be damned.

Prior to the sectionals, Aris overheard some girls complaining that others were not pulling their weight. He thought about the 2004 boys and how they had to settle their differences in open court—an encounter session in which weakness would be exposed and wrestled with. He decided to try the same approach with the 2006 girls. Could they handle it? "If you want to make an omelet, you have to break a few eggs," Aris rationalized.

Time and again, Aris found that overcoming the taboo of treating girls and boys as athletes—true gender equity—was one reinvention that stymied him. He never questioned his purpose. He never questioned his girls and their ability to handle it. "Complexity did not have to be a death sentence," he said.

11

COMFORTABLY NUMB

Don't get cocky the first mile. The race happens in the second half, when everyone is in a lot of pain. That's what we were trained for.
—*Mackenzie Carter, Fayetteville-Manlius cross-country runner*

2006 Season II

As much as he'd tried, Bill Aris could not rely solely on his psychological wizardry in coaching the Fayetteville-Manlius cross-country team. At times, he needed one of his athlete's emotional élan to help him.

In November 2006, confronting the championship events, the Fayetteville-Manlius girls still needed some Stotan polish to perform at their best. After the Section 3 state qualifier—assuming they qualified—the girls would face the two best teams in the country, 2004 Nike Cross Nationals champion Saratoga Springs and 2005 Nike Cross Nationals champion Hilton, in the State Public Schools Championship. No one in New York State figured F-M to run anywhere close to those teams, but with all the advanced training the girls had amassed in the past four months, it remained for Fayetteville to show its prowess as a seamless unit in competition.

After the boys went down to their aforementioned defeat in the sectional, Fayetteville's team success rested with the girls. The previous year, Fayetteville girls had placed sixth in State Public Class 2A. While Saratoga and Hilton waged a sensational 46–47 duel up front, F-M scored 132 points well behind in the nine-team field. But now F-M had a revamped squad empowered by Stotan teaching, and the girls would not tolerate weakness, in themselves or one another.

The ideas that Aris had bequeathed the girls so moved them that at this point in the season, facing the best in the country, freshman Molly Malone was hard-bitten enough to exclaim to any laggard, "The only reason your teammate is killing herself is for *you*. How dare you run only for *yourself*!"

Each girl had her own prescription for loyalty. The team's other freshman, Mackenzie Carter, abiding by nutritional dictates, refused sweets. Not even her favorite, Reese's Peanut Butter Cups. Not one.

Any F-M lapse, on or off the course, could always be met by an Aris tale from the dustbin of legend. Like the one among many about the all-time great Emil Zátopek who, a half century before, advised, "When you can't keep going, go faster."

A few girls in the Fayetteville lineup could do that more reliably in training than in a race. At Green Lakes, the closer, more intimate coaching, with team-mates around you, made for compelling urgency to keep up. In competition, a more diffuse environment, a girl could get lost in a crowded field and more acceptably lose face. To succeed, each F-M runner needed lock-solid adherence to Stotan pillars, not only regarding shared suffering but lifestyle as well.

Not every girl was abiding by the lifestyle. Play toys like Friday-night football, or staying out late, even on the eve of a meet, were too much for two F-M girls in particular to give up. It was not just that the girls' performances were suffering but that this development could spread to others. Aris decided to recruit his captain and most mature athlete, senior Jessica Hauser, to assist with the task of heading off the situation with diplomacy.

Hauser (whose middle name actually was Grace) readily jumped in. Aris, referring to the errant girls, told her, "I'll address the matter, but I'm just the coach. As a teammate, friend, and peer, you could be far more effective in bringing about change. The girls might be shocked and offended, but I think you'll get through to them."

First Hauser met with the compliant team members to reinforce what they already knew: "We're getting into the trenches of the season. Every decision that we make reflects on our commitment, and our love for what we are doing *for each other.*"

Then, another day, Hauser pulled aside the two offending girls, fellow seniors Hilary Hooley and Catie Caputo, and spoke with them in private after a workout. Hauser told them, "You guys are not measuring up and pulling your weight. We need a shift." The girls offered no objection. Hooley told me years later that she'd received her slap on the wrist as part of growing up. "It was uncomfortable but a reality of life," she said. "There was no antagonism, but we were told, 'If you don't want to be here, go . . . '"

There was no departure. Rather, said Carter, "We all put our hands on the burner."

At the sectional, the Fayetteville girls proceeded to have their best race of the season. Both Hooley and Caputo raced closer to teammates, in fact, close to Hauser, so that the trio of Hauser, Caputo, and Hooley were separated by only sixteen seconds, as opposed to fifty-two seconds the week before. F-M triumphed by twenty-one points as Carter again led the team with another second-place finish. The girls were on to state.

At times, Hauser herself would have trouble keeping up. "I trained better than I raced," she said. "In workouts, I could transcend boundaries." Hauser felt undermined by her own perfectionism. "If things weren't perfect in a race, like after the first mile I doubted myself," she said, "I couldn't push through the barriers."

Perfection had many overlapping faces. One was the inclination to "totalize" an experience when perfection, or how one framed it, did not materialize. As in: "My race isn't perfect right now, the whole thing is ruined, so why bother?" For this athlete, it was perfection or nothing.

As Jerry Lynch pointed out in *Thinking Body, Dancing Mind*, perfection was an illusion, a cover when self-worth was suffused with doubt. In that view, since you could never be perfect, you could never win; but you were still safe—not being perfect was not a failure either.

In this vein some risk was eliminated, and maybe that's what Hauser's racing conundrum was about: risk. Maybe the team leader, the head of F-M's UN, needed to offer herself something personal to work on when she wasn't putting out fires.

In his book *How Bad Do You Want It? Mastering the Psychology of Mind over Muscle*, author Matt Fitzgerald said that athletes may be affected by adaptive (positive) or maladaptive (negative) perfectionism. Hauser leaned toward adaptive, deconstructing her performances to try and stick closer to Carter and the team's solid number-two girl, Buchan.

However, going into state, with the team gaps being what they were, Hauser was the only runner typically without a racing partner—she was often in "no-man's-land," as Aris put it. When the team, boys and girls, traveled to Warwick Valley, in Orange County, for the State Public meet, the F-M girls lineup had solidified into Carter and Buchan leading, Hauser usually next by herself, and then a loosely bunched foursome of Chapman, Malone, Hooley, and Caputo.

In the boys Class 2A race, competing as an individual, Gruenewald faced off against Murdock, who'd transferred from Saratoga Springs to Shenende-howa. It was rare for a national headliner to switch schools in his senior year. While Murdock felt he needed a new team milieu, he also had little choice. At the time, his mother lost her job, his father was ill and not working, and, amid the housing collapse, his family lost its home. The Murdocks managed to find a place to rent in nearby Clifton Park, where Shenendehowa (an Iroquois term) was located.

In the excitement—the nation's two best runners going head-to-head—Gruenewald lost his Stotan cool and went out at a breakneck pace. "I was undefeated. I was the King of Van Cortlandt Park," said Gruenewald, mocking himself. "I was reckless." Murdock was poised to take advantage. Once known as a careless competitor himself, he felt his previous coaches at Saratoga, Art and Linda Kranick, had taught him discipline, and that his new coach at Shen (as it was known), Matt Jones, broke down running in a scientific way so that Murdock could learn to race smarter.

When Gruenewald hit the mile on the Warwick Valley 5k course in a sizzling 4:24, Murdock had the emotional tools to let him go. Biding his time, Murdock passed Gruenewald around two miles and sped to victory in 15:12. Gruenewald was fifty meters back in second in 15:20. King, in his best performance to date, took third in 15:29. "Bill talked to me about running a 'Stotan' race, and not being content to hang back," said King. "I ran with a different attitude."

∽

When the F-M girls lined up at the start, they were in a meditative calm. Peace became them. Their Stotan skin held one another close. They'd made it to states—hardly a given over the summer—and felt ready for reward, something to behold. But what? Could they be closer still?

Hilton and Saratoga keyed on each other. The running websites keyed on both—it was a long-awaited battle of the two national champions.

As the race took shape, the rainbow of colored singlets—teams wore sectional colors, not school uniforms—seemed out of place. What was Fayetteville up to trying to run with Hilton and Saratoga? Midway, coach Art Kranick of Saratoga, in an abrupt mental reversal, started yelling at his girls to "go after yellow," referring to Fayetteville's Section 3 uniforms (actually more gold than yellow) well placed among the lead runners. Seeing Kranick's panic alerted the Hilton coach, Mike Szczepanik, and he followed suit. "Go after yellow!"

Carter and Buchan, as reliable as Mantle and Maris, came home sixth and seventh with severity on their faces in 18:15 and 18:16. After that, welcome surprises: here was Hauser taking a risk to finish fourteenth as F-M's third girl; here was Chapman, seconds behind and, crucially, ahead of her fourth-scorer counterparts from both Hilton and Saratoga; here was Hooley—yes, *that* Hooley—doing the same to her fifth-scorer counterparts, improving her sectional time by sixty seconds.

When the girls did their barefoot cooldown and heard the results, they were stunned. Fayetteville-Manlius 67, Hilton 71, Saratoga Springs 73.

"Unbelievable," said Hauser. "We won without trying to."

"Astonishment," said Carter, who thought then about how her mom fussed with her custom dinners of salmon, sweet potato, and spinach the night before races. Malone thought about recent practices in the Green Lakes darkness while her "livid" dad waited in the parking lot with the motor running.

Tears of euphoria spilled from the girls. Chapman's joy, however, was colored by dread. Her thought, as an eighth grader, was, "Oh no, *more* training, *more* racing, the season's *not* over!" When Chapman, still thirteen, had first considered joining cross-country, she'd made a list of pros and cons. One of her cons was practice on Saturdays. What a laugh. Courtney had no idea her regular school day would be like this: up at 5:00 for a morning shake-out run (three days a week), breakfast, shower (if time), catch the bus at 7:10, classes till 2:06, homework for an hour, practice from 3:15 to 6:15, shower, dinner, homework, into bed by tenish. Now, after running closer than ever to Carter and Buchan, the baby of the team not only had more of the same on her plate but was *counted on* with new goals ahead.

That this disparate collection of young and older girls, the timid and tough, those with killer eyes and touching sweetness, could excel as one had some basis in a principle called "social placebo," in which supportive teammates together can effect changes in the athletes' brain chemistry. This alteration, according to an Oxford University study of rowers, helped a competitor better handle pain and fatigue.

After his setback, Gruenewald needed comforting. On the eve of the next week's State Federation Championship, he knew there would be no dinner at home, and his older brother would be out partying. Tommy took John Aris's offer to stay at his place. John prepared Tommy a salmon dinner just the way he liked it. After dinner, Tommy paged through a book of John's, *The Art of War*, an ancient Chinese military treatise, and then hit the sack. Tommy slept in John's bed. John slept on the floor.

The next morning, at Bowdoin Park, in the "Feds," a one-race grand finale with all state divisions racing together, Gruenewald led the boys field but this time held back while tackling the vaunted hills. He gauged Murdock and another contender, Brian Rhodes-Devey of Guilderland. When Gruenewald sensed his opponents' complacency, he took off, using his practiced speed, and gapped the two challengers.

On the final, flat, 1k stretch to the finish, with the Hudson River to his right and an Amtrak train whizzing by within yards of the park perimeter, Gruenewald saw Mackenzie Carter's mom, Marnie, cheering for him. "That was so meaningful for me," Gruenewald said. Referring to his mother's passing five years before, he said, "I didn't have a strong female in my life. Marnie was in tears, screaming, 'I'm so proud of you!' That powered me to the finish, where I fell into Bill's arms."

Gruenewald's winning time of 15:40.1 was just four-tenths of a second off the course record. While Geoff King also ran well, placing fifth, improving third-man Luke FitzGibbons had a shoe come off in the first mile and ran the rest of the race, more than two miles, in one spike, his foot torn to shreds from the rough ground. He would finish well off his usual spot, in thirty-second place. "Luke was writhing in pain the whole way," said Aris.

With the other F-M boys far back, Fayetteville wound up third in the team scoring and may have missed a Nike Cross Nationals at-large invitation because of FitzGibbons's mishap. Murdock told me he was sick all week, still throwing up right before race time, and only competed because his Shenendehowa team had a chance for a nationals berth. Indeed, led by Murdock's three team points, Shen scored ninety-eight points to win by fifty-three. Runner-up Collegiate, a Manhattan private school, had 151. F-M scored 154.

NXN selectors gave Shenendehowa, along with Christian Brothers of New Jersey, automatic bids from the Northeast (New York was part of the Northeast region at that time). Danbury, the New England champion from Connecticut, received one of the four boys' at-large bids nationwide. At the Manhattan meet a month earlier, Danbury had outrun Fayetteville by an average of a few seconds per man. But they'd competed in separate races, so the difference was negligible. FitzGibbons's lost shoe at Feds proved costly.

When the Fayetteville girls got ready to race Feds, they were inspired by claims of "fluke," the media meme following their state public meet triumph. Fluke: that's what was repeated in New York and beyond. How else to explain F-M?

Bowdoin Park itself seemed a fluke for its popularity as a cross-country site. The park—the "jewel of Dutchess County," so-called—seemed to fall off a cliff from the main road and drop down almost to the edge of the train tracks and Hudson waters. The park presented no defined running trail but a hodgepodge of connecting ups and downs, flanked by playgrounds and picnic tables. It took some work to make cross-country out of it.

Upriver, the Indian Point nuclear power plant, where the peace activist Pete Seeger once held vigil, could be seen in the distance. From the apex of the Bowdoin hills, the Hudson Valley opened up and so did its contrasts, from Sing Sing prison in Ossining to the Culinary Institute of America in Hyde Park.

Contrast enveloped the Federation girls race. Saratoga was the venerable champion with almost two decades of national standing. Hilton was the national newbie, burdened, said coach Szczepanik, by having to defend its NXN title. Fayetteville was a curiosity, nothing more.

To capitalize on his team's subordinate stature, Aris tried a new competitive tack to try to confuse and weaken the opposition: a sacrificial lamb. Molly Malone, a freshman, would be asked to give some blood on behalf of the team.

Aris presented this idea to her. "You're still young and thus far don't have the endurance to be in our top five," he said. "I'm looking for you to contribute something greater. If I had to pick a girl to lead the team to the top of the Bowdoin hills, it would be no one else but you. You have the speed, toughness, willpower, and competitive angst. If you decide to do this, serve as a sacrificial lamb, don't worry if you blow apart in the second half, because your job is already done: you will have sprung your teammates forward and inspired them with your courage." Aris added, "And you know what—it wouldn't surprise me if you refused to give in the rest of the race."

Malone was game. "Killing myself for the team made sense to me," she said. "I found that running balls to the wall from the gun was my best racing style."

Malone had come a long way since squirming over summer training as a child of Vermont. She told me that as "running became the thing I was good at," it defined her identity, drawing on inbred impulses while also presenting hard-won values. "Don't make excuses," she said, putting a stamp on a new virtue. "It affected every aspect of my life. Maybe I was more willing than others to hurt for the team."

At the gun, Malone shot out with the leaders, rubbing shoulders with opponents who'd run two minutes faster. No worries: Aris always said, "Pain is fear leaving the body." She took it all the way to the top. Carter and Buchan followed closely. Then, working the heavy turf was a quintet of F-M girls, bunched, for the first time all season—for the first time ever. Malone slipped back but not by much.

Buchan, her cheeks crimson like clowns' makeup, drove ahead of Carter, another first, as the pair finished as one in seventh and eighth, both in 18:49. Carter, her blond curls swaying and eyes like arrows, pushed forward to outrun future professional Emily Lipari of Long Island. Hauser nailed another race as the third F-M girl; Malone was fourth girl a stride behind Hauser in her first sub-twenty time; and Hooley, Chapman, and Caputo finished together—boom, boom—like training partners hearing John Aris's call at Green Lakes.

With the best girls-team performance in school history, Fayetteville put all five scorers ahead of both Hilton's and Saratoga's fourth girls. Fayetteville won with 103. Hilton took second (128), with Saratoga third (142). Fluke: over.

∞

The reach of F-M excellence, propelled by Malone's sacrifice, was what Aris had been hoping for since the girls' first eighty-minute runs over the summer. A compelling statistic: In the 2005 Federation meet on the same Bowdoin Park course, Carter had run 19:32; in 2006 her time was 18:49. Likewise for Hauser, who went from 20:55 to 19:57, and Hooley, who improved more than two minutes, from 22:17 to 20:13. And each girl had still more to give.

As expected, Fayetteville and Colts Neck of New Jersey received the two NXN automatic girls' invitations from the Northeast. Hilton was awarded an at-large berth. Saratoga Springs, in a controversial call, was left out. The other girls' at-large bids went to one team from California, and, unlikely enough, teams from two cross-country outliers, Alaska and Mississippi.

Saratoga—which had defeated Hilton in State Public Class 2A—had been the face of girls cross-country since the Kranicks took over the school's track

ABOVE: The visionary Fayetteville-Manlius cross-country program begins in summer 2004 with a week-long "Stotan" boys running camp in the Adirondacks. Based at the vacation home of runner Owen Kimple's family, at Lake Bonaparte, the eight athletes devour healthy meals, train twice a day, run sand dunes, and learn methods of mind power and team building. Standing on the Kimples' lakeside dock, from left: Assistant coach John Aris, Jared Burdick, Owen Kimple, Andrew McCann, Danny Marnell, head coach Bill Aris. Sitting, from left: Tim Page, John Heron, Tommy Gruenewald, Geoff King. *Photo by Emily Kimple.* BELOW: In addition to logging the long, hilly runs, the boys enjoy the lake, with Gruenewald, a sophomore, keeping the team afloat. The boys draw the attention of local girls who, one day, skim by on the lake asking neighbors, "Where are the track boys?" *Photo by Tim Page.*

The boys emerge from their Stotan camp empowerment with an unprecedented performance two months later, in October of 2014, in the Manhattan meet at Van Cortlandt Park in the Bronx. Fayetteville sweeps the first five places against national power Christian Brothers Academy of New Jersey with a "perfect" 15-point score. The team also shatters the five-man team time record that stood for 33 years. On the 2.5-mile course, Jared Burdick paces F-M, with (from right) John Heron, Tommy Gruenewald, and Owen Kimple a few strides back, and fifth man, Andrew McCann, trying to close the gap from behind. Nicknamed Bulldog, McCann lives up to his reputation with a surge on the home straight to secure the sweep. The baby-faced Gruenewald, the eventual individual winner, has his own nickname—Manchild. *Photo by Don Rich.*

ABOVE: Shortly after their record breaking Manhattan run, co-captions Owen Kimple (left) and Jared Burdick, along with coach Bill Aris, discuss the backstory of their victory with Marc Bloom. The boys emphasize team "love" engendered by the summer program. Aris elaborates on Stotan concepts, used in the 1950s and '60s by the legendary Australian coach Percy Cerutty. The new Fayetteville ideas will put them within grasp of the National title in December. *Photo by Don Rich.* BELOW: Bill Aris forms a seamless coaching duo with son John, a former team member, who serves as an assistant for six seasons. At the 2004 camp, John is enlisted to prepare nutritious fare for eight famished teenage boys and two hungry coaches. As motivation, John also runs with team members, especially when the F-M girls start taking on the Stotan ways in 2006; once John can no longer keep up, he uses a bike. *Photo by Marnie Carter.*

Pack running—"no one off the back"—becomes a Fayetteville hallmark practiced in workouts and forged in competition with a bold front-running style. Here, in a fall 2005 meet, the F-M foursome (from right) of Tommy Gruenewald, Andrew McCann, Owen Kimple, and John Heron pace the field, with fifth man Luke FitzGibbons right behind Kimple. This season the boys reprise their '04 Nationals' effort with another podium performance. *Photo by Marnie Carter.*

Joy and hardship often seem like equal partners in the F-M saga. ABOVE: In 2006, in their introduction to Stotan enhancement, the girls win their first team championship at Nike Cross Nationals, by 50 points, over the two previous NXN winners, also from New York. From left: Jessica Hauser, Mackenzie Carter, Kathryn Buchan, Hilary Hooley, Catie Caputo, Molly Malone, Courtney Chapman. *Photo by Marnie Carter.* BELOW, BOTTOM: In 2007, Bill Aris's 18-hour days catch up with him and after being hospitalized the night before in exhaustion he travels to Nationals with John taking the coaching lead. BELOW, RIGHT: In 2008, Molly Malone gets sick in Portland the night before Nationals. However, she proves in competition that it takes more than a stomach virus to keep a Stotan down. *Photos courtesy of Molly Malone.* BELOW, LEFT: The spring 2006 graduate Owen Kimple goes on to Cornell, takes a semester abroad in Australia in fall '08, and makes a pilgrimage to the Portsea site of Percy Cerutty's training camp. Owen tackles the same sand dunes that the Olympic champion Herb Elliott ran, if a bit slower. *Photo by Jen Gish.*

In 2008, in one of the girls' signature performances, Mackenzie Carter leads (from right) Hannah Luber, Meaghan Anklin, and Molly Malone across the finish in close order to dominate the NXN New York Regional qualifying meet at Bowdoin Park in Wappingers Falls, New York. The first F-M girl, Courtney Chapman, finished ahead. A week later at Nationals, the girls shock the assemblage at the weekend's Opening Ceremonies with a team video taken in storm conditions that displays their emblematic daring, confidence, and power. *Photo by Marnie Carter.*

ABOVE: In 2009, continuing to draw further away from all competition, the F-M girls, as one, take command of the Nationals field. From left, Molly Malone, Jill Fanning, Katie Sischo, Courtney Chapman, Mackenzie Carter. The five girls race to a record 17-second scoring spread for their fourth straight title. *Photo by Marnie Carter.* BELOW: In 2010, Christie Rutledge, a J.V. runner the year before, leads Nationals in the girls' most extraordinary performance yet—a record low 27 points to outrun the 2nd and 3rd place teams by about *60 seconds per scorer* and defeat the entire field of team runners if grouped as one all-star unit. Rutledge winds up second after Rachel Johnson of Texas, behind her, rallies in the last kilometer to triumph. *Photo by Marnie Carter.*

ABOVE: As a child, Christie Rutledge explores the wilds of Charleston Lake, Ontario, Canada, at her family's summer home. She runs, talks to the animals and digs for mussels to feed the fish. Later in middle school, her innocence is upended by a mean girls' culture and Christie will find her self-image shattered and lapse into recurrent health issues. *Photo by Bryan Rutledge.*

BELOW: Joining the F-M squad as a freshman in 2008, Christie is restored by true friends and solid values, and here, after her Nationals runner-up showing in 2010, she rejoices with teammates. Her health, however, is compromised for years to come until proper treatment finally puts her back on her feet, enabling Christie to graduate college with honors and enter medical school in August 2019.

ABOVE: Despite internal strife, the 2010 boys place second for their third podium performance at Nationals. After the race, Andrew Roache speaks with TV commentator Toni Reavis. On Roache's left are teammates Ben Thomas and Jules Wellner (with hat). *Photo by Marnie Carter.*

RIGHT: After the 2010 Nationals race, a climactic moment of resolution between antagonists Mark McGurrin, a senior (left), and Nick Ryan, a sophomore. McGurrin's combustible issues escalate to season-long friction with Ryan, in his first varsity season. In Portland, the two boys are able to overcome their feud as McGurrin is the first F-M runner, in 17th, earning all-American honors, and Ryan is number-3 (the third sophomore in the field), close behind Andrew Roache. Ryan, the first of four siblings to excel on the team, goes on to national-caliber performances in track and cross-country the next two years. *Photo by Marnie Carter.*

ABOVE: In June 2012, Nick Ryan, left, defeats Zavon Watkins of Liverpool, 4:05.24 to 4:07.24, to win the state track and field championships 1600 meters in a state-meet record, Section 3 record, F-M school record, and nationally-ranked time. Ryan also wins the 3200 meters in a sensational state-meet double. At right, in his senior year that fall, Ryan continues his record-breaking with a 15:27.0 Bowdoin Park 5k course record to win the NXN New York Regional by an astounding 25 seconds. *Photos courtesy of MileSplit.* BELOW: Bryce Millar, a two-time state cross-country champion, captures the 2014 New York Regional by 35 meters, a perfect lift-off for the boys' team making a Nationals title bid one week later in Portland. *Photo courtesy of MileSplit.*

In 2011, sporting new in-season uniforms and radiant smiles, the Fayetteville-Manlius girls celebrate their fifth straight Manhattan Eastern States Championship at Van Cortlandt Park in the Bronx. From left: Christie Rutledge, Alana Pearl, Heather Martin, Jill Fanning, Bill Aris, Katie Sischo, Katie Brislin, Annika Avery, Hannah Smith. Fanning is the individual Easterns champion, winning by 18 seconds in 14:03.8, the fastest F-M girls' time to date on the 2.5-mile course. Fayetteville triumphs by 48 points. Rutledge, injured, makes the trip to provide support. Martin soon suffers an injury and is also sidelined. Despite the key losses, F-M goes on to capture its sixth straight NXN girls' championship. *Photo by John Nepolitan.*

ABOVE: Despite the worst mud ever in 2012, the F-M girls capture their seventh straight Nationals title by a record 144 points and, as always, do their ritualistic barefoot strides after. *Photo by Marnie Carter.* BELOW: Alex Hatz, sixth at Nationals in 2008, rebounds from missing the 2009 cross-country season with a kidney ailment to win the 2010 national indoor (March) and outdoor (June) track and field championships in the mile. Here, Hatz first takes the Junior Mile at the 2010 Reebok indoor meet in Boston. Soon after, in his national indoor victory on the same Boston track, Hatz runs 4:05.50, then the third-fastest time ever for a high school boy indoors. *Photo by Victor Sailer/Photo Run.*

The girls who achieved the greatest cross-country performance ever—at Nationals 2010—cop some attitudes in a mid-season workout break that fall at their Green Lakes State Park training site. From left: Maggie Malone, Christie Rutledge, Jill Fanning, Courtney Chapman, Katie Sischo, Heather Martin, Katie Brislin. (Malone develops foot problems and is replaced on the Nationals squad by Emily McGurrin.) *Photo by Marnie Carter.*

Speaking of attitude . . . Home from college, from left, Molly Malone (she's in the neighborhood at Syracuse), Courtney Chapman (Villanova), and Mackenzie Carter (U-Washington, then transfer to SUNY Albany) have some fun with a "Biker Babes" motif at the base of the notorious Gulf Road hill. The image is enlarged and framed as a gift to Bill Aris for the pleasure of tackling the 1.5-mile ascent countless times in 10-mile training runs. *Photo, wardrobe and motorcycle acquisition by Marnie Carter.*

In typical Green Lakes conditions in late November, Bill Aris and the girls review final plans for the 2014 Nationals, two days before departing for Portland. All season, the girls have to work on team unity after personal conflicts in 2013 result in a disappointing second-place finish that season at Nationals. *Photo by Marnie Carter.*

The 2014 Nike Cross Nationals sweep. ABOVE: After several near-misses, the boys triumph by 48 points with a tight 23-second scoring spread. From left: Jonathan Abbot, Joe Walters, Peter Ryan, Adam Hunt, Riley Hughes; obscured Kyle Barber and Bryce Millar. BELOW: In their best display of team running yet, the girls regain the championship by 79 points with an 11-second spread, close to the "holy grail" of zero compression. From left: Reilly Madsen, Jessica Howe, Annika Avery, Jenna Farrell, Olivia Ryan, Sophie Ryan, Samantha Levy. The Ryan family has much to celebrate. Peter is the first F-M boy. Olivia, after struggling in the latter stages of 2013, is the first F-M girl. Sophie, a freshman, shows the beginnings of an enduring strength as the third scorer despite competing on an injured ankle. *Photographs by Marnie Carter.*

and cross-country programs in the late eighties. From 1993 through 2005, Saratoga girls were ranked number one in the country nine times by *Harrier*; three times they were number two.

With increasing exposure of girls running—national track meets, invitation races in big stadiums, internet videos, and girls training in skimpy attire on the roads and in public parks—unwanted attention became an issue.

In 2005, on Halloween, a man lurking on the sidelines of a Saratoga practice attempted to abduct a female team member as she went to her car to drive home. When the coaches saw the man trying to pull the girl into his van, he panicked and drove away. Art Kranick gave chase, and by the time he caught the perpetrator the police were on the scene to arrest him. Reports said the man was a forty-nine-year-old married father of three from Connecticut with a history of sexual assault charges. The following spring, the man pleaded guilty to second-degree attempted kidnapping and was sentenced to twelve years in prison.

With new product lines for young women, and a sleek clientele, high school girls' running outfits became more provocative. Standard issue in warm weather: Jog bras and revealing bathing suit–style bottoms known as bun huggers. In effect, this was running's version of a bikini, and, as girls were seen in these outfits, not everyone was happy about it.

In 1996, I wrote a story for the *New York Times* about "The Battle of the Bun Huggers," a dispute in Florida in which state officials disqualified a victorious girls cross-country team because of uniforms that, said one, "belonged in a Victoria's Secret catalogue." The controversy spilled into the finer points of French-cut briefs and girls' anatomy, and, as one coaching veteran at another school, a woman, concluded at the time, "Officials seem to be more interested in looking at girls' rear ends than their athletic prowess."

The intersection of female runners' power with the Lolita persona projected upon them had always been a threat to the male establishment. Claiming to protect women from the ravages of distance running, Olympic officials did not allow a women's event as long as the 1500 meters till 1972. And that was after years of American activism in which one US runner, ironically enough, shocked old fuddy-duddies at an AAU meeting by making her case wearing bikini-like togs that showed off her acceptably taut—but not too muscular for traditional tastes—physique.

In the early seventies, with reluctant liberties granted female runners here and there, a young girl out running could still generate antagonism. "I would get catcalls and have things thrown at me from car windows," said the running pioneer and F-M alumna Kathy Parker, after a male neighbor encouraged her to take her first strides in 1972 at age fourteen. "People didn't get it."

Around the same time, the Olympic champion Joan Samuelson once told me, when she started running as a teenager in Cape Elizabeth, Maine, "I was so embarrassed I'd walk when cars passed me. I'd pretend I was looking at the flowers."

When the high school athletes gathered for Nike Cross Nationals on the Nike campus, they would find not only a building named after Samuelson but oftentimes Joanie herself on hand to greet the assemblage.

While Saratoga Springs would not have the chance to compete in Portland in 2006, Fayetteville-Manlius, its potential successor as girls' running guidepost, set down its checklist for the big trip. First, Aris looked to Gruenewald, the team's 2004 and '05 NXN all-American, to help school the girls on what to expect. Meeting with the team in Aris's office at school, Gruenewald told the girls not to panic if they found themselves at the head of the race pack. "That's where you belong," he said. Then he came up with a phrase that the girls took to heart. "Give to gain," he told them. "Give everything you have, and you can have it all."

Next, with Green Lakes snowed in, the girls did an evening workout at the high school. In the darkness, Aris shined his car lights on the training ground. It was twenty degrees, if that, and Aris made it colder by hosing down the field to make it seem like nationals, with freezing water underfoot. Snow fell. "It was pure hell at the time," Hauser recalled. "But Bill knew something that others did not. Our training was not for weaklings. We became masters of our bodies and minds."

Finally, Aris dished out a special Pride Hill session on Thanksgiving morning. To simulate the muck-and-mire Portland Meadows racecourse, Aris had the girls train on a school field adjacent to Pride Lane, a long access road designated Pride Hill by the football team. Bill and John had gone to a farm and bought hay bales like they used in Portland, and set up a zig-zag training course that was as up, down, and all around as the girls would find ten days later.

After being warned by Aris not to stuff themselves with yams and pie at their Thanksgiving meal—everyone had to be lean and clean for nationals—the girls decided to find some release in an intimate, carefree run the day before boarding the plane for Portland. On their own, coaches not allowed, the seven girls, with giddy anticipation, ran four miles roundtrip from school to a secluded spot in Manlius called Mallards Landing. This run had been done by previous Fayetteville girls teams prior to big events and become ritual.

The girls typically raced with ribbons in their hair. When they ran to Mallards Landing, they wore ribbons from previous races. At the site, there was a small step bridge at the foot of a pond. In an act of solidarity with earlier teams and one another, they tied their ribbons to a post at the bridge, now filled with each girl's piece of flesh, as it were, potent reminders of success. Then they recited a pledge to prevail.

"It was a bonding experience," said Carter. "A happy moment, a last day we could enjoy each other before taking on the stress of a race."

Hauser was so taken by the occasion that, some years later, after she got married and had her first child, she returned to Mallards Landing with her husband and infant daughter. Jessica sat there fixed on the sacred canvas and clutching her child with tears in her eyes. "The memories gave me the chills," she said. Hauser vowed to bring her daughter back when she was old enough to understand the importance of the colorful insignia decorating the spot.

Late of Vermont, Molly Malone's father, Peter, took some time getting accustomed to his daughter's national-championship lifestyle. He once brought Molly a Snickers bar as a treat after practice. "Get that away from me. Don't let anybody see it," Molly shouted with alarm. Dad didn't understand the long practices ending with Aris lectures. He said, "I'm thinking, 'What's he telling them? It's left foot, right foot . . . '"

And then there was the coup de grâce before this year's Portland trip that caught Malone with his pants down. Since it was Molly's first year going to NXN, her parents were unaware of a team tradition that had started in '04. Team members not going to Portland posted encouraging signs—like Run Molly Run—on athletes' front lawns early on the morning of getaway day. Peter Malone was awakened at five a.m. There were people rustling in his yard. He told his wife to call 911, bolted out of bed in his underwear, opened the front door, and, in the darkness and early December cold, looked at one boy from the team and said, "Hey, don't I know you . . . ?"

∞

Portland was bone-chilling cold, an English cold, and Aris was obsessed with warding off team illness in every way possible. Socializing? There was only limited mixing allowed with the three-hundred-plus runners, who, said one F-M girl, brought their festering mono from snotty school gyms near and far. Food? Don't eat anything new. Sleep? Nap whenever possible. And always wear a hat. The hat was a tough sell. You don't mess with a girl's hair, even a girl who would give up sweets for a teammate.

Aris was unmoved by the girls' pleas. His rap: since you lose 50 percent of your body heat through your head, you're better off wearing a hat *all the time*, and have your hair flattened out, then losing body heat and risk getting a chill. *Okay, Mommy and Daddy!* The 2006 girls didn't come this far to let a germ from Yankton beat them. But they couldn't take the big boss *that* seriously. As an inside joke, they decided to wear their puffy hats everywhere, even indoors, even during meals. "In every photo," said Hooley, "you see us in hats."

As it turned out, the hats had limited powers. One day Kathryn Buchan's sister, Kris, brought along as an eighth alternate runner, came down with a migraine headache. Aris took her to a private room on the Nike campus to rest. She was allowed to remove her hat.

Even with team dictates, Chapman, the only eighth grader in the entire event, felt a new teenage freedom—being in a hotel without her parents. And with more than three hundred kids around, Chapman recalled, "I felt like Harry Potter at Hogwarts."

Checking out the racecourse with all the nationals competitors, the Fayetteville girls were not impressed. The much-talked-about, man-made "whoop-de-doo" hills were nothing, mere speed bumps.

Also testing the course was a team of Kenyan high school runners, boys and girls, brought to Portland by Nike as guests to race the next day's "open" event in a kind of valedictory. "They seem so stoic," observed Hauser that day. "It's ironic because that's what we were trying to be."

Aris chatted up another Kenyan, the dazzling Paul Tergat, world marathon record holder, five-time world cross-country champion, and United Nations World Food Program ambassador, who was again the weekend's keynote speaker. Apparently, the Kenyans and girls from Manlius had a similar training approach: never run slow.

What could go wrong? Fayetteville had beaten the defending champion, Hilton, twice in a row. Not ceding an inch, Hilton's final workout for nationals consisted of eleven miles' worth of four hundreds, eight hundreds, and mile runs to polish its own sword. Colts Neck had individual contender Ashley Higginson but had lost to Saratoga some weeks back. In a pattern that would continue to the present day, most of the buzz in Portland revolved around the California threats—Saugus and Corona del Mar. Both schools had excellent coaching but no experience in the harsh race conditions they would encounter on Saturday morning.

In the hotel on the eve of the competition, the girls reviewed the aggressive racing that had to be done while Bill and John made the goals personal. The girls were told to race for the departing seniors. *Run for Hauser, for Hooley, for Caputo.* Many girls wept. Hauser found it hard to contain her emotion. "We were touched, humbled," she said. "Bill never stopped believing in us."

Strategy was expressed in a new way, in something Aris grabbed from the Oregon wind at the last minute. A product of the 1970s, Aris was a big Pink Floyd fan. He remembered their iconic album *The Wall* and two of its tracks, "Comfortably Numb" and "Run Like Hell."

Aris instructed the girls, "For the first three kilometers, run comfortably numb. For the last two kilometers, run like hell." Aris also told Malone to use her assertiveness to try and link the second pack of five closer to the lead pair of Carter and Buchan. "This time," he said, "You're not a sacrificial lamb but possibly a key player in our scoring mix."

Comfortably numb: What did that mean? None of the greats—a Zátopek, a Prefontaine—ever devised such a plan. Percy Cerutty never spoke of it. "It means don't get cocky the first mile," explained Carter. "Don't let the hype of the race get to you and risk blowing up. The race happens in the second half when everyone is in a lot of pain. That's what we were trained for."

Was this latest Aris confection a concession to girls who might have trouble running like hell the entire race, or a shrewd tactic designed to foster team closeness in the final rush to the finish? Aris had to fine-tune—and fine-tune again: a thread could always come loose. In the morning shake-out run before breakfast, said Hooley, "I gave Bill a mini heart attack by lagging behind my teammates." Why so? "I was super nervous," she said.

"Competition is not friendly," said Aris. "It's nasty, the best and worst of human instincts. There could be no nice-nice."

At the starting berths, the Fayetteville girls said little. "There was a silent resilience," said Hauser. The girls did their final stride-outs. They applied baby oil to their legs for warmth. They were ready to go.

So was Tommy Gruenewald back in Syracuse. While disappointed he was not in Portland to race Murdock, Gruenewald wanted to give the girls a final underpinning from a higher power. Tommy knew that Bill's wife, Chris, a devout Catholic, would go to church before nationals to pray for the team.

Tommy arranged to accompany Chris to church and then help her pick out a Christmas tree.

"I was this young boy figuring out my life, figuring out my faith," said Gruenewald. "I had never prayed much, but there I was in church, on my knees, saying mass with Chris and petitioning God, 'Let each of these girls run her best race.'"

As planned, Tommy and Chris said their prayers at the precise time of the start of the girls race in Portland. Then, after getting the tree, they would go to Bill and Chris's home to wait for a call from Bill with the results.

∽

With the recent rain, the Portland Meadows course was as muddy as ever. But skies were clear, and the periodic sun was a treat. After the 1k checkpoint, Hilton led the scoring, but before long its top girl, front-running Allison Sawyer, lost a shoe in the mud. A girl from Eleanor Roosevelt of Maryland, the Eastern States runner-up at Van Cortlandt Park, also lost a shoe. Podium threat Yankton of South Dakota had one girl lose both shoes and another girl lose one. Midlothian, the Eastern States champion, had a girl break her wrist in a fall and taken out of the race by medics.

Sawyer, a steeplechaser in track, led the field past the mile with one shoe. Mud splattered every girl: legs, torso, face, hair. Uniforms were covered. Tara Upshaw of Southlake Carroll, outside Dallas, joined Sawyer at the front. Higginson, a steepler herself who would one day win the Pan American Games gold medal, surged into third. She termed the elements a delightful cross-country stew. "It allowed the race to unfold in a way that was true to the sport," she said. With her agility, Higginson moved into second over the hay bales as the defender, Betsy Bies of South Dakota, went by Upshaw and into third.

F-M, keeping its shoes intact, gained a small team lead at 2k. Carter and Buchan were positioned in the top ten. They toured the hills and hay bales and glopped through the lava-like mud and standing water as Aris watched, bundled up from a far corner of the course, yelling "Close the deal."

"I remember feeling shocked at how few people were ahead of me," said Carter. Only a freshman, Carter realized at that juncture the depth of her commitment and its purpose. "Bill made us hungry," she said. "We had a massive responsibility and a reason for existing, which many young teens our age could not say. Everything that came after was gravy—delicious, savory gravy."

It was not yet 3k, not yet time to run like hell, but Aris couldn't wait. The mud messed up everyone's calculations, and Aris wasn't taking any chances. A few places lost, a runner down . . . and pffft, the race was over. Carter kept drilling, not knowing that Buchan was close behind. Carter wouldn't dare look back.

"Close the deal." Every Fayetteville girl heard it. For Hauser, struggling in no-man's-land, it was not enough. "That was the most alone I'd ever felt in a race," she said. Risk-taking was not an option. The mud grabbed at her legs like riptides on the Jersey Shore. She could not see Carter or Buchan. Malone, after some early heavy lifting, fell back.

Hauser *was* alone. But she was not lost. She had the presence of mind to tell herself, at that moment, midway in the race with the team championship still up for grabs, "It's okay that you're alone." Then she let a comforting image overtake her. It was the team's "V" formation, like geese fly, that the girls had employed to stick together. Amid the chaos of mud spraying like horse dung on a bridle path, Hauser imagined the "V", and, in a brilliant dose of transference, imagined that the girls in front of her, from Albuquerque or Sioux Falls or Fairbanks, were her teammates, all of them together, the aloneness gone.

At 3k, Fayetteville had every runner in good position while other teams were strung out. Coaches gripped their personal PalmPilots, a Nike gift (on loan), to monitor team scoring and runners' positions every kilometer. While coaches searched for every tactical edge, Nike officials dug for every perk.

Hauser rallied. All the F-M girls did. At 4k, it was well past run-like-hell time. Bies of Yankton, who'd wept on the starting line in a gush of emotion, surged to the front, her cheeks caked, with Higginson challenging. Carter and Buchan were in close range with a shot at the top five. Hauser continued gaining ground, and now, with the finish in sight, Fayetteville was the only team with three girls well up there and another three in close ranks fighting Hilton and surprising Southlake Carroll for every inch of ground in front of the Portland Meadows grandstand for home.

"Close the deal. Close the deal." The Aris call, now barely audible, was like fog losing shape. He gave it all he could.

The girls filed in, first Carter and Buchan, among the leaders . . . then . . .

Hauser, in a dramatic rebound from solitary self-pity. "Where are my sisters?" she cried. She found Carter and Buchan, and the three embraced. Then Hooley and Chapman and Malone and Caputo finished, all seven in, and the embrace grew into a tearful huddle.

Hauser was taken in by the girlish Chapman, the weepiest of all. "Sweet little Courtney," Hauser said. "For her, so young, everything was intensified."

The finish area: No talk of scores, no talking to parents. Drinks. Sweats on. Barefoot strides. Yes, in the mud. The Kenyans did it. Hugs, tears, relief, uncertainty. *How'd we do? Did we make the podium?* Quiet, no talk of scores. Everyone waits.

At Portland Meadows, the mud tested everyone, including Higginson, who held on for an indelicate victory. At the finish, she'd tripped and fallen in a puddle the size of a kiddie pool while breaking the tape.

Officials corralled the top three teams to march onto the podium. The announcement: Southlake Carroll third with 187 points, defending champion Hilton second with 178, and the winner, the 2006 Nike Cross Nationals girls champion, Fayetteville-Manlius, 128. F-M captured its first national title, by fifty points.

∽

At a home in Manlius, New York, festooned with holiday decor, Tommy Gruenewald and Chris Aris rushed through the door with a Christmas tree and saw the phone blinking with a message. Tommy grabbed the phone, tapped "play," and heard the sobs of a hoarse fifty-year-old man who could barely get the words out: "We . . . won."

Gravy never tasted so good.

"Bill made us indestructible," declared Malone.

"It was a season of believing," said Chapman, who, later that night at the full awards ceremonies, was presented with the NXN girls Golden Anchor Award, for best fifth-scorer finish. Chapman was petrified walking up on stage by herself. The Hogwart received a belt buckle.

Carter placed fourth, the only freshman in the top twenty, in 19:34, just behind Hilton's Sawyer, not giving in to her shoeless foot. All runners' times were slowed more than a minute by the mud. Buchan took fifth, a stride behind Carter, in 19:36. Hauser finished twenty-ninth in 20:36. Then came the tight trio of Hooley, forty-fourth (20:53), Chapman, forty-sixth (20:54), and Malone, forty-eighth (20:57), with Caputo trailing in seventy-sixth (21:28).

During the awards, when Higginson came up to the stage as individual champion, she had the poise of one who would soon captain the Princeton University team. Among her future "body-perfect" cohort, Higginson would always confront physical issues, which came with the territory. Her teammate, Brianna Jackucewicz, in eleventh, pushed Colts Neck to fourth-place with 200 points. Jackucewicz went on to Harvard, where she was reminded she was no longer the little girl who won road races while her father pedaled beside her on his bicycle.

Gruenewald felt some validation when Steve Murdock, more or less his equal, captured the boys individual title. (Coatesville, from the Philadelphia area, was team champion.) Before the season closed, Gruenewald actually had a chance to race Murdock, the week after NXN, at the Foot Locker nationals in San Diego. Both boys had qualified in the Foot Locker Northeast Regional, held at Van Cortlandt Park the week between the New York "Feds" and Nike Cross Nationals.

Four days after coming home from NXN, Bill Aris, who'd been going nonstop for five months in his grand orchestration, hopped a plane again for the West Coast to be with Tommy. He went with John and Tommy's father. Gruenewald had little racing spirit left and placed twentieth, in the middle of the field of forty. Murdock took third.

Once home for good, Aris immediately turned his attention to 2007. What could he do to make it even better? Four of the top seven girls—Carter, Buchan, Malone, and Chapman—would return from their magical mystery tour. Who else could Aris find with killer eyes? By then, Gruenewald would be gone to college, but there was a freshman boy, Alex Hatz, who'd played fall soccer but had previously run track and looked pretty good. Maybe in the spring Gruenewald could help groom the youngster in the Stotan ways.

Aris could only manage to look ahead, not inward. Did he lack the capacity for self-reflection? Was he too enthralled with Stotan principles—and their success—to mentor himself? Could he go on like this: pushing day and night, roused at three in the morning with new ideas, dreaming up "V" formations, scouring the literature for themes of pain and suffering, adapting the lyrics of Pink Floyd or Jim Morrison into some competitive launchpad of beguiling virtuosity?

Something had to give.

12

HARD ROCKS AT OTTER CREEK

We were all scared. The sand hills had been built up so much. It was like a mystique.

—*Courtney Chapman, Fayetteville-Manlius cross-country runner*

2007 Season

On a sweltering August morning in 2007, the eight top Fayetteville-Manlius girls gathered at the Manlius YMCA parking lot to meet Bill and John Aris for a day trip to Otter Creek. It was five thirty, still dark. The Aris men had the girls do a twenty-minute shake-out run, similar to what they would do three mornings a week before school, and then go into the Y for some weight training, also part of their usual routine.

Before shoving off, Bill and John told the girls, "This will be the hardest running you've ever done, probably the hardest running you will ever do."

With that, the team of ten was on its way—four girls went with Bill, the other four with John—and the little caravan headed two hours north through the florid byways of Oneida, Rome, and Forestport, across the Black River, and into the Adirondacks.

"I remember watching the sun rise as we headed there," said Mackenzie Carter, starting her sophomore season after placing fourth at Nike Cross Nationals in 2006. "It was a pretty drive. I really like the woods. It's my favorite place to be, to run. That's why I enjoyed cross-country so much. We spent so much time in nature."

In that sense, cross-country running, at least in the New York wilderness, at least in the F-M covenant, thrived on a certain contradiction. The primitive, lush naturalness of the trails inspired reflection and introspection, stretching out time and pricking the senses, seducing the mind, as Thoreau said, to simplify life. In his yearning, Thoreau could never have imagined that nature's purity would one day find companionship with young runners restless to test their fortitude for intensity. With their pilgrimage, the F-M girls would immerse themselves in the comingling of beauty and, if you will, the beast—the sand hills.

Heavy sand offered the hardest running to be found anywhere. It's what Cerutty had done with Elliott at Portsea, what the Arises had done with the F-M boys team as a finishing touch to the 2004 Stotan summer camp. Running sand hills to build muscle, toughness, and team unity had worked for the boys. It was now the girls' turn. Bill Aris felt they were ready for it.

With the 2006 Nike Cross Nationals championship in their pockets, the girls *had* to come to Otter Creek. Discoveries awaited them. But in the simplicity of their surroundings, provocation festered. After losing three seniors, including team leader Jessica Hauser—"motherly," one girl called her—and bringing in three newcomers, there was a clash of personalities and sporadic impatience with any pedestrian conversion to Stotan ideas.

"There were a lot of new variables we had not dealt with," said Carter. "Every team dynamic is different. If you throw in just one new person who brings something different to the table, the whole flow of the team can be off."

Hauser went on to Brigham Young University to nurture her Mormon faith. Hilary Hooley went to Colgate, where she ran cross-country and track all four years. Catie Caputo, who was a member of the school's 2005 state-championship lacrosse team, continued lacrosse at Georgetown.

The same leadership vacuum that affected the boys in 2005 challenged the girls in '07. In addition to Carter, the experienced varsity runners were Courtney Chapman, a freshman who'd outgrown her eighth-grade puppy shyness; Molly Malone, a badass sophomore who had queen-bee friction with Carter; and Kathryn Buchan, who reprised her sixth-in-the-country 2006 NXN

performance with a 2007 New York State indoor track 1500-meter championship three months later.

Carter, Chapman, Malone, and Buchan: in terms of running capacity, no
team in the country could touch this returning foursome. The three new girls
in the varsity mix were Jocelyn Richards, the only senior, coming back from
injury; Buchan's sister Kristen (they were identical twins), an experienced
sophomore who had vastly improved; and Hannah Luber, a sophomore in
her first year of cross-country who had played soccer the previous fall and
lacrosse in the spring.

Earlier that winter, Luber had run indoor track as a freshman, prodded by
one of Aris's sell jobs. Luber had been taken in by the full-frontal Aris persona:
"The tall, misleading lankiness, the theatrical mannerisms, the animated facial
expressions and dramatic arm swings," as she described it. Oh, yes, one more
thing: "the heavy Long Island accent."

Aris had been taken in by Luber's athleticism, and he got her right. In her
first competitive season, in the winter of 2007, Luber took second, to Carter, in
the sectional 3,000 meters, and then, at state, placed second in the nonseeded
division of the 3,000, albeit with a pretty fancy time. In addition, Luber put
in a lot of training on her own—ten-mile runs, weight work—since she knew
she'd have to be ready for cross-country come summer.

With Luber on board, the Fearsome Foursome had become the Fabulous
Five. What could stop them?

Hannah Luber had three older sisters—Claire, Betsy, and Ellen—who had
all run for Aris and enjoyed teasing Hannah with horror stories, some true, some
exaggerated, about what she was getting into. The favorite tale was about when
Aris learned that one of the Luber girls had fibbed about missing practice, saying
she had a dentist appointment, when in truth she attended a friend's birthday
party. Aris, the story went, decided to teach the girl a lesson by showing up at
the party "and scaring the crap out of the girl." To set the record straight—it
was not a Luber sister but her friend on the team, and Aris did not go to the
party but confronted the girl by phone, at which point he scared the crap out
of her. "My finest hour," said Aris.

Either way, Hannah Luber suited up for cross-country with some trepidation. But she appeared up for the task. This was a girl who would one day
backpack through Southeast Asia, snowboard the French Alps, take a college semester abroad in Fiji, and teach science to impoverished children in
Guatemala.

But Luber's gritty, mind-of-her-own disposition did not always travel well. "Hannah could be a stubborn pain in the ass at times," said Aris. "She would be all over the place and needed to channel her energy."

While Luber readily adhered to Stotan ideas, relishing the prospect of "learning how to harness them," her initial training style went against the grain. As Malone recalled, Luber "would not show up for the first 80 percent" of a run—meaning she would run slower than required, like a warm-up. Then, in the last 20 percent, "she would blow us out of the water." Her teammates were furious. Malone revisited the girls' grievance, "*Now* you 'show up'? What the hell?"

Luber was a study in extremes. Aris would tell her, "Hannah, when you're bad, you're bad. But when you're good, you're excellent." She could get after teammates for not being "all in," or use her independent streak to do her own thing.

In her apprenticeship, Luber, self-conscious about lacking the natural speed of others, took more time to get her traction, serving up stored energy she was proud to use. Indulgence had consequences if not corrected.

✒

When the team arrived at Otter Creek, some sixty-five miles of interlocking horse trails, heaven on earth for runners, waited. The girls traveled light. John Aris, the chef, had packed food and drink. The group parked first at horse stables. The girls did their second run of the morning, forty-five minutes, another prelude, at a steady aerobic pace, on flat trails. Bill and John ran with them at the rear. "Looking at them," recalled Bill Aris, "I remember thinking how tall and imposing they were. We built on that."

After the run in the stable area, the team drove twenty minutes to a high point of the creek, where the entourage set up camp for the day. The girls sat on a stone rise, had lunch, and took out their notebooks. That season, Aris had the girls bring notebooks to practice like they were in class. With the sun rising and the rustle of wildlife in the thicket, Aris delivered a lecture on teamwork and selflessness and regaled the girls with stories about the Ethiopians, like the two-time Olympic marathon champion Abebe Bikila, whose first victory in 1960 at Rome was achieved barefoot. And the Kenyans—how they warmed up in sweatpants, even in the heat, and the girls should too. The girls scribbled notes while anxiety built for the *raison d'être* of the excursion: the sand hills.

"We were all scared," said Chapman. "The sand hills had been built up so much. It was like a mystique."

The eight girls—Chapman's older sister, Alexandra, was number eight—proceeded to run for eighty minutes on all manner of terrain, finishing with the sand hills, much the same workout the boys did in 2004. The heavy dunes, with their leg-devouring density and contained heat, drove the girls to new levels of exhaustion and, for some, satisfaction. "It was like running in place," said Malone. "My feet were on fire." There could be no point of letup. John Aris ran behind the girls, urging them on. Bill Aris ran to various checkpoints to monitor effort. Bill liked what he saw: shared suffering.

Bill was so inspired that he asked the girls to each find a stone in the woods as a memento of their experience. "Nothing ostentatious, just out of the dirt," he told them. "You are as rough and hard as rocks. Other teams have sleepovers. We're looking at rocks."

The girls could barely bend to pick out a rock without their legs buckling. Most would keep their personal *objets d'art* to the present day.

But they were not quite done. After a food break, the girls were assigned to finish up with their fourth run, an easy forty minutes around the periphery of Otter Creek. "We'd run over twenty miles," said Malone. "We were only jogging the forty minutes, but I couldn't do it. I fell off to a walk-run pace and tried not to cry."

Up ahead, Malone could see the Buchan sisters also struggling. One of them tripped on a tree root, fell to the ground, and just lay there. The odor of what horses had left behind was close. "C'mon," someone called, "we're almost done."

Chapman, still shadowing the "bigger personalities" (as she put it) but refusing to be babied, survived intact—and that was after skipping track for basketball the prior winter. A point guard who'd played in youth leagues since first grade, Chapman was on the school's "modified" team. After the season, her running prowess bare, she let go of basketball, prompting her to think after Otter Creek: "I can be the best on the team if I want to."

Carter had held that distinction in 2006. Now, "feeling expectations starting to creep in," competing emotions befell her, and she would have to reconcile the scandalous allure of being normal with the moral seriousness of her athletic pursuit. When the day's running was finished, said Carter, the girls were delirious with fatigue, but, for some, it was a blissful fatigue. "We could not feel our legs anymore," she said. "If there was ever a day when we experienced runner's high, it was during that last run."

Many had attempted to plumb the mystery of runner's high. Had these young girls discovered it in the coda of their exhaustion? "This was the year," said Carter, "when Bill and John Aris found out just how hard they could push high school girls."

For a grand finale, the eight girls leapt into the adjacent Black River for an F-M baptism on rough rapids—no life jackets, naked of fear—their rear ends skimming off the smooth rocks, rejoicing in the water's carriage to . . . no one knew where. From there, the day's agenda brought more bathing: a detour on the drive home to Luber's grandparents' summer cottage on Tully Lake, near Manlius, for diving and dinner.

The group got back at school by eight P.M. It was a fifteen-hour day, not just for the girls but for the Arises too. Father and son did all four runs with the girls. Bill thought nothing of it. That was the level of stamina he demanded of himself every day during the school term.

✑

When fall racing started, Aris held the boys out of the first meet, the Chittenango Invitational at Jamesville Beach County Park. They were not yet strong enough for competition. They were green, and Aris had to scale back workouts. Some of the faster girls could keep up with the slower boys. "It was futile," said Aris. Thinking back to past boys championships, he wondered, "Would we ever become *that* again?"

The girls ran Chitt, taking seven of the top eight places in a fantastic opener, but you won't find their performances in the official results. Fayetteville was disqualified for a starting-line violation. Officials declared that, one minute before the race, after the field was told to remain on the line with no more stride-outs, the F-M girls did one more stride-out, causing a "disruption and delay" in the start. The head official did not announce the decision until after the race.

Aris was out on the course and had not witnessed the alleged infraction. F-M took the DQ as more of a joke than anything. Aris felt the decision was preposterous but said in interviews that the official making the call (who ended up taking a lot of heat in the media) was a competent guy. Aris told the girls their performances stood on their own. A few days later, a package arrived at the high school sent by the coach of the "winning" girls team, Pittsford-Mendon, near Rochester. It was the first-place plaque. Aris thanked the coach for his gesture. Then he tossed the plaque in the trash.

The true individual winner was Fayetteville's Kathryn Buchan, fourteen seconds ahead of runner-up Luber. The eight girls who'd tested themselves at Otter Creek looked invincible. But days later Buchan came down with an ankle injury and was forced to the sidelines. According to Aris, instead of taking Sundays off to rest as he'd instructed, Buchan was a "closet trainer," doing her own workouts on the side. Aris learned from Buchan's sister that Kathryn would go to a forest trail outside Manlius where no one would see her, run for ninety minutes on rough terrain, and come home limping.

Discord followed Fayetteville to the next meet, the McQuaid Invitational in Rochester. Girls' bickering in practice reached Aris's ears. "Sharp edges," he called it. Aris delayed departure on race day and told the girls, "We are not getting on the bus till you resolve the issues. Find a quiet room at school and battle it out. I'll sit and wait. When you come back, I'll know whether we have a team or we don't."

"There was animosity," said Carter. It was about training, not the racing itself. "Certain people were underperforming some days but acting like they deserved to be treated like they weren't," Carter said. "They didn't understand the gravity of the situation, and how we were supposed to conduct ourselves."

The face-to-face sit-down worked. The reigning national champions did not rest on their laurels but held one another accountable to the greater goals of selflessness and ego crushing. "It brought us closer together," said Carter. "Some people just needed a kick in the butt."

When the girls emerged from school, there were stern faces and moist eyes. "Are we a team or not?" Aris asked. They were. But their unity would prove to be tenuous.

With his tough-love approach, Aris was consolidating a mosaic of proven ideas on teenage development into an all-or-nothing strategy. "That makes total sense to me," said Lisa Damour, PhD, director of Laurel School's Center for Research on Girls in Cleveland, when told about Aris's encounter groups for conflict resolution. "You can't treat girls as fragile," said Damour. "If you treat them as fragile, they act fragile."

In her child-psychology practice, Damour oftentimes saw "loving adults" trying to "protect" girls by telling them to avoid something difficult outside their comfort zone. However, since, as Damour said, "the adolescent brain can be readily hijacked by emotion," girls must be taught skills in conflict resolution as a way to gain control over their emotions and grow comfortable with them.

Since the Fayetteville girls were being held to such high standards—standards new to girls—some conflict was inevitable. The girls were able to contain it as racing picked up. With Buchan resting, Luber led the victorious F-M squad at McQuaid with her second-place finish, and then Malone paced the team at the Manhattan Easterns, leading Chapman and Luber across the line in a seamless trio at Van Cortlandt Park in the Bronx. Fayetteville dominated the team scoring.

The Otter Creek ethos of living beyond 80 percent continued. Mondays at Green Lakes, after a fifteen-minute warm-up, the girls would do a two-mile tempo run, at close to race pace, then as much as two hours of repeat hills and circuits. It would be "go do three repeats of this hill with a one-minute recovery." Then: "Go do three straightaways." Then: "Five of these . . ." Aris never told the girls what was coming next.

With the girls hungering for spent relief, Tuesday was supposed to be a recovery day. But it evolved into workout intensity and gained notoriety as an F-M signature. The "Gulf Road run"—ten miles, with a crushing mile-and-a-half ascent on Gulf Road midway. While Aris framed it as a steady run at conversational pace, the girls took to pushing one another with Stotan pride: Who could be first to the top of Gulf Road?

The hill constituted a workout unto itself. Malone, still learning to finesse the route, could not keep up. One day, fed up with getting her ass kicked, she told her teammates, "I'm going out hard for the first five miles. Let me go, and try and catch me on the hill." They did let her go, and they did catch her. Later on, after a few tries, Malone, scaling the peak alone, turned around and saw no one coming up from behind. She flew the second half back to school, covering the ten miles in sixty-one minutes, a girls record for the course. "They hated me for that," she said.

✍

It was around this time that F-M started to be hated—admired by some, hated by others—locally for their success. When they raced, they seemed to be a different species, not only in performance but in how they carried themselves. In the Section 3 state public schools qualifier at Jamesville Beach, Fayetteville swept the first five places (and seven of the first eight) in the Class 2A division for a perfect fifteen-point score. Luber notched another victory, twenty-three seconds ahead of runner-up Chapman. Kate Buchan returned to the lineup as number-three girl, close on Chapman's heels. Her cross-training had paid off.

With every advance, the girls were matching the 2004 boys, breezing through Van Cortlandt Park with a seventy-two-point victory margin over Saratoga Springs in the Manhattan Eastern States race. Aris, at this point, had thirty-five or forty training plans swirling in his mind, along with concepts like training cycles, quadric spheres, micro and macro. "It was my solar system," he said. "It was always fluid, dynamic, growing."

Still, Aris wrote nothing down. It was all in his head. How did he remember everything? "I have no idea," he said.

Never satisfied, Aris's probing could take him anywhere, like a retrospective film of the US-Soviet "Miracle on Ice" 1980 Olympic hockey final at Lake Placid. Though won by the United States, with a dramatic last-second goal, Aris was always impressed by the Russian style of play, whose originator was Anatoly Tarasov, considered the "Father of Russian ice hockey."

After World War II, Tarasov built the Russian hockey program from scratch and helped lead the national team to nine straight world championships and Olympic gold medals. The telecast specified the Russian style of seamless teamwork on the ice, which evolved from Tarasov's innovative passing system and training techniques. Tarasov did not take his best player and revolve the team around him. He did the opposite. He had his top gun *serve* the team. "That's it," Aris said. "That's us. That's how I coach."

The Aris method, four years in the works, was certified not only by its bold, new training but on new ways of teaching, of penetrating the teenage soul, which, day by day, was under siege from cultural madness. Daily, there had to be fiery preaching, even to the converted, because these kids, like any kids, could not get away from what Philip Roth called "the indigenous American berserk."

Or, what Aris would call, the American scourge of selfism.

In a fascinating treatise on teenage behavior in *Brandeis* magazine, former *Psychology Today* editor in chief Robert Epstein, PhD, wrote that "there is overwhelming evidence from multiple fields that adolescence is caused by cultural practices, not the brain. These practices do two things to young people well past puberty: infantilize them—that is, control and restrict them as if they were still children—and isolate them from responsible adults, trapping them in the inane world of teen culture."

Epstein, current senior research psychologist at the American Institute for Behavior Research and Technology in Vista, California, further noted that "the stage of life we call adolescence does not exist in many cultures." Epstein laid much of the blame on the corrupting influence of junk media.

Aris understood this from the start. He knew he could not just deliver work-outs. He had to disseminate something powerful to infiltrate the teenage mind warp. He landed on the most powerful thing of all: poetry. And with the most powerful framework he could summon: enlightenment.

Almost every athlete I spoke with recalled the Aris orations at Green Lakes as a sacred tapestry: an aesthetic carried on the wind through the trees, into the man's stews and plots, as Mackenzie Carter said, encrusted by the man's Long Island locutions, as Hannah Luber put it, and formulated, as Jessica Hauser stated, into "spectacular sermons with witty humor from literature and the great intellects of the world."

As trusted an intellect as John Dewey, the educator and philosopher, said that *how* we learn is more important, and enduring, than *what* we learn. I came across that notion in Neil Postman's 1985 classic, *Amusing Ourselves to Death*, a critique of television's debasement of society into an entertainment culture. I shudder to think what Postman would say today about the internet and social media. But back in the Reagan era, Postman traced the demise of the written word as our primary medium for enlightenment and understanding—our cultural transformation from the Age of Exposition to the Age of Show Business.

How quaint.

Fast forward to 2004 and beyond, and we have Aris, on little sleep and plenty of coffee, turning over stones, going back decades or maybe a century even, to make the spoken word golden. Cerutty. Elliott. Zátopek. Selflessness. Pain. Love. The grand exposition, with dramatic arm swings no extra charge. Aris could not stop because it was working, it was precious, and he knew no other way. The young athletes were seduced.

Never more confident, the girls took their sectional sweep to the North Country hinterland of Norfolk, close to the Canadian border, and left no doubt in state public Class 2A about who was number one in the country. Placing 3-4-5-6 within thirteen seconds, led by Chapman, Fayetteville vanquished Saratoga Springs, 23 to 71, in the nine-team finale. It was more of the same at the next week's State Federation Championship at Bowdoin Park. F-M ran 2-4-6-7, Chapman leading. The result: Fayetteville 26, Saratoga 80.

To qualify for nationals, Fayetteville had to return to Bowdoin Park the next week. In a dramatic change to the selection process, Nike Cross Nationals in 2007 created regional qualifying events while also separating New York into its own region, just like California. New York was deemed too strong to remain in the "Northeast." And Nike officials wanted to eliminate subjectivity from team selections. The two first teams in each of the nine regions would go to Portland. The at-large teams would still be chosen by committee. There would now be twenty-two boys teams and twenty-two girls teams in each race.

The decision was hailed nationally, but the extra race, especially on a rugged course like Bowdoin Park, could present a heavy burden. Fayetteville girls won the regional decisively, with Carter, Chapman, and Luber placing 4-5-6, but the pitched downhills made Kathryn Buchan's bum ankle worse, and she was the sixth F-M girl, just ahead of her sister and almost a minute behind Carter.

Make that one more thing on Aris's head. His head shook with the girls' lingering disputatiousness "over who was still not pulling their weight," said Malone. While the girls won big, there was still chirping over minor lapses, real or imagined. "It definitely wore on Bill," said Malone.

Aris had created toughness. And toughness tends to do its own thing. "We had the control," said Malone. "It was stressful for Bill to try and maneuver girls who were going to make their own decisions."

And then Aris had to deal with that pain in the ass Alex Hatz on the boys' team. Here was a sophomore considered one of Fayetteville's greatest running talents who, by his own admission, (1) "didn't particularly like cross-country that first year"; (2) "didn't always do well with authority"; (3) "could be abrasive"; and (4) "was somewhat of an angry guy" over his parents' divorce, living with his dad and, after a while, "my mom not in the picture."

After his track success as a freshman, Hatz left his close-knit soccer friends and took Aris's invitation to try cross-country in the fall, mainly because of guidance from Tommy Gruenewald and Geoff King, who'd taken in the brooding Hatz as a worthy cause. Then, Hatz had no Stotan blood at all, and the boys team was, Aris said, "messy."

Aris tried all season to "prop them up," but the boys missed their primary goal, which was to win the sectional and make it to the state public finals. In Section 3, it was Liverpool 56, F-M 58. Fayetteville did not run terribly: the first four boys had a taut twenty-second spread, but it was another thirty seconds to number five. The boys finished the season placing fourth in the Federation meet; Aris did not run them in the Nike regional. With both Aris men giving Hatz a shoulder, he managed to be F-M's number-one or number-two man all season, qualifying for state on an individual basis and placing twenty-seventh. Cross-country couldn't end soon enough for him.

For Bill Aris, however, the end almost came sooner than expected.

As the team prepared to defend its girls national title, Aris, now fifty-one, proceeded with what he did every day that fall and in years past: up at four thirty after three hours' sleep, run an hour in the darkness, do an hour of weight training at the Y at five thirty, home for a shower, wolf down breakfast in the car to the high school, put in an eight-hour day on his feet as an F-M school aide, supervise a three-hour practice into the evening darkness, and then back at home dreaming up more ideas for the team well into the night.

"I thought I was indestructible," Aris said. He felt so at ease at practice that when the team warmed up, he would walk around blissfully singing theme songs from the TV shows of his childhood, like *F Troop*.

What couldn't Aris handle? "I saw what had worked for me and the kids. I felt, 'Maybe if I worked even harder, we'd do even better.'" With his boundless energy, Aris met any notion of cutting back with this response: "Less wasn't more. Less was less."

⚬

And so it would be that on the eve of departure for Portland, during a Section 3 coaches' meeting that he cochaired at a nearby high school, Aris collapsed. When he got out of his chair to use the men's room, he got woozy . . . and that's the last thing Aris could remember. He'd fallen to the ground and passed out. EMTs were called. When Aris regained consciousness, he looked up, saw his son John, and cried out, "What am I doing here? What are *you* doing here? What just happened?"

Did Bill Aris have a heart attack?

Aris was taken by ambulance to St. Joseph's Hospital, where his wife, Chris, worked as a neonatal nurse practitioner. John was at his father's side waiting for a diagnosis. He'd seen his dad work himself ragged but thought nothing of it; dad did that every season. "He was like a hurricane," said John. Now, contemplating the worst, John said, "I was fearful for my father's life."

Finally, doctors reported that Aris was suffering from exhaustion and dehydration, nothing more, and should remain in the hospital for another twenty-four hours for observation and rest. Aris's blood pressure was high; his sugar levels were off. It was past midnight, and the early flight to Portland was hours away. He told the doctor, "I'm not going to wake up in the morning, look up in the sky, and watch my team go to Portland without me."

Despite the doctor's objection, Aris signed himself out of the hospital, went home for a couple hours' sleep, took Advil for his headache, and went with John to the airport at four A.M. for the team's six o'clock flight. His weekend plan: tell the girls nothing, tell their traveling parents nothing, have John take charge, do what he could to help. A few girls suspected something. Bill was unusually quiet and on the flight looked pale and rested his head on the tray table.

In Portland, the talk was how Saugus of California would give Fayetteville-Manlius a run for it. In 2006, sickness had swept through the Saugus squad, and the Centurians placed eighteenth in the twenty-team field. In 2007, Saugus was considered a cofavorite after winning its state Division 1 title by seventy-two points the week before with a course record 18:09 5k average at Woodward Park in Fresno. Woodward was considered a "neutral" course: some hills, nothing dramatic, good footing.

In California, cross-country could have sterility to it. Athletes rarely, if ever, saw rain or mud. Some fans, even within California, referred to running certain flat courses as a "track meet on grass." The fast times could be deceptive, especially when many California girls arrived in Portland in December with great tans.

Bill Aris laid low. He stayed hydrated, got a good night's sleep, let John run things, and by race time felt "half human." In many ways, John, as a coach, was an equal partner. He'd formed close relationships with the girls while running with them, working to exhaustion while corralling the girls into a fighting unit. On Pumphouse Hill, around Round Lake, up Gulf Road, elbows rubbed, shoes got clipped, breaths mingled with sweat and spit. When John could no longer keep up, or got injured trying, the girls' parents bought him a mountain bike to use. The bike was called "piranha."

Race morning in Portland was cold, damp, and windy. The Fayetteville girls wore black long-sleeved jerseys under their Nike-given green singlets, which Bill called "Ethiopian green," as the color was a perfect match for the green in the Ethiopian national flag. The girls also ran with gloves, some with headbands around their ears. They lathered their bodies with baby oil for additional warmth, a sensation that would give Courtney Chapman race jitters when she recalled it as an adult.

Chapman had something more as a coat of arms. Her race number was 300—an "Oh, my God" moment for her—since *300* was the name of a recently opened film about the ancient Greek battle of Thermopylae. In the film, three hundred Spartan warriors fought to the death to defend their Greek city-state of Sparta. Bill hailed Courtney's number as a symbol of Greek courage, no less than what the girls possessed as they grouped for a last-second huddle at the start.

After a few words from the coaches, Bill asked if anyone had a final thought before the fireworks display would alight and the gun would sound. Hannah Luber, her arms in a team embrace, looked up—the same Hannah who had cried on the last repetition of track workouts in the scorching wind, the same Hannah whose "godfather" was Bill Aris, her confirmation sponsor in church—and said:

"Let's go kick some motherfucking California asses!"

∽

Carter, Luber, Chapman, and Malone raced hard to the front, occupying the top ten in the first mile. John had told them, "Don't let anyone push you around" and "stay on your feet" in the crush of 154 girls off the line. Saugus had its top girl up there and a second girl in good position. Later their girls would tell an interviewer, "We were prepared for the weather." One wondered how. Saugus, situated outside Los Angeles, had summer-like conditions all season.

Fayetteville's top four kept pressing, with Buchan, her ankle no more than 50 percent, doing what she could in the number-five spot. Luber stood in the lead at one point, upholding her rallying cry but not dwelling on a thirst for first. Rather, she turned melancholy, thinking, "Oh, shit, I'm actually in the last race of my first cross-country season."

A girl from Iowa, Katie Flood, pulled ahead, leading a front pack of six with Luber at the rear. At 1k, Fayetteville led by eighty-five points; at 2k, the lead was eighty-one. Carter, her ponytail flapping like the wind-blown bunting, surged close to Luber. Flood, gloveless, pushed the pace, stringing out the pacesetters.

When the girls, in waves, tackled the tight, choppy whoop-de-doos, lined by evergreens and decorative shrubbery for effect, many were thrown off balance and needed to reset themselves. When they scooted the hay bales, set in neat rows like flights of hurdles, some girls tripped and fell. The field splashed through large puddles and standing water; there was no alternative. When snow flurries fell from the Oregon sky, spectators huddled like skiers on a chairlift.

A girl from Alabama, Madeline Morgan, surged to challenge Flood. She would say after the race that she hadn't seen snow in seven years. Perhaps training in inclement weather didn't matter.

At 3k, the Fayetteville lead ballooned to 108 points with Saugus second. Chapman ran the mud with an easy stride, the "300" on her chest and hip not forgotten. Luber led her teammates with a green ribbon in her hair, to be saved and pinned to history at Mallards Landing.

The event's announcers spoke as though the race were over. One heralded Fayetteville's "five number ones." The other said upstate New York was like East Africa.

While all but the few elite girls up front—those likely to get full rides from the college coaches in the audience—bounced around and in some cases could barely stay on their feet, the first five Fayetteville girls covered the ground with radiant authority: heads high, big strides, grinding arms, and with an attitude that said, "We've done this before. It's what we do at practice. It's what we've done since July."

Deep in their hearts, in the penetrating vacantness of competition, what the Fayetteville girls knew was this: what they'd done in training—how they'd grown and who they were as young people apart—was the central tenet of their experience. The race was secondary, a by-product. Training was where culture changed. The race was like a degree after years of study. That's why Mackenzie Carter would get upset when a teammate didn't understand the "gravity" of a workout. "How they'd trained," said John Aris, "exceeded any difficulty they would find in the race."

In the last half mile, with lightness in their feet, the trio of Chapman, Luber, and Carter grew tighter. They seemed linked by a current, the Ethiopian green, one, two, three, their black jerseys reaching, with the finish now in sight. *Crosswinds, snow, take a hike. We don't care.* Across the line they swept: Morgan outkicking Flood in 18:55, a Saugus girl, Kathy Dunn, fifth in 19:18, a second Saugus girl, Kaylin Mahoney, dueling with Chapman to the wire for seventh. Neither girl would budge in the home straight. Chapman and Mahoney, two freshmen, driving home with elbows brushing for team-point advantage. Mahoney, with a better lean, got it. Their times: 19:23.5 and 19:23.6.

Luber stormed to the wire right behind in ninth place—*ninth in the country*—in 19:26. Maybe now her parents, watching from the cordoned-off periphery, could understand why their daughter passed up time on the family boat and decided "to live Stotan." Then Carter arrived, also close, in a rare scoring tie, for tenth, every girl fighting for critical inches, *for one point.* Carter and her rival were given the same time, 19:30.8. The photo timer could not separate them, almost unheard of in cross-country. Then Malone, taking eighteenth, in another tie—had this girl-for-girl closeness ever happened before? Malone and her rival, a girl from Saratoga Springs, were also given the same time, 19:47.9. "I kicked home with every ounce of my being," said Malone. The multiple ties were uncanny, a testament to girls' fierceness.

In a bravura performance, the Fayetteville first four were separated by only fourteen seconds (Saugus first four: eighty-two seconds), and it was twenty-eight seconds back to Buchan, who would receive the Golden Anchor Award as the field's first fifth scorer, in 20:16. When the tally came out, it was Fayetteville-Manlius 83, Saugus 171, with Saratoga Springs third and another New York school, Burnt Hills-Ballston Lake, fifth. (F-M's sixth and seventh girls were Kristen Buchan and Jocelyn Richards, both well ahead of any other school's fifth runners.)

Eighty-eight points? Asses kicked? Check.

"So much crying," said Luber. "I was a mess." Aris grabbed Luber's shoulders and, through his own tears, said to her, "It was all worth it, Hannah, right? It was all worth it." Luber, her feet frozen, could not speak. Her thoughts, too, were frozen, as though frozen in time. Aris left her. There were more hugs and tears of conquest all around, especially when Bill told the girls the truth of his illness.

Later, when coherence returned to her, Luber, recalling her coach's entreaty, thought for a moment, and said to no one in particular, "Fuck, yeah!"

∽

In the first four years of Nike Cross Nationals, Fayetteville-Manlius had separated from the rest of the country. In 2004 and 2005, the F-M boys had taken second and third. In both 2006 and 2007, the F-M girls were victorious, the latter by a wide margin. (The boys 2007 champion was Neuqua Valley of Illinois.)

While this dominance inspired awe, it also generated curiosity, envy, and even anger. No one could imagine what a high school cross-country team could be doing to achieve such superiority. What did they know in New York that they did not know elsewhere in the country? After all, teenagers were . . . *teenagers.*

At Saugus, even before the meet, Fayetteville's intrigue had so captivated the coach, Rene Paragas, that he'd posted photos of the F-M girls in the team locker room. "These are their names. This is who they are," Paragas told his girls. "These are the times they've run. They have two legs like you. They get tired like you . . . "

It made sense for Paragas to try and frame the F-M girls as "just like you." I doubt any of the Saugus girls bought it. But there were times when Fayetteville girls found refuge in being both: intimidating *and* normal. In Portland, Mackenzie Carter, who'd clutched her rough stone from Otter Creek as an omen of grandeur, summoned a guilty pleasure in observing other teams "just happy to be there," envying them a little for their average-girl comforts.

"We were so young," she said. "I wanted the race to be over so we could go to the dance and be up all night."

13

FITS OVER F-M FOOTAGE

*I went to bed feeling fire in my stomach. I was ripped awake at
midnight to run to the bathroom and vomit all over the place.*
—Molly Malone, Fayetteville-Manlius cross-country runner

2008 Season

I f rival coaches were hanging pictures of the Fayetteville girls in their school
locker rooms like WANTED posters displayed on a post office wall, there was
not much reason for the team to try and amass even more of a psychological
edge for the national championships. Or was there?

It was the fifth year of Nike Cross Nationals, and event organizers continued
tinkering with their formula, seeking enhancements on and off the racecourse.
In 2008, adding to dramatic change the previous year of regional qualifying
meets, NXN decided to invite the nation's top individual competitors to go
along with team entries that had defined the event since 2004. The top five
"individual" boys and girls from each of the nine regions—those not among
the top five as members of qualifying teams—would come to Portland on the
same basis as the teams, with all expenses paid, free gear, and immersion in a
weekend of fanfare on the Nike campus.

The additional forty-five boys and forty-five girls would be added to the team fields, so that each race would now have 199 runners. The competition would be modeled after the NCAA championships, Nike's original plan, and the event's name would be changed from Nike Team Nationals to Nike Cross Nationals, reflecting the all-inclusive dynamic of the championships.

While the change was greeted with excitement, there were potential drawbacks. Could the Portland Meadows racecourse, already questioned for its poor drainage in the rain and quirky layout, handle the larger fields? Some coaches were concerned that pivotal spills could result on the muddy turf and tight turns. Coaches also had a new race complexion to deal with. The top individual qualifiers were much faster than most of the team runners. The individuals would start faster, presenting the field with a stepped-up pace, and many in the rank and file might not be able to avoid getting drawn into an early tempo too rich for them. As never before, teams would need to thread the needle in pacing strategy; plus, would they be able to identify chief team rivals with the forty-five individuals now crowded into the mix?

For his part, Bill Aris was elated. He liked that the event would have that much more gravitas. And as far as the new, faster runners—they would only give Fayetteville, especially the girls, more bodies to try and outrun to achieve their best. After all, F-M girls, based on their domination the past two years, could always use more runners to fight off.

There was one more critical issue for the new NXN. The additional individual qualifiers put Nike in direct competition with the next weekend's Foot Locker high school nationals, which had stood alone as an individual-only event for twenty-eight years. Early attempts to have the two events join were futile. But at least each had its own drawing card for the nation's elite individuals: run in the sun on a clean, reliable Balboa Park course with a hotel on the beach in San Diego; or venture into "true" cross-country in the Portland Meadows slop while enjoying Nike cachet on a corporate campus steeped in running history. Based on the qualifying-meet schedule of both programs, it was almost impossible to do both events. Could Foot Locker survive this latest Nike threat?

One thing was certain—Foot Locker could never match Nike when it came to entertaining the troops in the weekend's opening ceremonies. Nike meet planners wanted to greet the 398 teenage runners with something original, something with pizzazz, a tough call for kids used to click-a-second images and less-than-zero attention spans. The original Gong Show ideas had been retired to the Nike attic. This season, Nike had the answer: team videos. Each team would create a homegrown video that reflected on their locale and running persona. The videos would be shown to all on opening night.

The ceremony gave off red carpet anticipation. Here were the best teams in the country. Let's meet them up close and personal.

In the procession of footage, boys teams did bare-chested muscle poses, sat on fancy cars, hung out in the woods or mountains, paraded at the beach, wore silly costumes. Girls teams did gymnastics routines, said "howdy" in various regional dialects, attempted sexy poses, wore silly costumes.

When the F-M girls' video came on, this is what the audience was treated to:

Athletes in sleek, matching black uniforms from head to toe. A thundering shock-and-awe score. Running in unison. Running fast. Running through a snowstorm. Running in the rain through deep puddles. Running in darkness. Running up and over hills. No letup. No expression. No talking.

Just watch.

Watch the flashbacks to earlier races of domination. See the girls at the New York Regional in lime-green uniforms, singlets and shorts; see their imposing height, their mature, muscular bodies, powerful, thrusting arms and glutes; everyone together, a sea of lime, practically zero compression; then, cut back to the darkness, to the night, to the snow, the same girls in all black, all as one, running, running . . . running like they were born to it.

Silence.

No one in the Nike auditorium that evening would soon forget those two minutes and fifty-seven seconds. One hundred and ninety-two girls were shaking in their new Nikes. It was so intimidating that some girls coaches were angry and said so. Other coaches thought the video was a "fake." This brinkmanship further separated F-M from the crowd, frustrating a running community under siege from something they could not understand. Little girls presented like warriors—anarchy!

"It was Machiavellian, beautiful," said Aris. "All for psychological effect."

The girls had run for the video after a workout. They were on the high school grounds. In the Syracuse area in late November, it was raining and snowing, usually at the same time, almost daily. Bill and his son John found a drainage ravine, a Portland Meadows–style bog, for the girls to run through; they had the girls put their spikes on and run 150-meter sprints through the snow.

"It was cold, dark, and miserable," recalled Molly Malone, a member of Fayetteville's 2006 and 2007 championship teams. "But when the footage came on in Portland after other teams' 'happy to be here' videos, it had shattering impact."

The composite was an F-M family production. *Directors*: Bill and John Aris. *Featured players*: Kathryn Buchan (senior), Meaghan Anklin (senior), Mackenzie Carter (junior), Alexandra Chapman (senior), Courtney Chapman (sophomore), Hannah Luber (junior), Molly Malone (junior). *Videographers*: Mackenzie's parents, Mark and Marnie, and John Aris. *Film editor*: Mackenzie. *Still photographer*: Marnie. *Gaffer*: Tanner Carter, Mackenzie's brother, who had run for the team. *On location*: the new school access road at Fayetteville-Manlius.

Chapman said that in Portland, when the girls realized that their show had the opposition "scared shitless," they took it as an ironic joke in light of their actual "goofy" personalities, silly stunts, and bawdy style.

⚬

Luber and Malone, for example, were inseparable best friends. They'd clicked years before when Malone moved to Manlius from Vermont. The adventurous Luber liked Malone's "Vermont weirdness" and indefatigable sense of humor. Did their compatibility have anything to do with the fact that one summer day in Vermont, on a dare at a swimming hole, Malone had swallowed a frog whole and won five bucks?

Malone, disoriented in her New York newbie period, liked that Luber "was another girl on the team who didn't know what she was doing." They lived less than a mile apart. After training they would collapse in each other's homes, in Hannah's basement in the winter or on Molly's porch in the summer. They grew to share a disregard for convention. Malone was the one whose training spit found its way into John Aris's mouth. Luber was the one on the 2007 NXN starting line who implored, Let's go kick some oh-God-she-actually-said-that California rear ends.

So it was no surprise that a favorite pastime of the pair, in the summer, was a contest to see who could last the longest without showering or shaving her legs. "It was very competitive," said Luber. *Pause*. "Our families said we smelled."

Was this spectacle Aris's gender equity gone wild? Not really. Malone, who could never have imagined what the 2008 nationals would have in store for her, saw pragmatism in the girls' funny business. "In the summer," she said, "you woke up, ran, waited, ran again, went to sleep, and did it the next day. How many times am I going to shower in a freaking week? Soon I'm just going to get dirty again."

How long did the contest go on? "Too long," said Chapman. Actually, by all accounts, it was two weeks. Who won? Call it a tie.

When they weren't getting down and dirty, Luber and Malone were sneaking out the door at night to photograph one another doing handstands in the playground of a local church. They ran for F-M. They were in training. They were not going to be the Manlius townies sneaking out to a local bar with fake IDs. Handstands at Immaculate Conception: that was the girls' big night out.

With their indomitable strength and selective playfulness, the Fayetteville-Manlius girls of 2008 began to create something new. The previous squads had tortured growing pains. This team was older, wiser, and simpler, more commanding from the start. "My mom always said we were badasses," said Chapman, a team leader even as a sophomore. "We wanted to be looked at that way. We also wanted to define ourselves with our own identity and not always be compared with the boys team of '04–'05."

Bill Aris had no problem with that. "The girls were the new ambassadors of our initiative," he said.

It was an easy call. While the Fayetteville girls were winning NXN by fifty and eighty-eight points, respectively, the past two years, the F-M boys had not even made it to the state finals. In both 2006 and '07, they took their losses to Liverpool in the Section 3 state qualifier hard. After the 2004 and '05 Stotan transcendence, it was an embarrassment.

Soccer punk. That's what Aris had called the team's best male runner, Alex Hatz, returning for his junior year. As a sophomore in 2007, Hatz was out for himself. He sought the glory of the track while belittling the hard work of cross-country. The Green Lakes trails were no inducement. "Stotan" may well have been a dish in a Mexican restaurant.

The 2008 boys also featured Paul Merriman, a promising talent overshadowed by Hatz in '07, and Brendan Farrell, who continued playing Sunday lacrosse while running. When Farrell started in cross-country in 2007, he could barely run two miles, and after long Saturday workouts, he would have to sit on the couch all afternoon and "not move." Merriman and Farrell were juniors. With Hatz, this junior trio back in the fold for '08 had Aris smacking his lips. He plotted ways to make Stotan men out of them.

A fourth boy, sophomore Andrew Roache, presented more of a challenge. "Quite the weirdo," assessed Farrell. To Aris, Roache's long, unkempt hair, vaudevillian body language, and uncoordinated running form made him seem like the Kramer character on *Seinfeld*. Somewhat like Kramer, Roache would suddenly go missing. While running in a group at Green Lakes, Andrew would disappear, and return from a grove munching a crab apple while sprinting to catch up.

Roache apparently prized his long locks even more than a shiny piece of fruit. In the team's annual midseason trip to Van Cortlandt Park for the Manhattan meet, John Aris took to shaving the boys' heads into a marine cut the night before the event for ritual toughness. On the way down to the Bronx, at a truck stop for a bathroom break, Roache purchased a briefcase he fancied. It had a dial for a lock. After the head shaving, Roache gathered his cut hair and locked it in the briefcase. Once home in Manlius, he took out his hair and buried it under a pine tree in his backyard, where it remains to this day.

The briefcase? Roache now employs it to store books used to attain two master's degrees.

As the summer season began, Aris not only had to try and carve out new men but remake himself. The fall 2007 collapse had to be addressed. Aris decided to continue his school-aide position only one more year, that's it. Aris didn't want to spend his future days putting out fires, breaking up fights. He gave up his four thirty A.M. run and got more sleep. He did less running overall, focusing on weight training, and following his team dictates for better nutrition and a more harmonious lifestyle.

But what to do with these ramshackle boys? Back to the Adirondacks.

Not Lake Bonaparte or Otter Creek. This time it was Lake Placid. Merriman's father, Mike, had a connection that got the team cabin-type accommodations in the shadows of the Mt. Van Hoevenberg cross-country ski trails used for the 1980 Winter Olympics. Bill, John, and Mike Merriman went up with six boys: Hatz, Merriman, Farrell, and Roache, along with the only senior, John Cico, and a sophomore, Owen Strong. As usual, they brought food, drink, trepidation, and just enough courage.

Upon arrival on a Friday afternoon, the boys ran an introductory ten miles, having to walk on a mountain section they found impossible to negotiate. Saturday called for three runs, the first and third runs of six or seven miles at average effort, with hills thrown in. The key testing workout came in the middle. To emulate the patron saints, it was done on sand: about six miles of repeat runs of one or two minutes with minimal recovery.

"It was about how much pain we were willing to go through," said Farrell, who was happy just to break the five-minute mile, novice grade, in sophomore track the previous spring.

The mini camp's final run on a hot and humid Sunday morning was two hours, about seventeen miles, through a wild life preserve. "We were so tired," said Farrell, "that Bill, who was not in great shape, could keep up with us for the first hour." Hatz, by then in the process of converting from punk to prize, said exhaustion caused him to trip and fall three times during the effort. Still, Hatz's drip-drip maturity and emerging feel for distance cracked open a door for him. "It was a tough weekend but a defining one for the team and the season," he said.

Considering the girls' Otter Creek experience the previous year—a one-day Stotan camp with all the trimmings—Aris amped up their training. At Green Lakes, he dished out two hours' worth of "You can't be serious" cries from the girls, who were now becoming young women. Aris never doubted the girls' capacity, calling them "a fighting unit with conviction."

Start with a hard two miles. Take a breather. Go to the base of God's Country Hill. Run halfway up. Run near to the top where Aris can see you. Run to the very top, about three-quarters of a mile, four minutes of burning muscle. Repeat. Run from God's Country to the campgrounds. Repeat. Run a two-mile loop through a wooded area groomed for four-wheelers that spits you out back at the base of the hill. And more . . .

Bill: "Okay, good job everybody."

Girls: "Thank God we're done."

Bill: "And now for the finisher."

Malone: "I felt tears well up in my eyes."

This particular Aris finisher was a fast, "finely calibrated" series of hills and loops for over a mile—the burnishing; and a concluding cool-down jog that brought you back to the parking lot and the reward: your backpack with food. "All through high school," said Malone, "I would eat until I couldn't eat anymore. It was run, eat, and sleep." Plus the occasional shower.

Once Hatz got the hang of that idea, of no-frills enhancement from within, he would start to become one of the greatest Stotans of all. "That's when I fell in love with the process," he said.

Hatz had already shown a piercing talent. He'd ended his track season in June with a third place in the state 1600 behind victorious future pro Kyle Merber of Long Island. Hatz's time of 4:13.94 made him the nation's fastest sophomore of 2007. He was perfectly at home in the mile, or 1600, and was inspired by meeting the previous year's state champion, F-M's Owen Kimple, now at Cornell. Hatz looked up to Kimple, admiring his speed.

Not that Hatz lacked for any. "Alex could get out of bed and run a forty-nine-second four hundred meters," said Aris.

Wearing his confidence like a coat of arms, and with newfound fitness from a summer of feasting on the Green Lakes smorgasbord, Hatz was one dangerous dude about to make his mark on the nation. He first showed his virtuosity in, of all things, a half marathon. It was late summer, and Aris had an assortment of team members run Tromptown, the farm-country half marathon about twenty-five miles south of Manlius, in DeRuyter, that some early Stotans had done before. "It felt like the middle of nowhere," said Farrell.

It was an F-M invasion. Aris told his runners to do the first ten miles at a tempo effort, about 80 percent of maximum, and run the last 5k all out. Hatz, who had never before run a race longer than 5k, went out and won the darn thing in 1:13:25 with no one near him. Merriman was the second F-M runner in 1:16:59, followed by Cico (1:19:45), Roache (1:20:37), Farrell (1:20:37), and Strong (1:21:24). It was bravo for all except Farrell, who'd been training with Merriman but could not stick with him for the full thirteen miles.

Bravo for the girls as well. Malone was first, leading all women, in 1:22:16, a time that would win the women's division at most half marathons. She was followed by Chapman (1:25:22), Luber (1:27:25), and Carter (1:29:08), all well under seven minutes per mile in what was mainly a workout.

And nobody in the national landscape knew, because who'd ever heard of Tromptown? The Adirondacks, Green Lakes, Tromptown. It was like a collective wilderness inhabited only by Fayetteville-Manlius. Partake of its mighty gifts and risk being transformed.

So far, the F-M boys and girls had never made it to Nike Cross Nationals together in the same year. After the half marathon, Aris was starting to see a parallel path taking shape. Not just making nationals but winning. Crazy enough, he contemplated this brazen thought more with the boys than the girls. He kept thinking, "conversion." The boys were being converted. Hatz led. The rest followed.

The girls? While Aris was impressed with their power and unity, he sensed some strange karma he couldn't put his finger on. A cautionary whispering, perhaps, in the sacral silence of the Round Lake wood-chip forest trail, where the path narrowed, hikers were scarce, and sheltering shade of the cedars and hemlocks gave the route an eerie, seductive darkness. Allow your senses to shudder. Cup your ears and listen: What did these kids have in store for you?

Aris fretted. Maybe he just had too much time on his hands after not running at four thirty in the morning.

The girls varsity had two new members, both at risk. Katie Sischo, a former swimmer with butterfly shoulders, came in from an excellent eighth-grade track season for her freshman year. She survived the early tests with a couple of good races. But before long she had aches and pains that she kept to herself rather expose fragility. "You're a distance runner," she reasoned. "When do you *not* hurt?"

The other addition was Meagan Anklin, a senior with an injury-riddled career. Aris was forced to baby her with equal parts running and cross-training. She was barely running thirty miles a week, warm-up level for the F-M girls, while swimming and spinning almost daily.

Anklin had played soccer and lacrosse and joined the team as a freshman in 2005 after receiving a personal letter, handwritten and mailed in an envelope at the post office, from a senior team member, Hilary Hooley. Hooley and two other seniors, envious of the boys' success at the time, took it upon themselves to try and fill their own shoes with promising talent. Hooley had seen young Anklin running in the neighborhood and then at a Fourth of July 5k with her dad, a former F-M runner himself. Told she "could be a really good fit," Anklin hopped aboard.

By senior year, Anklin's injuries had not totally cleared up, and in late September, with racing underway, her parents had her go for a cortisone shot to try and arrest her ITB—iliotibial band—issues. Cortisone did not always work and could make a problem worse. "It was a big leap of faith," Anklin said. "I was desperate."

Desperate because Anklin so desired to live by the team's Stotan principles and find her way onto the nationals lineup. Desperate enough that on Thanksgiving, with a tableful of family and guests and heaping plates of food—and the regional qualifying meet two days hence—Anklin passed up the turkey and trimmings for her own homemade meal: a peanut butter-and-jelly sandwich. It was the tryptophan taboo—avoiding the amino acid found in turkey that is said to cause fatigue. While Anklin said she "didn't think twice" about her special meal, her parents were, like, "Uh, I guess the coach, uh . . . knows best."

This begrudging recognition was tested in the team's opening meet at Chittenango. With meager opposition, Aris held out the top girls, who trained instead, and told them to remain discreet during the meet so as not to flaunt their status. The girls decided to wear flashy, mismatched colors, "ironically curated accessories," said Carter, "to sell the disguise." Luber walked around with a bag of McDonald's. The spectacle caused a fury, and the girls felt a humbling that Aris then used to build character.

Anklin's treatment was successful. By early November and the Section 3 state qualifier, Anklin was strong enough on meager mileage to be the number-three F-M girl as the team swept the first five places (actually top seven) for a perfect fifteen points. "I was in awe of Meagan. We could count on her as a rock even though half the time she wasn't able to run with us," said Chapman, sectional winner by twenty seconds over Luber and Eastern States runner-up by a stride weeks earlier to a girl from New Jersey at Van Cortlandt Park.

However, the dark whispering in Aris's ear would become audible. Sischo, a solid varsity scorer, was running on the second of two loops at the sectional when, with six hundred meters to go on a down-and-up hairpin turn, she yelled to her coach, "I heard something pop."

"Her right leg snapped like a chicken bone," said Aris. Sischo, fourteen, would not relent with the team sweep at stake. She continued to the finish despite a stress fracture in the fibula—a bone in the lower leg—to place seventh in 19:24.

With Sischo out for the season and the championship meets coming up, Aris held an emergency meeting with the girls to settle minds and plug holes. Sischo showed up in a cast from knee to toe. Anklin was edgy. She now faced more pressure as a Sischo surrogate. Luber and Malone, the gruesome two-some, shrugged off the setback, saying each year it was one thing or another, no problem.

Aris, in a nickname mood, started calling Luber "Clubber," after the fear-some Mr. T. character Clubber Lang, in *Rocky III*. It was additional mooring for Luber, already smitten by the team's "cinematic perfection," the Aris style of bringing artistry to Green Lakes workouts, intensity welcome. "Hills, flats, roads, gravel, mulch, mud, shade. It was a runner's paradise," she said. "Parts of the Serengeti were completely closed to the sun. Every summer, it drew us all back."

When Luber was confirmed in her Catholic church, Aris was her sponsor. "Bill was my godfather," she said. More than she might have realized at the time. With their closeness, Aris drew up a handwritten, seven-page "boyfriend contract" in which Aris made prospective Luber suitors an offer they couldn't refuse. Read the contract, fill it out, and sign, agreeing to treat Hannah with respect and decency, and then maybe you could have Hannah's hand. The contract had stipulations for eating habits (healthy required), alcohol intake (abstinence required), police record (are you kidding?), and, of course, blood type and mile PR. "I thought it was hysterical," said Luber.

In perhaps her best race to date, Luber took third in the state public Class 2A championships, helping to secure Fayetteville's third-straight runaway victory as Chapman led the team with her first state title. Surging up Cardiac Hill on the tough Sunken Meadow course on Long Island, Chapman felt a second wind, left the field behind, and triumphed by a whopping thirty-three seconds.

F-M now had a second national figure to go with Hatz on the boys' side. Going into state, Hatz was not just Fayetteville's top man but was undefeated, except for a third at Manhattan, with his shaved head a look that seemed to click, at least in the Bronx. Meet officials finally listened to coaches' pleas to create an Eastern States boys race to match what the girls had had for years. However, in one of the regular non-elite varsity races, an outlier, Soloman Haile of Maryland, a recent immigrant from Ethiopia, broke Tommy Gruenewald's 2006 course record by four seconds with a 12:06.61 run on the two-and-a-half-mile Van Cortlandt Park course. Haile got into hot soup with questions about his age, identity, and whether he'd taken professional money at a road race. He was cleared on all fronts by the Maryland state high schools association and went on to win that season's Foot Locker nationals.

After leading the boys to a 28–76 sectional triumph over Liverpool to calm any nerves about a sectional jinx, Hatz paced the team to a state runner-up performance, 30–47, behind national power Shenendehowa. Hatz's victory gave F-M a sweep of the Class 2A individual titles, but he had none of Chapman's dominance, eking out a .3-second win, about a foot, in 15:59. More importantly, Fayetteville had a solid number-two man in Merriman, who placed third in the race, and a reliable number three in Farrell, who had his best showing at sectionals after overcoming an early-season bout of mono.

Aris was right: the three junior boys were cooking, and the boys and girls were on a parallel path toward nationals. However, the rabble-rouser coach had to go and make trouble when he decided, then and forevermore, not to compete in the next week's State Federation Championship. With the advent of NXN regionals the previous year, to Aris, and in time to others, the Feds became superfluous since both meets would have the same fields at the same site two weeks in a row.

The late-season schedule was already too crowded. The addition of the Feds made for six straight weekends of racing. Why risk injury in a meet that didn't really matter? "It was like playing with fire," said Aris, who felt it wiser to fit in more training and be sharp for regionals and nationals.

While the F-M athletes agreed, and Aris called his decision "pragmatic and brutally objective," the Feds had been a mainstay for thirty-five years, and the Aris pullout—downright blasphemy to some—went viral throughout the state and beyond. It was more fuel for those who already thought Aris was too much his own man and considered the Fayetteville team arrogant in its disregard for convention.

The personal attacks on Aris were of a piece with what Cerutty the renegade had gone through as public enemy number one in the Australian track firmament. "The great coach must be a heterodox," he wrote. "Often he is deemed a 'crank.' More often he is in conflict with authority, officialdom." Aris cleaved to Cerutty's answer that a Stotan must have the fortitude to withstand criticism and "cast them off as comments from the unknowing."

Aris put the finishing touch on the team's preparation for Portland with a two-mile time trial a few days before regionals. A menacing storm suddenly hit the area that afternoon, causing schools to cancel team practices. Aris would hear none of it. He told the runners they were welcome to go to Green Lakes "on their own" and that, coincidentally, he might just show up "on my own."

There were blizzard conditions: driving snow, ice, raging winds. Aris tweaked his planned course but went ahead with it. "You couldn't see a thing, we were falling down," recalled Hatz, who was outrun by Farrell that day. No visibility, no matter. Aris declared it a "cornerstone workout." Hatz agreed. "We got a lot of purpose out of it."

The girls, however, had trouble marshaling the stoicism embodied in their soon-to-be-produced badass video. "There was literally a foot of snow on the ground," said Chapman. Aris ordered the girls to produce no more than a twenty-second compression for their top five. They tried but failed. Their effort was wan. They were slip sliding away. "I'm disgusted," Aris told them. "Do it again."

"Insane," cried Chapman. "Why?" Because, said Aris, you might have similar conditions in Portland. And, by the way, Zátopek would never play it safe in the snow. This is the man who won four Olympic gold medals by doing intervals in combat boots, running with his javelin-thrower wife on his back, and thriving on workouts like 10 x 100 meters and 20 x 400 meters—twice a day—with another six miles on the roads for good measure.

After a short jogging break in the storm, the girls did the time trial again. *Better, good, you're ready.* "We were angry," said Luber, "but I got the sense that Bill knew our bodies better than we did."

The New York Regional demonstrated that. On a sunny day with comfortable forty-degree temperatures and mild winds off the Hudson, the Fayetteville girls went out and ran a White Moment race, the best girls race ever by F-M or any other team, a race comparable to what the original Stotans had run four years earlier on the same course. Chapman, not at her state-meet finest with a bug coming on, took third, but after her, following closely, came Carter, Malone, Anklin, and Luber, all together, boom, boom, a sight to behold, a dreamy unity fashioned before in the snow and now in the sun. The barely running Anklin was the new Sischo. While onlookers went gaga, Malone was nonplussed, saying, "That's what we're *supposed* to do."

Chapman (18:30), Carter (18:41), Malone (18:42), Anklin (18:43), and Luber (18:43)–placing 3-4-5-6-7—crossed the finish with a thirteen-second compression and twenty-five points. Luber called it "heavenly."

That same day in Fresno, at the California state championships, the Saugus girls, heralded all season as a match—this time, better watch out—for Fayetteville in Portland, ran the fastest California state girls race ever. With the event serving as the NXN California regional, Saugus, now in the state's Division 2 (based on enrollment), placed all five scorers in the top twenty to triumph by 109 points with an average 5k time of 18:02.

By comparison, F-M ran an 18:40 average at its regional. But Bowdoin Park's untamed terrain was like Harrison Ford escaping *The Fugitive* train wreck by running through the wilds compared with California's Woodward Park, a well-groomed site with nary a true challenge. Still, with NXN around the corner, the websites were calling Saugus "the greatest girls team ever," and its coach, Rene Paragas, the same one who'd posted the F-M faces in his locker room the year before, probably didn't think he needed the photos this time around.

That is, until he saw the opening-night video. Then the unknowing took on a new language.

Still, to some, the numbers didn't add up. Saugus's 18:02 versus Fayetteville's 18:40? But times often didn't accurately reflect terrain. Yet state "agents," as Aris referred to them, were feeling pretty confident that California dreamin' would come to pass on such an early winter's day. With New York girls teams having won all four Nike Cross Nationals championships to date, two-time defender Fayetteville felt an undercurrent of animosity, not admiration, in Portland, and Aris decided that he and his athletes would not do on-camera interviews before the race. When asked, he replied, "We'll let our running do the talking."

The opposition might have gotten false hopes when Sischo was seen walking around the Nike campus on crutches. Aris had invited her to make the trip, and she was eager to support her teammates. On the boys side, Paul Merriman was in much the same boat. At the regional, he'd suffered an avulsion fracture behind the knee, in which a tendon tore away from bone, and he had to drop out.

With Hatz winning the regional and Farrell having his best race, Fayetteville boys had placed second to qualify for NXN. Only eight points behind victorious Shenendehowa, F-M would have been a certain winner—and NXN podium threat—with Merriman healthy. Like Sischo, Merriman also came to Portland, and with a specific duty: "To help instill belief in your teammates," Aris instructed him.

At this point, Aris started calling 2008 "the season of adversity." New York coaches pissed at him for skipping the Feds. California advocates regarding him as cross-country's Satan. Everyone jarred by the scorched-earth video. Sischo's leg. Merriman's leg. And some F-M athletes hurt by family discord as though plucked from an Updike story. "It wasn't Shangri-la," Aris said.

At least this year Aris had not collapsed. But the year was not quite over.

∞

When the boys championship race took off at Portland Meadows, there was an immediate pileup on the first turn about a quarter mile from the start. Meet officials had not considered how 199 very fast runners—up from 154 in 2007—would merge like cars leaving a toll plaza when the turf narrowed and pinched them in around a sweeping curve. While the day was pleasant, without the dastardly mud, the course still had its spongy spots. A number of boys went down with the chain effect of a bike-racing spill. "We were lucky to escape that," said Farrell.

While every F-M boy was competing at NXN for the first time, they felt no pressure. The girls helped them fend off distractions and, once racing, without Merriman, it was, as Farrell put it, "a dry run for 2009." The boys' only goal was to acquit themselves with dignity and not place at the rear of the twenty-two-team field.

Hatz, a legitimate individual contender, held back early, content to follow. When Nike staffers had fitted him with shoes and asked for his race plans, he told them, "to win." That was bold for a guy making his first plane trip. In the race, Hatz moved up, hardly noticed, and used his miler's speed to gobble up spots in the last kilometer to wind up a satisfied sixth in 15:27, thirteen seconds shy of the winner, Reed Connor of Texas.

Farrell and the rest of the team ran as expected in the thick of the pack, and Fayetteville placed sixteenth as North Central of Spokane, a running hotbed in eastern Washington, was victorious. With Merriman running—hypothetically scoring about one hundred points fewer than the team's fifth scorer—F-M would have placed in the top five. But with a lineup of three juniors and three sophomores, F-M took the result with stoic acceptance and looked ahead.

The Fayetteville girls lined up with game faces that fired daggers. Except for Malone. She looked pale and disengaged. Aris attributed her demeanor to pre-race jitters. Luber felt fine, no swearing this time. When John Aris told her, "I'm waiting for the day when you fulfill your potential," Luber said, "W-o-o-o, I could really suck into that," and wrote John's words on her arm. Anklin felt fine, too, now playing for keeps. In 2007, she'd come to Portland to run the open race, follow the illustrious Kenyans, scout the course, and report back to the varsity. Anklin lost her shoe in the mud and still finished to deliver her reconnaissance strategy.

For Chapman, Carter, Malone, Luber, Anklin, Buchan, and Chapman's sister, Alexandra—the seven of them—the moment had arrived. With temperatures in the forties, little wind, and a blue sky, it was said to be California weather. Two upstate New Yorkers flew out ahead to gap the field—regional winner Danielle Winslow of Queensbury and Liz Predmore, a freshman from Shenendehowa, who Chapman had seen walking up Cardiac Hill in her state-meet victory back on Long Island. Chapman, a top-five threat, held back. Her head was a little screwed up. Everyone's head was a little screwed up. Everyone had a secret, unknown to Bill or John Aris.

Molly Malone was sick with a stomach virus. It had come on overnight. "I went to bed feeling fire in my stomach," she said. "I was ripped awake at midnight to run to the bathroom and vomit all over the place."

There were four athletes to a suite consisting of a bedroom and a den with a pull-out couch. Molly's roommates—Mackenzie, Hannah, and Kathryn—were roused by her cries. Kathryn was the first one to come to Molly's side. As Molly knelt on her knees at the toilet, Kathryn crouched from behind while holding Molly's hair back as she let loose. When Hannah walked in, Kathryn, standing vigil, told her, "I'm handling it. Go back to bed. We can't let everyone get sick."

Molly's nausea continued through the night. She threw up at least eight times. "Morning came and I could not stop puking," she said. "I felt like I got hit by a bus." Molly dressed for the team's predawn shake-out run in the mall parking lot across the street, trying to act like nothing happened, trying not to vomit, in front of Bill or John. She wanted to race. Chapman and the girls in the other F-M room had slept through the commotion. Molly told everyone to say nothing, the team would manage the ordeal. Self-governance, a Stotan standby.

At breakfast, for Bill's benefit, Molly pretended to eat. But all she could get down were three tiny Cheerios. En route to the racecourse, Molly still "felt like hell" and still wanted to race. Her teammates agreed: do what you can. Bill suspected nothing and after the start took up position around the 2k mark, about a mile and a quarter into the race. It was role reversal. Last year, Bill was the one with the secret illness.

Could Malone really run a race? Would she have to pull off to the side, vomit, and drop out? The sprawling Portland Meadows landscape lie ahead with bumps and jumps, twists and turns, a clash of 199 bodies vying for every inch, every point, doing everything they could to deny Fayetteville its third-straight championship.

Saugus would be breathing down the F-M necks. That's what people said. *Let the Californians show the F-M girls what they could do with their damn video.* Malone had been counted on for key points. Without her score, there could be a one-hundred-point swing, and Fayetteville would be out of it.

Malone had no plan, just to try and stay afoot. She had no fuel in her, no liquid. She was empty, "terrified," she said, at what would ensue. No runner was more prepared for the brutality of a 5k cross-country race. This was the same Malone who in training would leave her teammates on the torturous Gulf Road climb for the heck of it.

∽

At the start, in a captain's voice, Chapman gave an order: "Everyone needs to step it up." Malone heard nothing. Her senses were dulled. Oh, Vermont was never like this. *In Vermont I never felt like crawling into a corner and sleeping like a bear through winter.*

The race got off, and before long the 1k standings came up. Fayetteville was in front, but where was Malone? *How* was Malone? Could anyone spot her in the flash of bodies? No. Aris waited. Chapman, Luber, Carter, and Anklin all passed the 2k in squadron formation, like in the video, but what about Malone? Here she came. Her suffering could no longer be disguised.

"What's wrong?" Aris, arms open, shouted when he saw Malone running behind. "What the hell are you doing? You need to go." Malone broke into tears.

She felt ashamed. Aris could not know that the team's number-one hard-ass was upholding her formidability standard as she hurdled the hay bales and bounced over the whoop-de-doos despite a turbulent stomach crying, "Stop!"

Sun washed over Portland Meadows. The pair of New Yorkers at the front was overtaken by a pair of Texans. At 2k and also at 3k, Fayetteville still led the team standings. Saugus was second, its chances alive, while lopsided point totals up on the scoreboard suggested otherwise. The new technology was not yet sophisticated enough to filter the "individuals" while simultaneously registering team scorers at each kilometer; thus, points shown during the race were distorted, throwing some confusion into the team picture. This incongruity would be smoothed out at the finish.

Word of Malone's illness spread through the F-M camp. Buchan and Hatz had been dating, and Kathryn told Alex before the girls race went off. Alex told his parents, and his parents. . . . With a kilometer to go, Aris found out. His anger turned to awe. "Molly was in agony," he said. "She didn't want to worry me or make excuses."

At 4k, seeing Aris a second time, Chapman heard Aris implore, "Molly's way back. You have to do something!" Characterizing her effort as "truth through the lens of aspiration," Chapman did her job with a big rally to lead the team in seventh place, scoring three team points; she was eleven seconds ahead of the first Saugus girl that she'd finished closely with the previous year. Anklin, also with a late surge, ran the race of her life for nineteenth, ninth among the 154 team runners, thirty seconds ahead of the second Saugus girl. Luber, kissing the inscription on her arm like a mobster's pinkie ring, and Carter, in her third NXN scoring role, followed closely behind Anklin in twenty-first and twenty-fourth—the three of them seconds apart.

Across the finish, F-M had four girls well ahead of Saugus's number two with a four-runner tally of thirty-three points. Saugus had ninety-nine points through four girls. But if Malone collapsed or wound up finishing on all fours, like her position a few hours before with her head in the hotel toilet, Saugus, with a strong fifth runner, could win.

The F-M girls peered down the home straight looking for their blue-and-lavender colors to appear. Malone needed to finish. It didn't have to be a great finish, just midpack somewhere, to secure the victory. *Malone—where are you? C'mon, Molly, bring it home* . . .

"Team: no regrets," Malone kept saying to herself. Her figure emerged, like a vision, anguish on her face. *C'mon, Molly.* Driving the final yards in desperation,

Malone fell across the line and into the waiting arms of teammates. She was the fifth and final Fayetteville scorer in sixty-third place—one second ahead of the fifth Saugus girl. But that edge was merely symbolic given the huge F-M lead. With a pounding head and growling stomach, Malone was ushered to the medical depot to get checked out.

Malone had outrun two-thirds of the championship field. Her time was only thirty to forty seconds off what she was capable of. Later that night Malone would be given the Golden Anchor Award as the leading fifth scorer. She had no memory of it.

What would be seared into memory was how Malone and all the girls used their braided intimacy to bring Fayetteville-Manlius its third-straight Nike Cross Nationals championship by a margin of sixty-nine points. It was F-M 66, Saugus 135. The Centurians did all they could. With its second through fifth scorers finishing within five seconds of one another, and outrunning the bronze-medal team, Tatnall of Delaware, by forty-seven points, Saugus probably *was* the best California team ever.

Yet, Saugus felt stymied. They trained sixty miles a week. They broke all the course records at home. But, at NXN, F-M outran them by twenty-three seconds per scoring girl. Saugus's average time from Woodward Park in Fresno to Portland Meadows went from 18:02 to 18:41. Fayetteville's average from Bowdoin Park to Portland Meadows went from 18:40 to 18:18. The F-M video revealed something—that Fayetteville-Manlius inhabited "Pet Sounds" while everyone else still lived off "California Girls."

Malone left the medical tent without help. The bug had passed. Her head spinning eased. Her stomach settled for a long-awaited meal. Malone's mind swirled with images: God's Country Hill. The Serengeti. Bowdoin. The time trial. The hotel bathroom. Bill's pleading at two thousand meters.

Aris had no voice left. He was like a cell phone losing power in the mountains. When the girls congregated to leave Portland Meadows after the brief trophy ceremony, Aris, in tears, growled, "Stotan . . ." and, drawing the girls closer, a whisper, "This is the sweetest one of all."

⟢

Aris found that he could never have Stotan purity all the way—teenage whimsy of handstands and hair burial came with the territory—but that didn't matter. A tidy compliance resulting in perfect angels was never attainable, nor the real goal. What Aris could do was teach kids that by contributing to the greater good of their community, their team, they could in their selflessness find inspiration and the truths they sought.

In reaching deep to touch the runners' authentic selves, Aris had turned over abandoned texts as though reviving a dead language, like a choral lyric from the ancient Greeks, with its hymnal beauty. His was the language of faith, proving potent to the teenage ears: follow me, believe, and shared suffering—through the glory of hard running—will save you.

Ironically, runners with little natural talent, like Luber, had the most to gain. Luber marveled at the "gazelle" grace of a Chapman or Carter, who flew over mud that sucked her in. With "meat on me," Luber said, it took her longer to find a groove, but once in flight her endurance kicked in, and her grit, and she discovered a different talent.

When the broader, more inclusive qualities took up stake, Aris could enrich the piquant teenage thirst for what Herb Elliott held about "running for the sake of running," that's all that really mattered. Malone, consecrating Stotan essence, was its poster girl. "Winning was beside the point," she said. Malone could not recall any of her race times or details of races. Well, maybe one.

That's why Malone's Anchor Award, to her, was a throwaway. It was why attention bowed Fayetteville runners, and the stage was an affront. Drilled in humility, Chapman recognized that the "high platform" of the season would always bring a doubting voice that had to be pushed away—let out like a scream that fused into acceptance. "We actually did this," she said. "Yet vulnerability sticks in my mind."

The coach could work with that.

What impelled Bill Aris, what made him say "Do it again" in the Green Lakes blizzard, was articulated in an eloquent essay on child-rearing by Adam Gopnik in *The New Yorker*. "The private sense of mastery," wrote Gopnik, "the hard thing suddenly made easy, counts for far more in their inner lives than does the achievement, the competition won, the reward secured." Gopnik called this hunger a paradox. "The mystery of mastery," he wrote, "felt in a child's mind or muscles . . ."

What mastery was yet to behold these young runners? Certainly it had not yet played out for Alex Hatz, his talent erupting as he looked to the track season and his senior year. "After cross-country," he said, "I was a more complete runner. But the mile was still my thing." Hatz could not know as he boarded the flight home from Portland that his mile antecedent was kicking up some sand on his behalf on the other side of the world.

14

PILGRIMAGE TO PORTSEA

In going through tough times, I would recall what I did in high school, like the Junction Boys Workout. Even to this day, it still lives in me.

—*Owen Kimple, Fayetteville-Manlius cross-country alumnus*

2008 Encore

After his transformative experience at Fayetteville-Manlius High School, Owen Kimple never forgot his Stotan upbringing. He never forgot about Percy Cerutty or Herb Elliott. He never forgot about running the sand hills in the Adirondacks just as Elliott had done at Portsea in Australia. In college, at Cornell, if Kimple's running hit a dry spell and he felt lost, he would summon the memories of his younger self when all seemed possible, when, in some magical way, those sand hills had propelled him into manhood.

"In going through tough times," he said, "I would recall what I did in high school, like the Junction Boys workout." He would recall the rigor, the satisfaction, the teammate's youthful blasphemy that led to the empowering effort. "Even to this day," he said, of the enduring enrichment of that day's lessons, "it still lives in me."

Once at Cornell, after his races, Kimple would phone Bill Aris for counsel. Kimple never forgot how, in his senior track season, in 2006, Aris had given him solo workouts to teach him how to train himself. College running was not like running in high school; certainly not like running at F-M. Team closeness was elusive, and coaches rarely demonstrated a personal touch. Kimple would be more on his own at Ithaca.

And, most of all, Kimple would recall his best high school race of that season, the best race he would ever run—an *Elliott* race crafted by Aris that embraced the competitive cornucopia of the Cerutty stewardship. It had come in the mile.

Herb Elliott was probably the greatest miler ever. With an Olympic gold medal in the 1500 meters in 1960 at Rome, world records in the mile (3:54.5) and 1500 (3:35.6), and firsts in every mile and 1500 of his career, Elliott had no peers—he'd done it all.

The mile. It was *the* race.

After Kimple had concluded his high school cross-country running at F-M with a disappointing performance at Nike Cross Nationals in the fall of 2005, he defused his letdown by remembering what Bill and John Aris had drilled into him since he'd first "gotten the running bug" as a yearling: "You could be a great miler."

Milers possessed speed and strength, and Kimple had both. He regarded Elliott as his hero and touchstone. Elliott had run his first sub-4:00 mile at nineteen in 1958. But Elliott was not precocious. He was *made* into a miler.

What Kimple saw in Elliott was what Bill Aris hoped for: unwavering commitment and toughness—the qualities Kimple earned at the 2004 F-M summer camp based at his family cottage on Lake Bonaparte. Each component of the Elliott constellation was ingested like scripture by Kimple and his teammates along with their salmon filets and tuna steaks: Elliott's fourteen-mile morning runs around the Portsea golf course in southeastern Australia followed by sprints to exhaustion up an endless sand dune with a sixty-degree slope; his devouring of fruits, vegetables, oats, and nuts for fuel; his rebound at seventeen after an accident in which a piano crushed his foot; his savage racing style infused by spiritual grounding, a love of nature, and a contempt for pain.

Elliott was everything Kimple wanted to be. And now Aris would offer Kimple his chance to emulate the master. Doing his best training ever in track, in the spring of 2006, days before graduation, Kimple was set to run the 1600 meters—essentially the mile distance, four laps of the track—at the New York

State championships. The meet was held in the far north, at St. Lawrence University, in the rain.

Before the race, Aris told Kimple he was ready to run an "Elliott mile." Discarding common wait-and-kick tactics as beneath him—beneath the honor of the mile and his Stotan learning—Elliott's *style de course* was a commanding surge on the penultimate lap. With a dramatic burst of speed from the Stotan handbook, Elliott would challenge himself, and the field, to run at a punishing pace. That's how Elliott won the 1960 Olympic 1500 in world-record time. With seven hundred meters to go, he raced ahead with finality to triumph by 2.8 seconds as the competition gasped from behind. It was the largest margin of victory ever in an Olympic 1500 final.

Owen Kimple would attempt to do the same forty-six years later in the sleepy college town of Canton, New York, twenty miles from the Canadian border. First, Aris showed Kimple a clip of the Rome final. "Think of the audacity," Aris told him. "Elliott blasted clean and won in a world record." Aris said, "As a high school runner, you are as prepared as Elliott was as an Olympian." Aris instructed Kimple to do as Elliott had done: "Blow the doors off the field with seven hundred meters to go."

Sensing Kimple's fear, Aris tried to sharpen him with language from the '04 Stotan camp, language uttered within Kimple's own walls. "I want you to risk failure and deal with your internal demons," Aris told him. "I want you to conquer them."

Clothed in the Fayetteville forest green of that season, and running on a slow, puddled track, Kimple shot out into second place behind the favorite, Brian Rhodes-Devey of Guilderland, a fierce kicker. Rhodes-Devey's 400 split was 60.4 as the two boys pulled away from the field. On the second lap, BRD (as he was known) opened a five-meter gap on Kimple and drew past the 800 in 2:02.19.

On the next turn, Kimple drew back up to Rhodes-Devey with a crisp stride and confident bearing. "I was feeling inexplicably good," said Kimple. "No pain. Floating. I was perfectly peaked."

At the top of the backstretch, with seven hundred meters left, Kimple unleashed his Elliott tsunami, tore into first, and raced with abandon to crush the field. Kimple's margin of victory was even bigger than Elliott's in Rome as he crossed the finish in a dazzling 4:07.71. Rhodes-Devey was 3.69 seconds behind, close to thirty meters, in 4:11.40. It was another twenty meters back to the trailing runners as fourteen boys broke 4:20 in the deep field. While he was not seeking records, Kimple set an all-time Section 3 best with a time that made him the sixth-fastest high school miler in the country that season.

Years later, referring to his evolution as a miler who'd finally been able to squelch fear and summon Stotan strength, Kimple called his state-meet triumph "a profoundly beautiful culmination of it all."

~

Cornell welcomed Kimple. But his first two years were disappointing. In cross-country, Kimple did not adjust well to the longer college-racing distance of 8k, about five miles. In track, he was not running any faster than in high school. He found himself burnt out, he said, almost ready to quit.

On the Big Red squad, he couldn't the find the brotherhood he'd relied upon in high school. When Kimple would speak with former F-M teammates, he would hear the same lament: things were not quite the same in college. Kimple felt a measure of comfort at a cross-country meet in the Midwest when, midrace, he came upon former teammate John Heron, now at Coastal Carolina, and gave him an F-M slap on the rear as he ran ahead.

Feeling out of place in Ithaca and in need of a life-changing jolt, Kimple decided to take a semester of study abroad, in the fall of 2008, in Australia. It was the start of his junior year. Kimple would take classes in his field, economics and management, at John Cook University in Cairns, in Far North Queensland, gateway to the Great Barrier Reef.

How much farther away could Kimple get? When Kimple presented his plan to the Cornell men's head coach, Robert Johnson, at first he took a hard line. He'd recruited Kimple, a high school star and F-M luminary. College runners could take a couple of years to find their groove. But Kimple needed a break, at least for a while. Johnson came around. "Take as much time as you need," he told him. "Then come back to running."

But . . . *Australia?* Wasn't that the home of a certain coach and miler still drumming in the pit of Kimple's soul? Kimple told me his chosen sunburned country had nothing whatsoever to do with Cerutty or Elliott or any of that. He said he needed to go far, take a risk, and do something audacious. In fact, part of Kimple's master plan was to give up running for a time. That summer, on July 4, Owen Kimple stopped running.

There was a girl. Isn't there always? Kimple had a girlfriend he'd met at Cornell, Rachel, who'd supported his idea and wanted to come along. In late August of 2008, Kimple picked up with Rachel, who hailed from Portland, Oregon, and two of his male classmates, and the four of them set off for Australia.

In Cairns, Kimple found tropical heat and nature in abundance. He trekked through the Daintree Rainforest, and on his twenty-first birthday, Rachel presented him with a helicopter ride over the Great Barrier Reef. At John Cook, his classes were pass/fail. "It was freeing," he said, "to be in such a distant environment."

So freeing that before long, in October, Kimple resumed running and worked up to eighty miles a week. He felt refreshed and strong, and when classes ended in mid-December, the American foursome traveled by train to Sydney and Melbourne to see more of Australia. They were in Melbourne at the time of a half marathon. When Kimple chatted up Aussies at the race and mentioned Herb Elliott, their response, fifty years after Elliott's first sub-4:00 mile, was like a bow to royalty.

Kimple got to thinking. Portsea was not all that far from Melbourne, was it? In fact, it was sixty miles south, a ninety-minute drive along the Mornington Peninsula, as breathtaking a ride as tooling down California's 101. Kimple and his friends rented a car the next day. Driving on the "other" side of the road, Kimple curved along the sinuous coastal forefoot of Port Phillip Bay, akin to the Italian boot, and arrived at the seaside town of Portsea, on the tongue of the peninsula's western tip, Victoria state, with South Pacific waters crashing the shore. Kimple looked toward the sea and took a deep breath. "It felt like the edge of the world," he said.

With the confluence of the Indian Ocean, South Pacific, Bass Strait, and Tasman Sea, indeed it was. Such a place of little but land and sea and a peering out into empty vastness presented a vision of how running immortality could have been emboldened there in the 1950s. Cerutty himself described the setting as beautiful but modest. "Deep blue waters, golden sands . . . the whole beach is no longer than three quarters of a mile. . . . Everything was clean and gay. Surely a favoured place."

The Portsea of 2008 was pretty much as Cerutty had left it: a place in which to surf, snorkel, and down a pint; a place to sit on a pub deck with a lobster sandwich and watch the boats go out. Portsea had modest cottage homes, easygoing hotels, a golf course, a beach. Well, not *a* beach. *The* beach.

Kimple knew what he'd come for. From the moment he'd gotten the idea in Melbourne, Kimple knew: he had to run the dunes.

Kimple walked up to the first local he saw, a Portsean walking down the street, and asked, "Do you know where these big sand dunes are?" The man answered, "Oh, yeah, that's where Herb Elliott used to train." Kimple was stunned. The man showed him.

Could this be true? Kimple stood on the unspoiled beach, at the foot of the dunes, alone but for the seagulls, and imagined: this was the spot, in 1956, after the Melbourne Olympics, when the eighteen-year-old Elliott came to meet his master—"a wiry, tempestuous man, with a leathery face and flame-white hair," as *Sports Illustrated* called Cerutty—to learn the ways of history and make history that, he, too, would learn a half century later as a teenager in Manlius, New York. It was where Elliott slept in threadbare "ski huts" while doing the commando training that made him the best ever.

Flushed with the imprint of Bill Aris evangelism and Cerutty-and-Elliott Stotan footprints all over the place, Owen Kimple took off his shirt and shoes and got ready to run. "I was in awe," he said. "I didn't expect the dunes to be so big."

Surely the dunes would not lose their museum quality or ecological authenticity if just a little sand went missing. Before embarking on his workout, Kimple took a large mason jar from his car. He felt like Indiana Jones poised to excavate a precious find, protect it, mother it, and bring it to those back home who would appreciate its meaning and value.

Some young men turning twenty-one mark the occasion by sowing some oats, getting drunk or stoned, or perhaps going *Easy Rider* with a motorcycle trip across the desert. Kimple ran the dunes at the edge of the world.

With the late-afternoon sun still harsh, and the frigid, emerald waters of Bass Strait to his back, Kimple—like Elliott himself in the classic photos that illustrate the Cerutty texts—proceeded to churn up and down the unruly, cliff-sloped dunes, one after the other, to exhaustion. Kimple would sprint to the top of each climb, then jog back down the dune, traveling in reprieve a bit farther to the water's edge to moisten his feet for traction. Still, he said, every stride up was met with a half stride back. Kimple did this nonstop for forty minutes until he could do no more.

Each ascent took Kimple about thirty-five seconds. Consider: thirty-five seconds for a twenty-one-year-old with eighty miles a week in his legs to run barely eighty feet. That's how steep and consuming it was. Back in the day, it took Elliott less than half that—fifteen seconds tops per climb. Elliott's record number of repetitions at one time: forty-two. Kimple did twenty. In his last runs, he watched the sun set from the barren, windswept beach.

In his push up the dunes, Kimple kept thinking, "I can't believe it. Herb Elliott. Here I am." He thought about the F-M "machine" and the 2004 Stotan camp, the Aris lectures and the Lynch book. Kimple said he found the texture of the Portsea sand "bizarrely similar," fine and loose, to that of Otter Creek, the F-M litmus test where the Stotan camp that mirrored Portsea climaxed. It all came back to him. But even more so than Otter Creek, or anything F-M did at Green Lakes during Kimple's era, at Portsea the rawness of the setting, the leap into history, and solitary effort to depletion conspired to make Kimple believe, "That was the best workout I ever ran."

Maybe so. It was certainly Kimple's most emotional workout, and, perhaps for the young man searching inward, his most pivotal. Afterward, as darkness fell and Kimple collected his friends, his feelings gripped him anew with an odd blend of muse and melancholy. It was time to go.

Practically shaking in wonder, the only thing Kimple could do was retrieve his mason jar and fill it with Portsea sand. Could Kimple keep his prize under wraps on the long journey home, beyond the scrutiny of airport watchdogs?

The foursome drove back to Melbourne for a couple of last days in Australia. Then it was on to New Zealand—Arthur Lydiard country—as a fitting finale to Kimple's four-month South Pacific odyssey. Kimple's sand was still safe, secured in a suitcase, traveling the world.

Running in Auckland, on some of the hilly North Island trails that had their own rich legacy, courtesy of Lydiard, Kimple reflected on the physical and intellectual merger that Aris had espoused, a concept borne of Cerutty, who cleaved to "excellence," not "athletics," and devoured Tennyson, not training manuals. Elliott said it himself, "Poetry makes you a better man by giving you an appreciation of beauty." Even at eighteen, Elliott was reading Hindu texts on self-mastery and conquering ego. For Kimple, the Lynch psychology book took care of that.

It was all coming together for Kimple: Aris. Cerutty. Elliott. Stotan . . . and himself.

Aris called it "the twine of history." The lessons of the generations in one coherent tableau. As in 1952 at the Helsinki Olympics, when the greatest distance runner ever, Zátopek, happened to share accommodations at the Olympic Village with the man who would become the greatest coach ever—yes, Cerutty. Cerutty, without proper credentials, had crashed the Games primarily to meet Zátopek and learn from him. Zátopek had three races to run—the 5,000, 10,000, and marathon—and needed his rest. Yet, Zátopek offered Cerutty his bed in the Village while Zátopek, in the course of capturing the Olympic distance triple, took refuge in a sleeping bag in the nearby forest. Soon after, Cerutty would open up his cottage in Portsea to the athletes he trained.

∽

Kimple's jar of sand made it all the way back to Syracuse in one piece. It was Christmastime, and all seven of his former teammates who'd attended the 2004 Stotan camp with him were home from college on winter break. Kimple got hold of small baby-food jars, filled them with Portsea sand, and presented one to each of the guys. The gifts came as a wonderful surprise and filled the day with old stories and one version or another of what was proving to be true in their young lives, as Elliott once put it: "My weaknesses are going to be challenged as I try to improve myself, and I mustn't give in, otherwise I'm a lesser human being."

Kimple saved some sand for himself and some for one more gift. He went over to Bill Aris's home and gave him a baby jar with the sacred sand—what had signified to Aris uncanny promise years before. Oh, Lord, it *was* Christmas. Aris was enamored with his gift and overcome with joy that an original Stotan had ventured to Portsea and stuck himself in the earth as an emissary of the team. What more could Bill Aris ask for?

Aris placed the jar on a shelf where he could see it daily. Aris would not open it, not yet; not until he could think of a purposeful use for it. His current athletes deserved to physically touch a grain of their heritage, finger a piece of Portsea, but how?

Kimple returned to Cornell. Coach Johnson embraced him and was glad to have Kimple in shape after he'd trained bountifully Down Under. Indeed, Kimple's running took off. In 2009, his junior-year track season, Kimple earned various accolades, which he linked to his bold journey. "I was twelve thousand miles from home," he said. "For the first time in my life, I learned to truly take care of myself, and I did so while feeling this magical place that had played such a big role in my development as a runner."

In his senior year, doing his best college running, Kimple had one last chance to get the mile monkey off his back. Kimple's Elliott-inspired 4:07.71 in high school was still his best time, achieved in the slightly shorter (by 9.3 meters) 1600 meters. That he'd not improved upon that at Cornell weighed on him and was a factor that led to his decision to flee to distant shores.

Kimple's shot at redemption came at Princeton University that April of 2010. With his Cornell graduation close at hand, Kimple ran the 1500 meters, Herb Elliott's Olympic event, at the Larry Ellis Invitational. This race would be no jewel, no Elliott runaway, nothing even close. Kimple, competing for time and guarding his pace, finished far down the field but got what he so desperately sought: a time of 3:48.77, equivalent to a 4:07 mile, about 4:06 at the 1600 mark. Any way you looked at the fuzzy math, Kimple had done it. He had improved upon his high school best.

At twenty-one, heading out into the world, Owen Kimple was still a damn good miler.

Even after college, however, Kimple was not quite through with Nike Cross Nationals or Fayetteville-Manlius. Nor was the teenage Alex Hatz, sixth at NXN in 2008, yet through with trying to emulate Kimple as a miler and a man. With their shared suffering in the sand dunes, Hatz and Kimple and the twine of history sped on.

15

RISKING FAILURE

Nobody giving an inch to anyone in a workout. Nobody giving an inch to anyone in the country.

—*Katie Sischo, Fayetteville–Manlius cross-country runner*

2009 Season I

Plattsburgh, New York, site of the 2009 New York State cross-country championships, was an unlikely place for running history to be made. A city of twenty thousand in the northeast corner of the North Country near Canada, it was noted mainly for its branch of the State University, where the state meet was held. Nothing much happened in Plattsburgh, but that was about to change. Gale-force runners from a town four hours away, from a place called Manlius, would soon line up to race the flat course on the university grounds.

Plattsburgh's notable former residents included John Lloyd Young, a Plattsburgh High graduate who, three years earlier, won a Tony Award playing Frankie Valli in the original Broadway cast of *Jersey Boys*. The first line of one of Valli's signature hits, "Can't Take My Eyes Off You," was, *"You're just too good to be true."*

For Fayetteville-Manlius, that lyric could have been the theme of the state championships, and indeed the entire season and beyond. With their superiority and grandeur, the F-M runners—girls in particular—seemed too good to be true. Genius, it seemed, had its drawbacks.

After five years of the Fayetteville-Manlius conversion, Bill Aris could talk all he wanted about Stotan humility. But while his athletes had learned the hard lessons of letting go of the self—the inconsequential self, as the philosopher Derek Parfit had it—Aris found himself stuck with his own ego, which by this time could betray him.

The team's national domination threatened the very fabric of high school running, and some people, coaches or whoever, couldn't handle it. They had no idea what Aris was doing with his athletes, only the startling vision seen every year of F-M girls taking the country by storm and looking so darn cool doing it. What could any team do to buckle down and challenge Fayetteville?

As the team's "sheen of success," as Aris called it, lost its novelty and morphed for some into a source of frustration—as Fayetteville-Manlius became like Norway at the Winter Olympics—scornful naysayers would fill up the internet with wild accusations about the team and its coach. Hard work? Mind-body mastery? Nah. Something devious? Bingo.

Aris had let this destructive meme get to him. He felt his coaching under attack. He could smell the stink across time zones. With time on his hands after leaving his school-aide position after sixteen years, Aris could apply his ingenuity to bringing the athletes that much closer to zero compression. He was also more vulnerable when contentiousness came his way.

But Aris would grow despairing no longer. As the season began, he ceased caring about the cloud, as it were, and found peace in insulating himself from the chatter. Aris boiled off the impurities of the outside world, finding what Parfit referred to as the "open air."

His runners were ahead of him. The girls had discovered their better angels and as never before merged as latticework, each one an arpeggio in a Bach toccata. With Green Lakes workouts spun off like pizzas in the air, each burst up God's Country produced a convoy of five, the prong of zero compression growing as a vision of perfection that might soon be realized.

If he needed reprieve from impure threats, Aris, as refuge, would dreamily recall how this season's formidable girls had tickled him from their first runs with a sweetness they would never quite abandon.

Mackenzie Carter, now a senior, had joined the Fayetteville-Manlius team in seventh grade and run her first race on the day of her thirteenth birthday. It was a junior-varsity 1500 meters on the indoor track at Syracuse University. On the day of her official flowering as a teenager, she would celebrate with seven and a half laps around Manley Field House, placing in midpack, and a birthday cake, fashioned by a teammate, of wrapped PowerBars stacked high with a candle on top. Carter would nibble at the PowerBars, and the taffy-like boost must have helped. Soon after, Carter would win her first race, at 3,000 meters.

When Hannah Luber, also a senior in 2009, was in sixth grade, she'd listened to her three sisters tell stories about Aris at the dinner table. To Hannah's twelve-year-old ears, Aris sounded tyrannical. "I'll never have to worry about this Aris fellow," Hannah said to herself. "I'm a soccer and lacrosse player."

After moving from Vermont and joining the team as a freshman, Molly Malone, the third senior on the 2009 varsity, took a lot of shit from friends and their parents about Aris being "crazy" and pushing the runners too hard. "This pissed me off. I had bought into the program and it paid off," said Malone. "I finally gave up trying to defend myself."

In eighth grade, when Courtney Chapman decided to give up basketball and invest in the running mandate Aris offered, she saw the difference between herself and her peers and "began to fester a deep desire to do something great in my life." Once overcoming her fears, Chapman, a junior in 2009, went to practice every day consumed by the feeling "of having the power to control a race."

As the cross-country season took shape, Katie Sischo, a sophomore, had yet to experience that. The previous year, Sischo had watched her teammates win their third-straight Nike Cross Nationals championship while on crutches that sunk into the Portland Meadows mud. She'd felt a voracious void after suffering a stress fracture in her lower leg in the last month of the season.

It was the hunger of missing out that propelled Sischo into 2009, when this group of five girls—Carter, Luber, Malone, Chapman, and Sischo—were, with their experience and maturity, a new team "growing up," said Aris, "before my eyes."

Differences, yes, still. Malone: hard-ass. Luber: hard-ass but mercurial. Chapman: ice water in her veins. Carter: always in conflict. Sischo: thorn turned hero.

As a group, they had struggled through every test in the mud, on hills, in the snow and darkness, with sleet like nails piercing their faces, year after year, but the greatest test had always been one to one: who kept up, who gave in, who had to be called out with tears shed and feelings hurt. "How much browbeating could we do?" Aris had wondered.

From their naivete as "little girls," to their personality conflicts as developing teens, to their ultimate embrace as family—*look what we've been through, for crying out loud*—the Fayetteville-Manlius girls could finally accept one another as equal partners, their individual egos drifting away like ragweed in the wind.

"It was empowering," said Sischo. "Nobody giving an inch to anyone in a workout. Nobody giving an inch to anyone in the country." Even hard-ass Malone felt a new comradeship that season. "We were all on the same page," she said. "Once you get on that page, it's hard to get off it."

‰

In 2009, that page would be filled with Gulf Road ten-milers. The Gulf Road hill itself, a mile and a half long, was so steep that town trucks were unable to plow the road after winter storms. The snow just sat there. For the girls, the ascent was alluring, and during cross-country they turned Gulf Road—twice a week, sometimes three—into unspoken competitions. The girls were so strong they couldn't resist. And everyone wanted to achieve the fastest times—well below seventy minutes.

At times, Sischo was forced to give an inch. Female complexity was not totally erased. Sischo was no longer wet behind the ears like the team's newcomers, freshman Jillian Fanning and sophomore Heather Martin, but she did not quite fit in with the older girls; early on that fall, Sischo still needed to earn their respect. "I was in a funny spot," she said. "I wouldn't say we were all buddy-buddy 24-7."

With her broad swimmer's physique and Eric Heiden quads, Sischo could not find lightness up Gulf Road. She would do her best training on hill repeats at Green Lakes, where, after a hard few minutes, a short break gave her stacked muscles a reprieve. She also did not take well to the loud, urgent calls from Aris or teammates to step it up, get your ass moving, rah-rah, and all that. Sischo said she was a different style of learner, motivated by a softer patina of "talking through" ideas and enrichment. After practice, while waiting for a pick-up, Sischo was moved to contemplation with Aris when discussing the latest book he'd recommended, like the one about the guy who went to Africa and had tires made into running shoes for needy children.

Sischo's hard-baked older teammates were not always patient with her deliberate progress. However, the leathery Luber felt chastened by her own inner voice. Luber's racing became tepid. She said her mind didn't let her perform as usual. She couldn't figure out why. Self-governance saved her, at least for one meet, and it was a big one. In the midseason Manhattan meet at Van Cortlandt Park, Luber placed second in the girls Eastern States Championship. Luber led Fayetteville to meet records in scoring, twenty-two points, and average time, 14:35.5.

While trembling before the race, Luber found peace once in flight and a goosebumps quiet amid the solitude of the Back Hills. Leading her teammates onto the home straight—now switched from the parade grounds' edge to the Broadway side of the park—Luber raced to the finish with calmness she hadn't felt all season. "I was able to take my thoughts out of it and just run," she said. On the bus ride home, she leaned over to John Aris and told him, "This was for you." It was John's birthday. It was also his last season of coaching.

Luber could not sustain her coherence and lapsed into lethargy with championship season coming up. Two days before the Section 3 meet, as darkness fell on the school grounds, Luber found herself as the seventh girl in a workout with her "legs not moving." Malone came up to her and said, "I don't know what's going on, but get your shit together." Bluntness from her stable mate kicked Luber into gear, and she raced the sectional in a tight pack with her teammates as F-M swept the first six places.

By then Malone had become the team's most complete runner and lacked for nothing, mind or body. The previous spring, Malone had run a 4:30.70 1500 meters for fourth in the state championship behind three girls that would eventually turn pro, set a sectional 800 record of 2:09.93, and clocked a fifty-eight-second leg on a winning 4 x 400 relay. Excellence from the 400 to 5k cross-country was something few girls in the nation could match.

Malone was so fearless that at Plattsburgh, in the state Class 2A championship, she considered testing her will by attempting to run ahead of the field with Chapman, the state favorite who'd led the F-M contingent by eleven seconds in the sectional. Malone had a proven record of fearlessness in state competition. It was three years before, as a freshman, when she'd taken up Aris's proposal of being a sacrificial lamb on the long, punishing ascent at Bowdoin Park in the Feds.

The state meet, run by the New York State Public High Schools Athletic Association, was first held in 1950, for boys, in Schenectady. The distance was

2.2 miles. Girls were added in 1975, running two and a half miles; by then, boys ran three miles. Both boys and girls would race a 5k course starting in 1978. A primitive state forerunner, if you will, was held from the early 1920s to the early '30s, according to a bit of history provided by Perry King on milesplit.com. King said the event ceased because of financial strain during the Great Depression.

In 2009, the Plattsburgh course, called Rugar Woods, had little going for it. Some flat, wooded paths and loops around a baseball field. The F-M camp preferred hills where the athletes' strengths could set them far apart. Carter, alone, welcomed the tabletop flatness. She felt she had only a few cross-country races left in her. As always, she'd gotten a slow start over the summer, where her options included leisurely stays at her family place on Lake Ontario. Each season, she said, cross-country and track, one right after the other, started to feel burdensome, smothering what was left of her childhood. "I was a little bitter about it," she said. "I had mental struggles more than the other girls. It had to do with my own chemistry."

In addition to the established top five, the state-meet lineup included Fanning and Martin, two girls with different properties on the F-M periodic table. They both took to the Stotan lifestyle of good food and early nights. Fanning had running in her blood and followed her sister, Kathryn, a senior, onto the team. In just a few varsity races, Jillian became a key scorer and was the second F-M girl in the sectional sweep. Martin, on the other hand, was a sprinter without a lick of distance in her system when Aris convinced her to try cross-country. After conquering her fears—not of hills, but of Aris, who initially "terrified" her—Martin worked up to seventh position on the varsity. When Aris started kidding her about her thick eyebrows, Martin was able to relax.

The team's biggest kidder turned out to be young Jillian. She would drive the team into stitches by imitating Aris: with sweatpants pulled above her waist, pacing the Green Lake grounds, slumping posture, hands behind her back; then, growing animated, as though the girls passed on a run, throwing her arms out, fingers separated and pleading for more. Jillian would perform her act while shadowing Aris like a lion cub. "She was like a little Bill," said Malone.

∾

When the season began, the boys looked to join the girls in casting their lot in Plattsburgh as a nationals liftoff. After the disappointment of the previous year, when Paul Merriman's injury erased hopes of Nike Cross Nationals podium contention, the boys team that assembled for 2009 was enriched with sure-footed experience and as much pizzazz as any F-M team that had come before. It was not hard to imagine that, when all was said and done, both boys and girls teams could stand atop the Portland podium in the first NXN team sweep.

It was also not hard to picture the team's top runner, Alex Hatz, now a senior, competing for the NXN individual title. After his sixth at NXN in 2008, Hatz had since become a premier miler in track. He ran his races in the style of Owen Kimple, who'd raced in the style of Herb Elliott. Hatz may well have had some of Kimple's treasured Portsea sand sprinkled on him as an anointed protégé.

That spring of 2009, as Kimple had done two years before, Hatz took on an Aris challenge to "risk failure." It happened in early May at the Chittenango Invitational. Hatz was set to run the mile against a worthy local rival, Chris Stogsdill of Marcellus High. For added drama, the race would be held at night, under the lights, like the Grand Prix races in Oslo or Stockholm.

When Aris sat down with Hatz to map out strategy, he told him that if he ran a typical sit-and-kick race, a safe race, he would probably win. "But my question to you is this," posed Aris. "Would you rather win or grow as an athlete? What I'm proposing is far more of a challenge to your ego, your sense of pace, your abilities, toughness, all of it." Prior, the subject of a future four-minute mile for Hatz had been broached. Aris continued, "Do you want to learn how to run a four-minute mile in the years to come? I'm not saying you will ever do it. But if you want to learn how it feels instead of just sneaking up on Stogsdill at the end and outkicking him, it means risking failure. You may well lose the race. You must be prepared to accept that."

Hatz agreed. "I wanted to try and push my limits," he said, "and sub-4:00 always excited me." Since Roger Bannister ran the first sub-4:00 in 1954, with a 3:59.4, the goal had been a touchstone of greatness. Only one high school *junior* of appropriate age had ever broken four minutes—Jim Ryun in 1964. Hatz was certainly not ready for that.

But Hatz was ready to get a taste of it. In practice, Hatz had "played around" with sub-4:00 by running a 1200-meter time trial, three laps of the track (slightly less than three-quarters of a mile), in three minutes even, close to four-minute-mile pace. He would follow that, after a bit of recovery, with a set of four-hundred-meter sprints.

At Chittenango, the night lacked for Scandinavian bouquet. Rain and lightning delayed the meet. Warm-ups were adjusted. The athletes grew edgy. Finally, two hours late, the mile was ready to get underway.

Aris told Hatz to take the lead and try to run the first quarter mile in fifty-nine seconds, continue that pace through the half in about 1:59, and through three quarters in three flat to 3:01. That's how sub-4:00-milers did it—and they had enough maturity and power while under duress to marshal a last-lap kick of under sixty seconds.

Hatz went for it. His splits were on target: 59, 1:59, and 3:01. Stogsdill, a senior, let him have it. With a lap to go, Stogsdill was twelve meters back, hanging on for dear life. At that point, Aris didn't care who won. Hatz did. But he found he could not satisfy his dual agenda: the risk *and* the victory. Hatz, nothing left, soon faded—"the wheels came off," he said—and Stogsdill caught and passed him with about two hundred meters to go for the win. Stogsdill, to his credit, clocked an exceptional 4:07.93. Hatz struggled home in 4:10.80, still his best time to date.

"That's when Alex Hatz grew up," said Aris. "After that, I started calling him Alexander the Great."

Hatz didn't feel that great, not yet. "Losing was not an easy pill for me to swallow," he said. The next day at practice, Bill and John took Hatz aside. "You ran a man's race," they told him. "Don't brood about it. Take it like a man and learn from it." Hatz did. "I knew I'd made a mental breakthrough," he said. "That set me up to one day have a chance to run sub-4:00."

Alexander the Great continued his junior track season with a state championship 1600 victory, bettering Kimple's time, in a 4:06.11 performance and Section 3 record. After taking the SATs that morning, Hatz cruised the first half of the race before shattering the field with a 58.85-second last lap to triumph by forty meters. Hatz would face Stogsdill again at the next weekend's high school nationals in Greensboro, North Carolina, a mile rematch. In a slow-paced tactical race, Stogsdill held off Hatz, 4:06.70 to 4:07.28, for the title. Hatz's racing legs had been compromised the previous day on an eleven-hour drive from Syracuse to Greensboro with his dad at the wheel and Bill and Molly Malone in the car. "Not ideal," Hatz said.

Hatz was able to dismiss the loss. But not the pain he'd felt in his lower back after competition. The more he drank to stay hydrated, the more the discomfort. In early-summer cross-country workouts, Hatz grew concerned about spoiling the team vibe. Merriman, along with fellow senior Brendan Farrell and juniors Andrew Roache and Mark McGurrin, were all in good shape and expecting a big fall season.

Roache, the team oddball, was ready to make headway. He still snatched crab apples on the run, and his buried locks remained untouched in his backyard.

But Roache's antics belied his toughness. "He was a relentless competitor," said Aris. "Obstinate in confronting pain."

Roache loved Green Lakes, especially the secluded Round Lake trail with its cushy wood-chip path protected from the sun on hot summer days. Roache had grown his hair back, and long, and a beard too, and in training couldn't wait to duck away from the heat of the open meadows and into the cooling shade of the lake's pillowy perimeter. The dreamscape setting with its mirrored reflection off the water inspired awe. A misty haze rose above the aquamarine surface, enhanced by its glacial lineage. Round Lake, as well as Green Lake, was among the few "meromictic" lakes worldwide—they were deep and stable and did not experience seasonal "turnover," the mixing of the upper and lower water masses.

Seasonal turnover did occur *around* Round Lake. Park staff would put down a fresh layer of wood chips at the start of summer. Like measuring the seasons by leaf color, Roache took delight in noting the time of year by the virgin quality of the woodsy grounds.

Roache's natural stimulus was not new to him. He'd joined cross-country as a freshman, he said, because he "liked being outside." Plus, he'd had enough of playing tuba in the school band.

∽

With summer training barely started, Hatz labored behind Roache and the others. His back pain grew so bad that he had to stop running and see a specialist in New York City. Tests showed Hatz's right kidney not draining properly (hence the drinking issue), an ailment known as UPJ obstruction. "A plumbing defect," Aris called it. Hatz was told he was probably born with the condition and that the only treatment was surgery. Hatz's summer training was over. Could he salvage the season?

Hatz underwent "robotic" surgery in mid-August at NYU Medical Center. Hatz also had a stent put in for a month to keep his urethra open. Hatz spent four days in hospital. Running was out of the question, at least until the stent was removed.

Fayetteville reverted to damage control. Unable to count on Hatz, the boys needed a solid fifth man. The candidates were senior Joe Hartnett, junior Owen Strong, and sophomore Ben Thomas. None had shown much. In 2008, Hartnett, as sixth man in the NXN lineup, placed 186th in the field of 199. He was laid back with no evident Stotan fire.

By the end of September, fully recovered, Hatz resumed running. He'd put on a few pounds and ran like it. Two weeks later, Aris agreed to let Hatz test himself at the Manhattan Easterns, where he competed in training shoes. Plattsburgh was a month away. Among the Easterns' preseason favorites, Hatz now just wanted to see if he could stick with teammates. He couldn't. Hatz lumbered down the Van Cortlandt home straight, a pitiful sight in fifty-fourth place, twenty-six seconds behind the team's fourth man.

Season over? Not quite yet.

There was some good news. Fayetteville still placed second, ten points behind old foe Christian Brothers, with the F-M top four putting together a terrific ten-second spread. However, Hartnett, the sixth man, was twenty-one seconds behind Hatz on the two-and-a-half-mile course and not looking like a fifth-man solution. Eleven days later, in its league meet, an easy F-M win, Hatz was the team's number-seven runner in 18:04, almost three minutes behind victorious Farrell and slower than the winner of the JV race.

Season over? Not quite yet.

Soon after, unrelated to the kidney issue, Hatz came down with a case of shingles, a severe rash more common in older people. Hatz's doctor told him the condition was probably brought on by stress, whether from the surgery or the attempted comeback or both.

Now, season over.

16

SWEEPING SIGNALS

Clean. Whole. Stotan. We lived for each other, for that moment, for the team.

—*Molly Malone, Fayetteville-Manlius cross-country runner*

2009 Season II

I n Plattsburgh, as teams from Long Island to Buffalo gathered for the state finals, it was a warmish North Country day with a bit of drizzle. In large-schools Class 2A, the boys race was set to go off first. When the F-M bus arrived, one boy was missing. Not the postsurgical Alex Hatz, who'd come for support. It was Andrew Roache, who'd gotten sick earlier that week.

"It came on quickly," he said. "I was light-headed, feverish, wiped out." Roache tried to run a workout but had to stop. He went to the doctor, who delivered the verdict: swine flu, which had been going around and was labeled a pandemic. Roache was given medication and warned not to run.

Roache wouldn't hear of it. Ultimately, the doctor told Roache, do what you want. His parents, resigned, said the same. Aris, too, told him, "It's up to you."

On the day before the state meet, Roache came to practice on the school soccer field. "It was cold," he said. "You could see your breath in the air." He did some easy running and left early. His status for the meet was still uncertain. Before leaving, Roache deposited a brief note he'd written to the team in Aris's office. After practice, once Aris saw the note, he gathered the boys and read it aloud. Roache's note said: "I plan to run. I'm not sitting it out. I'd rather die than let my team down."

Roache was too sick to ride the team bus, and he didn't want to risk spreading his flu. So instead, bundled up, he made the four-hour trip with his parents to Saranac, near Plattsburgh, to stay the night. On race day, at five A.M., they drove to the team's motel. Roache sat in the car and waited. At six o'clock, Aris and the boys came out for their three-mile shake-out run. Roache joined in, keeping his distance.

In Plattsburgh, at the race site, Roache remained covered with blankets in the car while his teammates warmed up on the course. He would have to race "blind," without seeing the course. Fayetteville took the line. Roache was feverish and felt stomach distress. He was undeterred. "It was my duty to make it hurt as much as I could that day," he told me. "Just run my brains out."

Roache took the start with his teammates. He had nothing in his system but running "jelly beans" and a sip of juice. The race went off. The light rain muddied the course and some runners lost footing. Roache stayed on his feet. Could he actually finish a 5k in his condition? Roache tried to follow runners he knew, even from other teams.

Some sixteen minutes later—what must have felt like sixteen minutes of hell—Roache crossed the finish. His time was 16:11 and his place, in the field of 108, was twenty-eighth. More critically, after displacement of "individuals," Roache scored fourteen team points and was the fourth F-M runner across the line.

Once done, Roache was in no position to sort out the scoring math. He darted to a garbage can, put his head in it, and began to vomit. Not giving up yet, he attempted to do the team cooldown. He had to stop midway and vomit some more. Then he retreated to his parents' car, got his blankets, and waited for the results.

With Farrell taking sixth and Hartnett finally delivering a clutch fifth-man performance—only thirty seconds separated Farrell and Hartnett—Fayetteville won the Class 2A championship by fifteen points over North Rockland. Without Roache, it would have been a toss-up.

When we spoke, Roache traced his irreproachable toughness to childhood. He grew up with a learning disability, dyslexia, and could not read well. "I made up my mind, if anyone would be able to help me, it would be me," he said. "I had the sense of pulling myself up, overcoming and pushing through it." Roache would adapt to his disorder and, by high school, "had learned how to cope with it."

Aris was so impressed with Roache that he started calling him "Vlad the Impaler," in reference to the fifteenth-century Romanian warrior who used draconian measures in conquest. Maybe it wasn't the most charming sobriquet, but Aris liked it. What's more, Aris took Roache's note, made a poster of it with Vlad the Impaler on it, and pinned it to the front of his office door at school. Teachers passing by were not amused.

Who knows how Roache managed to complete that race. But, for context, Aris could have gone right to his patron saint, Cerutty, who taught Elliott that a footrace was "not a test of athletic skill but human character." Elliott once said that he sought to harness spiritual strength before a race, not for it "to dominate the body" but rather as a tool of transcendence that would melt away.

∽

When the Fayetteville girls lined up to race, Malone gazed out to the Plattsburgh course. "I had this moment," she recalled. "This was going to be a good one. Everyone coming together. Everything Bill fed us. We all believed it."

The girls were besotted with a convergence of ideas—some felt, some understood, some just out there like crab apples to be snatched at Green Lakes. Elliott never studied his opponents. He immersed himself in poetry and music, the forests and the solitude. That is where he could find his truth, his spirituality, his mastery.

As the truth seeker Bob Dylan once said, "The songs are my lexicon. I believe in songs." Dylan was an alchemist. He created new art.

So, too, with Aris. He created a new art form for his runners. Aris felt this bluesy rush from the first days of the 2004 Stotan camp when old ideas became fresh again. Those crazy kids wanted something important, "points of fixture," as the French philosopher Alain Badiou wrote in *The True Life*. The Aris lexicon—art and philosophy and more—stirred up a belief system that the young runners craved like nothing else. This is what other coaches, admirers, and skeptics alike could not understand. F-M success was not based on endless miles but endless ideas.

The great minds of Aris's Greek heritage, from Socrates to Plato, called for youth not to be condemned by social customs, to rise above the life given to them as commodity, and take risks. Today's neuroscientists tell us that by age fifteen one's reasoning faculties are more or less developed. Andrew Roache knew what he was doing.

Chapman, the defending state Class 2A champion, took out the pace and led the girls field. Malone said, "Screw this," refuting her subordinate standing, and joined her. Their message to the opposition: come chase us. Her bravura notwithstanding, Chapman still harbored doubts. Humble to the core, the spotlight did not seduce her. "I was still trying to figure out who I was as a runner," she said.

Malone knew who she was. "It didn't even feel like a race," she remembered. "I was, like, 'Wow, look what my body can do.'"

The pair strode the open grounds, then disappeared through the wooded section and around the ball field. They heard no footsteps from behind. "Holy shit," Malone said to herself. "We're leading the state championship by a large margin!" The course brought them back around the field, through the same woods again, and then into the open, around a bowl, to the home straight.

It was all Fayetteville. First, second, third, fourth . . . . *sixth* . . .

Where was Saratoga Springs? Saratoga, F-M's perennial rival, the 2004 NXN champion and '05 runner-up that the week before had won its Section 2 title with seven of the top twelve places—Saratoga, number-two ranked nationally at that moment—where were their girls? The Blue Streaks had their first runner, sectional winner Keelen Hollowood, a freshman, in the top ten. The next four Saratoga girls were spread out far behind.

Could it happen? Could the number-one team in the country sweep the number-two team in the country, and the entire field, in the state championships? Could Fayetteville take the first five places ahead of Saratoga's first girl and everyone else's? Could F-M register a perfect score of fifteen points? Nothing close to that degree of domination had ever happened in cross-country.

In the closing apron of turf, it fell to Katie Sischo to secure the F-M sweep. Chapman had drawn away to a repeat state victory by nine seconds in 17:26. Then, within touching distance, came Malone, Fanning, and Carter. F-M had its first four in. With fifty meters to go, Sischo had already passed Hollowood and taken command of sixth place. Ahead of her, in fifth, was the prize—Nicole Irving of Shenedehowa, whose muscular countenance gave nothing away.

Bill and John watched from a nearby bluff. "Oh, my God!" they blurted out to one another. "The fangs came out," said Bill. "Katie was moving like a wrecking machine."

At the race start, Sischo had been pinned against the bunting marking the course. She fell back and had to work hard to make up ground. She would pass one girl, then another, then one more. Finally, she could see the front of the race. "It was all gold," she said, referring to the Section 3 shirts worn by F-M. Sischo hated those shirts. They looked like the garish, ill-fitting freebies given to joggers at road races.

Sischo loved to sprint. She was an 800 specialist. "I can do this," she said. "I can do this." Practically riding Irving's back, Sischo worked her arms and sprung off the wet ground with her sledgehammer thighs, fists clenched, forearms ripped, calves bulging, and that god-awful shirt tucked in as the rules required. Irving looked gorgeous: a hungry, textbook stride, perfect posture, loose hands, arms swinging, animalistic in her own right.

Irving drifted left, hemming in Sischo against the flagged boundary. Sischo, entranced by her reading of running literature, swung right. She drove ahead like a swimmer touching the wall to take fifth by four-tenths of a second, about eight inches, and complete the F-M scoring and unprecedented sweep. "Katie closed the deal," said Carter. "She won our approval."

"Oh, the humanity!" Bill cried. He looked at John. They smiled. They hugged.

"Looking back," Malone said, "it still makes my heart stop. A segment of life was redefined."

Bill likened the tour de force of the girls' tighter-than-ever eleven-second spread to the sweet spot of the "swing" in crew. As the sportswriter Paul Gallico, a collegiate rower, described it almost a century ago: "Eight oars whip out of the water in unison; eight oars dip again and one feels a great exultation in one's breast."

The past three years, since the F-M girls emerged on the national scene, they had won state Class 2A over Saratoga by scores of 67 to 73 in 2006 (Hilton second, 71, SS third, 73), 23 to 71 (2007), and 22 to 48 (2008). This year: Fayetteville 15, Saratoga 59. The F-M times to the fraction: Chapman 17:25.4, Malone 17:34.7, Fanning 17:35.3, Carter 17:36.0, and Sischo 17:36.7. The F-M team average, 17:33, was thirty-five seconds per girl faster than Saratoga. That margin would only grow.

With Chapman's four years of varsity experience and two state titles, what questions of identity nagged at her? She'd just defeated an all-star field leaving luminaries like Lizzie Predmore of Shenedehowa, sixth nationally in 2008, seventeen seconds behind. Chapman was still trying to process the gaudiness of Aris's language, how he would tell the girls to dig into their souls "to find collective meaning." Chapman said, "I would hold Bill's words in my palm." She would then simplify their essence, her need to link aptitude with ideas, and think, "Oh, yeah. Let's kill this workout."

As with any artist, Aris's catalogue was open to interpretation. In his decorous fluency, Aris always presented a bit of mystery. It was the perfect invitation, serving what the Irish poet John Banville wrote about childhood and "its constantly recurring astonishment."

∽

Roache recovered in time for nationals. But swine flu was still a health issue, and Malone got an idea. She went to her father's office at a pharmaceutical company, pilfered some surgical masks, drew animal faces on them, and distributed them to teammates to wear on the flight to Portland. It was half serious, half ribbing Aris, who was always over the top with health concerns. Seems he had good reason to be.

Imagine if the girls wore them *in* Portland in front of the Saugus girls from California, again billed as an NXN threat. *Ahha! So that's the Fayetteville secret!* Saugus, winner of its fourth-straight state title, by thirty-five points with a near-record average time, was already smarting from a midseason brouhaha with Fayetteville.

Saugus had decided to come east for the McQuaid Invitational in Rochester in October. Fayetteville typically ran McQuaid. Saugus savored a chance to race the Stotans on a flat course in predictably good weather—California conditions—where their track-style attributes might be put to good use. The Centurians, said Aris, planned it as a sneak attack. McQuaid officials were in on it. They kept the Saugus entry quiet.

But what the Saugus coach, Rene Paragas, had not known was that Aris had decided months earlier he was skipping McQuaid this year; Manhattan was the week after, and he didn't want his team racing two big meets in succession. Naturally, the internet lit up with claims that Fayetteville was ducking Saugus. "It was a covert maneuver," said Aris. "All they had to do was ask me."

Later, Aris called Paragas and told him, "We weren't ducking you. My decision had been made in June." Besides, if the Saugus trip was kept a secret, who was F-M ducking? When I asked Paragas about it, he insisted there was nothing coy in his plans. "It wasn't, 'Let's ambush them,'" he said.

In any case, Saugus got a chance to stretch its legs with a runaway victory at Genesee Valley Park. After that, the team paid a visit to nearby Niagara Falls before heading home. The Californians could relish some success right in the F-M neighborhood.

In Portland, the boys went off first, and based on their New York regional showing—victory by forty-two points with another strong fifth-man run by Hartnett—the team still hoped for a podium shot even with Hatz, last year's New York regional champion, left at home. Hatz, back running again but in no position to race, fell into tears when the team departed. Aris gave him an assuring talk. Hatz had handled his illnesses with Stotan courage. The mile beckoned. He would soon unleash his "pent-up competitive rage," Aris said.

If only the boys' team had some of that fire at Portland Meadows. Merriman, instructed to lead the group with a hearty start for good positioning in the sloppy footing, ran a mild pace off the mark. "We got crushed," said Roache. "Too many bodies." A half mile in, one of those bodies drew up on Farrell and clipped his heel with a spike, taking Farrell's shoe off. Farrell couldn't run freely, got stuck in a pack where points piled up, and blamed the mishap on Bernard Lagat, one of the world's greatest runners.

The night before, Lagat, a native Kenyan who'd become an American citizen in 2004, had come into the boys' hotel room to offer advice. In 2009, Nike had its sponsored athletes serve as regional "captains," and Lagat was assigned the New York boys. He regaled them with a story of how once in a big race he'd gotten spiked, lost his shoe, and still finished with a good performance. "That was our jinx," said Farrell.

Farrell's shoeless foot would plunge in and out of the frozen mud. Temperatures were in the low thirties. He saw runners from New York that he'd beaten well ahead of him. He almost lost his other shoe when he got spiked again in the last mile. Farrell finished 114th as the team's fourth man and was rushed to the medical tent for treatment on his numb foot. A heater applied to his foot shocked his chilled body, and he almost passed out.

With Merriman placing 75th, McGurrin 78th, Roache 79th, and Hartnett close behind Farrell in 124th, Fayetteville, with a twenty-one-second spread (Farrell ran a remarkable 16:25 "on one leg"), ran well as a unit. The boys-team places, thirty-ninth to eightieth, however, were too far back, and they wound up ninth with 270 points. The what-if math was painful. Farrell's missing shoe cost the team about fifty points. And with a healthy Hatz in the mix, that would have further reduced the F-M tally by close to eighty points. Fayetteville could have reasonably been expected to score 140, no worse than 150. The winner, Boerne of Texas, had 195.

∽

In the chill, the girls coated their bodies, as usual, with baby oil, and also wore long-sleeved shirts under their lemon-yellow singlets, and gloves as well. For guidance, Aris urged the girls to embrace the holy trinity: risking failure, self-governance, and zero compression. They had won the regional, 41–77, over Saratoga. Chapman was sick then and far back, enabling Fanning, the freshman, to be the first F-M girl, with Sischo close behind. Luber improved from her poor state run when she almost dropped out in embarrassment.

Who was Fayetteville competing against at nationals? Saugus? By this time, the Californians were probably psyched out beyond repair. F-M competed only against perfection. Zero compression. It was the only foe left. "We knew it wouldn't happen, but that was our intent," Aris offered. As a last spur to the girls, he said to them, "When have we ever run a *careful* race?"

Malone heard him. Plattsburgh, Portland, no difference. Malone bolted to the front of the nationals field with Chapman by her side and the eventual winner, Katie Flood of Iowa, a stride back. The F-M pair pressed through standing water around the first turn, bodies splashing, elbows jabbing, shoes soaked a minute into the race. Queensbury's senior twins from New York, Brittany and Danielle Winslow, boldly shared the front. With F-M holding court, the lead group passed the first kilometer in 3:13, close to five-minute-mile pace. The effort was suicidal—what was the point? Fayetteville led the early scoring by a huge margin. That was the point.

"We had no right to be so far up," said Malone. "But . . ." she paused to consider the celestial impact, "I didn't feel superexhausted."

Inevitably, Chapman and Malone drifted back, and were then visible to Carter and Fanning, with Sischo charging from behind and Luber close enough, restoring her confidence. The six girls, entering the realm of "zero," had no worries, no rivals, nothing between them and a fourth-straight championship. Hay bales, roller coaster hills, mud, puddles the size of Lake Tahoe. Nothing mattered. Two k, 3k, 4k . . .

Around the last bend and the long straight for home, Sischo was the strongest—Sischo, the state-meet closer who'd watched the year before on crutches, swept ahead and was the first Fayetteville girl across the line. Malone, second, didn't see her go by and thought she was first—her hope as a senior in her last cross-country race. Chapman, Fanning, and Carter followed within seconds. It was a few more seconds to Luber, and then a bit of a gap to Martin, the converted sprinter, the fastest seventh girl in the field by twenty-four seconds.

Afterward, after the results made it official—that F-M had done it again, with 74 points, well ahead of runner-up Saratoga, 147—the victorious girls linked arm-and-arm for photos and interviews. With their radiant glow and buoyant smiles, they were tickled with life. When a reporter asked Sischo how the team had assessed its chances coming into Portland, she replied, "We don't predict. We prepare and perform."

Fayetteville won with no girl in the top twenty. Their scorers placed twenty-first through thirty-sixth (eleven through nineteen in team points) with a record-smashing seventeen-second compression. It was Sischo 18:15, Malone 18:17, Chapman 18:20, Fanning 18:24, and Carter 18:32. (The course, typically slightly longer than five kilometers, measured 5,083 meters.) Saratoga's spread was sixty seconds. F-M's top five girls finished ahead of Saratoga's second girl and came within twelve seconds of again sweeping the number-two team in the country. Saugus wound up fourth.

The three Fayetteville seniors, Luber, Carter, and Malone, their high school cross-country odyssey over, pulled off to the side for a private, emotional huddle. I summoned Malone that day, asking for a last word as officials broke down the course. "We perform how we live," she told me with moist eyes. "Clean. Whole. Stotan." Looking back years later, Malone could easily return to that purity in her breast, saying, "We lived for each other, for that moment in time, for the team."

In their connections, in the feeling of family that the girls spoke about that day in Portland, there was, perhaps above all else, an underlying "will to meaning," as defined in the existential work of psychologist Viktor Frankl. Life was a quest not for pleasure or power, posited Frankl, but for meaning. It was to possess the spiritual light in which to surrender your ego and live for another. "Your strength lies within your teammates," Malone said.

After the race, boarding the bus back to the hotel, even Carter dwelled on intimacy. "This was the most like family we ever felt," she said. Carter had fought for that—fought herself for it. She'd lived, as she put it, an alternative life, a life of constant challenge, of Power Bar birthday cakes and Thanksgiving unturkey. When she crossed the Portland Meadows finish line for the fourth and final time, she felt spent relief. "Oh, my gosh," she told herself. "I did it."

17

PLAY DATES IN FAIRYLAND

When I couldn't keep up, I was embarrassed to tell Bill and would
go into the woods and cry.
       —*Christie Rutledge, Fayetteville-Manlius cross-country runner*

2010 Season I

The young girl from Manlius was always active, running whenever
she could. She loved nature and ran in the woods at the back of her
home. She would run in bare feet and she would climb trees in bare
feet, thrilling to the earth and bark and everything primal and free. She had a
secret spot where there was a canopy of vines over the tops of the trees. The girl
would think nothing of climbing up and around and swinging from the vines,
much like the animals she treasured.

"When I would come in for dinner after a day of playing," the girl recalled,
"I would be scraped up and covered in dirt and leaves and totally exhausted
and so happy."

In the summers, she would run lap after lap around her family's vacation
home at Charleston Lake, about two hours north, near the Thousand Islands, in
Ontario, Canada. "I wanted to see how many laps I could do," the girl recalled.

At the time, she was six, seven, eight years old, and . . . "I ran like a maniac. My feet got muddied and I had huge callouses."

The girl would take to exploring the lake's shoreline and the broader locale, Beecher Island, always barefoot, stopping to savor the plants, like ferns and moss, and making friends with the wildlife. Her confidants included "George The Great Blue Heron," and "Ralph The Red Squirrel."

She would swim in the lake and play with her older brother on the family dock and diving board. As she got a little older, the girl learned to scuba dive. She would descend with her dad to the lake's bottom, crushing up zebra mussels and feeding them to the fish.

The girl's name was Christie Rutledge.

At the time, in the early 2000s, when Christie's world included learning all she could about whales, especially killer whales, Bill Aris was learning all he could about the Stotan ideas and formulating his view that girls and boys on the running course should be nurtured with the same opportunities for excellence.

In 2006, when the Fayetteville-Manlius girls won their first national cross-country championship, Rutledge entered middle school and found a "mean girls" culture that shattered the little girl in her that still found sanctuary at the tops of trees. "I lost some of my playfulness," she said. "I became self-conscious and suddenly realized it wasn't cool to wear boys' clothes and play in the dirt and be obsessed with whales."

Rutledge felt lost. What self-respecting middle school girl would dare to be seen running in the woods after school, and without the right haircut or makeup or snotty attitude? Feeling her innocence under siege, Rutledge became withdrawn and confused, fearing what life held in store. With a failing self-worth, she sunk into the beginnings of an eating disorder, which would plague her, on and off, for years. In seventh grade, she restricted her food intake, lost weight, and tried to fit in.

Rutledge thought middle school soccer would be a refuge, but she got cut. After that, Rutledge tried "modified" cross-country in eighth grade and liked it. She could run without risk. Entering F-M in the fall of 2008, Rutledge embarked on her freshman season, feeling, "It was a safe haven for me." She said, "I no longer had to worry about saying the 'right' things and being popular." Rutledge felt at home with barefoot drills, running in the woods, and exploring far-off trails at Green Lakes. Mostly, she liked the family atmosphere and thoughtfulness of the Stotan philosophy.

Hard work and humility were paramount. In time, no one would work harder than Rutledge. She liked that personal quirks were respected and even used by the coach as a way to fortify team bonding. Each girl's qualities were valued.

Christie could play all she wanted. "I wasn't looked down upon for the fact that I would often pick up twigs and run with them in my mouth, and it was okay that I was always smiling weirdly on steady runs."

In that first year of 2008, Rutledge was seen as "Smiley Christie." She typically placed dead last among the twenty or so F-M girls in a meet but always had a smile about her. She started out running thirty-one minutes for 5k and worked her way down to twenty-seven minutes, still a jogger's pace. Time? Place? No matter. Christie would be the teammate swooning with cheers, hugs, and high fives for the older girls she held in awe and kept at a distance. "I didn't think anyone knew who I was," she said.

In training, Rutledge was wracked by the new sensations of mile after mile at a brisk pace. She found it impossible to keep up with other freshmen, like Katie Sischo, a friend since middle school. Once, when Rutledge had to stop, a boys' team member scolded her for "cutting" the course. Other times, she would find refuge in private. "When I couldn't keep up," she said, "I was embarrassed to tell Bill and would go into the woods and cry."

Rutledge was safe for the time being: Bill Aris didn't notice. However, she did catch Aris's attention the next year, when, as a sophomore, she started completing workouts, even long runs of ninety minutes, while learning the gravitational tricks of the Green Lakes hills. Rutledge's 5k times plummeted to twenty minutes. It was a remarkable seven-minute improvement, fast enough to win a JV race.

Her teammates were startled to see Rutledge cross the line first. "We were all, 'What the hell just happened?'" said Mackenzie Carter, a senior that 2009 season. "Christie looked like she was *racing*. We'd never seen that in her."

Rutledge shrugged off the win. Even later, she never cared about competition or who was first, second, or third, only that she was part of something "bigger than just you." In her mind, a race was not about beating anybody, but being covered in dirt like you'd just run through the brush at Charleston Lake.

With renewed confidence, Rutledge's eating issues quieted down, for the time being, and she ran track in the winter and spring of 2010 while continuing to polish her virtuosity as a concert pianist. She'd been playing piano since age four and had a baby grand at home. Cross-country and piano did not go well together. "I'd come home from a workout and my hands would be frozen," said Rutledge. "I had to go straight to piano practice. It was hard to play."

Rutledge worked on a selection for a concerto competition. The winner would be given the opportunity to play with the Syracuse Symphony Orchestra. She spent hours perfecting Beethoven's *Concerto no. 1 in C Major*, as well as the cadenza, an ornamental flourish near the end when the orchestra stops and the pianist plays solo. It's a moving piece, unveiled in Vienna in 1795, and to watch Leonard Bernstein conduct the Vienna Philharmonic at the height of his career—doing this very Beethoven work—is to surrender to a resplendent beauty, life's wonder crystalized in the maestro's uncontained joy.

Rutledge devoured the piece but did not win the competition. Her father, Bryan, thought she had more to give. One day after picking her up from cross-country practice, he said to her, "I don't know why you're trying so hard at this," referring to cross-country. "Why don't you just stick with piano?"

Rutledge demurred. She followed her heart, putting running first. That spring, she made a breakthrough, running the 3,000 meters in track in 10:30, her best time by over thirty seconds and a respectable showing for a sophomore. "Hmmm," said Aris.

Seeing his daughter's progress, her father, an ophthalmologist, offered her one thousand dollars if she could make the F-M varsity team competing in the national championships. Instead of getting an allowance, Christie and her brother would receive a monetary prize if they could achieve the hardest goal they could think of, something seemingly beyond reach.

Rutledge had no interest in the possible windfall. She could not imagine running nationals. But she did yearn to stick with the top girls. A blessing in disguise led to that. Rutledge developed a foot injury that aborted her track season. Aris had her do cross-training on a stationary bike. Rutledge biked as much as ninety minutes a day every day for three weeks. "My legs burned," she said, "but I got strong." After biking she would join the team for weight training and core work.

When summer training started for the 2010 fall cross-country season, Rutledge dared to try some modest runs alongside all-Americans like Sischo and Carter. Rutledge still felt awkward intimating that she was a worthy runner.

∽

After the girls won their fourth-straight Nike Cross Nationals in fall 2009 with their best championships performance yet, the ensuing track season presented more of the same—dizzying success in winter and spring for both boys and girls in every major event on the high school circuit.

Alex Hatz—"Alexander the Great"—lived up to his moniker. Fully recovered from his debilitating fall ailments and training through the winter on the hilly roads near school for strength and the Syracuse University indoor track for speed, Hatz captured the national indoor mile title in Boston in March. Hatz ran 4:05.50 to set a state indoor mile record, shattering a twenty-four-year-old mark by two seconds. Hatz thus became the third-fastest US high school indoor miler of all time. He completed his F-M career three months later with a national outdoor mile title, running 4:08.09 in Greensboro, North Carolina.

Hatz went on to the University of Wisconsin in Madison. He yearned to run the sub-4:00 mile Aris had groomed him for with Stotan bravery that spring night of his junior year. Though college running lacked the structure he'd been accustomed to, Hatz found his moment one February day in 2012. He was then a sophomore—actually a redshirt freshman.

It was the Tyson Food Invitational on the University of Arkansas indoor track. The meet was a college and professional event in one. Hatz lined up for the mile in a three-race field that featured three members of the Kenyan national team—a pair of sub-3:50-milers and the prior year's world outdoor championship 1500 silver medalist. The Kenyan trio ran 1-2-3 in the pro race. Hatz won the faster of the two college races in 3:58.68 as the next four runners also broke four minutes. He remembered that rainy night in Chittenango.

Oh, yes: The Arkansas city in which Hatz achieved that sub-4:00? Fayetteville.

Matching Hatz's national high school mile sweep in 2010 were the Fayetteville girls in the 4 x 800 meter relay. After taking the national indoor title, the outdoor race offered the F-M girls even greater reward. The week before, F-M had been beaten by Garden City in the state meet. The anchor runner, Molly Malone, shouldered the blame for a tactical blunder. In Greensboro, Hannah Luber led off with a so-so 2:17.04, putting F-M in sixth. Mackenzie Carter's 2:11.48 brought the foursome up to third. With her snazzy 2:10.39, Katie Sischo handed off to Malone in first. But this time Malone would be patient. In a frantic final baton exchange, she slowed just enough to allow the Garden City anchor to draw ahead. "I knew she would take the bait," said Malone. Aris had told Malone, "Whoever is the last to kick is going to win."

With Garden City leading around the final turn, Malone, as planned, slingshot onto the home straight, gained an advantage, and won with a brilliant anchor, 2:08.08. Malone's time would have placed her second in the championship individual 800. Aris had said it before and said it again: "Molly Malone is the toughest athlete, male or female, I've coached." Fayetteville's time of 8:46.98 was the second-fastest ever run.

That same month, at her graduation party, Malone, staying local at Syracuse University, presented Aris with a parting gift. Malone was an artist. For a senior AP art project, Malone did a portrait of her coach in charcoal. She gave Aris a curious *Venus de Milo* grin, well worthy of his Greekness, and had the work matted and framed for him. "I was blown away," said Aris.

The work was also something of an inside joke. Malone never liked it when outsiders referred to Aris as a tyrant. Molly knew the inner Bill—the Chevy Chase kind of Bill with deadpan humor who would racewalk the Portland airport against team members upon arrival at nationals. "I could never beat him," said Jillian Fanning, a sophomore in 2010. "I would be laughing too hard."

Luber, going on to the University of Iowa, also had a gift for Aris, not fashioned until her junior year. One night out on campus, Luber got dressed up. Her attempt at donning high heels caused her to take a bad fall, resulting in a spiral fracture of her left fibula, a bone in the calf. After one surgery to insert a plate and several screws into her leg, and a second surgery to take out one screw, then weeks of rehab, Luber was her old self. She took one of her X-rays, framed it along with the original, extricated screw, adding the warning, "Hey kids, don't wear heels," and gave it to Aris as a Christmas gift.

⚭

Summer brought a rebuilding year for the girls. The graduation of Malone, Luber, and Carter—the "warriors," said Aris—left a huge void. "We had pieces, unknowns, question marks," he said.

One piece was Rutledge, moving up from the JV. She rejoiced at Green Lakes, taking the hills, she said, "like a mountain goat trying to navigate rocks and the roots." Another piece was Fanning, who'd placed sixth in the previous spring's state championship 3,000. Fanning embraced Green Lakes "as escape from reality," and lived up to her nickname, "Prancer," for her grace on the tortuous Gulf Road climb. A third piece was junior Heather Martin, the seventh and last runner at NXN in 2009. The sprinter cum distance runner worked on "expanding" her speed—carrying it over greater distances—and bolstering her athleticism with Aris's weight-training program. The team did dead lifts, cleans, jerks, and squats among other exercises. Martin, at first glance petite, could eventually deadlift 225 pounds.

The veterans counted on to lead the squad were Sischo, now a junior, and Courtney Chapman, the team's only senior on the cusp of national stature. Sischo had matured, and the girls now called her "Mom." "She was good at keeping us in order," said Rutledge. Sischo applied her leverage with custodial care. "I was not a fiery person," she said.

Sischo didn't have to be. By midsummer the girls shared a joie de vivre wherever they trained. Toward the end of a Saturday long run of two hours at Green Lakes, their muscle fuel nearing empty, the girls would treat themselves to a remote trail beyond Round Lake, beyond God's Country Hill, where they would stop for a moment and gaze at the valley below, no one speaking, their devotions as one. "We could see all the way to the Erie Canal," recalled Fanning. "We called the spot, 'the End of the World.'"

Three other girls were Stotan ducklings: sophomore Katie Brislin, who lived in the district and transferred from a Catholic school; sophomore Maggie Malone, who had a touch of her sister Molly's brashness; and junior Emily McGurrin, whose older brother Mark led the boys' team, soon to devolve into rancor.

Should any girl lack for Stotan crackle, they would be reproached by the ghostly presence of their foremothers, who, earlier that summer, had marked their training turf like cheetahs on the savanna. Malone, Luber, and Carter, before departing for college (Carter hauled off to the University of Washington in Seattle), went to training sites and spray-painted telephones, trees, whatever they could, in pink and green, so their F-M successors would see their treasured touchstones and feel the same inspiration they had. "It was not a jokey thing. It had a serious purpose," said Malone.

The trio marked the apex of Gulf Road, Round Lake, spots all over town. "We loved it, seeing that," said Sischo, "It was a stake for the places we held in such reverence. The symbols helped the young girls feeling their way."

While Rutledge soon found she could keep up with anyone, she was still young in temperament, framing a Green Lakes meadow as "a magical fairyland" and demonstrating a pain threshold rarely seen in all the F-M years. Her hard-driving style—she knew only one pace, fast—perhaps masked a festering turmoil, returning her to childhood impulses.

Christie's "refusal to give in," as Aris put it, would alarm training partners. Fanning, concerned at how deeply her friend pushed through pain—yes, the Stotan mandate, but *every day?*—would warn her, "Make sure you're not killing yourself."

Not to worry. How could you kill yourself engaged in play? Play suffused the imperishable need to live in beauty, wrote the Dutch historian Johann Huizinga. To live, we *had* to play.

So it would be that Rutledge, who hid her face when the girls watched scary movies together at the Chapmans' place, shocked everyone, including herself, in the team's first summer time trial at Green Lakes in late July. When Rutledge passed Chapman, took the lead, and won in 18:10 for 5k, a hush came over the finish straight on the Serengeti. "I'm still in shock thinking about it," Rutledge told me. "I always felt it was a fluke."

Aris thought it was a fluke. After the run, he said to himself, "Is this the same girl who ran thirty minutes two years ago? Did the other girls have a bad day?"

Chapman was second in 18:14, followed by Fanning, 18:18, and Sischo, 18:28. Darn good foursome. Brislin led the ducklings in twenty minutes even. Aris called Brislin "Kabaa." (Don't ask.) Next, Malone in 20:07. Aris called her "Dibaba." (Don't ask.)

Rutledge won the next time trial and the one after that; and the one after that. Then she won the Gulf Road ten-mile time trial in 63:30, one of the fastest ever by a girl and faster that day than many of the boys. Aris referred to the ascent's bottom half as the "honeymoon" section. Hah. The second half reached grades of 18 percent. The run was the team's ultimate testing rite. Show courage on the tiered switchbacks of Gulf Road, and that's how you'll run the last mile at nationals. Show weakness—pal, you've work to do, mind and body.

Chapman finished ninety seconds behind. If Chapman, with her national credentials, was now the team's number-two girl, who could complain? But soon Chapman was on a flight to Paris with her F-M French class, a trip postponed from the previous spring when volcanic eruptions in Iceland cancelled flights all over Europe. Chapman returned home sick as a dog. She had fever, aches, and shakes and could not get out of bed for three days.

Aris gave Chapman shortened workouts and cross-training. Chapman's symptoms, milder yet draining, persisted. No doctor could offer a firm diagnosis. She would run, get into bed, run. . . . It was her senior year. She insisted on running an early-September time trial on a humid, ninety-degree day. Chapman placed fourth on the squad, twenty-six seconds behind the front-running Rutledge.

Chapman's fate, and now the team's, was uncertain. Thank goodness Mother Sischo could provide some leadership. Sisco helped Rutledge grow comfortable in the glare of success. *It was okay to be first. You were safe.* Christie continued training with twigs in her mouth. She played Brahms with hands stained from splattered mud. She shielded her eyes from fright. One day at Green Lakes, she happened to come upon Mark McGurrin running by her.

"Hi, Mark," Christie called out.

"Bug off," McGurrin told her.

∽

At first, as a freshman, McGurrin wanted to be a pole vaulter. "I liked the idea of flinging myself up in the air," he told me. Before long, he found his mettle in running. In his junior year, 2009, McGurrin's talent was evident, and in Portland, he was the team's number-two scorer. However, at the same time, by his own admission, McGurrin became a divisive influence, inflaming his relationship with the coaching staff.

In 2010, McGurrin's senior cross-country season, the situation worsened. McGurrin dissed the girls because he felt they were favored by Bill Aris. He was pissed off at encounter groups in which the athletes had to air differences close-up. "I won't say it was not effective," said McGurrin, "but I don't know if it was worth it." He tangled often with the sophomore Nick Ryan—Nick the young buck, perhaps a mite full of himself, and Mark feeling he'd been around too long to take it. A late-season confrontation over some crude joke resulted in the two boys fighting in the snow at Green Lakes with Nick, according to Mark, "stomping my face."

"We were beside ourselves on a daily basis," said Aris. "McGurrin was unpredictable and out of control."

"I could be a nasty, brutal jerk at times," McGurrin said. "I was a stupid teenager."

When I spoke with McGurrin years later, he was about to complete studies in England to become a brewmaster after graduation from Brown University, where he'd run track and cross-country. He seemed to carry the wounds of his youth; he was sometimes resentful, other times remorseful.

The son of two physicians, McGurrin said he attended private school until fifth grade and was bullied constantly. "I spent a lot of time being called names," he told me. "If you want to know why I would be in people's faces," he said, referring to his later years, "it's because I genuinely don't like people." He paused and added, "I'm tougher on myself than on anyone else."

It was into this emotional cauldron that Aris tried to create a semblance of competitive literacy. Ryan had been an unconvincing JV runner as a freshman, his season aborted by an infected blister. As a sophomore, he came close to quitting the team after being whipped by Gulf Road and finishing his first ten-milers in a staggering ninety minutes. Andrew Roache—he of the buried hair—returned to his final cross-country season after some excellent track running. But as a senior he, too, skirmished with Ryan while siding with McGurrin when disputes arose. "Mark was more the leader," said Roache about their kinship. "I was more the lackey."

With the powder keg ready to catch fire, Aris pulled McGurrin aside and read him the riot act. Either he apologized to the girls, who were upset by his toxic behavior, or he was off the team. McGurrin, hardly contrite, agreed.

Young Ryan provided some good news. He cut out sweets, lost weight, and, with a summer growth spurt, became a svelte five-feet-eleven, 154-pound force on the running trails. In competition, Ryan joined McGurrin and Roache to create a solid up-front trio. Ryan showed his promise as the first F-M boy at the midseason league meet, placing third in 15:49 on a muddy 5k course, twenty seconds ahead of McGurrin. Fayetteville went on to win the Section 3 state qualifier, but in state championship Class 2A, F-M would face Eastern States champion Shaker, from the Albany area. Aris told the boys that Shaker was "younger and hungrier" than they were.

At Lakeside Park in the Dutchess County town of Pawling, not far from Bowdoin Park, F-M ran its weakest state race since the pre-Stotan era. McGurrin had spent the night vomiting with the flu. (Aris had put McGurrin and Ryan together as roommates, hoping they could finally come to terms.) Ryan had no business leading the entire field, but he did, falling back after the mile when he hit the ascent, Toboggan Hill. Ryan still went on to pace the team, but there was little to speak of. Roache and McGurrin followed wanly with the next four guys well back. It was Shaker 58, Warwick Valley 78, and F-M 80.

Aris, fuming, gathered the boys into a meeting and told them "if this is all you've got" there's no point going to the regional qualifying meet for nationals. He told them their racing capacity was not the problem. It was their poor attitude and lack of cohesiveness. "We have to talk straight up. Truth has to come out," Aris said. "I need input from each of you. Let's do it without a fistfight. Where do we go from here?"

Ryan, still relatively new to the operation, spoke up. "I've watched some of you guys blow off runs, taking it easy, walking when the coach can't see you. I've done everything I could. Not as well as some of you, but I've tried. I'm sick and tired of it. Coach, I agree with you. I don't think we deserve to go to regionals."

The boys were stunned at being called out, especially by the team's youngest member. Aris beamed. He said aloud how much he appreciated Ryan's honesty and told the boys, "This is how leaders are born."

Feeling a cathartic moment—at least Bill did—the boys moved on to regionals, again meeting Shaker, then a big favorite, and the rest of the state. Ryan's assertive stance may have settled everyone down. The boys had one of their own, not just the coach, to answer to; and more of an identity not pricked by the illustrious girls.

After two weeks of blameless training, the boys attacked Bowdoin Park, delivering their best race of the season. McGurrin and Ryan roared into the front pack, held position, and went on to place fourth and fifth—first and second among team runners—for optimal points. Knowing they'd qualified for nationals as individuals, even if the team didn't make it, McGurrin and Ryan hugged at the finish, telling one another, Disney-like, "We're going to Oregon!"

Roache was close behind in ninth, the top three separated by fourteen seconds—16:09, 16:15, and 16:23—good enough to overcome the distant placings of the last two scorers. F-M had outrun Shaker at six of the seven positions to triumph, 45 to 59. The whole team was going to Oregon. McGurrin was the hero. He'd led the team into nationals. He scored one point.

Would the boys find only temporary reprieve from contentiousness? Did they just say, "screw this" and come together? Was it something deeper, something Nick Ryan offered that touched doubt and longing, a way to disperse teenage distress signals? Did that finish-line hug really count?

The next day, a Sunday, the seven boys met for a two-hour run at Green Lakes. It was McGurrin, Ryan, and Roache plus the second pack of Andrew Veilleux, Ben Thomas, Eric Billinson, and Jules Wellner. It would be their last long run before nationals. It was a lovely late-fall day. The turf was dry, the skies blue. The boys started running. After twenty minutes, they happened to hit the golf course. One by one, they stopped running and lay down on a pristine green. The seven of them, all prone, looked up at the blue sky. For a time, nothing was spoken. The boys could hear each other's soft breaths.

Then one boy said, "We made it." Another offered, "I'm tired, but it's really cool to finish in Portland." Then they resumed running but only back to their cars. They'd done enough.

"We seemed like a team again," Roache told me. As every season, Roache had grown out his hair and beard. When F-M boarded their flight to PDX, Roache looked like Tom Hanks in *Cast Away*.

The pre-NXN rankings had come out. The consensus had Fayetteville between tenth and fifteenth in the country among the twenty-two teams. The first thing Aris told the boys upon landing in Portland was, "You guys suck."

18

WINGS ON THEIR FEET

I wanted him to have new stories, new cross-country myths about the girls team, about amazing athletes coming together to achieve inhuman feats.

—*Courtney Chapman, after her fifth nationals*

2010 Season II

A girls' rebuilding year? That was a good one. Fayetteville dominated every 2010 meet, some with close to perfect scores. Jillian Fanning, Christie Rutledge, and Katie Sischo were an unimpeachable top three, with Courtney Chapman up and down depending on her lingering weakness. Heather Martin was closing in but concerned that she was now counted on for more. She was relieved when Chapman told her, "Don't be afraid to pass me even though I'm more of a distance runner than you are."

Granted her freedom, Martin did pass Chapman at the Manhattan Easterns in the Bronx as the team's fifth scorer. Fanning, in a breakthrough, took second to that season's Foot Locker national titlist Aisling Cuffe. She raced Cuffe elbow to elbow for the first mile at Van Cortlandt Park, thinking, "What am I doing here?" F-M put all scorers in the first eleven finishers for thirty-two points.

The year before, in her first Manhattan trip as a freshman, Fanning was all nerves. Her roommate, Hannah Luber, found a way to relax her. With lights out, the two girls went to the team stash of PowerBars, took them into the hallway, and constructed "teepees" out of them outside the girls' rooms so they would see them in the morning. Fanning felt better.

The third-place Easterns team in 2010 was actually from the West. Great Oak of Southern California made the literal cross-country trip to get their first look at F-M, never mind the Bronx, in an omen for the future. In a few years, the Wolfpack would surpass Saugus as California's premier squad and assume the responsibility of "trying to unlock the NXN mystery," in the words of Saugus coach Rene Paragas.

This season, Saugus had its best team ever. No matter how well F-M ran, Aris warned the girls about Saugus. "Bill managed to convince us we were in trouble for nationals," said Sischo. "It was always Saugus this, Saugus that. We knew he was trying to motivate us, and it worked."

Saugus, situated in Newhall, a middle-class suburb of Los Angeles, did everything it could to try and dent Fayetteville dominance. Paragas took a page from the F-M playbook and had his girls train in sand at a riverbed, what they call "washes." Instead of making only a summer trip to Big Bear Lake, known for its ski resort and mountain trails—and where the world-class marathoner Ryan Hall had grown up and trained—Paragas made two additional fall trips for the altitude training. The elevation was close to seven thousand feet. Paragas knew a few days were not enough to enrich the runners' red blood cells, but he liked the hills and cold temperatures and opportunity, he said, "to train like Stotans."

The team's work paid off. Saugus won its fifth-straight California state title with a record low score, twenty-three points, and a record-low team average, 17:53 for 5k, at Woodward Park in Fresno. The Centurians placed all five scorers in the top ten in Division 2 with a spiffy compression of twenty-three seconds. Maybe this time Saugus *was* a team to be reckoned with.

Fayetteville proceeded to also win its fifth-straight state title with another Class 2A sweep of Saratoga Springs, considered the equal of Saugus. In a pattern so striking it was starting to revamp notions of what excellence meant and what female runners could do, F-M outran Saratoga by forty-two seconds per girl on the Pawling course. The winner was none other than Rutledge in 17:31. Rutledge's favorite part was Toboggan Hill. Likewise for Fanning in second. Prancer and the girl who once cried in the woods couldn't get enough hills.

Bill Aris obliged. The team did its Gulf Road staple as well as the cliff-like Townsend Road, also with an 18-20-percent grade at its steepest, plus the almost-mile-long school access road, with speed bumps like hay bales—whatever hill or mountain Aris would fancy. Most any run from the school put the team deep into remote climbs—thank the Onondaga escarpment—within minutes.

The terrain that F-M lived on made the most brutal racecourses seem easy. Aris characterized Bowdoin Park, feared by all for its uphill first mile, as a speed runner's course. Fanning said she "absolutely loved it" and showed her love when she won the NXN New York Regional at Bowdoin in eighteen minutes flat as F-M defeated Saratoga easily and this time by a margin of forty-four seconds per girl. Aris still expounded on a Saugus threat.

The girls fulfilled their prenationals ritual of running to Mallards Landing, reciting an affirmation, and tying their race ribbons to the post at the pond adorned with ribbons from the past. "It had religious importance," said Sischo. This time they wound up doing it in the six A.M. darkness before boarding their flight to Portland. In the rush, they took a shortcut through thorny bushes, and Rutledge got all cut up and bloodied. But for her, it was another day at the office.

&

In Portland, the Fayetteville boys were nobody. "To the world we didn't even belong there," said Aris. "You guys suck" became the weekend mantra. "I thought Bill meant it in jest," Andrew Roache recalled, "but he said it with a serious face." The Aris zinger was meant to rally the boys when it was easy for them to accept the assessments of the cross-country gossip mill. Mark McGurrin readily took it on. "We were being disrespected," he said. The online favorites were American Fork of Utah and Arcadia of California.

Nick Ryan was just thrilled to be there for the first time. He hung with Andrew Veilleux, who'd run NXN as a sophomore two years before as the team's seventh runner. "We made it our mission to explore every part of the Nike campus we could sneak our way into," Ryan said. While the 398 teenagers were closely supervised, it was, in effect, open season on campus, where some five thousand Nike employees worked. Ryan says they found no doors locked, nothing secured. They walked unmolested into private quarters. They walked into a room filled with prototype shoes in the process of design. Did Nick Ryan fly home with Nike secrets?

The F-M girls withdrew into the gentle currents of their Stotan ways. By this time, it was something they inhabited. Their orchestral design was about to burst through the curtain and onto the national stage once again. Aris leaned on lyricism to illuminate his gathering force. "Let's go to classical music," he said in Portland. "You have the great composers of the past. Today's composers take their music and add to it." He referred to the great coaches, Cerutty and others. "I take the tenets of each, add to it, and put it all into a tapestry."

But in Portland, music would serve as more than a metaphor. It—art— would be needed to help explain Fayetteville-Manlius when all else failed. The girls would soon run, and logic would soon fail us. A soaring, ethereal voice would be needed—a way to touch the senses and signal something new. Where would it come from?

Chapman, the girl running nationals for a record fifth time, had told the team, "Let's run this one for Bill." Aris turned that around at the team meeting. He'd become aware of what Courtney had proposed. He held his walking stick, his Bernstein baton, in his hand. "Let's run this one for Courtney," he said. "She's been a team player since eighth grade, she's been our best runner, she's carried you, and she's been under the weather. You dedicate this race to *her*." Thinking back, Courtney said, "I'm not an emotional person. But that day I cried."

When the boys took the start, they knew two things: First, Owen Kimple was in the house. Second, they still, well . . .

Kimple, who'd helped define all things Stotan in 2004 and '05, whose family cottage hosted the Stotan summer camp that gave F-M its liftoff, who went to Portsea and brought Cerutty's pearls back to Manlius, was working on a Nike internship after graduation from Cornell. Nike assigned Kimple to help with NXN. He became the only NXN "graduate" to have a hand in planning one. No Gong Shows, he guaranteed.

The boys race went off. It was overcast, forty degrees, with whistling winds. The course was soaked from monthlong rain. The announcers spoke of the favorites. Arcadia, American Fork. The team from Manlius? Not a mention.

For the first time, the individual race superseded the team competition. Two of the greatest and most dynamic high school runners ever—Edward Cheserek of Kenya and New Jersey, and Lukas Verzbikas of Lithuania and Illinois—dueled at the front.

Only months before, Cheserek had come dirt poor from his homeland on a charity program to a Catholic school in Newark. A legend built around his casual remark that in Kenya he'd once run for sixty miles through the brush after getting lost. When I'd visited Cheserek for an interview at his school, St. Benedict's Prep, he spoke in a whisper and seemed the picture of childlike innocence—much like the Kenyan high school runners who were NXN guests in 2006 through 2008 and awed by their first plane trip, their first time riding an escalator, their first taste of technology. But behind Cheserek's quiet whisper was a fierceness and deceptive speed.

Aris always told his runners: take what the Kenyans go through as a gift to inspire you. You don't have to walk two miles for a jug of water to survive. But don't walk the school halls like you've got it made, either.

By midway, Cheserek and Verzbikas fronted the lead pack. They moved back and forth, testing one another. Also up in the mix were Ammar Moussa, Arcadia's top man, whose parents were from Morocco and Egypt, and Elias Gedyon of Loyola of Los Angeles, whose father was from Ethiopia. Plus one good old boy from Texas: the defending champion Craig Lutz. It was the high school Olympics.

Verzbikas presented an exotic figure. A triathlete by trade, he was world ranked in the junior division, coached by his father, and well versed in physiological principles. He ran few races, preferring to build up training reserves from swimming and bicycling—to complement his running—in a pro-style program.

The first Fayetteville boys were about a minute behind. In the furious start and lumpy grounds, Ryan and Roache, working to stay on their feet, saw a number of runners go down. McGurrin had mud fly into his eye and blood running down his shin from a spike wound. At 4k, the three of them found one another. "Ten more guys," Aris yelled. He meant: each of you, catch ten more. That was probably too much to ask, but they did fight off one another. The antagonists Ryan and McGurrin racing one another to the NXN finish—justice on a muddy platter.

As the F-M trio hit the long home straight, Verzbikas gave credence to cross-training by outrunning Cheserek to the wire, 16:00 to 16:02. Verzbikas, a senior, went on to the University of Oregon, quit, and then suffered various life-threatening bicycle accidents in triathlon training. Cheserek, a sophomore, also did his college running at Oregon, graduating in 2017 after winning a record seventeen NCAA titles.

The "you suck" boys did okay for themselves. While Moussa, coated with mud, took fourth for two team points, McGurrin, Roache, and Ryan placed seventeenth, twenty-seventh, and twenty-eighth, all ahead of the second Arcadia runner. The last two scorers of each team would determine the national championship.

Andrew Veilleux and Ben Thomas ran decently from behind, but their Arcadia counterparts were well ahead, and the California school nailed the state's first NXN title with ninety-two points. What about F-M? What about all those top-ranked teams, from Illinois and Indiana, Utah and Colorado? Even in midpack—87th and 101st—Veilleux and Thomas achieved more than they could have imagined. Their 47 and 58 team points finished off a Fayetteville total of 135, good enough for *second place*. Third at state, *second in the nation*. That's how F-M rolled.

But . . . wait. Second in the nation and thirty points ahead of third? Second at NXN just like Kimple's '04 team that had shocked the world with its Manhattan sweep of CBA? These 2010 boys, with all they'd gone through, were probably the most unlikely team ever to climb onto an NXN podium. But some crazy last-ditch unity pierced the boys, propelling McGurrin—McGurrin!—to seventeenth in the country, and with Roache and Ryan, the threesome ran its best at nationals.

Give some credit to the boys' pastoral cohesion, six days before, in the meditative quiet of Green Lakes. Ryan, de facto team leader, credited Aris. "'You suck' revved us up," he said. If these unpolished rascals could get this close to victory, how much longer could Fayetteville be prevented from winning the boys title and sweeping the national championships? So far, in five tries: second, second (third on a tiebreaker), sixteenth, ninth, second.

At the evening's awards ceremonies, it was Owen Kimple who came on stage to present the F-M boys with their trophy. Kimple's Stotan odyssey was finally complete.

McGurrin's place earned him top twenty-one, all-American status. "It meant the world to me," McGurrin said, quickly adding, "Not that I deserved the world." Some questioned whether this team "deserved" second. McGurrin deserved the last word. "I loved those fucking guys," he told me. "Even Nick at that point."

∽

Let the music play. Watch the girls enter the shimmering light of myth.

Boom: Rutledge, Sischo, and Fanning charged out to lead the nationals field. One, two, three in their black-and-gold singlets. "A mass of talent," the announcer cried. In the cold, F-M wore black long-sleeved jerseys underneath, black gloves, and black hair ribbons being sanctified for Mallards Landing. After the long, opening straight, negotiating some of the worst of the mud, Rutledge, in her first NXN, the JV girl from last year, surged ahead. Two minutes gone, and the race was hers. Could she hold it?

"Nothing was planned," she said, thinking back. "I felt it in my feet: the hay bales, we had practiced that, and the hills, the mud. I just loved it."

Rutledge ran with a cool look, unperturbed, out front on her terms. She was a picture with elbows in, erect posture, a quiet stride. "I kept thinking I would die out," she said. "I was in disbelief. This can't be real. But I just kept going."

She could not see the clumsy F-M near miss behind her. Sischo tripped over the first set of hay bales and slammed into Fanning. Both girls almost fell. They possessed the composure to grab one another and say, "You okay?" They were. They proceeded to work together, plying from around fifteenth place. Each girl had more to give. To gain ground, they told each other, "You go and I'll go, too."

In the collision, Sischo had a shoe come half off. The pair moved up, now in the top ten. They could see Rutledge ahead. "I knew she would hold it," said Sischo, her shoe upper fastened to her foot by the gummy guck. "The mud sucked you in," said Fanning. "There was no bounce."

Rutledge knew Sisco and Fanning would hold it. "I had to smile. I couldn't help it," Rutledge said, when she noticed her teammates close. "Then I went back to racing."

They came upon Aris screaming. 'Saugus!" he yelled. "They're coming! They're right behind you!" Sischo didn't know whether to believe him, but she wanted to, anything for a spur. "Jill and I made an audible noise and turned the wheels on," she said.

When the intermediate team scores were announced, they were too absurd to be taken seriously. Did Saugus ever show up? They did, but before the race Paragas had whispered to me, "We're running for second." I had never heard something like that uttered from a top coach before.

Martin, running the race of her life, the race that made her equal parts sprinter *and* distance runner, was the fourth F-M girl, and within sight of Sischo and Fanning. The timid little girl who had once been scared shitless by a growl from Molly Malone kept thinking, in the middle of Portland Meadows, "Wow, this is so much fun." Opponents' bodies were caving in around her, there were no Saugus girls to be seen, and Martin was having a ball.

And it was a no-guilt treat, putting her ahead of Chapman, who'd encouraged it. At F-M number five, Chapman, holding her team gift close, knew her mono or flu or whatever-the-heck-it-was senior destiny was sealed, and so her only focus was, "Pass one girl, then another, then . . ." In her new role as closer, she had time to think and realized, "I don't always have to be the strongest. I don't always have to give. I can take, too."

Finally, Rutledge had company. The South Regional champion, Rachel Johnson of Texas, drew up to her. Johnson, a senior at Plano High, outside Dallas, was the latest Texas product to rise nationally. In 2008, a Texas boy and girl swept the NXN individual titles. In 2009, a Texas boy, and boys team, triumphed. Johnson had started cautiously and found her fitness midway. In fact, Johnson's stamina seemed unlimited. In 2009, she'd run both NXN and Foot Locker, and both regionals, four races in a row, and was doing the same this year.

Johnson, competing as an individual, used aggressive arm action to stick with Rutledge. Rutledge pulled away by ten meters. Johnson pulled her back. Rutledge was still baked in disbelief. Then play got rough, subduing her. "I didn't feel a need to 'beat' her," Rutledge said.

In the last kilometer, after one more round of hay bales, Johnson inched ahead and used her sub-5:00 mile speed to gain a decisive edge. Rutledge had no pure speed. "She was probably the slowest varsity girl I ever coached," said Aris.

As the two girls, the Texan and the New Yorker, ran for home toward Nike's Finish on Empty banner, Sischo, down the finish straight, felt her shoe finally slip off. "I was relieved, but I think I could have done better with two shoes," she offered.

Johnson won it in 18:19. Rutledge finished second in 18:22. Sischo and Fanning came into view. Rutledge was in tears. It was Sischo, fourth in the country, in 18:50, and Fanning sixth, in 18:52, for seven team points thus far. Martin was coming. And Chapman! The top five were either in or coming, everyone . . . across the line. Martin placed sixteenth, ahead of many state champions, and *every Saugus girl*, in 19:13. Chapman completed the scoring in twenty-ninth, running 19:37. She had learned to *take* with serenity and grace.

Where would the soaring voices come from? Perhaps from the girl whose concerto fingers struggled against the cold while dabbing her moist red cheeks.

Give the poets their say, but this one belonged to Ms. Rutledge, encapsulating five years of Fayetteville-Manlius outwitting the modern world. In harvesting her desires, she revealed a bit more of the F-M exploration into the teenage human.

Christie Rutledge: from last on her team to second in the nation. She'd found her true self in the coalition of goodness that was the Aris mission. Didn't all these girls find that, treated like athletes who could do anything? There was no model for what these girls had become.

Rutledge could feel realness all day long. Tickled by morning runs before school when she would pop out of bed at five o'clock to embrace the dawn; bliss at dusk coming home from practice muddy and exhausted. "It was everything I could ask for, everything I needed," she said.

"I still can't believe it," her mother told me that day at Portland Meadows. "My daughter taught me a lot."

Beyond the finish-area corral: tears and hugs. Hugs from Bill. *Daddy, grandpa, coach, psychologist, philosopher, preacher, teacher, maestro*. Mud everywhere: on eyelashes, noses, earlobes. Energy gone: finish on empty. Paradoxes: flawed perfection. Luminous chaos. Legs bloody from spike wounds, the blood congealed by cold.

All of Portland Meadows knew the F-M girls had won. They mounted the makeshift stage—Rutledge, Sisco, Fanning, Martin, and Chapman, along with their sixth and seventh runners, McGurrin and Brislin—for the on-site awards in bare feet after their cooldown. Saugus and Saratoga Springs joined Fayetteville on the podium.

The announcement came: Saugus third with 117 points, Saratoga second with 104, and Fayetteville-Manlius, champion for the fifth year in a row with . . . *twenty-seven points.*

It was almost too much to bear. Among the 154 team runners, F-M had scored 1-2-4-8-12 for five of the nation's top dozen team places. Twenty-seven points, an inconceivable score. Twenty-seven points, *beating the entire rest of the country scored as an all-star team*, 27–30. Twenty-seven points, achieved by outrunning Saratoga by fifty-nine seconds per girl in a 5k race, and Saugus, the greatest California team ever, by fifty-six seconds per girl. Team averages were Fayetteville 18:59, Saratoga 19:58, Saugus, 19:55. F-M swept the runner-up Saratoga, placing all five scorers ahead of Saratoga's first girl.

That last coup was cemented by the fifth scorer, Chapman, less than capacity but thirteen seconds ahead of Saratoga's first girl. "Instead of Bill telling future teams about the original Stotans," said Chapman, referring to the tales she'd heard at her first nationals in 2006, "I wanted him to have new stories, new cross-country myths about the girls team, about amazing athletes coming together to achieve inhuman feats."

On this day of discovery, of symphonic power, Sischo also saw the lessons of history come to bear. "We ran that race for the years and years of Stotans, male and female, that came before us," she said. "Also for the Stotans to come. And for Bill, who had fought for this. It was a gift for him. We were athletes, but we were also high school kids. He gave so much to us, and we wanted to be able to give something back."

Fayetteville-Manlius Defeats the Nation
If Assembled As One All-Star Team

Fayetteville-Manlius	Time	Pts	The Rest of the Country	Time	Pts
Christie Rutledge	18:22	1	Haley Pierce (DE)	18:51	3
Katie Sischo	18:50	2	Caroline Hardin (MT)	18:54	5
Jillian Fanning	18:52	4	Samantha Nadel (NY)	19:02	6
Heather Martin	19:13	8	Annemarie Maag (OR)	19:13	7
Courtney Chapman	19:37	12	Erin Hooker (CO)	19:17	9
	TOTAL: 27 points			**TOTAL: 30 points**	
F-M average time: 18:59			*Nation average time: 19:03*		

19

EMOTIONAL RESCUE

I will never forget the rush. I'm thinking, "Oh my God, I'm leading nationals."

—*Jillian Fanning, Fayetteville-Manlius cross-country runner*

2011 Season

A kid from Texas who played middle school football moved to Manlius and appeared on Bill Aris's doorstep as a freshman. Summer training was almost over, and the cross-country doors were closed. The kid begged to join the team after realizing that at five feet eight and 120 pounds he was too small for high school football, even in New York. Aris gave him a shot. But the kid couldn't hack it—any of it, like racing in the snow, which he'd never seen—and quit after the fall season. He disappeared for three years, returning to the team as a senior having undergone a metamorphosis. He was now a mileage junkie, said Aris, one who would drive himself beyond warning signs. Late in the season, the kid suffered a stress fracture and had to walk with a protective boot, which he discarded to compete in the championship events, crucial to team success.

"In Houston," the kid said, "cross-country was not a respected sport."

A top girl on the team who fielded criticism for her sacrifices and hard work from friends playing volleyball and field hockey fell asleep in the F-M tent, taking an unintended nap, before the biggest race of the regular season. She made it to the starting line, flew into the lead, but panicked since there were no course marshals directing her on the descending switchbacks of the wooded trails. Weeks later, at championship time, when the boy in the boot competed with a fractured metatarsal bone, the girl ran with the initials of two teammates penned on her wrist as a reminder of who she was running for and what the season had become.

"I was powered by selflessness," she said. "Every race was run for my teammates."

Forget the girls' historic twenty-seven points. Throw out the boys national runner-up performance. That was then. This was now: 2011. "No legacy," Aris always said. Like "risking failure" or "shared suffering," "no legacy" was a team standard. Aris started calculating the next season after the paint was barely dry on the previous one.

No legacy ran through Stotan precepts like rainwater flooding the Portland Meadows turf. No complacency. No big heads, only big hearts. Feast on the process, plan anew. Each season's end was a new beginning: new learning and, hopefully, even greater empowerment. Each team was like a new family—brittle, vulnerable, irresistible, hard to read, harder to transform. Each kid took time. New ideas, always, and never let them become dogma.

That's why Aris wrote nothing down. He wanted a blank canvas.

Were these the F-M girls who'd won five national championships in a row by record point scores, record victory margins, and record team times, sweeping away running's limits? Were these the boys with three NXN podium performances and two more appearances in a seven-year stretch? In the craw of the opposition, yes, but not in the Fayetteville-Manlius locker room or weight room, in the coach's office, and certainly not on Gulf Road, where mortals dare tread only with hundreds of miles in their legs.

"Each team," said Aris, "was a totally new operation. I could not take the idealism of the original 2004 boys and just put a Stotan label on the new bunch as though they were the same. I had to speak with a subtly different dialect each year. This also kept it fresh for the athletes and for myself. Each athlete perceived and interpreted Stotan concepts in a different way."

And often, as the years went by, with less enthusiasm to start. Bedrock Stotan families did not always materialize, and teenage culture became less resilient, vexing Aris. He used to mold the athletes to fit Stotan principles; now, more often, he did the opposite: adapting the principles to fit the team. "Training was the easy part," he said. "The hard part was unlocking the doors of each kid's mind."

Even Green Lakes was different, or so it seemed. Was it the wind or morning dew, or did the hills feel steeper yet? Was it the athletes and how they ran God's Country or Pump House or circled Round Lake, taking command or giving in, knowing themselves or questioning? Maybe it was the team, all together, how they strode the Serengeti, with a new vitality or a laboring, reimagining the sumptuous trails with a welcoming spirit or dread.

Either way, one's mind had to be fertile. As Cerutty said, first cultivate "purity, beauty and logic," and only then will you possess the breadth to seek excellence and know what it takes to achieve it. Aris started from scratch. Which minds were open, and which needed work? How would he cultivate a boys team with only one proven runner; and a girls team of veterans poised to inculcate the next generation but not expecting the need for emergency measures and T-shirts expressing their emotional fortitude?

∽

The kid from Houston was Matt Deyo. "I didn't even know who he was," said Nick Ryan, now a junior. "But Matt became the biggest catalyst for what our team had." Ryan was keen on regaining the state title that had eluded the boys in 2010 and prompted his calling-out monologue after the race. Referring to 2011, Ryan said, "Our other guys were not focused on working hard. Deyo loved to work. Every idea I had he backed up and then some."

What had driven Deyo from the team as a freshman was not only the snow. He competed in one meet that twice took the field through a freezing, waist-high creek like soldiers negotiating a river in a war movie. Deyo didn't even have spikes, which did not endear him to Aris. In his last JV race, Deyo ran 22:24 for 5k, placing forty-fifth out of sixty-nine, and called it a season.

Word got around a year later that Deyo had taken to running the roads on his own. The grapevine exaggerated his running to the point where Aris heard that Deyo "was doing gargantuan mileage." When I caught up with Deyo years later, he said he did forty miles a week, nothing more, and enjoyed road racing against adults. He would run about thirty road races his sophomore and junior years, from the 5k to half marathon. He notched some victories while breaking sixty minutes for ten miles and seventeen minutes for 5k. A favorite was the Ithaca Skunk Cabbage Half Marathon.

Deyo was now ready for cross-country, and when he bumped into Aris at a road race, he took the coach's invitation to return. By this time, Deyo was a top student with a keen intellect, inspired to serve team and country whenever called. For now, team was enough, and Ryan was delighted to have Deyo at his side after the tumultuous 2010 season in which, as Ryan looked back, different "friend groups" based on talent, age, and personality could not settle their differences.

Deyo's gung-ho approach was a mixed blessing. He was a closet trainer, according to Aris, doing extra runs on his own. "My challenge was to keep him healthy," said Aris. Deyo had his own challenge: "Never complain, never show weakness."

In track the previous spring, Ryan had run a 9:11.86 3200, making him the third-fastest sophomore in the country in 2011. Ryan was excited to be named one of the cross-country captains for fall and took that stature into racing, winning the opening meet, the Vernon-Verona-Sheril (VVS) Invitational, on the season's state-meet course. With Deyo in third twenty-two seconds behind, F-M had the strong one-two it hoped for. The rest of the team—"peripherals," Aris called them—wasn't half bad. Fitness levels varied, and varsity positions were in flux. They all ran under seventeen minutes.

Ryan carried his gallantry, and Deyo his optimism, into the Manhattan Eastern States championship at Van Cortlandt Park. All of cross-country, in the Bronx and beyond, was keyed on whether Edward Cheserek, the mighty Kenyan from New Jersey, could better twelve minutes for the two-and-a-half-mile course. The record stood at 12:03.77. Sub-12:00 at Vanny was high school cross-country's four-minute mile.

Risking failure to see where he stood against the nation's best, Ryan followed Cheserek and his breakneck pace into the hills until, about a kilometer out, he could take no more. Ryan sunk back practically into Deyo's arms, and the two of them raced closely to the finish as Cheserek achieved his Roger Bannister moment: 11:55.39, winning by twenty-five seconds. Ryan was fifth in 12:50.20 and Deyo eighth in 12:55.00.

Deyo was ecstatic running so close to Ryan, and Ryan was pleased that he'd learned what he needed to do to try and get closer to the likes of Cheserek. Ryan also liked that with Deyo on his tail, he was no longer "untouchable" in the minds of teammates, who now took shots at him at practice, making everyone that much stronger. As a team, Fayetteville placed second to old nemesis Christian Brothers, ranked in the top five nationally.

Two years later, Deyo would have been able to converse with Cheserek in his native tongue. Then at MIT, Deyo was an aerospace-engineering major, as well as a member of the air force ROTC. Deyo was sent in a group mission by the US Department of Defense to spend a summer traveling through Kenya while learning Swahili. "It was considered a 'strategic' language," said Deyo. Ironically, while running track and cross-country for the Engineers—a Division 3 all-American and team captain—Deyo barely ran a step in Kenya.

With Cheserek's historic run, I could not help but think back almost a half century to when the first high school runners broke *thirteen* minutes. The course was slower then, pockmarked with debris, and cross-country had no panache, rather like its status in present-day Houston.

After meets, officials would repair to a local joint known as the Dutchman's. Pints flowed, some in recognition of the city's Dutch heritage, notably the Van Cortlandts, their burial plots near Cemetery Hill. The crypt itself, on what's called Vault Hill, is an unkempt, gated square on which a sign reads:

MY BODY I COMMIT TO THE EARTH TO BE BURIED IN A FAMILY
VAULT WHICH I INTEND TO BUILD ON MY PLANTATION . . .
FREDERICK VAN CORTLANDT, 1699–1749.

Eventually, the Dutchman's became no more, replaced as a landmark by a bakery known for its carrot cakes, situated across the finish line on Broadway. The bakery became a tourist attraction, especially after a 2010 *New York Times* story told of its international popularity as it filled orders from China, Costa Rica, and points in between.

At its races, the Van Cortlandt Park Track Club typically awarded the shop's carrot cakes instead of medals or trophies. The high school crowd stuck with hardware, and as the Fayetteville girls lined up for the Easterns, they raced for a fifth-straight title. The winning trophies, taller than a high hurdle, stood as regal endowments in Aris's office back in Manlius.

After her Bronx nap, a premeet first, Jillian Fanning, now a junior, emerged from the F-M tent and into the sunlight. With more than three hundred schools competing, there were at least a hundred team tents, from bare-bones operations to those with catering setups, and maybe some of that carrot cake. "I was completely calm," said Fanning.

Fanning had every right to her autumnal bliss. The previous season, in track—after placing sixth in the country at NXN—Fanning ran on F-M distance medley relay foursomes that won indoor nationals and Penn Relays and took second at outdoor nationals in state-record time. It was an unprecedented DMR triple. Fanning ran the anchor 1600 on the first two and the lead-off 1200 on the last one, as departing senior Courtney Chapman was assigned anchor duty in Greensboro before going on to Villanova. The other two girls in the relay lineup were Katie Sischo in the 800 and Heather Martin in the 400.

Fanning (9:43.20 3,000), Martin (2:11.28 800), and Chapman (4:23.01 1500) all captured state outdoor championship bronze medals that June. Chapman's time ranked her fifth in the nation. She'd competed against Mary Cain, fast becoming a cause célèbre as a fifteen-year-old Bronxville High sophomore in suburban New York. With an array of age records starting in middle school, Cain won in a state-record 4:17.84, with more fireworks to come, on and off the track, before long.

For their performances going back to cross-country, Fanning and Sischo, along with 2010 national runner-up Christie Rutledge, had all attended the annual Nike Elite Camp for high school distance runners on the Nike campus in Beaverton that summer of 2011. The camp was mainly a preseason honorific, with about ten girls and ten boys from across the country. No team had ever had three invitees from the same gender in the same year.

Martin was supposed to come as well, but camp organizers lost their nerve about having four athletes from one school. It was more bad luck for Martin. At indoor nationals at the New York Armory, her bag with her uniform and spikes was stolen shortly before the race. Martin cried. Aris panicked. A teammate gave her a uniform, and meet sponsor New Balance came through with a pair of spikes that Martin got to keep. She raced angry and fast.

This Fayetteville quartet, Fanning-Sischo-Rutledge-Martin—the 2-4-6-16 national placers the previous year—was a returning armada never imagined for one cross-country team. With F-M keeping to itself at NXN in 2010, Sischo found it a treat to mix with Nike camp peers in the summer of '11. They took the opportunity to try and uncover F-M techniques. "We don't have any secrets to tell you," Sischo would answer. Based on what Sischo found, one "secret" was apparent to her: "We saw others not living the lives we were living."

When the campers would go out for runs, Rutledge, however, could not join them. The previous winter, doing sprints at the end of a road workout, she'd slipped on a patch of ice and felt intense pain in her right leg. Rutledge limped back to school and took a couple of days off. The pain worsened, affecting her hip, gluteus, and low back. She proceeded to see one doctor after another, even traveling to New York for gait analysis. She underwent physical therapy. Nothing worked. No running for weeks, then months.

Without running as an emotional safety net and depressed over not being as engaged with teammates—her true friends—Rutledge fell back into the eating disorder that had developed years before. "Running was so natural to me," she said. "Now it was taken away."

Rutledge agreed to speak openly with me about her disease. I have written often, in the New York Times and elsewhere, about the scourge of eating disorders.

Christie's physical pain and emotional pain would be joined for years in a cycle of turmoil and despair. She only wanted to be herself, the little girl running barefoot in the woods, unrestrained by the judgements of others.

Christie was bulimic and went for counseling but hated it. She was embarrassed, attempting to mask her issues. That season, Christie, five feet five, found her weight plummet to ninety-five pounds, twenty pounds less than normal levels. Her parents insisted she gain weight. Doing her best, Christie would get back up to 110; then, she would fall back down into the nineties. At the Nike camp that summer, when everyone else was running, Christie would go vomit.

Once back in Manlius, Christie managed to get in some modest training. Not one to lean on teammates or the coach, she would keep her problems to herself. However, Christie's severe weight fluctuations and general listlessness were apparent. Her close friends on the team, as well as Aris, had seen eating disorders in the sport before and sensed Christie had become a victim. Because of the complex issues involved, no one attempted to intervene for fear of intruding on Christie's delicate psyche and risk making her situation worse. Besides, Christie herself tried to summon optimism. "I would just hope," she said. "If I just ignored it, maybe it would go away." With her training modified, Christie was still able to take second behind Fanning in the VVS meet, running 18:23. Afterward, Christie could not hide her limping. "I was so sad," she said. "I would go cry."

❧

Fanning's Bronx calm didn't last long. Leading the Eastern States from the gun, she climbed Freshman Hill then shot across the bridge above the Henry

Hudson Parkway and into the pressing ascent of the Back Hills. Then it was up and over the last ridge and onto the creviced downhills, a test of daring with a bit of orienteering thrown in. Course markings were not always evident at race pace. "I kept thinking, 'Please, God, don't let me get lost back here,'" Fanning recalled.

The thought of it—Fanning flying on steep, curvy pitches and doubting her way—gave Aris fits. "I love tough courses," he said. "But Van Cortlandt was the most treacherous course I'd ever seen. How do I tell a kid, 'You can't be afraid, you can't backpedal. You have to attack.' Yet I do it every year."

Fanning found her way, body intact, and raced to victory by nineteen seconds in 14:03.8. She thus established herself as a national contender. Fayetteville was a 45–83 victor over Tatnall, a rising Delaware private school. Sischo, freshman Annika Avery, Martin, and junior Hannah Smith completed the F-M scoring. Because of the downhills, Aris kept Rutledge out. Soon, seeing her condition, Aris put a stop to her fall season.

Two weeks later, at a Green Lakes workout on Halloween, Martin felt pain on the outside of her right foot. That night she sat in her kitchen with her foot in an ice bucket while trick-or-treaters rang the doorbell. With continued pain, Martin went to the doctor, but an X-ray showed nothing. A day later, an MRI revealed a stress fracture in the cuboid bone, which helped stabilize the foot. Martin embarked on standard protocol: a protective boot for six weeks with crutches for two weeks, and no running for eight weeks.

The girls felt lost. The healthy ones cried over the injured ones; the injured ones felt guilty leaving their teammates. It didn't take much for Rutledge to feel guilty. She was always blaming herself for something. How would the team make up for the losses? Aris relied on his Nietzsche quote: "That which does not kill us makes us stronger."

Sischo was the only senior still running. She realized it was her team now—hers and Jillian's. She had looked to the older girls, like Chapman, brimming, she said, with emotional intelligence. "Now the younger women were looking to us," she said. "You never know who will be in the top seven."

That was never truer as the state championships approached. Sischo, who herself was dealing with plantar fascia issues, schooled the apprentices on everyday discomforts. "When you become a serious runner, 'everything' hurts," she told them. "You're a Stotan, you power through." They learned to distinguish between pain and fatigue. Aris called that precipitous understanding the "razor blade walk."

Earlier, Aris had assigned the team to read *Unbroken*, the bestselling World War II saga of the Olympic runner and air force pilot Lou Zamperini. The girls decided to dedicate their performances to Christie and Heather. They had T-shirts made up with the saying UNBREAKABLE, and inscribed the two girls' initials on it.

In addition, Bill's father, John, had taken ill. Two days before state he passed away. Bill was back and forth to his parents' home in Connecticut, comforting his mother and helping with final arrangements. He would try and make it to state. "I'm having a hard time," he told the team at practice. "I want you to know because you're like members of my family. I don't want you to feel bad. With or without me, support each other on Saturday."

The team was now running for Bill and his father as well.

With Fanning winning by an astounding forty seconds, Fayetteville scored a perfect fifteen points in state Class A to sweep runner-up Saratoga Springs for the third-straight year. The VVS course was muddy, and Fanning pushed as never before. Aris was able to be there. At the finish, Fanning collapsed into Bill's arms, telling him, "This one was for you." Aris wept.

After Fanning, and Sischo, the team's second finisher, the rest of F-M was like a summer-stock troupe taking the Broadway stage: Avery right behind Sischo, then, close enough, Smith, sophomore Alana Pearl, junior Katie Brislin, and the plucky eighth grader, Jenna Farrell, the team's number six.

As the team's seventh runner at NXN the previous year, Brislin was the only one of the five with nationals experience. She lived in Manlius and had attended Christian Brothers Academy in Syracuse for three years before transferring to F-M in 2010. With his nicknaming predilections, Aris decided to christen Brislin "Kabaa," after her CBA lineage. The name seemed innocent enough at the time.

At state, the boys could only envy the girls' depth. Ryan captured his first state championship by twenty-six seconds. Deyo, fit from biking, tossed his fracture boot aside and came through admirably in third. It was twenty seconds back to F-M's number three, Ben Thomas, and another twelve seconds to freshman Bryce Millar, the fastest ninth grader of the meet.

Deyo had kept up with Ryan early on as the VVS course wound through a cornfield and forest. Finding the pace too rich, Deyo eased back to the chase group, securing Ryan's lead by exerting control over the tempered opposition—which at one point could no longer see Ryan. It was impressive strategy for the kid from Houston, who finished a few strides out of second in taking the bronze medal.

The crucial fifth-man position worried Aris. Juniors Connor Farrell and Colin FitzGibbons—both had older brothers run for F-M and contribute at nationals—placed sixty-fourth and sixty-eighth with times over eighteen minutes. "Two peas in a pod," Aris said dismissively. Seventh man Mike Malone, a senior and brother of Molly and Maggie, was the caboose; he couldn't carry his sisters' spikes. The team result: F-M 63, Rush-Henrietta 64. A win, but . . .

To shore up for regionals, two weeks later, Aris took the team into sharpening mode: shorter runs, some added speed, and targeted hill work with emphasis on recovery, sleep, healthy meals, and stress management. Flowery lectures tightened up, touching on the ancient antagonism between instinct and reason: how gut sense melded with evidence at hand.

The boys took that battle cry on to Bowdoin Park. Everything had been accounted for. Even their weight training had been adjusted, from two sessions a week to one. Whether lifts or squats, the program was designed to build not only muscle—the muscle used in the running movement—but also energy and access to it. In all weight exercises, boys and girls alike lifted the greatest weight they could handle with perfect form for a maximum of five repetitions. This approach (as opposed to common practice of three sets of ten reps at lower weight), said Aris, produced the same A-lactate energy developed in sprinting, while enhancing use of that energy and "every other aspect of your running."

On regionals morning, the team rose at five for its shake-out run in the hotel parking lot. It was nothing unusual, said Aris, but Ryan recalled it as including some up-tempo work that seemed jarring with a big race hours hence. Maybe Ryan was just edgy. He told me he not only wanted to win but try for the course record of 15:35.5.

As the boys race unfolded, Ryan, with Deyo in tow, took a wide arc as the field funneled to the switchbacks and then the steep climb to the park's interior. Ryan pushed the pace at the front. Deyo hung on. Behind them, FitzGibbons and Farrell were walking the hill, praying, maybe for the nightmare to end, for a spark of life, for something. In the last mile, Ryan couldn't hold it and, as he put it, "the wheels came off." It was just enough for Deyo to see him and pull closer. Ryan still pushed on for the victory in sixteen minutes even and "was completely spent." Deyo took seventh in 16:16. Since the injury, he was doing his best racing. Not so counterintuitive: the overzealous workout fiend probably needed to get off his feet.

Where were the peripherals? FitzGibbons and Farrell got moving, found redemption, and, with Thomas, gave Fayetteville the minimal scoring punch necessary for second. The F-M boys earned their sixth trip to nationals. Shaker, the winner, scored 78 points. F-M had 93. Rush took third with 114.

In sync with the setting's unruliness—not a crisp foot plant to be had, river currents whipping up, trains hauling, frozen spectators huddled around an open fire—the athletes, for the first time all season, could wear whatever the heck they wanted, and not even have to tuck in their shirts. "We're not the uniform police," declared meet director Paul Limmer. "Watches, earrings, all okay. You can wear three thousand dollars' worth of jewelry if you want."

In the girls race, a revitalized Saratoga Springs team pushed Fayetteville as never before in the Stotan era. Fanning, her ears bejeweled, went out and dominated the race, running 17:48 to leave the Millrose Games mile champion Samantha Nadel of Long Island twenty-seven seconds behind, and the mile superstar, Mary Cain from New York, another five seconds back in third. While Sischo and Smith placed sixth and seventh, strides apart, Saratoga attacked Fayetteville at its own game, packing four girls within twenty-two seconds ahead of Fayetteville's fourth and fifth scorers—Pearl and Brislin.

This was serious. After Smith, it felt like an eternity before Pearl and Brislin emerged from the last curling path and onto the Bowdoin home straight. The pair allowed thirty-five and thirty-seven seconds to amass behind Smith as Fayetteville snatched a 43–57 victory. Fourteen points was nothing. In Portland, a slip in the mud could account for it.

This time, Aris did not need to use his California scare factor. While Saugus girls had collected their sixth-straight state crown, the Stotans had their hands full with Saratoga. What elixir of emotional craftsmanship could Aris concoct with four girls who had never been to Portland—an eighth grader, Farrell, the youngest girl in the field; the freshman, Avery, who'd run miserably at Bowdoin; sophomore Pearl, who'd lacked consistency; and Smith, running well but green? And a fifth, Brislin, who, fortunately, was not informed of the uproar her nickname had left behind.

Early on getaway morning, teammates not on the nationals squad did their usual due diligence by posting signs of encouragement in the athletes' front yards. Brislin's sign, naturally, was KABAA. However, it was displayed at the wrong address, the home, as it happened, of an Islamic family. There was shock and outrage.

The Kabaa, in Mecca, Saudi Arabia, is one of Islam's sacred shrines. It is a stone building within the center of the Grand Mosque, considered the House of God—the very mosque to which Muslims the world over face in prayer. The

Manlius family took the F-M sign as a religious affront. The police were noti-
fied, and while the Fayetteville runners were competing in Portland—unaware,
as was Aris—the school's athletic director spent the weekend putting out fires.

∽

Once in Portland, Ryan stayed put. No snooping around Nike corporate board-
rooms. One morning at breakfast, the Fayetteville boys got some idea of what
they were up against. They saw the favorite, Futsum Zeinasellassie of Indiana,
and watched what he ate. Zienasellassie had come to the United States from
Eritrea in 2007. African runners were known for their healthy diets. "He had a
big plate of bacon," said Deyo. "Nothing else, just bacon. We took that to mean
if he can eat whatever he wants, we're not real competition for him."

Ryan decided to test that theory. He was fitter than when he'd raced Cheserek in the Bronx. This year Cheserek was skipping NXN in favor of the next
week's Foot Locker Nationals, which he would win. For the time being, Ryan
had Zeineselassie, who would also run Foot Locker, to himself; or was it the
other way around?

It was dry, cold, and gray. Portland Meadows had seen worse days. Ryan
raced out to the lead. In no time, he would gap the field. At the half mile, Ryan's
split was 2:11 and he was ahead by fifty meters. The pack, Futsum included,
let him have it.

Ryan sought to get "a low stick," that is, one point for his team. Most in the
trailing pack were individual competitors. Ryan reasoned that the team runners
with the most to lose would be scared off by his hard pace. That proved to be
the case. Not a single team runner would chase after him.

Instead of the nationals race having a deliberate tempo that would build
toward a climax, Ryan, who lacked the primal kick of others, defined it from the
start. Would Futsum catch him at will and blow home? Aris was all for Ryan's
strategy. "You beat the kickers with brutal strength," he said.

But fifty meters? That took some chops. Futsum (what most people called
him) had won the NXN Midwest by fourteen seconds and his state finals by
forty-four seconds and had a "speed rating" (a calculus devised by Tullyrunners
webmaster Bill Meylan) that was off the charts. When Ryan breezed through
the whoop-de-doos at around three-quarters of a mile, his fifty-meter advantage
bordering on disrespect, he saw Aris. Ryan could tell that his coach was not at
ease because he said nothing and gave him a "Bill look."

Unbeknownst to Ryan, his low stick had to go lower than a limbo bar because Deyo had "froze up" at the start, slipped, and watched 198 runners dash off ahead of him. Deyo just about welcomed the challenge. "I worked and worked and worked," he said. "I enjoyed passing people." Through the hills and hay bales and looping contours, Deyo passed all of his teammates save Ryan, whom he could see challenged by Futsum midway. Ryan and Futsum briefly ran side by side. The announcer referred to Futsum as "the total package." Indiana started cross-country meets in August, and this was Futsum's thirteenth race. Might he tire?

By 3k, Futsum was gone and Ryan struggled to hold on to second. Christian Brothers and Southlake Carroll of Texas waged a two-team duel for the championship. Nike added another wrinkle to the team contest by having each team's presumed fifth scorers wear identifying wristbands so the fifth men (and women) could compete against one another for crucial points. Nice try, but the idea didn't have its desired effect. Neither did the year's Nike slogan: "Hope less. Kick more."

At least not for Ryan. He let Futsum go to conserve energy in case any team runners came up on him. In the last kilometer, three more individuals pulled ahead, but Ryan's plan worked. While Futsum won going away in 15:03, Ryan's fifth place in 15:31 was more than enough for a single team point. The second team runner, from Miami, was twentieth.

Despite his fall, Deyo capped his season only twenty-three seconds behind Ryan—closer to Ryan than Ryan was to Futsum—in 15:54. Soon he would be able to get rid of his boot. Deyo would eventually take his master's in computer science, combine that with his aerospace background, and work in the new field of "vehicle autonomy engineering."

Fayetteville placed twelfth, about as expected, and everyone in the F-M camp was happy. Perhaps happier than in 2010, when even second place could not cleanse the bad taste of the season's infighting. Ryan was happy because he felt he could come back the next year and win nationals as a senior. Aris was happy that every boy had run up to par and five of the seven would return for 2012.

Thomas (16:36), FitzGibbons (16:53), and Farrell (16:55) filled out the five scorers. Young Millar, in his first nationals, was close behind in 17:05 and showing sparks of Stotan command. In what became something of a family joke, Mike Malone's only goal was not to finish dead last. He placed 197th out of 199 with twenty-five seconds to spare. His sisters would still razz him.

In a tight team contest, CBA prevailed over Carroll, 91–95, to bring New Jersey its first championship. No other team was close. Fayetteville boys would see a lot of Carroll the next year but with tempers flaring.

∞

Malone's sister Maggie had come to Portland along with Rutledge and Martin for team support. The three girls roomed together. Martin no longer had crutches, only the boot. Rutledge, the reigning national runner-up, had nothing. "It was embarrassing," she said. "People would ask me, 'Why aren't you running?' I felt I was letting people down."

Sischo took her teammates' disappointment personally. "Two of my best friends were devastated," she lamented. "This should have been their peak, a celebratory farewell." Sischo had to contain her emotion. She had a job to do. Sischo had to make sure the new kids knew the deal—knew that "if you are not practically passing out across the finish, you had too much left."

Sischo herself would drive so hard for home she would "black out every year." With this impression of team lore, what was the child in young Jenna Farrell to think? "Growing up," Farrell told me, "Molly, Mackenzie, and Courtney were my idols," she said, referring to the Stotan badasses Malone, Carter, and Chapman that she'd watched. "To be honest, I was scared of them."

Who wouldn't be? Earlier that season, over the summer, when the three girls were home from college, the idea came up that wouldn't it be cool if the badasses posed for a reunion photo worthy of their reputations. Mackenzie's family owned a car dealership, and her father, Mark, got hold of three Harley-Davidson motorcycles. Her mom, Marnie, by then an F-M assistant coach, as well as team photographer, picked up some black leather jackets, jeans, and boots.

The girls put their outfits together and, with Marnie, went to the base of the Gulf Road climb for the shoot. The Harleys were waiting. With come-hither attitudes, long hair flowing, and, taking possession of the bikes, the girls depicted *The Wild Ones*, gender equity version. After several takes, and silly faces giving way to perfect pouting, the girls nailed it and so did Marnie.

A twenty-four-by-thirty-six-inch framed photo with inscriptions would hang in Aris's office for all to see—or, rather, bear witness. The image must have scared the pants off Farrell. In Portland, she said, she was also fearful of Fanning and Sischo. She saw how opponents would regard them with awe. They were young women. Fully grown, muscular, the next generation of badasses.

Fanning could sense Farrell's angst. Before the start, she told her, "Think about Gulf Road, how you didn't think you would finish."

The girls assembled to race with CR and HM written on their arms. "It was nothing like 2010," said Sischo, referring to her injured teammates. Katie Brislin was now expected to play a larger role. At regionals, she was the crucial number-five scorer but only ten seconds ahead of Farrell. Was Brislin still crying on Gulf Road? "Not as much," she said.

The cannon boomed, and shortly off the line Brislin went flying. Positioned in front of Farrell in the starting "box," Brislin's back leg was clipped from behind by Farrell's spike. Brislin somersaulted. "I saw my shoes and socks up in the air," she recounted, "and everyone was gone."

Brislin lay on the ground shaken. She was not hurt. Her muddy shoes were intact. Brislin rose, and with the field including Farrell sprinting away, she proceeded to do her best Lasse Virén imitation and give chase. In 1972, Virén, of Finland, famously tripped and fell in the Olympic 10,000 meters, sat on the track, got up, caught the field, and won in world-record time.

To Fayetteville, Portland Meadows was the Olympics. Brislin passed one girl, then another, then three more. The new somersault strategy! Even Aris hadn't cooked up this one. "It took the pressure off," said Brislin. "I just ran for my life without thinking."

Up front, Fanning was where she should be: in the lead pack holding steady after Samantha Nadel—the Long Islander Fanning had defeated by twenty-seven seconds at regionals—raced to a risky lead. Nadel, who'd placed ninth in 2010 and would later join Heather Martin at Georgetown, was eventually sucked back as a front assembly of five took command.

In the field's natural flow, at midway Fanning found herself a few strides ahead with Katie Knight of North Central in Spokane at her side. Then Fanning drew a meter or two on Knight. "I will never forget the rush," said Fanning, "I'm thinking, 'Oh my God, I'm leading nationals!'"

They went through the mud and hurdled the hay bales. "The Kenyans go over them seven hundred different ways," remarked commentator Lauren Fleshman, a Nike-sponsored elite runner, on the minimal hurdling finesse of Kenyans who dominated the steeplechase in track. Fleshman's point: power trumped finesse.

Not always. Coming off the second tour of the whoop-de-doos, Fanning was off-balance and her foot jammed, causing an old back-and-hip problem to reappear. "I felt it immediately," said Fanning. "My whole body shifted." Aris saw Fanning's form change; he saw her face grow weary. "Survive or surrender," Aris thought to himself.

There was a mile to go. For Fanning, first place was gone, but with Saratoga breathing down the F-M necks every team point was gold. Brislin made it all the way up to Sischo. In the second half, Pearl, Smith, and Farrell were all close by, the five of them separated by seconds. How did the fifty-second gap from Sischo to Farrell at regionals shrink by two-thirds in one week? *Every* girl running her best? On the *same* day? In *Portland*?

Was it acquired Cerutty purity, the consumption of Aris grandiloquence, or the urgency of living up to the ghostly precedent of the Biker Babes? Probably some of each, filtered through basic survival instincts in meeting peer approval.

Teammate influence, current or past, whether in muddy spikes or leather boots, can produce a two-pronged effect, according to psychologists. One is "behavioral synchrony," that in working together for peak performance athletes' brains produce greater amounts of discomfort-suppressing endorphins, than if working alone. Second, being watched by friends activates teens' reward centers; this has a snowballing effect—more watching (i.e., validation) brings more seeking of reward.

A new leader, Sarah Baxter of California, emerged, building a lead in the last kilometer. "Just finish," Fanning told herself moments later. "Eight-hundred to go. Just finish." The hope of holding that early lead, of using what Van Cortlandt had taught her, and state, and regional—runaway victories over formidable opposition—had vanished. Fanning slipped to fourth. Her body listed.

Baxter, her state's pride and joy all season, came through unchallenged with a twenty-five-meter victory in 17:38. Fanning held fourth in 17:50 as she fell into Aris's arms. Sischo and Brislin raced one another down the stretch. Sischo, black waves stealing memory, had the legs, placing twenty-first, her third-straight year as an all-American, glooming credentials to take with her to Providence. Their times were 18:26 and 18:30. Brislin ran her best race ever, a massive regionals improvement.

It was necessary. Three Saratoga girls were mixed in with the two Katies. The Blue Streaks had all five scorers in the top thirty. But with Pearl and Smith at 18:35 and 18:39, the F-M gap from Sischo to Smith was only thirteen seconds, and, adding up the team points, Fayetteville won its sixth-straight national title, 60–84, over Saratoga. The third-place team, Tatnall, was ninety-eight points farther back. Three California schools placed eleventh, twelfth, and thirteenth—that was Saugus.

With a bit more cross-country arithmetic, Fayetteville was found to achieve another can't-believe-it distinction. Take away F-M number-one Fanning and the team still would have won. The next five girls from Sischo through Farrell (who ran 18:40 on Smith's heels), if scored as a team, tallied seventy-eight points. Farrell, of all people, brought her team a sweet flourish.

"That race mimicked our whole season," said Aris. "Against all odds."

The triumph in its aftermath had a different feeling than others past. While the girls amazed themselves—"I couldn't believe we pulled it off," said Sischo—the enterprise was not quite whole. It bore conflicting emotions, a lingering tug of regret.

When the seven F-M girls took the on-field podium for the awards, they made sure Martin and Rutledge joined them and also received victory jackets presented the winning teams. Martin, her boot wrapped in a Wegmans bag because of the mud, looked ahead to her recovery when she could run track and get ready for college. Martins's first run back would be one mile on Christmas Day. Rutledge looked empty but tried to strike a positive chord. "Things will get better," she told herself. "I'll be fine."

∽

In track that senior year, Rutledge ran through pain while still in the throes of bulimia. "I tried to suck it up," she said. Doctors still had no diagnosis for her pain and, as such, never told Rutledge not to run. In order to race, she would mask her condition. Rutledge had some good performances, at 3,000 meters, but after, she said, "my right side would shut down." While at times thinking the pain was "in her head," she was often massaging her right glute, to the point where teammates told her she had "grumpy butt syndrome."

Rutledge still managed excellent grades and went on to Dartmouth. In 2012 cross-country as a freshman, she ran two excellent opening races as the Big Green's number-two woman behind NCAA champion and would-be 2016 Olympian Abbey D'Agostino. Former Olympic marathoner Mark Coogan was the Dartmouth coach. He gave Rutledge a freshman award for her early performances.

However, Rutledge's leg pain and bulimia worsened, and her cross-country season ended. After that, still hiding the worst, she managed to run two early-season indoor track races, a 3,000 and a 5,000. Her season ended again. Rutledge underwent therapy with a Dartmouth "treatment team" but to no avail.

In the spring of 2013, with no other options, Rutledge left Dartmouth on a "personal leave" for a residential treatment center in St. Louis. It was a three-month program. She said the corrective measures were "too fast" to be effective, but as an "eager-to-please, perfect patient," she gave therapists the impression she was better.

Rutledge returned to Dartmouth but not to running. She relapsed, and got depressed and sick. In late summer, Rutledge left Dartmouth again for another residential treatment center, this time in Miami, where she would stay for a year and a half. She was monitored constantly. One day Rutledge felt so claustrophobic she escaped the facility and hid by climbing a tree. "I just wanted to move and be free," she said. After a few hours, before the police were called, Rutledge returned.

But, Rutledge said, in those eighteen months she gradually got better. Rutledge left the center in 2015, stayed in Miami, and got a job in a bike shop. She got hooked on cycling and felt her best in years. She even resumed running and started swimming. She met like-minded people of all ages who became her friends. She decided to resume college at the University of Miami. Rutledge felt she never "fit in" at Dartmouth and transferred her credits. Her major was psychology with a bio minor. She was premed.

Rutledge became a member of three training groups. Her new friends talked her into triathlon. She did "brick" workouts like ten-mile runs after long bike rides. In April 2016, Rutledge won the age twenty-to-twenty-four division in a Half Ironman, known as 70.3, in Miami. Her time was four hours fifty-six minutes, and she'd qualified for the world championships in Australia. She didn't go.

After the race, Rutledge's physical pain returned. Months later, finally with a diagnosis, doctors told Rutledge she had fractures at the bottom of her hip bones, labrum tears on both sides, and torn hamstrings on both sides at her gluteal attachments, known as the ischial tuberosity. Her longstanding nutritional deficiencies probably played a role in her musculoskeletal breakdown, she said. In 2017, Rutledge underwent two rare "double surgeries,"—right side, then left—in May and August, to attempt to mend her back to normal.

When we spoke, Rutledge was several months into aggressive daily rehab. She'd started a little biking. After the intensive therapy she had learned to come to terms with her issues of identity and self-image and felt renewed freedom to be who she wanted and do what nurtured her soul. She better understood what she valued most: a connection to people who would embrace

her without condition and to be fully engaged in . . . "some *thing*." A passion, she said: being able to serve the need to move her body, as she had as
a child, as she had with her teammates at Green Lakes, running to the end
of the world.

During a tough spell in therapy, Rutledge had called Bill Aris for support.
He told her to think about how she went from a thirty-minute 5k runner to
second in the nation. She could conquer this, too. "That's how I got through my
treatment," she said. "I told myself, 'You can be good from here.'"

At last check, in the spring of 2018, Rutledge, twenty-four, had graduated
from Miami and was applying to medical school. She told me her eating issues
were gone. Rutledge wanted to become an orthopedic surgeon specializing in
sports medicine. She said she had a perfect GPA and had nailed the MCATs.
Like swinging from the trees.

20

MUD IN YOUR EYE

We are strong. We are free. How high is up?
—*Fayetteville-Manlius cross-country runners screaming*
out on the Serengeti plain

2012 Season

Scene I:
How do you choreograph a dance in the mud, perhaps the worst
mud ever for a cross-country race? Create a ballet no less. If you're
Bill Aris, you send off running ballerinas impervious to the tumult
in their midst.

Scene II:
How do you contain chaos in the mud? Prevent punches in a
swamp? Mud wrestling had come to Nike Cross Nationals, but this
was no fraternity prank. Macho madness lashed out like a primal
scream as arms and legs battled furiously for space, and no one gave
an inch. Aris was helpless.

∽

"Mud and goose crap," Aris said. "Sloppy, disgusting, warm, liquid mud."

"We were trained in mud for that kind of race for six months," said Katie Brislin, a senior in 2012, shrugging off the ubercrazy nationals conditions at Portland Meadows. Brislin, who used to devour Sour Patch Kids at races before learning the healthful Stotan ways, got herself into such fitness that year she led the girls in a sixteen-mile training run on roads that swooped up and down mountainous terrain to a radio tower. Brislin averaged 6:35 per mile—a darn good half marathon and then some.

That fall, Nick Ryan was so fit he did his average daily training runs—the lingua franca of nonworkout days—at 5:45 per mile and was being talked about as a nationals favorite. But before he could act on it, Ryan was facedown in the runners' goose-crap stew, a Portland Meadows specialty that would finally lead to a change of venue two years later. "I had mud underneath my contact lens," said Ryan, a senior in his last cross-country season for F-M. "I couldn't quite see."

What the Fayetteville runners would always see were the elements inseparable from the running, the blessings bestowed by life's wonders—the feel and taste and perfume of nature—presented by their coach. For Fayetteville, and Fayetteville alone, Nike Cross Nationals was not a two-part engagement: practice all season in the unfettered world of institutional design and then—ooops—jump into goose crap. F-M walked the walk, ran the run, deep into the uncivilized world, day by day, always with a little mud under their fingernails if not their contact lenses.

Like the time late in the season when the team added a flourish to a Serengeti workout at Green Lakes. Pressing at championship-level race effort, the runners climbed one sopping hill after another for over an hour, relentless in pursuit of exhaustion. Then, feeling they could do no more, the athletes were awarded an Aris provocation: the finisher.

Aris had the team meet him on a section of the lower Serengeti at the junction of the Cerutty Trail and Lydiard Trail in the back of the park. The Serengeti; Cerutty; Lydiard; the names alone summoned one's best. Harkening back to a workout the original Stotans mastered in 2004 and prefacing it with nuggets of Stotan folklore like truffles from a Viennese table, Aris instructed the boys and girls to tackle one last hill, a steep, rocky pitch, and wait for him at the top.

The effort would not end with the last gasps of air.

"From that perch at the top of the hill," Aris told the troupe, "look at the landscape below: the towns and the homes. Look at the sky and horizon." On a clear day you could see all the way to Lake Ontario. "Soak it all in," Aris said. "Look and listen. Think of the work you've done for months, summer and fall, and how you are ready to conquer the running world."

The coach was not done.

With a specter of light finding its human target, and the runners' faces a coppery glow in the dusk, Aris delivered a closing decree even Cerutty never thought of. "I told them that when they took in the landscape, the fading sun, the colors, nature at its best," said Aris, "they should think of something meaningful to them as individuals, something to inspire their teammates, and they should scream it out to the world and across the horizon to the heavens."

The athletes, boys and girls, ran the last long ascent with newfound powers. And, with Fayetteville and Manlius, and Skaneateles and Syracuse, below—with the sky above and the mud below—they screamed out to the darkening sky.

"I can picture it," said Alana Pearl, a junior who'd joined the team as a freshman after her family had moved from Virginia. "We affirmed the seriousness of the endeavor. And of our friendship, how much we enjoyed each other." Brislin agreed, saying, "We put a stamp on the workout."

The runners did not shout en masse. They took turns spontaneously, calling out declarations one by one at the summit of the Serengeti plains: "We are strong." "We are free." And, an Aris rhetorical favorite, "How high is up?"

"It felt good to yell," said Jillian Fanning, a senior team leader who'd run on the last three national-championship squads but was now struggling with injuries. "We always had targets on our backs. Screaming out all together felt empowering."

∽

When Ryan finished his junior track season a few months before, the target on his back could be seen for miles. In the state championships at nearby Cicero-North Syracuse High School, Ryan ran the 3200 in the meet's opening day and came back in the next day's 1600. Ryan's workouts predicted fast times. "Destroy nine minutes," said Aris, referring to the 3200. "That's what we'd trained for."

To achieve that goal, Ryan had to mirror the ballsy, front-running pace of his Stotan predecessors—Owen Kimple, Alex Hatz, and Tommy Gruenewald, his role model. That was the plan. But at the start Ryan decided on his own to sit and kick, and as he passed the halfway point in a timid 4:38, Aris was stunned at the surprise before his eyes. What happened to risking failure? Aris expected Ryan to run a Herb Elliott–style race. That's what F-M runners did. Instead he ran "normal."

Ryan breezed home with a 4:25 second half to win comfortably in 9:03.81, for his first state title. He knew Aris hoped for more. "Bill thought I could run 8:50," Ryan said. When Nick boarded the team bus the next day for the 1600, Aris offered salvation, telling him, "Your sins will be forgiven if you break 4:06."

In the 1600, Ryan atoned. In the rain, on a puddle-strewn track, he went out hard, controlled the race from the front, and came home in a nationally ranked 4:05.24, a state-meet record and faster than Kimple, Hatz, and Gruenewald had ever run. Aris had no patience for art—the running art—that was not taken seriously. "Bill gave me a big hug. I've never seen him so excited," said Ryan.

The field had not lied down for Ryan either. He had to outrun the Millrose Games indoor mile champion, Zavon Watkins of Liverpool, one of the nation's top 800 runners. Speedwise, Watkins could run rings around Ryan. Ryan had to burn him off, and he did by two full seconds, a good fifteen meters. "It was the greatest track race I've ever witnessed by a high school boy," Aris declared.

Weeks later, Ryan, along with Fanning, took a return visit to the summer's Nike Elite Camp in Oregon. The session was keyed to the Olympic Trials in Eugene, where the campers ran a celebratory mile, more showcase than competition, and both Ryan and Fanning placed in midfield. "We were eating pizza and ice cream the night before," said Ryan.

In the starstruck milieu of Hayward Field, Fanning found herself watching the trials competition one day while steeplechaser Evan Jager, track's rock star (at least to teenage girls), sat behind her. With her pulse racing harder than it did in the camp mile, Fanning took a picture with Jager, who made his first Olympic team in 2012 and, years later, broke many hearts when he married his Swedish girlfriend.

Ryan had rock-star qualities himself. But he would not let his accolades define him. While Ryan had to do the most rigorous workouts on his own, he collected teammates in need of a boost for the team's aerobic base work, the hour and two-hour runs and everything in between. "Nick may have been elite, but he wasn't elitist," said Aris.

As the first of four Ryan siblings to join the team, Nick brought a dutiful upbringing into the program. His father, Tim, was a school superintendent at a nearby district. His mother, Pat, worked at a YMCA as group-exercise coordinator. They had swimming in the family, and that's how Nick started out. Once Nick was running and the Ryans were informed about clean Stotan eating, Pat emptied her pantry of premade, packaged foods that were convenient with four kids to feed.

While Nick was trim, he was also powerful from F-M weight training. He could deadlift 345 pounds. Nick carried his size well, moving with grace on the toughest hills, even on Gulf Road. On some runs he collared the rising sophomore Bryce Millar, who'd played middle school football in seventh grade, and the two of them would cut quite a brawny figure running the Gulf Road ten-miler in a startling fifty-three minutes as teammates struggled to keep them in sight.

The rich pace was a risk for Millar. It was a long season and he was barely fifteen. Other boys, too, tried to join the party, on less audacious grounds. Teenage impulse would create a pack, but all at once? Aris worried that the boys' agreeable hunger for more had a "suicidal" edge that the team could ill afford. Ryan, after all, was the only established runner. The other boys returning from the Nike Cross Nationals lineup—Colin FitzGibbons, Connor Farrell, and Millar—had placed 149th, 157th, and 166th respectively in Portland in 2011.

With Ryan highly recruited and taking his college visits in September, Aris decided that for the first time the varsity squad would not begin fall competition until October with the Manhattan meet at Van Cortlandt Park. The boys Eastern States race featured a rematch between Ryan and the record-setting defender Edward Cheserek. This time Ryan had a chance.

Cheserek and Ryan broke quickly from the field across the opening flats and funneled into the narrow Cowpath. It was a two-man race. "It was strange," said Ryan. "I'm big and Cheserek's a little guy, but he kept pushing and elbowing me."

The odd couple ran together on the clean cinder path, almost immaculate thanks to well-funded Parks Department upkeep ("Cross Country Trail Maintainer," thirty-two hours a week, pays up to sixteen dollars per hour, must be able to lift at least fifty pounds), and into the Back Woods a half-mile out. On the curvy ascent, up and up, with a little down, under a canopy of red oak and hickory trees, intersecting nature trails left and right, one boy pulled ahead, then the other. The rest of the field was ten seconds behind. Quick feet and alertness were Back Woods currency. The hills, a point of pride in Van Cortlandt legend, were somewhat overblown; terrain was short and fast, quick bites like running for the bus on Belmont Avenue in *The Bronx Tale*.

At the crest of the climb, Cheserek surged, using his compact size to advantage on the descent. "His turnover was s-o-o-o fast," said Ryan, envious of Cheserek's leg speed and daredevil style. Once out of the hills and onto the home straight, Cheserek led by twelve seconds. Ryan closed some ground, but Cheserek took the victory in 11:58.7 for another sub-12:00. Ryan held second in 12:05.7 and declared himself "the world's fastest loser."

True enough, but Ryan gained street savvy as he looked ahead to Portland. "I tested myself. I knew where I stood," he said. "Now I could take a serious look at winning a national title."

Ryan received excellent Manhattan support from Millar, who placed seventh in 12:27.2 as the first sophomore in the race. The other F-M boys were bunched about another minute back, and the team placed a pedestrian fourth with 218 points. Defending national champion Christian Brothers scored ninety-four to triumph by over one hundred and take back the course record from Fayetteville with a 12:44.5 scoring average on the two-and-a-half-mile course.

At the finish a memorial stone paid tribute to pioneering distance legend Peter McArdle, who'd trained at Van Cortlandt and died there of a heart attack in 1985 at age fifty-six. McArdle was a running hero in his native Ireland who came to America in 1956. He trained 150 miles a week while holding down a full-time job. McArdle competed in the 1964 Olympic Marathon at Tokyo, placing twenty-third.

In the surprise of the day for Fayetteville, another Irishman, the second boy of the Ryan clan, Peter, a freshman running varsity, clocked 14:21.4 as the squad's seventh man. It was not Peter's time that signaled Stotan promise but his courage. A freak accident two years earlier led doctors to wonder whether Peter would ever walk properly, let alone tackle the Van Cortlandt Park cross-country course.

Leaving middle school one day after practice in seventh grade, Peter was slammed in the heel by a door whose metal base sliced through his Achilles tendon to within a fraction of an inch of severing it completely. Peter underwent two surgeries and a year of rehab to completely heal. Still, his physician said he might end up with a permanent limp. Peter proved him wrong. Van Cortlandt was his springboard. There would be more to come.

∞

In a summer workout, Fanning had "overextended" on a downhill and injured her left quadriceps muscle. She went for chiropractic care but to little effect. As girls leader, she found she could take care of her injury and cross-train when necessary, without concern for teammate lapses.

If anything, Fanning's setback made the team more accountable. The girl who'd been sixth and fourth in the country the past two years was now in damage control. Others had to step up. "I tried to stay positive so the girls wouldn't lose faith," she said.

Fanning's sunny disposition seemed to help. Brislin was no longer tearful on Gulf Road. Pearl had overcome an iron deficiency the previous year to excel in track, especially in the steeplechase, and rated selflessness her foremost cross-country guidepost. Jenna Farrell, mature for a freshman with a sisterly closeness to Pearl, saluted every training command. Varsity newcomer Mary Barger, perhaps the toughest of the lot, provided quiet leadership of her own while only a sophomore.

Aris kept Fanning out of Manhattan rather than subject her to Van Cortlandt's jarring downhills. Fanning came along to help coach. "I tried to keep Bill calm," she recalled. "He was a mess." How so? "Our first race," she said. "It was nerve-racking."

Tatnall of Delaware, a dependable national power, took advantage of Fanning's absence to outrun F-M, 81–90, for the Eastern States Championship. Pearl and Brislin were the first two Fayetteville girls across in 14:46.2 and 14:48.3, eighth and ninth, respectively. Pearl had grown more confident after reading the mind-body work *The Inner Game of Tennis* that Aris had given her. The other F-M scorers were well back.

The last Fayetteville girl to finish, more than a minute behind Pearl, was a dazed Barger. Her undoing would prove to be an asset. Barger led with gallantry, never more so than at Manhattan, where she ran with a stomach virus. Though dehydrated, Barger would not give in. At the finish, Barger collapsed, barely uttering "Did we win?" as Aris picked her up in his arms and carried her to a Porta-John. "That was love for your team right there," said Fanning.

Aris was not bitten by the loss—first fall meet, missing pieces—but he had his limit. On the bus home, Nick Ryan, abetted by Connor Farrell, pulled out some contraband, "an insane amount of candy," devoured some, and passed it around. Ryan felt heady from his performance and also a craving after his parents had disposed of what his mom called "all-American food." When Aris happened to walk back to the cheap seats, he caught the youngsters off guard; everyone froze, especially the girls, who, at that moment, had their mouths and hands full of chocolate caramel. Aris bore down on the girls only, the same girls who just got beat.

Nick and Connor had dodged a bullet. They looked at each other with their eyes saying: "Thank God it wasn't us."

∞

A fuzzy uncertainty pervaded the team as championship season approached. Ryan knocked off more victories with Millar a solid second. But the other boys were stuck far back in close containment. At the finish line, it was, "Where *are* they already?" More to the point: Why? They trained hard. They heard the lectures. Their chocolate binge was over. Aris tried to be patient with them.

While the girls had no friendly fire—callouts not necessary—and their unified training gave them an infectious serenity, questions remained. Fanning returned to the lineup but lacked her previous power. Brislin had a terrible race trying to sandwich college visits between hard workouts. "I was fried," she said.

At the state championships in Buffalo, more worries: Fanning had to compete with bronchitis and a sinus infection. She kept it from Bill but told the girls, which spurred them on. During the race, Fanning could barely breathe; every little hill felt endless. At the finish, her teammates tended to her as she wheezed and fought off leg cramps.

Doing her finest warrior pose for eighteen minutes twenty-four seconds, Fanning was the number-four F-M scorer, seventeenth overall, as Fayetteville defeated Saratoga 32–56, for its seventh-straight Class A championship. Pearl led the team again with her best race in 18:07. Unpredictable freshman Annika Avery followed with Barger close behind. Brislin unfried herself for the fifth-scoring spot a stride behind Fanning. This was the F-M everyone knew: an eighteen-second compression, a week to regionals, two weeks to nationals.

The boys required more patience than anticipated. Ryan creamed the Elma Meadows Park course record, winning by twenty-two seconds in 15:08. Millar placed fourth in 15:41, another beauty. The other F-M boys were in it until fading in the last quarter mile, when a tight Saratoga team delivered a closing blow for a 57–58 victory. Saratoga had raced to an eighteen-second spread and placed its third, fourth, and fifth scorers ahead of Fayetteville's FitzGibbons, Farrell, and sophomore Adam Hunt for the decisive points.

As if that wasn't enough, before the team scores came out, F-M parents, not keyed in to the late-race developments, hailed their sons like they'd won, with victory poses and pictures galore. Aris, irritated, tried to calm them down. Then he ducked into the scoring booth, got the official word, and presented everyone with the bad news. "It was funny and sad at the same time," said Ryan.

With Cheserek bypassing NXN for Foot Locker again, Ryan affirmed his status as the favorite for Portland with a 15:27 course record at Bowdoin Park, winning the New York Regional by twenty-six seconds. Millar nailed another hot run himself, placing eighth in 16:09. Millar, quiet as they come, was a good student. He learned from Ryan. He'd also gotten an earlier talking-to from Alex Hatz after some sparkling middle school track running. Once on the F-M varsity, Millar read up on Stotan ideas and liked what he saw. "I'm not a party guy," he told me.

Okay, we're waiting . . . Colin, Connor, Adam, *whoever?* While still thirty seconds and more in arrears to Millar, this time the F-M trio was threaded closer to its Saratoga counterparts, and Fayetteville turned the tables with an 86–98 New York triumph. Fayetteville ran the regionals with four seniors and three sophomores, an odd mix, and two of the sophs, Hunt and Riley Hughes, needed to find their inner Herb Elliott pretty soon.

The girls had their inner everything polished, ready for viewing, the unveiling of something new, even to them. The earth waited. Or maybe, for cross-country: Earth waited. Bumps were smoothed like rocks in a river. Fanning felt better. Medication had cleared her up. Her optimistic side glowed.

You could never know when Aris's Stotan romance would reach its emotional depth and make a girl feel it in her nerve endings, and maybe every girl would feel it at once, and then every Cerutty talking point would be like a Serengeti scream. When, after the weeks and months, it all made sense. Moral ambiguity, gone. What else could you do but scream?

That's how it unfurled at Bowdoin Park: the feeling in the air, from the trees, on the rickety trails, in the uppsy-downsy terroir, sweeping the girls on a carpet ride of ease and indulgence—what the Norwegians call *friluftsliv*, or open-air life, a phrase coined by Ibsen. Scream because you are home, the only place you want to be:

Running cross-country.

The Fayetteville girls ran, four together, one a sliver apart, the scoring five. The four brushed and touched and spoke, each a leader, each a provocateur. They occupied the back of the field's top ten with the finish coming up. Pearl noticed two Saratoga girls nearby. They were on the flat horseshoe loop with a half mile left. "Go . . ." Pearl instructed, and the four F-M girls ran faster. "I remembered Bill saying 'every second counts,'" she said. Bill's every word was like a promise to Pearl. "This is how we're supposed to run. What we always talked about, zero compression."

The four—Pearl, Avery, Brislin, and Fanning—raced to the tape, as close as they could be without bumping into each other. In their dazzling precision and clean carriage, it was ballet: elegant, lyrical, powerful, a hundred Green Lakes workouts in the making. It was a sight to behold.

"I've always thought of cross-country as a violent, operatic ballet," said Aris. "Our operatic crescendo comes into play during championship season. Think about opera: violence and grace come together. We use that. Running is 'violent,' but also artistry when done right."

The girls placed eighth, ninth, tenth, and eleventh. Their times were 18:49 to 18:51—in effect zero compression for the four—with fifth scorer Barger twentieth in 19:02, for an actual thirteen-second compression for the scoring five. Aris's "zero compression" mantra was something of a misnomer. For a team to cross the finish with the same time, the individuals would likely have to slow and modulate their pace and practically hold hands across the line—an insult to their competition. Zero compression was part ideal, part aesthetic.

The score was Fayetteville 28, Saratoga 59. Saratoga was rated the second- or third-best team in the country. Could there be any doubt about F-M expectations at Nike Cross Nationals? There was talk of a team from the Dallas area, Southlake Carroll, with the greatest girls team ever seen in Texas. And, from California, rising power Great Oak was the new Saugus.

In their seventh season of dominance, the Fayetteville girls were changing running's Western canon. Nobody knew what to make of them. They arrived in Portland after rising up to meet nature on equal footing—*that* was the victory, what Aris had in mind all along.

∽

Then came the mud. Race day at NXN was clear and sunny, but in the days and weeks prior Portland Meadows had soaked up rain like rice paddies in a third-world nation during monsoon season. In addition, the facility's regular maintenance staff faltered, and it was left to Nike hired hands like Ryan Canning of Boise, course manager at this point, to try and rescue the operation. Canning had come to Portland that summer to dig out trenches and install French drains but to no avail.

The boys-team favorites were the same schools that had dueled to a close finish the previous year: victorious Christian Brothers and runner-up Southlake Carroll; the Texans qualified both boys and girls teams almost every year. Fayetteville boys were rated around tenth. Aris figured the boys at their best could make the podium or even win. Nick Ryan felt the same. The mud could mess up the morning line. "It was a crapshoot," said Ryan. Quite literally.

Moments after the gun, Ryan was rolling in it. The urge to get out fast and not be left behind in the sucking turf fueled the start, and barely one hundred yards down the opening straightaway, as 199 bodies fought for position, a collision occurred. Ryan tripped and fell, or maybe he was pushed from behind; who could tell. In the domino effect, Ryan knocked into teammates and opponents. They too plunged into the mess. Within seconds, dozens of boys had gone down including most of Fayetteville and most of Southlake Carroll. Aris, watching from behind the start, couldn't see it.

Ryan panicked. Realizing the race had left without him, he dug himself up and sprinted furiously to the front, pulling to and ahead of the leaders by the half-mile point. He remembered 2011 when he led the nationals field from the gun, fading midway to finish a gallant fifth. It was a remarkable display of bravado. "There was not a sadness about that," said his mother, Pat, proudly. This time, as Ryan would fade again, a mother hurt for her wounded son. "It was horrifying," she said.

Ryan realized later that teenage impulse, and a measure of anger, made him squander energy in pursuit of the lead. Once in front, he pushed even harder, feeling, "The NXN race was mine to lose." In the last mile, after filtering back to around twentieth, Ryan felt crushed by the whole bizarre situation. "It was surreal," he said. "The whole race was surreal."

Nothing made sense. Ryan finished fifteenth as victory went to the Midwest Regional runner-up Sam Wharton of Ohio, in 17:06. Millar had a miserable race more than a minute behind Ryan. The other F-M boys were also far back. They could not make up ground after the crash, and Fayetteville placed sixteenth. Neither could Carroll in taking eighth. CBA managed fourth. Arcadia of Southern California, hardly considered mudders, won its second boys title. In the Portland Meadows archipelago, times were slowed by two minutes and more.

Ryan threw off his jersey and sat down in the slop to consider the bedlam. "I felt like something had been ripped from me," he said. Ryan wanted to rip somebody's head off, maybe the Carroll kid who was later heard boasting of his aggressive contact with Nick. Perhaps that was so much bluster. But when Aris pieced together the episode, he saw fault on Carroll's part and brought that grievance to the attention of Nike meet director, Drew Haberkorn. Haberkorn said that from where he'd stood he could see the whole thing, and no one individual or team was to blame. The Carroll coach, Justin Leonard, summed it up to me as "mass chaos" with everyone "in a panic running for the first turn."

In time, Ryan cooled off and went on to have a sensational track season, running an F-M record 8:55.93 3200 and achieving another wondrous state-meet double—an 8:58.28 3200 win followed (the same day, as bad weather compressed the meet) by a runner-up 4:07.55 (the winner ran fresh). Ryan went on to Syracuse University, where he could keep close to his three siblings who would soon star for F-M, but not before visiting twenty-six countries on a live-by-your-wits European adventure.

∽

Leonard never saw Fayetteville as a target but source of wonder. When the Carroll team engaged Fayetteville in the girls race, the Dragons were like officers of the Texas branch of the F-M fan club.

After the 2010 F-M NXN victory in twenty-seven points, Leonard said, "It was the most remarkable team accomplishment I've seen in any sport. It was unexplainable." Leonard searched for comparison and came up with the University of Connecticut women's basketball team, which at that point had won seven NCAA championships with four undefeated seasons. "But," said Leonard, "UConn recruits the best high school players in the country. Bill Aris has no control over who shows up."

Not so. Aris handpicked a few basketball players with killer eyes.

Fanning, who had to find her fiery side, rallied the girls with her best Knute Rockne pep talk on the eve of the nationals race. "Conditions don't matter. Run your hearts out. Kill it."

The next day, at the start, the Fayetteville girls got left behind. Positioned on the obscure far outside of the twenty-two teams and forty-five individuals, finishing their leg spray and shoe taping, the girls didn't realize the gun was about to fire. Crack. The field left, and, for an instant, seven F-M girls looked at one another like, "What just happened?" F-M was like a sprinter "left in the blocks."

Well, so what. They took chase with their dancing shoes on. Their choreographer patrolled the course without a care. Mud, schmud. The top four Fayetteville girls, the Bowdoin Park ballerinas, settled in behind the race leaders forging a second wing in close order. Other teams were buried, who knew where; it was, as Pearl put it, a "whirlwind." A wall of mud came up and covered Fanning, but she held ground, pacing her team, denying her quad injury.

When the first scores came up, F-M had a huge lead with Carroll second, and the announcer said, "Manlius is putting hurt on the field." Give Carroll credit. When NXN began in 2004, Texas was still running the two-mile distance for girls, claiming they couldn't handle the 5k. Leonard had to take his team on a seven-hour bus trip to Fayetteville (that again), Arkansas, for an invitational girls 5k race. Carroll girls made NXN that first year, made the podium the next two years in third, and only missed qualifying once through 2011. In 2012, when Texas finally adopted the 5k for girls, Carroll won Class 5A with a state-meet record of thirty-two points and 18:12 team average.

In the Portland mud fest, Carroll was beating every team in the country but one. Aris always told the F-M girls to "make the race boring for spectators." They were carrying out their duty over the whoop-de-doos and hay bales and trench-like water, but in the crazy mise-en-scène they were unaware of their boring lead. With contestants' uniforms and race numbers covered in mud, it was impossible to ascertain anything concrete, except the race "at the top of the spear," as the announcer had it—Mary Cain versus the defending champ from California, Sarah Baxter.

As the lead pair raced the last mile well ahead of the trailing pack, one of the commentators, Nike-sponsored world-class runner Kara Goucher, offered, "These are two future stars of American distance running." Goucher should have known better. Elite young female runners rarely sustained their success. Cain and Baxter turned out to exemplify young women's growth issues that often predicted downfall.

Baxter went on to the University of Oregon, where, so far, she's done little running, let alone anything remotely comparable to her high school success. Cain, at the time of NXN, was already a cause célèbre. She competed as an "unattached" runner, not for her New York high school, as she had decided to turn pro and take the opportunity to be coached by Alberto Salazar, the Nike coach of Olympians at the Oregon Project, right there in Portland.

I'd gotten in the middle of that decision weeks early at the Manhattan meet. At Van Cortlandt, I heard that Salazar had visited Cain at her Bronxville home. After Cain's race, I questioned her about it. Cain confirmed that she'd seen Salazar. When I tried to delve into that, her father, a physician, cut the interview short, and I responded with some coarse remarks that I later regretted.

I knew I had a story that I would write for one of the running websites. Unsolicited, Salazar called me the next day to make sure I had my facts straight. He was not thrilled about my story but knew I would go ahead with it. We'd been friends since Salazar's own high school days and had a longstanding respect for one another. When the story appeared, it made noise in the running community. A teenage girl training, racing, and traveling with pros?

To make a longer story short: Cain soon achieved world-class stature and record breaking, especially in 2013 and '14, at age seventeen and eighteen, during one period living in Portland and taking college classes. After that, her performances slowed, she eventually moved back home, and disappeared from the track circuit. A lot of track fans got to say, "I told you so."

Girls' adolescent-development issues of weight gain, hormonal change, and psychosocial transformation never seem to hold weight when the next round of superstars emerges. The tease of success takes over. Cain was only the latest precocious female distance runner to be seduced by early prominence—or, if you will, captured by it—and then as her body grew find success aborted. Maybe it's easy to say in the aftermath, but Cain might have enjoyed a different outcome had she been groomed more for the long term. She could have stayed with her high school team and its well-regarded coach, done some open racing while remaining amateur, competed in college, let her adolescent body (and mind) flower, and, as a young adult with ideas of her own, have less to live up to and a more natural pathway into whatever peak efforts awaited her.

In that scenario, Cain might have missed out on some early records and making the world-championship team at seventeen, but how does that notoriety stack up against being a more satisfied young woman in her early twenties, with adult-level goals, graduated progress, and the likelihood of longer years of success—and perhaps world- or even Olympic-team membership down the road?

We can only speculate. The predicament facing the female phenom has no pat answer. Every girl and her circumstances differ. While Aris himself has never coached an athlete of Cain's caliber, he has had a number of national headliners in the girls' ranks. His selfless, team-based approach, in which individual stardom is frowned upon, has minimized the chance that any F-M girl would step out into a spotlight that might eventually betray her.

In Portland, Cain's ungainly posture did not seem to serve her on the muddy day. Baxter, however, looked graceful and triumphed in 19:17 for a repeat championship—the only runner, male or female, yet to do so. Cain took second in 19:21. When I saw Cain's father, we shook hands, and I said something akin to "sorry about our misunderstanding at Van Cortlandt."

While Baxter was telling reporters she wanted "to go lie down and soak my legs," the Fayetteville girls solidified like alpine hikers nearing a peak and filed across the line in another boom-boom F-M moment. All five scorers within thirty-seven seconds. Fanning was first girl in, twenty-first in 20:12 and, speaking for the group, said, "The mud didn't really faze us." But they, too, rhapsodized about soaking their feet in warm water, which they did once back in the hotel, whose staff was on guard for the messy spoils of cross-country.

Barger was right behind Fanning, twenty-second in 20:13. Brislin was next, 20:22, in twenty-ninth. The finish-area chaos forced cockeyed thinking. "I thought we lost," said Brislin. "I wanted to cry." Pearl and Farrell finished the scoring, thirty-fourth and fifty-first, respectively, with Avery and senior Michelle Duffy completing the lineup as numbers six and seven.

Unsure of the outcome, Fayetteville was called to the podium along with Carroll and Carmel of Indiana. The F-M girls were subdued, holding earned emotions dear. The announcement came: Fayetteville the winner with fifty-four points. Their victory margin was a record 144 points. That was almost twice the previous record margin, set by F-M in 2007. Carroll, in second, scored 198. Great Oak placed sixteenth, almost *one minute forty seconds* per girl behind Fayetteville.

Who wins a national cross-country title by 144 points? Carroll, making the podium for the third time, showed a brio of its own. But, still . . . "The best team in Texas history got demolished," said Leonard.

It was asked again that evening on the Nike campus: How did they *do* it?

One hundred and forty-four points! Did Fayetteville-Manlius run above the mud while others sank? Walk on water? What happened to regular flesh-and-blood kids we could understand.

One hundred and forty-four points! Fayetteville-Manlius had won their seventh-straight championship by fifty-three seconds per girl, and what Alana Pearl wanted to convey most was, "We didn't gloat about it."

One hundred and forty-four points! In the thirty-seven-year history of the NCAA women's cross-country championships, the greatest margin of victory was ninety points, by Villanova in 1990, during the Wildcats' string of six-straight titles under coach Marty Stern. But, as with UConn basketball, Villanova recruited the best runners out of high school. The '90 team included the likes of future Irish Olympian and world cross-country champion Sonia O'Sullivan.

One hundred and forty-four points! Did these girls have Kenyan or Ethiopian lineage or sleep in a fancy hyperbaric chamber to enhance oxygen consumption? Did they feast on turtle soup, ascribed as a magic potion for Chinese women world-record breakers some years back?

In their seeming unreality, in the way the girls could transcend and soar, there was perhaps a touch of magical realism to Fayetteville-Manlius. A tincture of García Márquez, an illusion showing what truth is and could be. Singing and dancing and intoxicating scents: the beating heart of free will. In transforming teenagers, some willing, some resistant, what had Bill Aris discovered? Perhaps what the Nobel laureate novelist knew about life and love.

"Stotanism has elements of brutality," Aris said, "but also grace and style. When the kids come together for each other, there's a oneness about it. When I look into their eyes at that moment and feel that they get it, that's my fix. Then there's one heartbeat among us."

It was something to scream about.

21

REMEMBER THE ALAMO

We were using the past to guide us. But this was a whole different team.
—Annika Avery, Fayetteville-Manlius cross-country runner

2013 Season

When the Fayetteville-Manlius runners started their summer training, even louder screams could be heard on the Green Lakes trails. But they were not screams of unity or empowerment. This time the screams brought to mind the haunting work of Edvard Munch, the Norwegian expressionist, whose 1893 painting *The Scream* became a timeless emblem of anxiety in the modern age. Bill Aris could have posed for it.

From the moment Aris received a phone call from one girl's mother informing him of the family's impending move, he wanted to fly up that gravel road himself and scream out in frustration—the master of grand orchestration at his wit's end over how to form a team with eight young ladies who could not get along.

And the girl who started F-M's emotional avalanche was not even there.

Her name was Mary Barger. As a sophomore in 2012, Barger had been Fayetteville's number-two scorer in the girls team's seventh-straight Nike Cross

Nationals championship. Barger finished her race in Portland practically in unison with FM's top scorer, senior Jillian Fanning, who'd placed number four in the nation in 2011. Fanning, Barger, and another senior Katie Brislin, had formed a commanding top three in Portland, separated by only ten seconds, especially impressive in the event's worst-mud-ever conditions.

Then, F-M lost Fanning, the team's primary leader, and Brislin, a steadying influence, to graduation. At least Barger was expected back. She was counted on for key leadership in 2013.

Fanning went on to Providence, where, as a sophomore in an indoor mile race at the New York Armory, she would suffer a complete fracture of her left femur. She was carried off the track to New York Presbyterian Columbia University Medical Center across the street. In surgery a titanium rod was inserted into her leg, from the hip to the knee. The injury was a freak occurrence. Fanning always ate a healthy diet for strong bones. Tests to determine the cause turned up nothing. After that, Fanning's running was never the same.

Brislin enjoyed a marvelous senior spring track season as a Fayetteville miler. With many victories to her credit, Brislin made the state finals in the 1500 meters, placing a close second in 4:29.25, equivalent to a sub-4:50 mile. She went on to Villanova and after three semesters transferred to Le Moyne, Aris's alma mater, in Syracuse, where a bad case of mono would derail her momentum.

When Brislin left high school, she held closely to a life lesson she felt as a converted Stotan: "I got to the point where, I won't say I didn't feel pain in a race but in a way thrived on it and was able to push through it. That taught me what I was capable of, in running, in anything."

Barger was that same kind of kid. She couldn't be broken. She had the type of personality where a mere glance in a teammate's direction could work magic. As summer approached, Aris valued Barger's calming personality no matter the circumstances. "You couldn't make Mary angry if you tried," he said. Jenna Farrell, a sophomore that season, agreed. "Mary was consistent and never freaked out about anything," Farrell said.

But then, poof, the girls' glue was gone. Aris got the call from Mary's mom informing him that her husband, a bank executive, had been transferred and the family would be moving to the Rochester area. Even though Rochester was a commutable seventy-minute drive from Syracuse, the Bargers were moving on out.

Aris's first reaction: shock. "Mary was liked and respected by everyone and could be a conduit to different factions of the team," he said. "She was like the axel with spokes going out to each of the girls. After that, we had no backbone."

The girls' first reaction: shock. "We all panicked," said Farrell. The shock was magnified when Barger trained with F-M over the summer before departing for Pittsford-Mendon High School. "It made us feel Mary was still with us," said Farrell. Come fall, the girls found it perilous to face cross-country without her.

Leadership on a high school cross-country team, especially one with national aspirations—especially one with Stotanesque standards of how to conquer pain, commit fully and live the life—required a mature athlete to steer with cunning and finesse when personalities clashed and conflicts arose. Barger's void came at a time when Fayetteville's needs were never greater. This was the weakest F-M girls team since before the Stotan era.

Senior Alana Pearl and junior Annika Avery returned from the 2012 NXN team along with the sophomore Farrell, experienced as a varsity contributor since eighth grade. They'd been the team's number four, five, and six performers at nationals. As fall competition got underway, five other girls were in contention for NXN team berths. The thin ranks of established runners along with newcomers under pressure to perform proved a toxic mix. The girls fought. Aris fumed.

The other five varsity contenders were junior Jessica Howe, sophomore Megan Menz, sophomore Samantha Levy, freshman Reilly Madsen, and junior Olivia Ryan—a third Ryan sibling—in her first cross-country season after running track and captaining the Fayetteville swim team.

Olivia Ryan faced an arduous summer. A self-professed "trackie" who felt at home in the sprints, Ryan's parents told her she had to quit swimming because F-M had no pool and the late-night logistics of swim time at another school became impossible to manage. Olivia's brother, Nick, had been a national star; her other brother, Peter, was currently on the squad. Enter Olivia, who had to learn distance running as though learning French. She had stamina from swimming. Aris would try and work with that.

Howe had a touch of varsity experience from the previous year but was never counted on then, nor had she been in the lineup for state or regionals. Madsen was new. Menz and Levy had run JV. Levy had broken both legs in a skiing accident as a child and had to relearn how to walk.

A vegetarian, Levy was smitten by running, embracing Stotan values and questioning those who did not. Every girl's emotional weakness was magnified by what Levy called "a leadership disaster." The way Levy saw it, a rift developed between the older girls, the veterans, and the newer faces who struggled to learn the ropes. The vets were impatient: accustomed Fayetteville scaffolding was rickety. The youngsters, some immature, felt mistreated, their voices not heard.

There was no Mary Barger to settle things down and make everyone feel good about herself. Aris tried, fielding the girls' complaints, their venting, trying to find common ground. "Glue?" said Aris. "It was not even Elmer's glue. Talk to one side, talk to the other. I felt like a contortionist."

An assertive and selfless peer was needed to set things straight. In *The Captain Class* by Sam Walker, he wrote, "The most crucial ingredient in a team that achieves and sustains historic greatness is the character of the player who leads it." F-M never had to worry about that. From Jessica Hauser to Courtney Chapman, Molly Malone to Katie Sischo to Jill Fanning, the girls, from 2006 through 2012, had their bases covered.

In *Untangled*, about teenage girls' adolescent trauma, author Lisa Damour stressed the crucial role of "tribal" belonging. The tribe functions as family, she said. At F-M, "Do I like my tribe?" and "Does my tribe like me?" became *everything.*

Fayetteville's tribal warfare spilled out onto the training ground. If some girls dogged it on a run, others took it personally. "We tried to teach them," said Avery, who'd embraced the Aris adage that "pain was your friend," "but they pushed back on that." Pearl would roll her eyes. She couldn't truck any hint of style over substance. Once, a girl's fashion-plate mind-set emerged. Molly Malone would have had a shit fit.

The team's first big meet, the McQuaid Invitational in Rochester in late September, was a reckoning. Avery took sixth with Pearl twelfth and Farrell fourteenth—decent if not great—but the last four scorers (Menz, Madsen, Howe, and Ryan) were well back in a performance that Aris would term, "remember the Alamo." Levy did not compete. She had a stress fracture in her right foot.

The scores: Unionville of Pennsylvania 45, Fayetteville-Manlius 79. Team dissension had not suggested a much different outcome. But seeing the numbers in black-and-white was a slap in the face.

Unionville outran F-M at all seven positions. The winners were led by their victorious all-American, Courtney Smith, in 16:47 for three miles, twenty-seven seconds ahead of Avery. Unionville, from the town of Kennett Square, about an hour west of Philadelphia, was unique among top teams for its reliance on cross-training—even more so than Fayetteville.

The coach, Mark Lacianca, a physics teacher with a scientific approach, kept girls' mileage low, at thirty-five a week, while adding up to ninety minutes a day of spinning or swimming at high intensity. Lacianca calculated the girls' overall fitness to be "worth" over seventy miles per week. The girls' reduced running meant less risk of menstrual dysfunction. Lacianca, with parental help, kept tabs on the girls' monthly cycles to ward off irregularity.

Dr. Kate Berg, the Cincinnati physician specializing in amenorrhea, said that a girl typically needed a BMI, or body mass index (a measure of body fat based on height and weight) of at least 18 percent for menstruation to occur. For example, a female runner five feet tall weighing one hundred pounds would have a healthy BMI of 19.5, according to formulas; that same girl weighing ninety would have a BMI of 17.6.

While Unionville had no prior national standing, it had its best team ever and relished the chance to race Fayetteville. For its last workout before McQuaid, Lacianca had painted a Ghostbusters-style logo on its running path with an "FM" and red line of submission through it. "The girls enjoyed that," said Lacianca.

Aris grew desperate. The next week at the high school he pulled out one of his greatest hits: the boys 2004 Stotan-camp encounter group, used then as a soul-searching enhancer and in later years as therapy for emotional discord. Once practice ended, Aris told the top eight girls, "I'm putting you all in my office with the door closed. I want this problem solved. You don't have to love each other. But you do have to respect each other. And get along for our common goal. If you're not willing to do that, what are we doing here?"

"It was not pleasant," said Avery. "Alana and I tried to have everyone speak. It became confrontational."

"No calming of the seas," said Aris. "But we just had to move on."

Aris hoped for not only reconciliation but also a democratic capacity for acceptance of team roles. A few generals with willing support troops were the ideal. Or as Aris would have it: killers and cuddly. Like his dogs. If the dearly departed Oliver, a chocolate lab, came upon a deer at Green Lakes, he would "frolic with the deer" all day long, said Aris. If the current Chloe, an American Staffordshire, saw a deer, given the chance, she would hunt it down. "You need ruthless competitors together with those who go with the flow," he said.

Turbulence continued. The veterans blamed the McQuaid defeat on walking the racecourse at length in the morning heat all because the newer runners were confused about the route. "We felt drained by race time," said Avery.

Something else drained the team, something that would plague the girls right up until nationals. Unlike past years, no definitive top five or top seven emerged, and, after the secure front-running trio of Avery, Pearl, and Farrell, the other five slower girls were in a constant state of anxiety over where they fit in and who, in the end, would be left home when the team went off to Portland. At the outset, when Ryan signed up, she rocked the boat as an eighth girl in the mix for nationals.

Amid their uncertainty, the outliers focused on the result, not the process, while taking team success for granted, according to the veterans, and not respecting the training magnitude that went into the entire enterprise.

Two weeks after McQuaid, in a heralded rematch between the upstart and standard-bearer, Fayetteville fought back against Unionville in the Manhattan Eastern States Championship at Van Cortlandt Park. Six out of the seven Unionville girls outran their F-M counterparts, but this time Fayetteville managed to keep it close. It was Unionville 89, Fayetteville 92. Avery, Pearl, and Farrell were again F-M's top three. The team's top-five scoring compression of seventy-two seconds for the two-and-a-half-mile course was nothing to cheer about.

Still, comparing the two losses, Aris latched on to any thread of hope. "You see," he told the girls after the Manhattan race, "you can do this." It was more urging than affirmation.

༄

The F-M boys also placed second in the Easterns but without any of the girls' contretemps. Lock solid in effort and disposition, they were led by Bryce Millar, now a junior, a runner of national standing and one of the toughest son of a guns ever to pound a cross-country course. With his size, muscularity, and fierce countenance, Millar conveyed the message: do as I say, and stay out of my way. "Bryce was a warrior," said Aris.

But he was not arrogant. He just had that aura. In fact, Millar readily latched on to Stotan selflessness, telling me when we spoke that season: "Stay humble. Don't start thinking you're better than anybody."

Millar placed second at Van Cortlandt in 12:22. The annual Christian Brothers–Fayetteville championship rite resulted in a 90–114 CBA victory.

The Colts, breaking their team-time course record, were again rated a nationals threat. F-M also had a national-level squad, boosted by Peter Ryan, moving up from the freshmen ranks to excel as a sophomore.

Millar felt a little crowded when Ryan was able to stick with him in a summer time trial at Green Lakes. Peter was a risk-taker like his brother Nick. In another breakthrough workout, on the high school soccer fields, Peter held the front at the finish of an hour's worth of fast-paced fartlek runs. By this time, Bryce and Peter were friendly rivals playing games to see who would cry "uncle." In one two-hour run, the pair found their paths diverge. The other boys followed Bryce. Peter charged after the pack. When he caught up, Bryce and Peter raced off on their own, hammering race pace. After thirty minutes, neither giving in, Bryce looked at Peter as if to say, "We good now?" Peter looked back: "I would say so . . ." Then the pair dropped their pace to cruising speed.

Ryan, who looked like a young Elvis ("My hair was pouffy then"), loved the action but admitted, "Everyone knew Bryce inherited the team."

The second F-M man at Manhattan, and for most of the season, was Andrew Bergé, the team's only senior. Bergé, clocking 12:28 in fifth place, was running Van Cortlandt for the first time after missing his junior fall season with a hip injury. He'd brought it on. Bergé had taken a week that summer to go camping with his father in the Adirondacks. No problem. But after Bergé slept on the cold floor of his tent for a week, and then resumed team workouts, "everything seized up," he said, and Bergé was unable to compete after running one fall race.

In 2013, Bergé (pronounced Bur-JAY, with family roots in the Alsace-Lorraine region of Germany), trained in Millar's shadow, thriving on the hilliest trails like the Cerutty Loop. Millar, Bergé, and Ryan gave F-M a cracking top three, with juniors Adam Hunt and Kyle Barber providing dependable backup in the four-five positions.

At Manhattan, Ryan could have run with Bergé, but Peter usually had some nascent injury to watch out for and Aris had him hold back with Hunt. Ryan finished in 12:58 with Hunt a few strides behind. Barber was fifth man in 13:08. Riley Hughes and freshman Patrick Perry completed the seven.

Barber had been a slow Stotan convert. He'd quit running in middle school because his thirteen-year-old instinct told him "there was no glory in it." He'd also suffered from Osgood-Schlatter syndrome in both knees because of growth spurts. At F-M, Barber grew to six feet two and he was running-slim at 145 pounds. In time, Barber took the Aris messages to heart. Every new run, from Green Lakes to Gulf Road, along with team friendships "made for a strong and powerful blend" that gave Barber the goal of trying to get closer to Millar in practice by 2013. "He was the man," said Barber.

Close to Millar but not ahead. This deference would concern Aris. It seemed that no one, not even Ryan, dare think he could outrun Millar in competition. Millar defined team performance. However Millar raced—a great day, so-so day—the team raced. F-M had one killer and six cuddlys. The cuddlys let Millar take charge and assume full responsibility. Aris later regretted that perhaps he let that happen. It was convenient at the time. Plus, so much of Aris's energy was drawn to the girls.

By the state meet at Queensbury, in the Lake George area, the boys were humming along with few equals nationally, and the girls had managed to leave their ill will in the locker room, or so it seemed. Avery, Farrell, Howe, and Pearl placed 6-7-9-13 within fourteen seconds, 17:54 to 18:08 to defeat Saratoga, 31–67, and by thirty seconds per girl. That's how you win nationals!

The first three girls delivered their best race of the season while Pearl, tired from college visits, did her share. Number five, six, and seven? At this point, three weeks before NXN regional qualifying, the pecking order seemed clear-cut. Ryan and Menz, while far behind Pearl, were close together as a solid five and six.

Menz, pure of heart and demeaned by some for her innocence, represented a link to past glory. Her cousin was the Stotan standby Heather Martin, who'd inspired her. Martin had been pure of heart, too. Menz gave Aris a gift of freshness as he tried to retain his optimism.

Behind Menz, Madsen, the freshman, was another thirty-three seconds back as number seven. The injured Levy was back in training and, if ready for regionals, a likely replacement for Madsen in Portland.

Anxiety . . . *over?*

Not for the boys in their state race. Halfway, on a two-tiered hill in the Queensbury woods, Millar, Ryan, and Bergé, all in the lead pack, got swept up in race triage to preserve an eventual team triumph. Bergé got pushed—twice— by an Ithaca runner and was off balance and about to fall. Millar, ahead, saw the mishap and grabbed Bergé's arm; Ryan, behind, also saw Bergé falter and yanked him by his uniform from the other side. With two teammates holding him up, Bergé was able to maintain stride and go on to finish fourth.

Millar's keen instincts were also needed to save his own skin. In a sensational three-man duel that was still talked about years hence, Millar roared onto the home straight with Mikey Brannigan of Northport on his right and Mickey

Burke of Rush-Henrietta on his left. With one hundred meters to go and all three runners at their agonized limit—Millar's mouth agape and eyes fighting it—Miller powered to victory in 15:06.3. All three youngsters broke the course record. They were one second apart. Millar credited his year-round weekly swim with helping him "to not get out of breath at the end of races."

Millar couldn't know it at the time, but he'd outrun a future international star in Brannigan. Then a junior, Brannigan was autistic, and he and his family were open about it. High functioning on the spectrum, Brannigan started running in fourth grade and became a role model for special-needs athletes. He would go on to break the four-minute mile—3:57.58—and capture a number of world and Paralympics track titles.

In addition to Bergé in fourth, only ten seconds behind Millar, Ryan placed ninth with Hunt twenty-third and Barber twenty-eighth for a decisive Fayetteville victory. As with Olivia Ryan, Barber's strong suit was speed, and in track both runners excelled in the 400 meters. While Barber's athleticism was evident on the cross-country course, Ryan was still a work in progress. She'd moved from number-seven girl all season to number five at state but was still thirty-nine seconds behind Fayetteville's number four and only two seconds ahead of Menz, at number six.

Ryan was known to have a mind of her own, and even her mother, Pat, said Olivia could be "a little out there." It was not her style, said her mom, to "fall right in with the group." Ryan had experienced hip pain and, said Avery, told her she suffered migraine headaches. In class together, Avery would see Ryan struggle and lay her head on her desk. "Olivia was unpredictable," said Avery. "She seemed to be fighting her own demons."

As an independent thinker, pulled by both team and family, Ryan was probably looking for transparency at a time when clouds were in her coffee. Conditioned to dismiss Aris's effusive lectures on life and lactate by Nick, who'd grown weary of them by senior year, Olivia seemed out of sync with what was expected of her in her cross-country debut. "One time," she once told me, "Coach gave an entire speech about different kinds of airplanes, and nobody knew what he was talking about."

Aris realized even before this season that the task of capturing every athlete's heart and mind had grown tougher. Still caressing every angle of conversion, he witnessed Ryan's difficulties when, leading up to regionals, her training fell apart. "Olivia was tired mentally and physically," said Aris. "The quality was not there." Her brother Peter saw it, too. "She was tapped out," he said.

At the NXN New York Regional, the Fayetteville boys rocked the nation with a performance that had White Moment written all over it. F-M crushed the Bowdoin Park team-time course-record average set by its 2004 boys *by thirteen seconds*—an average of thirteen seconds faster for each of its five scorers. The '04 team performance had made F-M the national favorite; the boys, overwhelmed by first-year NXN hype, wound up second. Now, with a 16:02.4 team average on the nation's hilliest regional 5k course, was there any team in the country that could stand up to Fayetteville?

Millar and Bergé ran virtually even in fourth and fifth. Their times: 15:45.2 and 15:45.7. It was twelve seconds to Ryan. Barber and Hunt were close enough for F-M to achieve a team time never thought possible on the demanding course. Even Christian Brothers had to bow to Fayetteville. In the same meet's Northeast Regional, victorious CBA averaged 16:15.

F-M saw personal breakthroughs, too. In running virtually even with Millar, could Bergé become more killer than cuddly if need be in Portland? Ryan as well—could he put his Ryan-family headstrongness to use a week later? Aris felt yes, and yes. Barber drew new life from feeling more connected, within sight of Ryan around the final bend—using his height to see his teammates ahead in the crowd—and recently, in practice, giving nothing to Millar.

It was snowing when, in "box workouts" on the school fields, Barber had run every repetition with Millar, prompting Aris to say aloud, "Now that Kyle Barber's believing in himself, we have a shot at something." Barber would carry that affirmation to Portland. "It was so bluntly powerful," he said.

The girls' day at regionals was filled with tension. Levy was back in the lineup, her first race since September. To make room for her, Aris, for the first time, put a girl still under consideration for NXN—the freshman Madsen—in the event's "open" race for JV-level runners. In doing so, Aris gave himself a possible numerical nightmare. How would the slowest of the seven varsity runners compare with Madsen's time? Would elements other than pure times be factored into Aris's decision on the final seven? The open race was easier to negotiate with no do-or-die team contest at stake and plenty of room to run with thinner ranks at the front. Eight girls would race: seven varsity, one JV. Assuming F-M qualified (a given, really), seven would go to Portland. One would stay home.

Aris would have little time to sit back and contemplate his options. An hour after the competition, coaches had to give Nike officials their nationals lineups so travel arrangements could be made. The New York and Northeast athletes would be flying in four days.

Avery, feeling she had to carry the team at the front, went out and ran the race of her life to win the New York Regional by twenty seconds in 18:06. Avery charged up the hills and "cycled" back down, saying her legs churned as though bicycling, in a performance worthy of top ten at nationals. Pearl followed Avery and ran her best race, placing third in 18:34. The last three scorers did their jobs: Farrell, Howe, and Menz all under nineteen minutes and twenty-one seconds apart. Comebacking Levy, not expected for much, was a creditable number six in 19:34.

Things were looking up. But . . . what happened to Olivia Ryan? More than a minute later, in 20:37, Ryan crossed the finish. She'd almost dropped out. She was crying, wailing. She was saying things like she couldn't run anymore. Aris asked her, "Tell me—what happened?" Ryan couldn't say. Madsen, in the earlier open race, had placed third in 20:17, twenty seconds faster than Ryan, and without any drama.

Fayetteville won, 32–88, over Saratoga while running forty seconds faster per girl. Whatever the final F-M lineup, the team would be favored in Portland.

Parents hovered. Aris let it be known: he would try and make an objective decision on whether Levy, Ryan, or Madsen would be out. Aris consulted with his assistant coaches, Dave Davis and Jim Nixdorf. Putting it all together, Aris named Ryan. He felt he was doing her a favor, that Ryan's meltdown was evidence that she needed rest, that her long first season had overcome her. Olivia saw it otherwise. So did her parents. So did Nick and Peter. Bill had words that day with Olivia's father, Tim. The next week, before the team left for Portland, Bill and Tim smoothed things over.

Crazy thing was: with the boys team as strong a favorite as any, if the girls ran nationals as they had state or regionals, this could be, finally, the year of an F-M sweep. The girls national-team landscape did not appear as formidable as in years past. Great Oak of California was talked about again. Unionville, early-season F-M conqueror, won the Northeast regional but had one girl with mono and another with a ferritin deficiency.

✑

In Portland, one regional winner generating little attention was the Heartland girls champion Wayzata of Minnesota, situated in the Minneapolis–St. Paul suburb of Plymouth on the shores of Lake Minnetonka. The team had acquired a bit of Stotan ingenuity but was easy to overlook.

The state's largest high school, with a grades nine-to-twelve enrollment of about thirty-five hundred, Wayzata took the mid-November regional, in Sioux Falls, South Dakota, without the services of its top runner, senior Anna French. She had gotten sick and been sidelined for two weeks. In training, said Wayzata girls coach Dave Emmans, French had put pressure on herself to do more than necessary—apparently more than her body could take.

The prior year, in the 2012 state championships, French had placed second in Class 2A as Wayzata triumphed. It was Emmans's first state cross-country title in twenty years of coaching. Wayzata went on to take seventh that season in its first appearance at Nike Cross Nationals. The Heartland region, comprised of the Dakotas, Iowa, Kansas, and Nebraska along with Minnesota, had not had a girls-team podium contender in years. While Wayzata had six of its top seven girls back for 2013, the week before NXN, French ran the Foot Locker Midwest just to get a race in and placed thirty-third.

Wayzata had other problems. French was also a Nordic skier, a major sport in Minnesota that began the day after Heartland. French, along with two other team members who skied, could only run twice a week, as dictated by the ski coach. In addition, Emmans was concerned about the girls' dry-land training. He thought two-hour "ski walks" on snowless trails were a little much. A fourth runner, five-foot-nine McKayla Evans, played basketball. That, too, was underway by mid-November, and the basketball coach let Evans out of the gym *once* a week.

Emmans thus had only three girls training normally with nationals around the corner. On top of that, in a state demanding rigid adherence to postseason rules, Emmans and his coaching staff were disallowed from any direct contact with the team after the state finals—Wayzata triumphed by almost one hundred points—which fell a month before NXN. Two of the girls' mothers who'd run in college were assigned as, let's say, liaisons. This rule extended to nationals itself. In Portland, Emmans would have to be an outsider.

For final workouts at home and mental resolve on NXN weekend, the Wayzata girls, in their biggest race ever, had to cup their ears and listen for Emmans's "suggestions" floating somewhere above the din. If they heard something, it was not about winning but team unity. When Wayzata took the line, skiing and basketball were put aside, and a disarming calm enveloped the team—call it Minnesota nice—projected by Emmans, who, to listen to him tell it, had to fight himself to become the coach, and man, he wanted to be.

"I went through a stage of my career when I was kind of an ass," Emmans told me. "My controlling personality drove kids away." Finally, Emmans recognized this thing called selflessness. "I shrunk my ego. I gave up enough to allow the girls the freedom to see what they could do."

At the race start, the NXN fields were given an innovation designed to alleviate the crowded quarters and the falls that came with it. Course official Ryan Canning of Idaho came up with the idea of a "split start," which he'd employed successfully at a big meet in Boise. A flagged divider was set up from the start to the first turn—the problem point—for about three hundred meters. "An alley," said Canning. In a random selection, eleven teams were placed on one side of the alley; eleven on the other. The separation would hopefully delay convergence and sort out 199 bodies fighting for limited space.

F-M and other teams on the far outside right felt a disadvantage having to run on an angle toward the left turn, but Canning said the curved start was carefully measured, and everyone, inside or outside, raced the exact-same distance. Aris felt a better solution, with a traditional start, would be to put all the superior individual qualifiers on the inside, allowing them a clear path to get out ahead of the mostly slower team runners.

Emmans, however, called the new idea a "game changer" for his girls. Remembering 2012, he said, "This time we didn't get buried."

When the cannon sounded, French flew right out with the leaders. Emmans gasped, "Holy cow!" and, forgetting his required reticence, yelled to the other girls, "Anna's in the top ten!" as a motivator. When the other six Wayzata girls passed by in tantalizing, close formation, Emmans exclaimed to the team mothers—or was it to his assistant coaches; rules were out the window by now—"Are you kidding me?"

What was Wayzata trying to do, imitate Fayetteville? Actually, Wayzata never thought about challenging Fayetteville. Emmans felt F-M was indestructible. "We suffer unto truth," said the ancient Greeks. Emmans understood that F-M had passed that test long ago. "They can always see the final product," he said. "For F-M, it's never chaotic."

It was eighteen degrees at race time. Space heaters in the team tents were a godsend. Just before the start, F-M had tried something new: running through freezing puddles to get their feet accustomed to the cold so it would not come as a shock on the course. Apparently, the girls didn't mind soaked spikes.

Aris wanted no shocks of any kind. This was a not a time for inspirational oratory but simple steadiness. "You have to come together," he told the girls. "Run like you have in your best races. You don't even have to run better."

However, the girls' dissonance had not melted away. "It was underlying," said Pearl. "We were not together," said Levy. "Everyone had their allies."

Avery came to realize why she and Pearl could not bring the team together. "We were using the past to guide us," she said, referring to the regal style of leadership they'd been given by Kate Sischo, Fanning, and other members of F-M royalty in their cross-country gestation. "But this was a whole different team."

Avery and Pearl tried to lead for a last time—in the race. They pushed out into the top twenty or so, behind French and ahead of the rest of Wayzata. At the first kilometer, F-M paced the field with seventy-two points. No other team was close. Wayzata was not in the top five.

Much attention focused on the individual dual among a trio of superstars: two-time defender Sarah Baxter of California, national indoor-mile titlist Elise Cranny of Colorado, and Alexa Efraimson of Washington State, the past summer's World Youth Games 1500 meter bronze medalist competing in Donetsk, Ukraine. They raced well ahead from the start in their own orbit. "Alpha dogs," the announcer called them.

It was sunny and dry at Portland Meadows. Single-digit overnight temperatures made the mud freeze over. The turf was uneven, some sections were icy, and runners needed to find some bounce, exemplified by the high-kicking Efraimson. She attended Camus High just across the Columbia River from Portland and was the crowd favorite.

Avery and Pearl raced back and forth, each one drifting ahead. "It was my last high school cross-country race," said Pearl. "I told myself, 'This is it—everything you got.'" Farrell, Howe, and Menz followed from behind. Levy had pink eye and her vision was blurred. By 2k, Wayzata was on the board—Fayetteville 77, Wayzata 142—but Aris liked what he saw. Just hold it, he thought to himself.

They couldn't. When the 3k scores were announced, it was F-M still ahead with 101 but Wayzata closing with 128. Emmans kept saying, "Holy cow!" Aris kept saying, "Where is . . . ?" as he searched for some in his top five. The F-M girls seemed shopworn as the final "k" approached, and the team race turned into a toss-up. Wayzata rallied, French was still well placed, and the rest of the Trojans solidified as Fayetteville had done so many times before. "*Where is . . . ?*"

It was bellowed again by the tall man holding his good-luck stick. Did F-M have anything left? The tall man tossed the stick away.

Back in Manlius, Olivia and Nick, now a Syracuse University sophomore, were on the phone together while watching the webcast. They were still so upset about the Aris decision that they were not exactly pulling for the home team. There was a point to be made. Nick rationalized, "Bill always said, it was 'God, family, school, running.' I had to be in Olivia's corner."

While Emmans still felt somewhere in the middle of the NXN learning curve, he knew enough to isolate his greatest task—what he'd believed F-M had perfected. "Cross-country," he said, "is about dipping your toe into chaos, always testing the limits. The human body does not like all that chaos. It wants to go back to what it knows."

That day, no one knew more than Efraimson, giving off heat with her smoky breaths on the home straight. Looking gallant after holding back, she finished well ahead of the runner-up, Cranny, in a course-record 16:51. Baxter, third, needed help staying on her feet in the chute. Following Mary Cain, Efraimson would turn pro while in high school and sign with Nike.

A renewed Anna French could not be denied. She placed eighth between two other future pros (Katie Rainsberger of Colorado and Dani Jones of Arizona). Her layoff was a blessing, said Emmans. French found a way to bargain with herself for serenity. At NXN, "probably for the first time ever," said Emmans, "Anna ran free."

It was a freedom Fayetteville could only envy. They filed in: Avery twentieth, in 17:59, making all-American, Pearl twelve seconds behind her in twenty-ninth. The other five girls—Farrell, Howe, Menz, Levy, and Madsen in that order—were all over the map. In the final kilometer, F-M had hemorrhaged points. It was long past the time for group hugs. While it was easy to blame one or two particular girls, Pearl, the senior, wouldn't have it. "It was no one person's fault," she insisted.

In the team corral, once defeat was apparent, Pearl was disoriented. The usual postrace victory rituals belonged to others. "I didn't know what to do," she said.

Able to dispel chaos, Wayzata's next six girls after French exceeded their wildest imaginings. With a degree of team closeness out of the F-M mold, the six girls raced home within a shoulder-touching ten seconds in one big communal stamp. They'd heard Emmans's call and appropriated Stotan thunder for the victory.

It was Wayzata 108, Fayetteville-Manlius 120. The F-M girls' seven-year streak had ended. Aris was not angry. He'd seen it coming. He was happy for

Wayzata and told them so. He saw how grateful they were, their humility and glee during interviews, and their personal closeness. "That," Aris said, observing the Wayzata demeanor, "is what we were lacking."

Emmans was dazed. "To beat the New York Yankees of our sport . . ." he said. Holy cow!

∽

In the boys race, Fayetteville joined CBA and Northwest champion Gig Harbor of Washington as chief contenders. With the new start setup, maybe the race, for once, would get off cleanly.

F-M took off, briefly, like contenders. Millar went after the leaders. Bergé was close behind. Barber, too, was well positioned. But Hunt fell right away and picked up a spike wound. Then Ryan took a fall in a pileup a half mile out near the whoop-de-doos. The ground was so frozen that when a boy in front of Ryan kicked a flagged stake marking the course, the stake snapped in half and shot out like a weapon into the runner's legs, tripping them up. Ryan stepped on a competitor's head, rolled onto his back, then sprung up, all in one move. "You guys gotta get going!" Aris shouted.

Barber, buoyed by Aris's ode back home, looked for more to drive him. "We were trying to emulate the gods," said Barber, referring to the original Stotans of 2004 and '05. "That's what coach talked about. We could be the next ones."

Into the heart of the race, the boys used Millar as a touchstone. Millar led. Others followed. The boys were stuck, safe within the race womb. Where was the Ryan of fartlek fame, the Barber of box-workout prominence? The worst of the season's guarded malfunction, acquiescence, emerged to contain these capable F-M boys.

The 3k scores came up: Gig Harbor ahead with 123, Christian Brothers second with 128, and Fayetteville third with 160. Bergé moved up on Millar, now nothing like the animalistic competitor seen back home. "I tried to work with him as long as I could," Bergé said. When Millar let go, Bergé finally moved ahead—the first time anybody but Millar had led F-M all season.

Ryan could see Bergé take charge, and he, too, moved up on Millar. Barber fell back, confused over who to key off as uniform colors of various teams blurred into sameness. Hunt tried to find a groove, eyeing a distant Barber as the race seemed to get lost on Fayetteville. The second half was mostly damage control: late moves that fell flat.

It was a memorable day for Washington State. Taylor Wilmot of North Central, in Spokane, gave Washington a second-straight NXN individual title and, with Efraimson, an individual sweep. Wilmot ran fifteen minutes even in what would be the last NXN at Portland Meadows. Gig Harbor held on for the team victory with runner-up CBA and surprising Brentwood of Tennessee also on the podium in third.

Fayetteville scored 216 for fourth, forty-two points behind Brentwood. Bergé came across in 15:36 to lead the team. Ryan followed in 15:42. Millar, dejected, was third man in 15:56. Barber and Hunt completed the top five. Ryan felt he could have done more.

While Aris had seen internecine warfare among the girls, he saw timidity among the boys. Bergé, a dutiful lieutenant, "could have left Millar in the dust," claimed Aris. The next spring in track, Aris appeared to be proven right. Without team positions to honor, Bergé ran a 4:10.52 1600 for fourth in the state finals—further evidence of his prowess from fall.

After his combative season, Millar needed peace. His teammates let him be. What turbulence had confronted him? He'd been steady, a rock, indeed loved like a rock. "He was the guy who did everything right," said Barber, a close friend. "But he put a lot of pressure on himself."

Barber and the others had been to Millar's home. Bryce's parents prepared lavish breakfasts for the team after Saturday long runs when the boys alternated from Dave's Diner. "Their house was like a shrine to Bryce," said Barber. "Walls filled with running photos. The parents were wonderful people but maybe into it to the point where it affected Bryce."

*

"You take a deep breath and become logical again," said Barber of training and racing for five months, running nationals, crossing the finish, and letting your emotions out. Aris had to do that, too. On the trip home, his mind turned away from the letdown. Instead, it spun with ideas, a corrective, for next season.

This was not the last Fayetteville would see of Wayzata. In 2015, another girl's family move would link to the immutable resonance of Stotan power. Annika Avery's father got a job transfer to Minnesota—to Wayzata. While Annika went on to the University of California, Berkeley, the Averys picked up and moved to Wayzata, where Annika's mother, Kerry, became a middle school track coach. The girls she worked with fed into Dave Emmans's high school program.

When Annika as a college freshman went home to Wayzata on winter break, she met and ran with Anna French and other girls from the team that had defeated Fayetteville. Annika was invited into their homes. She met Emmans. She saw in Wayzata a touch of what she'd experienced at F-M, something missing from her college team: selflessness.

Even in defeat, Fayetteville-Manlius could take pride in its role as a citadel of greater purpose—delivering a contribution of lasting relevance. Emmans and the Wayzata girls had learned it, prevailing with their own version of Stotan. They had seized on "the unlimited unity of the all," as the philosopher Adam Kirsch has written. At times, truth and realness were uncomfortable dogma, but offered to a civilization in need. It was there, over the seasons, on display for everyone.

22

POET WARRIORS

You will remember this day later in life, this little memory, when you pick up your children from kindergarten, and you breathe in the air. You will remember that night when you were a kid and the world was perfect.

—Bill Aris

2014 Season II

On the Monday after their triumphant New York Regionals in Wappingers Falls, two days before their flight to Portland for the 2014 Nike Cross Nationals weekend, the Fayetteville-Manlius runners did their final tune-up workout at Green Lakes. With the nationals races now moved to a golf course, Aris took the team to the upper reaches of the park, beyond the lakes and the Serengeti, beyond the Cerutty and Lydiard trails, to the site's "masterpiece" golf course. Aris had been waiting all season for the golf course to close for the winter.

"It was an otherworldly day," Aris recalled. "Snow twinkling down. Magical." He gave the team a race-simulator workout, one that would mirror the conditions at the new site, Glendoveer Golf Course, for nationals. "I wanted them

to see what a fairway would feel like. Feel the inclines and declines topographi-
cally. Feel the mood and the ambiance. Feel the synergy of working together
toward a common goal."

With light fading and the snow getting heavier, Fayetteville had the park
to itself. The wind picked up, and ice crystals assaulted the runners' faces,
sticking like bold, white freckles. Only the warmth of a hard effort could
hope to melt them.

Together the boys and girls ran up and down the pitched fairways, about a
half-mile loop, eight times, with a few minutes' jog recovery between runs. "Long
accelerators," Aris called them. As usual, Aris did not time the runs. He instructed
the team to work hard, work together, and commit the terrain's subtleties to
memory. It was like test prep before the SAT. It was too late to learn anything
new, but a time to brush up and reinforce good habits.

Still, junior Peter Ryan remembered the effort as grueling, perhaps too aggressive only five days before nationals. "Guys were coming out of it exhausted," he
said. He added that they'd done harder workouts that fall, but as a race tune-up
"it seemed a little much."

The snow grew dense. A howling wind blew down from the Adirondacks,
ripping off the deep bunkers and swaying the hemlocks bracing for winter's
arrival. Visibility was all but gone. During the workout, many of the youngsters
slipped and fell, laughing as they lost balance. Few could hold their strides in
the closing-sprint finishers designed to replicate the rush off the starting line
at Nike Cross Nationals.

The seven boys and seven girls, their chests a unified drumbeat, stood in the
falling snow. A merciless wind cut their stinging cheeks raw. Soaked jerseys
stuck to their bodies. One girl, lacking proper support, felt a delicate abrasion.
Where was the Vaseline when you needed it?

The work was done, and the foreboding feeling lifted. Aris was pleased. His
team was ready for Portland. At that moment, and not before, a thought crossed
his mind: a benediction.

The coach addressed his athletes: "Everyone please be quiet. Stop talking.
Just listen." He gestured to the fourteen hearts and lungs still at work. "It was
completely silent except for the sound of our breathing," said Jenna Farrell. "It
was getting dark, it was just us and no one else anywhere."

In the darkness, in the collective stirring of their hearts, each boy and girl
could realize the climactic alchemy of their ending sprints. Then, as their hearts
retreated to rest and their breathing quivered to a contented quiet—in their

affirming moment of relief, and *belief*—the man in the hooded parka waving his newfound stick delivered a closing hymn:

"You will remember this day later in life, this little memory, when you pick up your children from kindergarten, and you breathe in the air. You will remember that night when you were a kid and the world was perfect."

∞

In Portland, the F-M boys and girls moved about with confidence at the Tiger Woods Center on the Nike campus. They sipped water, munched fruit, grabbed naps. They made only a token appearance at the social hall—the music, media, Ping-Pong, and the like, Aris felt, could suck the life out of you. When Woods's philandering was made public, Nike stuck by him. When Lance Armstrong's drug conspiracy made headlines, Nike took his name off the campus fitness center across the soccer green from Tiger Woods.

While Nike's business depended on international star power, on this weekend its core sport—running—took center stage with its most fundamental of all endeavors: high school cross-country. Nike's CEO, Mark Parker, who'd succeeded Nike cofounder Phil Knight, made a point of speaking to the runners and presenting the awards after the races. Parker's wife, Kathy Mills Parker, in her early running days in the 1970s, witnessed the confusion and conflict as young women sought emancipation through running. On the US world cross-country team that Parker represented in Europe, the women's squad was managed not by a coach but a female "chaperone" assigned to teach the athletes "manners" and how to comport themselves "like women." She told me that male world-team members took advantage of the more naive, inexperienced women on the squad in what might be considered sexual harassment today. Despite the affronts, Mills and her running sisters prevailed, paving the way for the freedoms taken for granted by girls and women later on.

Parker was an F-M alum and Aris considered her pioneering heritage an omen. Parker's nationals presence gave the Fayetteville enterprise a certain historical symmetry. It was a girl from F-M who'd helped break down barriers to equal opportunity for girls in running, and now, forty years later, the F-M girls were shattering every performance standard—every level of excellence considered revolutionary for young female runners.

Along with the Nike CEO and his wife, Fayetteville could also count on athletes' parents, grandparents, brothers, and sisters, former F-M runners in college or married, along with a few old codgers from the Syracuse area, to make the trip to Portland. They would see barely a few seconds of the actual running as the fields whizzed by, but, after all, this time they were present less to witness a race than a coronation.

Would Fayetteville race to one championship crown or—for the first time—two?

To listen to the background chatter, none. With the F-M girls' defeat in 2013, their detractors were writing them off. The F-M dynasty was over. Great Oak, the latest California girls team to rise up as a challenger, had a flashy statistical resume that was undeniable. It was easy to forget that in cross-country, stats were consumed by character and will.

While the F-M boys, again led by Bryce Millar, were rated a contender, their NXN near misses over the years—going back to 2004 and 2005, when the team emerged as a national force—as well as Millar's disappointing race in 2013, made their chances suspect. At least this time every boy in the F-M top five was groomed to lead.

With his decisive state Class A and New York Regional triumphs, Millar, big for a runner at six feet two and 165 pounds, had enjoyed as fine a season as any boy in the country. In races, Millar liked to go out at breakneck speed, coming up with that approach in team time trials on the Serengeti. He found that charging out in an "insanely fast" sprint, as he put it, even uphill, gave him confidence.

In Portland, Aris still played down the possible sweep. With competition about to unfold, however, he found he could no longer hide from it. Better to get the sweep on the table, but in the proper context.

To convey his message, Aris sat the boys down and told them about a particular *Seinfeld* episode. It was the one in which Jerry and George write a TV pilot and meet with the network producer, a Mr. Dalrymple. While waiting in his office, the producer's well-endowed teenage daughter comes out in a low-cut blouse, bends over, and captures George's attention. He can't keep his eyes off her décolletage. Just then the producer walks in and exclaims in anger, "Getting a good *look*, George?"

After that, back at Jerry's apartment, with no TV deal, Jerry says to George, "What the heck were you doing? Don't you realize that looking at cleavage is like looking at the sun? You take a quick glance, and then you've got to look away." In the telling, Aris added, "Sweeping nationals is like looking at the sun. Stare at it for too long and you go blind."

Aris told the girls more or less the same story, filtering the cleavage part. He added, "You all know a sweep is a possibility. We've never been a goal-oriented team." Aris paused so the girls could reflect on what he meant and what they knew—that the process of learning, growth, sharing, and excellence was the goal. "I've tried to get you both, boys and girls, physically and emotionally ready to run your best at nationals. I know what's going to happen if you do that."

With that teasing admission, Aris gave license to his athletes to think like "warriors," as he said, "going into battle." The fury of a cross-country race demanded it. Straddling the line between purity and conquest, Aris allowed himself a rare brazenness, hoping it would be a last bit of armor for his teams to prevail.

Would anything less than the boys and girls meeting that challenge as one be acceptable? In treating his team as a society apart, Aris fashioned a new model of teenage life. The mixture of the two sexes into one family created not only mutual respect, a stronger work ethic, and higher standards but a gender enlightenment that appeared to have legs.

"I've talked with girls on other teams," said Jenna Farrell, "and they think it's the most bizarre thing to be training with a guy. But it's empowering because you know you work just as hard and are just as strong as they are, and there's no being put down because you're a girl."

Every Stotan girl felt the same. "I could not imagine it any other way," said Samantha Levy. "The boys are a part of us. They add richness to the program that we wouldn't have if Bill only coached girls."

Peter Ryan had seen the gender dynamic from a unique perspective. He'd had a older brother, Nick, and older sister, Olivia, on the squad and, now, kid sister Sophie. Peter prized the Aris approach of not feeding female stereotypes of weakness, delicacy, or appeasement. The coaching fraternity's well-worn script of, "Be careful what you say to a girl," was not, Peter said thankfully, part of the Fayetteville lexicon.

The Aris model, perhaps best of all, diffused the complexities of teenage vulnerability, mystery, and fear. The Fayetteville boys had a natural and sincere regard for girls as rigorous athletes no less hungry for success, no less willing, said Ryan, "to lay it out there every day."

At every turn, Aris had taken on broad assumptions based on weary ideas and cleaned them up with Stotan simplicity. "Living a Stotan life," said Jenna Farrell, "requires you to strip away all the complicated things and focus on the simple parts of your life. I attribute all of my breakthroughs to keeping things simple."

In Portland, Stotan values were like a tasting menu with abundant choices, each one cooked up and timed for the perfect moment. Whether in the hotel, on the Nike campus, or in practice at the racecourse, Aris's mind was rip-roaring with ideas hitting him like ice crystals at Green Lakes: How would he give the kids one last emotional boost with the roar of a NASA launch? How would he assemble every Stotan lesson into one succinct message to assure that these fourteen kids would not fail?

∞

On race-day morning at five forty-five, before breakfast, the fourteen boys and girls gathered outside Aris's room for their ritualistic morning shake-out run. They sat on the ground, waiting. When Aris emerged, he took a long look at each athlete, one by one, making eye contact. Then he said, "Let's go." The group scurried down the stairs and out through the hotel kitchen and a back-door exit to avoid notice by Nike security guards.

"Just like *Goodfellas*," Aris said, in reference to the scene in which the gangster played by Ray Liotta leads his date through the kitchen of the Copacabana to a front-row table in the nightclub. And Aris didn't have to tip anyone.

With the coach in tow, the team scooted into the darkness and down to the Washington Square mall, all done up for Christmas. They entered the sheltered, empty, outdoor parking lot. "Run the perimeter," Aris instructed. As the team did several loops, interspersed with drills like high-knee lifts or back kicks, Aris ran back and forth, nonstop, shouting motivational messages, forcefully, insistently, relentlessly—his greatest hits echoing off the cavernous interior. With the thundering erudition of an ancient Greek orator delivering a speech from the Forum, Aris, in running shorts, his spindly legs darting every which way, bellowed whatever thoughts, on the spot, entered his mind:

You've been working for this since June 29.
Run for each other.
Love each other.
Pain is the purifier. Embrace it.
Walker. Jogger. Trainer. Racer. Killer. Stotan.
Cerutty said, "Setbacks are a spur for good."
We're in our own world now.
Be humble.

Hear your hearts beat.

Love each other.

Be poet warriors.

You're not nice little kids anymore, if you ever were.

Nietzsche said, "Whatever doesn't kill us makes us stronger."

You are now part of Stotan lore. You can hear the echoes of 2004.

You have joined ten years of Stotan history.

You're going to do what's unreasonable, not reasonable.

Do it for love.

Don't look at the sun.

Break through to the other side—the other side of suffering.

Seek freedom.

Accept pain.

Pain is your best friend.

Move beyond pain to greatness.

Aris then invoked a lyric from "The End" by Jim Morrison and the Doors, released in 1967. Rephrasing a passage to apply to the team, Aris cried out, "The Stotans awoke before dawn . . . put their spikes on and walked on down the hall . . . chose their singlets from the ancient gallery . . . and they walked down the hall . . . !" When performed, the song starts like a séance; then, it erupts like a race start.

After his declaration, referring to the fact that NXN was a postseason event in which, technically, the athletes represented clubs, not their schools (so that various high school sports officials wouldn't freak out), Aris told the kids, "We're out of school and I can say what I want. God is good and so are you."

It was still dark, about four hours before the day's competition would begin. Aris asked the athletes to line up, side by side, for their closing sprints. Before each run, Aris called emphatically, "Who's this one for?" The boys responded with one of their names. The girls responded with one of their names. Aris called, "Set . . . go," and the kids raced up a slight ascent to where Aris was standing. They did seven sprints, so that each of the seven runners on the boys and girls squads would hear their names called in one last powerful affirmation.

When they ran back to the hotel, Aris made a point of saying, "We go through the front door now." As the team entered the communal dining hall for a light breakfast, Aris leaned over to me and said, "My work is done now."

⁓

At the racecourse, Aris walked the carpeted Athletes Village, a converted indoor tennis center, as the national-meet officials put their final touches on the team starting corrals. Aris felt exhausted. His parking lot performance had left him as spent as a runner in the finish chute. He had barely touched his breakfast.

What was Aris really hoping for? What mattered? Who was he? Was the whole point the purity of the effort or the conquest of the opposition? Was it really all about the nobility of the process, as he'd preached, or sticking it to the doubters showing their envy in the media? What separated the love from the guts, the poet from the warrior, humility from the adulation? In his elevated society, in his Stotan culture, in his convictions and yearning, how did the pure outrank the impure in what Aris wanted his kids to take from their hard work and implausible rise since the end of June?

With his mind reeling, Aris needed to lie down and compose himself. The F-M girls had completed their warm-ups, and in the final moments before being called for the introductions, they were huddled in their private team dressing room with the curtains drawn. Each team enclosure had intimacy, perfect for last-minute communion.

"We were in lockdown," said Sophie Ryan.

At that moment Aris decided to lie down on his back on a massage bench about thirty feet from the girls' room. He chose to say nothing more. No more quotes. No more high-and-mighty mantras. "At this point," he thought, "all I could do was screw it up."

He looked up at the ceiling and closed his eyes, trying to quiet his mind. Rival coaches looked at him with amusement. A few sneered at this latest Aris gimmick. Who did he think he was? Photographers snapped pictures. Aris ignored the attention. "I just wanted to be calm," he said later.

Aris thought about a book he'd read, *Mastery* by Robert Greene, which talked about ways to bring out greatness in oneself and others. Aris thought about how he'd been trying to achieve that since the summer of 2004 Stotan camp in the Adirondacks. He thought about the teams that had followed, the boys and girls, how they'd touched him with their strength and beauty, and he thought about what he'd had to do this summer and fall, every summer and fall, to prepare for this moment. He thought about his team lacking in natural running talent, not what other teams had, and requiring nothing less than his relentless and comprehensive urging—an impetus for the athletes' minds and souls to accept his language, his "something extra." He thought about the morning shake-out run when his oration included subtleties articulated to address the particular emotional vulnerability of each of the fourteen kids.

Most of all Aris thought about the main reason for his awkward body language amid the hubbub of his public viewing. With pre-race anxiety in the air, Aris wanted to show the team that he didn't have a care in the world, that there was nothing to worry about, everything was under control. Float. Say nothing. Do nothing. He had to quell his own emotions and convey mastery.

"I wanted the kids to see me at peace and feel an assuredness," Aris said. "I wanted them to feel more connected to themselves as self-determining young runners. I wanted self-governance."

Aris had borrowed the idea from Alfred Hitchcock. When Aris had strolled around the arena earlier, he remembered a story about Hitchcock, the meticulous film director, conveying such confidence in his actors that at times during action on the set he would fall asleep in his director's chair.

That was Bill Aris: practically asleep with the first race coming up.

When the girls pulled back their curtain, they could see their coach and the curious people around him. "It seemed like Bill doing his normal crazy thing that you can't really describe or explain," said Jenna Farrell. "I guess that was his way of relaxing." Sam Levy saw a greater purpose. "We took it to mean he was letting us do our own thing," she said. "He was letting us be self-reliant."

When the athletes were called to race, they would need that self-reliance. No one knew Sophie Ryan's secret about her tender foot. No one suspected that Bryce Millar, who'd carried Ryan on his back for two miles through the forest, would be running on empty.

23

HERE COMES THE SUN

My mind shifted. There was no way I would let the team lose.
—*Peter Ryan, Fayetteville-Manlius cross-country runner*

2014 Finish Line

When the Fayetteville-Manlius girls left their quarters in the Athletes Village to head for the starting line of the 2014 NXN championship, Annika Avery was worried. Not about the new course they were about to run. Glendoveer, a welcome change from Portland Meadows, had drawn raves. No one expressed the view that the hay bales or whoop-de-doos would be missed; certainly not the mud. And Glendoveer was spectator friendly, with well-marked contours that were easy to follow. Family cheers would be heard during the races. Avery's parents, brother, and grandmother had made the trip.

Avery, a senior, derived some security from the last rituals back home. The girls had run over to Mallards Landing and tied their racing hair ribbons around the post at the creek. They'd stopped on Green Lakes runs to find twigs and construct teepees to leave in the woods, turf markings for future teams. They'd sung chants to one another, secret recitations never to be revealed.

And while Avery had received Bill Aris's world-is-perfect elegy in the snow-storm as a "beautiful moment," she could not fully savor his touching send-off because of a headache. "My head was cold," she said, as if wintry conditions were new to her. She'd pressed her fingers to her temples for relief.

Perhaps it was more of a troubled mind that had preyed on Avery and, in its own way, preyed on everyone in the F-M circle all season. There had been a lot at stake from day one.

Aris had offered new ideas, a "corrective," to cleanse the girls of their 2013 debacle. Six of their top seven runners were back. Aris also had correctives for the boys. They, too, had six of their top seven back. Would these new ideas work? Would teen extremes allow for selflessness to harvest? Fayetteville had a legitimate chance of sweeping the national championships. Would F-M gush gender equity in team sports as never before?

The goals for 2014 had been set almost from the moment the previous season had ended. Aris had told the young men, "We've never had a boys team win NXN. You're capable of running the table. If you want it, it can be done." Then he paused for effect and added, "If not now . . . *when?*"

The girls caught the same vibe. In fact, the girls quaked for the boys as much as for themselves. This, in part, is what drove Aris to frame the team's perfect world amid the captivating tableau of the whitening Green Lakes grounds. The boys and girls had forged an unspoken bond. Prior to Aris's salutation, he'd lined up the athletes for a drill and had the boys elbow the girls off the mark as a touchstone of what to expect in Portland. The girls took it as tough love.

Some on the team had valued history among them. The fathers of Riley Hughes, Kyle Barber, and the graduated Jillian Fanning had all been in the same fraternity together at Clarkston University up near Canada. In Manlius, as neighbors, the families would socialize with backyard barbeques, and the kids would get into trouble, like the time Jillian ate fish food and Riley broke his toe playing soccer.

Now, in the races that could announce it, would each wing of the squad hold its bonds as a sacred truth?

With all the Fayetteville dominance, the concordant closure to the Stotan principles that Aris had sought at Nike Cross Nationals had never quite been fulfilled. The 2004 boys team that swept Christian Brothers at Van Cortlandt Park and soared to the White Moment at Bowdoin Park, only to be undermined by the Gong Show in Portland, could still unearth hurt a decade hence. Even the 2010 girls that defeated the entire nation as one team with twenty-seven points carried a "what if?" because of the injured leading lady Courtney Chapman, a minute off her game giving it everything she had.

For Aris, perfection was fluid. Who dared speak of it? Even think it. Now, as two victories were sought—presented like jewels locked in glass—perfection took on its most profound purity: not one gender but both, not one leader but many, not one study in selflessness but another, once and for all, for every F-M boy and girl in the twine of history that ran.

"You will remember that night when you were a kid and the world was perfect." Aris pondered his season's mantra, "If not now . . . when?" It was like an oath, but was it too much to ask, even of F-M, of *this* F-M?

Avery, the lead returning girl, had worries from the first day of summer practice. She fretted about the gap left by the graduation of Alana Pearl, the number-two runner from the prior year. Pearl was consistent, in both performance and personality. Avery treasured consistency, the predictable. Where would those qualities come from?

Once the season got going, Avery worried about the Ryan sisters, Olivia and Sophie. It had taken time but Olivia, a senior, had finally let go of the bristleness that accompanied Aris's decision to leave her off the 2013 nationals squad. She committed to cross-country in 2014, but her distance conversion also took time, and her early racing was spotty. But that's not what threw Avery off-kilter. It was that Ryan still had a certain go-her-own-way style that made any attempt to tie a bow around the girls' collective unity fruitless.

Sophie, a freshman and the fourth and last Ryan sibling in the program, also had an independent streak but at this point followed her sister. She'd come up from her eighth-grade running as a "clueless" middle schooler, she told me, in "my own little world" of swimming, soccer, and lacrosse. "It was a challenge," said Avery.

When the girls lost the early-season McQuaid meet in Rochester for the second-straight year—to an unheralded Elmira team—Avery worried that the entire season might be doomed with setbacks just like '13, just like the blows in Portland. Avery ran a good race that day as the number-two Fayetteville scorer between Sam Levy and Jenna Farrell, but the Ryan girls were far back along with Jessica Howe and Reilly Madsen. Three reliable runs out of the seven? That messiness played with Avery's head. Farrell's too. At practice, Farrell recalled, there was too much giggling.

On the tail end of the season, Avery herself struggled after some stellar performances. Taking her college visits as far as away as California while demanding her best in her last high school cross-country races, Avery got sick, lost her edge, and was nothing like the girl who'd won the New York Regional with room to spare the year before.

Avery seemed to find solace more in wildlife than people. Even with her national track standing, Avery preferred the cross-country trails. "In some of my best races," she said, "I'd get to a point on the course, in the back woods, where I could hear the birds chirping, and I could hear my breathing with it. I loved that."

Nature never left Fayetteville. Nature was an assistant coach.

∽

To try and refresh the girls and quell any trespass, Aris reached as far as he could for daring ideas. Even, he said, "ideas I don't agree with because that stimulates my thinking." Aris could find his muse anywhere: like Paul Simon, who once found the title of a future hit, "Mother and Child Reunion," on the menu of a Chinese restaurant.

Aris put together his own menu, a tablet. From management studies he looked into, Aris decided to give all athletes, male and female, leadership roles. They would be chosen by one another each month with out-front discussion of each runner's personal qualities. Everyone, regardless of performance or experience, would have a stake in day-to-day operations. "If any leader faltered, another could step up," said Aris.

He told the team, "There is no cardboard cutout of how I want you to lead. I'm looking for each of you to bring out your best. This is going to be a test tube of learning—about commitment, work ethic, team love and accountability; about your responsibility to one another in a race. If you inspire others to do better, how can we fail?"

Levy, a junior and the number-one F-M girl in the first two meets, felt the broader leadership gave the team more "conviction." Farrell, also a junior, agreed. "Even if someone was not a true leader, at least she would have a say," she said. Farrell herself made a good impression. "Jenna was my go-to person," said the freshman Sophie. "She always knew what she was doing." Farrell, who'd followed two older brothers onto the team, helped Sophie learn how to "use teammates" in competition.

Avery the worrywart remained unconvinced. While the Aris corrective helped everyone feel accountable, she said, "We were not necessarily getting along better." Avery wanted birds to sing. But, remember, Aris had told the girls the year before—you don't have to get along, but rally around a common goal.

If there was a serious breach, like letting the pace dawdle on a crucial Saturday-morning long run while the coach was away visiting family, Aris would pull out an ace from *Chariots of Fire*, the award-winning 1981 film about the 1924 Olympics. After scolding the girls as they sat quivering at the Green Lakes pavilion, Aris referred to the pious Eric Liddell character that refused to compete on a Sunday. Liddell satisfied officials, if not himself, by switching events and still winning a gold medal. Clutching his medal and asked about his decision, Liddell said, "Do I have regrets? Yes. Doubts? No."

"I could treat you like little girls having a cuddly pillow-fight sleepover, but I won't," Aris told the young ladies. "This is the real world." Aris then put on his grandpa hat. "Coming down on you keeps me up at night, but it's necessary." Then, drawing upon Liddell's sentiment, Aris told them: "Do I have regrets? Yes. Doubts? No."

Using 2013 as a learning tool, Aris told the girls that the melting pot theory of bringing different people together was the backbone of the country, while in the salad bowl theory people coexisted while not uniting, emphasizing their differences. "Think about 2013. Think about this year," Aris said. "Which do you prefer?"

The Aris measures started to cohere in midseason when Fayetteville rebounded from its McQuaid setback to reclaim the Manhattan Eastern States Championship at Van Cortlandt Park. It was Avery who led the team, placing second in her best race of the season. F-M won by thirty-three points over La Salle of Rhode Island. Olivia Ryan finally showed her talent as the second F-M scorer, just ahead of Levy.

Down the home straight Avery chased after a tiny dynamo from Virginia by way of Eritrea, Weini Kelati, who ran 14:21 to Avery's 14:25 for the two-and-a-half-mile course. Avery had no idea who Kelati was. Who needs more worries?

The latest African to impact American high school running, Kelati carried a greater mystique than even that of Edward Cheserek. After representing her country three months earlier at the world junior track meet in Oregon, Kelati, who spoke no English, found a way to lose the homeward-bound Eritrean delegation and move in with a cousin in Virginia. She attended high school and, joining the cross-country team, outran all the boys.

When I spoke with Kelati's cousin at the time, I found out how desperate Kelati was. Her small village where her family still lived was under siege. Warring factions were everywhere: from Ethiopia and Sudan; ISIS, too. Kelati went on to win the 2015 Foot Locker championship, run for the University of

New Mexico, and contribute to the Lobos' back-to-back NCAA women's team cross-country championships.

The real world . . . don't you forget it.

Three weeks later the muddy earth in upstate Canton moved as a Ryan girl—Sophie—led Fayetteville to its ninth-straight state Class A title with a third-place finish against nationally ranked opposition. It was a near sweep: F-M 20, Saratoga 85. Ryan clocked 18:05, twenty-six seconds ahead of F-M number-two Levy; afterward, Ryan's pride was subdued by history. After all, she said, other F-M girls had *won* state.

With November snow blanketing Green Lakes, the team turned to its uberworthy alternative, Gulf Road, for their heady ten-miler, whose upper switchbacks swirled like the head of a soft ice cream cone. "The top half," said the 2004–'05 Stotan Owen Kimple years later, "still haunts me."

Indeed, this season, a haunting presence near the Gulf Road peak attempted to do what the racing opposition could not: stop Fayetteville in its tracks. A woman who lived near the crescent would blast her ratty car up the narrow, winding road with a cigarette dangling from her mouth threatening the runners, who dared tread on "her" turf. She complained to the *Post-Standard* in a scathing letter to the editor, which the paper chose to print without checking any facts with Aris. "It was sensationalism at our expense," steamed Aris, who took a stand by not speaking with *P-S* reporters for two years.

A break in the weather afforded the team a last chance to hit Green Lakes before regionals. The athletes devoured the Cerutty, the Lydiard, the terraced climb in the Valley of the Hills. They flew the sylvan meadows. At Round Lake, on the loop's magic carpet, on the offshoots, with the late-afternoon sun all but gone and shadows hiding potential peril, Sophie Ryan tripped over a tree root on a downhill pitch and went splat.

"I heard a 'pop,'" Ryan recalled. "I'm like, 'Oh, my God, I broke my ankle. My season's over.' I tried to get up and walk it off, but it hurt really bad and I started crying." Avery, slight of build, carried Sophie down the hill to lie on a bench at the lake. They were miles from Aris, who was waiting in his usual spot in the parking lot for the team to return. The boys were also running but nowhere to be seen.

"All of us were panicky," said Farrell. "We didn't know what to do."

It was twenty degrees. The girls decided to have Sophie place her ankle in the frigid lake as an ice bath to try and reduce the swelling. As Sophie sat on the gravel embankment at the water's edge, she waved the girls off to continue their run; they would check on her every few minutes.

Olivia stayed with Sophie trying to comfort her. A north wind scattered the fallen leaves and Sophie felt exposed. Warblers sang from the tulip tree canopy. It was not a happy tune. Sophie drew closer to Olivia, who clutched her sister around her waist as their chilled sweat mingled.

Within minutes, just as Sophie removed her frozen right ankle from the waters, the boys team ran by, stopped, and came to her aide. Millar, with the chassis of an Abrams tank, did the yeoman work in hoisting Sophie a couple of miles back to the parking lot, where Aris was greeted with the news. Team support kept up Sophie's spirits. "It showed how much the boys and girls cared for each other," she said.

Later that night, at home with her brother Peter while the rest of the family was out, Peter spoke to Sophie as both brother and surrogate coach. The two were close. Peter told Sophie the ankle was not broken and just needed time to heal. Sophie received a text message from Aris. She read it over and over. "He told me I was going to be okay, that I would be able to run regionals," she said. "I saved it."

Aris had to reassure his athletes. But the girls had only five solid runners. After number five, there was a big drop to number six. Earlier that evening at Green Lakes, after the parents had collected their kids and everyone left, Aris launched his new stick into the woods in frustration.

Sophie iced her ankle, took an anti-inflammatory when the pain flared, and told me—an admission, really—that on a scale of one to ten, her continuing discomfort was seven and a half to eight. How could she run the regionals when Bowdoin Park was frozen, the downhills would crush a tender ankle, and the opening straightaway was a moonscape of ice chunks? Focus on the race, let adrenaline carry you, and forget the ankle. "The team needed me," she said.

At the finish there was no time to think about the ankle. Sophie was the number-three F-M girl, and big sister Olivia achieved a breakthrough as the top Fayetteville scorer in the team's seventh-straight NXN New York victory. One year: tears, anguish, fury; the next: joy. "Olivia had fully arrived," said Aris. She placed fifth in 18:53, eight seconds ahead of Levy. F-M had all five scorers in the top twenty with an improving thirty-five-second compression.

Fayetteville in effect now had five first women. Olivia, Sophie, Annika, and Sam had all won races, with Jenna, in one race, a second behind. Bring on the nationals!

∽

In Portland, as the girls stripped down, Sophie's ankle was still a seven and a half to eight. She'd stopped icing. "Screw it," she said. "We were not planning on running bad." The girls were left on their own. Self-reliance ruled. Aris, his bench-nap-meditation-zen-offering complete, searched for spots to watch it all unfold. He had found a new stick.

Olivia, the "new Olivia," told her mom, "I'm not leaving this in the hands of anyone else."

Avery had already dismissed Sophie's ankle, saying, "She was always twisting it." At this point, Avery was not worried about the Ryans. It was the others. "I paid attention to small details," Avery said. "If someone looked uncomfortable, I would try and help them." She had customers. Levy was so nervous she barely touched her breakfast. "A bite of banana," she said. "Nationals were always scary," said Farrell. "Would you have a great race or blow up?"

The girls had done all they could. One day they'd run loops on the hilly Cerutty Trail totaling fourteen miles. "The more you're hurting," said Levy, "the more you're getting closer to excellence. With more pain, you're purifying yourself of the 'bad' runner and becoming the runner you were meant to be. Fourteen miles. A race . . . oh, that's just three miles."

The seven girls huddled in their cherry-red singlets with spikes on. They stood in a circle with arms folded around one another's shoulders. They spoke of how hard they'd worked, how much the season meant, and, said Levy, "how much we loved each other."

Levy raced out hard among the leaders with Olivia at her shoulder. It was fifty degrees, grey, no gloves needed, no jersey underneath. Olivia used her broad shoulders from years in the pool. Levy ran with grace. "I have good posture," she said. Her nerves were gone.

Compared to Portland Meadows, Glendoveer was like a shiny, new toy, surgically clean. One section was called the Lollipop Loop. The course had no main hill or pivotal corner. It was simple and serviceable. From a degree-of-difficulty standpoint, Aris gave it a laugh. Compared to what F-M ran back home, Glendoveer would hopefully be an eighteen-minute joyride for his girls.

Prepping the new facility gave Nike officials pause. While it was dry on race day, the course had soaked up a lot of rain in recent days and weeks. Course manager Ryan Canning and his staff had worked through the night on Thursday and Friday pumping the water out, especially in one spot that was knee deep. They also made use of squeegees from the tennis courts; they aerated the grounds. After leaving Portland Meadows, Nike needed to get Glendoveer right: this change was forever.

Nike had no control over the shrill talk on social media. The meme this time was that the new course was fair to all, as opposed to Portland Meadows' quirky slop that somehow favored Fayetteville. F-M's time was up. The polls had Great Oak of California as the favorite. Great Oak girls had dominated their state meet, and there was delight over the anticipated F-M drubbing.

That notion was put to rest at the 1k split. F-M led Great Oak of California by almost a hundred points. Sophie and Avery were in the second pack. The soft footing was kind to Sophie's ankle. Avery, seeing Levy ahead, told herself, "Okay, great, one less person to worry about." Avery listened for parents' cheers. Not her own parents but those of teammates. That would ease her mind that the girls were close.

The leaders included Stephanie Jenks, a world-ranked junior triathlete from rural Iowa. Her shoulders were bigger than Olivia's. Jenks traveled the world to compete, with her mom as coach. Stephanie told me she did eighteen workouts a week in run, bike, and swim. She was joined at the front by a girl half her size who looked half her age: Allie Ostrander of Alaska. Ostrander showed promise after winning the junior division of a July Fourth race up an Alaska mountain in which she beat all the boys.

By midway, Olivia was still far up but had ceded the pace to Jenks and Ostrander. Levy drifted a touch behind. Sophie closed on her sister, telling herself, "I gotta get up there." Sophie was prompted by confusion over uniform colors. She thought the individual qualifiers wearing the same colors per region represented a school team that, to her, was ahead. At 9:20 on the running clock, Sophie drew even with Olivia and the two, side by side, climbed a small hill near the finish to complete the first big loop. The sisters pushed each other. Neither would give an inch.

Ankle? What ankle? Sophie surged ahead of Olivia and now led all of F-M. "That was scary," she said. "To be in that position at nationals." Watching her daughters from the sidelines, and referring to young Sophie, Pat Ryan said later, "That girl's got no quit in her."

Aris darted from one kilometer to the next with his new stick, watching the girls trade positions, closing ranks. "They were like an accordion," said Aris. "Stretching and contracting."

The field covered the rolling terrain, all grass, a hill here, a turn there—patterned like Green Lakes loops but nothing anyone would call the "Viper," another choice Aris hill back home. Parents followed their kids. Brothers and sisters jumped the flagged course dividers. The announcers could be heard in a muffled way, as in a New York subway station. "The screws are being tightened," one called. It was a tumultuous scene, as always, but the F-M girls, with the finish near, felt a luminous calm, touching one another with their splendor.

Olivia passed Sophie back. Farrell moved to Sophie's side. Levy trailed by a few strides with Avery behind her. The five girls were barely seventy meters apart. Only one Great Oak girl was visible, just ahead of Olivia. Howe and Madsen, the expected six and seven runners, filled out the Fayetteville lineup about a minute farther back.

After FM's early aggression to stake its claim, the superior individual entries swarmed ahead: ten across the finish led by victorious Ostrander in 17:19; another bunch with the fading Jenks in nineteenth; then, into the thirties and forties, the first team runners. Spectators filled both sides of the home straight craning for a look, hoping to be dazzled by their own.

Then they came like the arrival of royalty: Manlius, as their uniforms read. Olivia first, the eleventh team runner, in 18:35. Avery next, the twelfth team runner, in 18:38. Avery second? She was the fifth F-M girl approaching the finish-area staging. Prompted by the team's connective tissue and schooled in what Aris taught as climactic "chute speed," Avery roared to the line. She said, "Up the last hill, I was thinking, 'We may have had our differences, but this is what we were working for.'"

Then it was Sophie next, the twelfth team runner, also in 18:38; Farrell after her, the thirteenth team runner, in 18:39. Four together, as one, the cross-country dream . . . *it can't happen, no one's ever done it, not at NXN.* The fifth? Where's the F-M fifth? That's what the announcer kept saying, almost with glee, and he was right there at the finish: *We haven't seen F-M's fifth!* Sorry, you missed her. It was Levy next, the fifth scorer, twentieth team runner out of 154, a few seconds back in 18:46.

An eleven-second compression at nationals. No individual "killers," just a pack of wolves. The scores: Fayetteville-Manlius 70, Great Oak 149, and Carmel of Indiana 173 in the twenty-two-team field. F-M won its eighth NXN championship in nine years, by seventy-nine points.

"Our worst moment," said Aris, referring to 2013, "was turned into our best." Aris paused and offered, "There's always hope that you can reach kids. You can never give up on them because you want to catch them at their point of understanding. They're growing every second. You never know when you hit it."

When you do, nothing is off-limits. Keith Richards of the Rolling Stones, referring to seamless teamwork, expressed the exaltation of comradeship with a verbal guitar lick in his excellent autobiography, *Life*. "There's a certain moment when you realize that you've actually just left the planet for a bit and nobody can touch you. You're elevated because you're with a bunch of guys that want to do the same thing as you. And when it works, baby, you've got wings."

After the earthly hugs and tears and rejoicing—after coaches with *how-do-they-do-it* looks marched their teams back to the heated comfort of the Athletes Village—Sophie Ryan needed help taking her shoes off for the team's barefoot strides. Her ankle hurt. Her feet were cold. She shrugged it off. "The season's over," she said.

But she knew it wasn't: the boys race was coming up. More nerves for Avery. More nerves for all of them. "We had little time to bask in the joy of our victory," said Farrell. "Coming off the podium, we saw the boys run right past us on their way to the starting line. They looked fearless. It felt like we had an understanding. We did our part, now it was time to do theirs."

∽

If not now . . . Kyle Barber had come down with mono over the summer and missed a month of training. Riley Hughes started summer from scratch after missing all of spring track with what he called "fake mono." After a lingering sore throat, Hughes got checked out, was diagnosed with mono and told not to run, only to find out later that his blood work was handled improperly. Adam Hunt had a knee problem. All three were seniors. Patrick Perry, a promising sophomore, had a hamstring problem.

Peter Ryan, now a junior, had suffered stress fractures in both femurs during the prior indoor track season and also missed spring track. He cross-trained with swimming, pool running, and stationery cycling, the usual team regimen, and over the summer, once back, if the team did a seventy-minute run, Ryan did half that.

Aris was undeterred. To try and inspire the boys as never before, Aris the film buff fell back on the silver screen. Remember *Ben Hur*, the 1959 film about the ancient Romans and Jews starring Charleton Heston? Remember that it won eleven Academy Awards including best picture? Remember the famous chariot race? The boys didn't either; in fact, Bill was only a toddler himself when the film came out.

But he'd always loved it. Remember the scene when the Roman ships, propelled by exhausted slaves in chains rowing in the hold, were preparing for battle? The commander called for faster and faster effort, moving from "cruising speed" to "battle speed" to "attack speed" to "ramming speed," as the slaves fought for their last ounce of strength.

Aris instructed the boys to watch the film on YouTube. Most did. Then Aris gave them a workout using the warship terminology as the boys ran faster and faster to reach "ramming speed." Aris likened the four speeds to "tempo effort," "workout effort," "race effort," and "finishing effort." The idea had psychological underpinnings: the triumph of good over evil, "us" versus "them" with the championships coming up; and, be ready for anything: there are no rules in the arena.

Aris had the boys take charge of their own workouts. Instead of using his whistle to signal pace changes on the school fields, Aris told the boys to decide when to run faster and longer with numerical callouts; *they* would decide on ramming speed. *They* would decide when to "inoculate" themselves against the pain expected in racing. Aris dished out "reverse ladders" on the Serengeti: faster, harder, pain is your friend, do every run like it's your last one. Patrolling the delta, Aris and his assistant coaches, Davis and Nixdorf, were in awe.

Early-day bike racers bit into tire tubes in desperation when pain proved too great. Fayetteville boys chewed on philosophy from their tasting menu: any nugget of deliverance, salty meaning, distillation of the greats, or maybe a spark from someone else: not Aris or Cerutty or Elliott, but the embrace of a local gentleman with a big heart who attended all the meets including nationals, Jerry Bisson.

Papa Bisson was Jillian Fanning's grandfather. He'd been a runner and coach and was the kind of person who uplifted everyone, not just his kin. Even before Jillian or her sister, Kathryn, ran for F-M, they'd go to the school track on Thanksgiving morning with other kids, like Barbour and Hughes, and run laps in a holiday gesture fashioned by Bisson. At the end, recalled Hughes, Bisson would present the participants with trophies that he'd won. He was Stotan through and through. "A saint," said Aris.

With people like Bisson in their corner, and armed with peerless confidence, Fayetteville boys marched into Van Cortlandt Park for the midseason Manhattan Easterns. There was nothing canny or coy about them. They just up and blew you away. Millar was at his best, taking second in 12:02, the new all-time "fastest loser," closer yet to Cheserek country (a Connecticut boy won in 11:58). Barbour was F-M number two in 12:23, running down a rival from Liverpool.

Ryan, half-runner/half cross-trainer, was told to hold back and stay with Hunt, who crossed in 12:38; Ryan was credited with 12:39. Ryan's femurs were better, but he'd picked up tendinitis in the knee, missed another two weeks of running, and had to wear a brace. He took off the brace to race; after, he put it right back on.

"I was very underweight," said Ryan, who then was five feet eleven and 120 pounds. "I didn't have the resources to build myself up." Ryan told me he fell into a cycle of always trying hard to rebound while not eating enough; being on the short end of calories in, calories out. On a spin bike at the Y, Ryan would gun it nonstop for over an hour. "Pete dripped so much sweat," said Aris, "you needed a mop to clean it up."

The boys left the Bronx with a shattering team-time course record of 12:32.4—*taking twelve seconds per man off the old mark*—in a performance that made everybody think: "Yep, the 2004 sweep of CBA." Hughes, solid fifth man in thirteen flat, said that together with the girls' victory, "It felt like a foreshadowing." All in due time, my friend. "We were not full of ourselves," said Aris. "It was part of our continuum."

A month later at state, the boys were so fit they were about to explode. Millar repeated as state Class A champion in 15:31. Barber ran his best race for third in 15:39. Hunt, keen on ROTC with a military future, ran his best race in 15:55, taking eighth right behind the all-American trackman Mikey Brannigan. Ryan was fourteenth in 16:05 with Joe Walters, a sophomore, edging Hughes for fifth scorer.

The Fayetteville boys scored a record-low twenty-four points, triumphed by seventy-six, and *swept* runner-up Shenendehowa, by placing all five scorers ahead of Shen's first. That's with Ryan adding to his reputation as having the devil at his side. A mile into the race, sitting in fourth with Millar leading on a steep gravel hill, a runner in front of Ryan swung his arm back to prevent a thorny branch from hitting him and smacked Ryan square in the eyes. "I couldn't see," said Ryan. He swerved, hit a tree, and went down, scraping his legs and hips. Once on his feet, Ryan said he couldn't open his eyes for over a minute. "I was running blind," he said.

Three weeks later, Ryan managed to stay on his feet in the team's perfunctory regionals win, as Millar triumphed cleanly and the boys arrived at nationals with the attitude, let's get this thing over with. They'd been swept up by the Aris blessing at Green Lakes, sweetened with the *Seinfeld* tales in Portland, and pumped up with the final, staccato Stotan commandments in the morning shakeout in the parking garage. At breakfast, with an Embassy Suites buffet worthy of a hotel on the Rue Rivoli, Riley Hughes ate personalized granola brought from home. Not everyone thought of that.

The boys knew the girls had won when they took the start. They understood Stotan history: that the 2004 team just missed, ditto for 2005; the Alex Hatz surgery that derailed 2009; the unlikely runner-up rise of the 2010 enfants terribles; the 2012 boys that got whacked into the mud; that they themselves had let an opportunity pass in '13. Eight Fayetteville boys teams had competed at NXN in ten years. No victory. No Stotan closure. No lordly culmination after sweeps and records and White Moments and saying to hell with weird shit that seemed to turn up when they weren't looking.

∞

The race was on. Millar went out with conviction. He'd led Fayetteville in every meet. He won the New York Regional by forty meters. He was a nationals favorite. His expression said: I dare you. The dense front pack gave off thunder as they hit the mile in 4:55. One commentator, noting the soggy surface, said, "Don't ask too much of the ground." The only leader wearing gloves was Tanner Anderson, a big, strong redhead from Washington State. He pushed the pace, and halfway, with the pack thinned out, Millar and Ryan ran side by side as a pair in eighth and ninth. The 2k scores were Fayetteville 69, Liverpool, seventeen miles north in Onondaga County, 120, with American Fork of Utah third.

Aris was relieved. He'd walked the hotel halls at two o'clock in the morning. Thinking, fretting, "getting off some edge," he said. Was this the day? He'd walked through the lobby and into the kitchen. Did he want a snack? He pondered his shake-out speech, to come within hours. A decade of wonder and dazzle flashed before him. After ten years, how did he get to this point?

One hundred and eleven miles in the Adirondacks. Encounter groups. The Junction Boys workout. Girls growing up. Stotan courage. Stotan letdowns. Gender equity. It was almost too much.

Barber, coming from behind, saw Millar and Ryan, and Hunt "mixed in," and felt a boost. At the start, an opponent to Barber's right had tried to manhandle him by grabbing his wrist and pushing him back. Barber swung the boy back to get free. "I had to move too quickly to be angry," he said.

Barber got another shot of adrenaline at about 3k. Millar started to fade. His face gave off turmoil. His body wavered. Would Millar even finish? "Seeing Bryce fall back, my race was now amplified," said Barber.

Aris had molded an entire team of leaders. They could no longer exist under Millar's spell. "Everyone looked up to Bryce," said Hughes. "If I did my warm-up strides close to Bryce, his presence would calm me."

With a mile to go, savagery was needed. Who would take charge with the grasp of victory coming loose? "My mind shifted," said Ryan. "There was no possible way I would let the team lose."

Peter was so much a Ryan: taking some hits but overcoming, always with the endgame in focus, stoic. He'd driven to Green Lakes in an old Dodge pickup with bags of ice in the cargo bed. He'd set up a makeshift ice bath for the boys, and they'd all soak in it on a summer day when their legs were tired.

How long ago that day seemed now. Ryan knew that no boys team had ever won NXN without at least one scorer well up front. Ryan pressed hard and passed Millar. Barber, too, chased after Millar, who dug for energy from the tyranny of an empty body. Barber passed Hunt, who remained close. Hughes held pace. His granola was working.

The F-M girls were in a race of their own, their second of the morning, following the boys. "We might have been breathing harder chasing the boys than in parts of our own race," said Farrell. "And most of us lost our voices screaming for them."

Avery, never one to let nuance escape her, said, "When we were watching the boys race, we were the most together that we were the entire season—even in our own race." How could that be? "The boys were so integral," she said. "We trained together. The boys pushed us, and we pushed them. We needed their team to complete it."

Curving through the last kilometer with the finish in view, the four of them—Ryan, Millar, Barber, and Hunt—were all close, just like the girls; not *that* close, but close enough—as a desperate Millar courted every blurring stride to the wire.

After Anderson sewed up the victory in 15:11, the third straight for a Washington boy, Ryan led F-M across the line in fifteenth in 15:40. Millar finished looking dazed in sixteen flat. Barber caught Millar at the line, also in sixteen flat. Hunt ran his best race, running up on the pair in 16:03. A twenty-three-second spread for the top four, yielding fifty-six team points. That's wiggle room. But fifth scorer Hughes didn't need it. He ran his best in 16:29, ahead of more than half the field. The sophomore Walters was on Hughes's heels in 16:32. Jonathan Abbot, a senior, completed the Fayetteville lineup at the rear.

Millar walked off to the side brooding. Barber retrieved an energy bar for him. Had personal issues gotten to Millar for the third year in a row at nationals? Family members said he had low blood sugar, which some wondered about. "They came at it from a loving point of view," said Hughes, of those closest to

Millar. Once home in Manlius, Millar, who went on to run for the University of Indiana, texted his six teammates, "Sorry for letting you guys down . . ." Barber texted him back, "No worries, we could not have done it without you."

Fayetteville scored 111 for the victory. Wayzata of Minnesota was second with 159. Anderson's team, North Spokane, was third (178). Liverpool held on for fourth (191). The F-M margin of victory was the largest yet for boys at NXN. The Nike Cross Nationals team sweep, ten years in the making, was secured.

Fayetteville's girls joined their boys on the podium. They lined up boy, girl, boy, girl for hugs, tears, and pictures. "Every hardship all season was instantly worth it," said Barber. "I would have been a fool to have asked for more from that race."

Certainly all the Ryans felt the same. Three of their own were central to the sweep. Peter, on one good leg, led the boys. "Picking up the flag," he said. Olivia, from hurt to redemption, led the girls. "I'd never seen so much happiness in one place as I did on that stage," she told me. Sophie, her ankle put to rest, trembled with tears of joy and the recognition that fury and rawness could go together. Nick, too, who'd come before and taught the others. He joked that he, the family's best runner, was the one without a national championship.

At the Saturday-night awards on the Nike campus, F-M humility was the gold medal as the boys and girls took the stage for their honors. They looked almost embarrassed to be up there, as though material reward were an insult. "They're a million miles from cocky," a longtime coach and official from New York, Dan Dougherty of Pearl River, told me. "That's a credit to Bill. That's what Bill's like."

Aris walked around with a half smile: controlled euphoria. "I was at peace that the boys finally finished the task we started in 2004," he said. "All of it came gushing back to me. My heart was full."

♾

Sometime later, I sat with Bill Aris on a brilliant morning at the Green Lakes pavilion, where every season began. Aris would come back to the park after Portland to meander the trails, sit at the picnic tables, and see the kids' faces, hear their voices, savor the spot where every Stotan youngster had listened and learned.

"When I ceased being interested in being liked in favor of being respected, I became a better coach," he said. Aris had to buck every trend, and break a few eggs as he liked to say, in helping kids to overcome what the columnist Roger Cohen called, "the incurable American excess."

While the Aris program seemed an overnight success when it emerged in 2004 with the dramatic Manhattan-meet boys' shutout of Christian Brothers Academy, it was actually years in the making: a tapestry of Aris's values learned from his humble upbringing, a work ethic embossed with marathon training in the Syracuse winter and principles developed during his assistant-coaching years when he first saw what could tickle teenagers and make them soar. "The 2014 NXN sweep," said Aris, "was a culmination of my journey not just as a runner and coach but as a man." It was a validation of all Aris held dear—humility, clean living, faith, and devotion to team ideals greater than oneself. "All these things rang loudly to me that season."

So did the recollection that, a decade earlier, Aris's upending of conventional wisdom almost didn't get off the ground. Had Andrew McCann, with his fancy threads, poison ivy, and bag of bananas, shown up just a little later to start the 2004 Stotan camp in the Adirondacks, Aris, demanding punctuality, would have packed everything up and told the other seven boys, "Sorry, I tried, but . . . let's go home." It was McCann of course who, nine weeks hence, ran his chops off to secure the record-breaking sweep at Van Cortlandt Park.

The camp, with its hard lessons and Percy Cerutty–style sandhill running, never would have worked had Aris, as a runner himself, not pushed to the limit, overcome weakness, and realized, "There's a place for you in this world if you're willing to dedicate yourself in every way." While training for the Boston Marathon on meager talent, Aris would run a hilly eighteen to twenty-four miles every Sunday and, midweek, after work, starving and exhausted, push himself out into the icy darkness for his second long run of the week, up to thirteen miles. Once back home, his two kids would break into laughter: daddy has icicles hanging off his beard.

If Aris made any discovery in his decade-long odyssey, it was that the teenage years did not have to be trivialized and dumbed down. Kids wanted more. When Aris gave them more, he discovered something else—"that average kids could do above-average things." The youngsters could elevate themselves, said Aris, because their governing strength was more than physical. "It was the heart and mind," said Aris. "*That* was the discovery."

The boys and girls would land on Aris's doorstep as confused and frightened teenagers, starting to see of the hazards of conformity, with zeal to be tapped, energy to expend. Jerry Lynch, the sport psychologist the team learned from, said it over and over, that kids wanted community, a connection, some meaning, an anchor. Aris himself was as unspoiled as the youngsters he invited into his separate society. He hadn't known otherwise as he saw, day by day, the dreamy, coltish runner, with a piquant charm, empowered by virtue.

"What Bill taught," said Nick Ryan, "is a good example of how you would want to lead your life."

Aris tinkered constantly with the right mix of dictate and tenderness. "Teaching," wrote Gilbert Highet, in his 1950 classic, *The Art of Teaching*, "is not like inducing a chemical reaction: it is much more like painting a picture or making a piece of music. . . . You must throw your heart into it."

Aris did. He could affect the course of the young and impressionable, like Samantha Levy. As a tenth-grade runner with a martial-arts black belt, Levy could still be lured by the high school crowd's superfluous social whirl, and looked the part. Bill, Sam, and her father had a meeting. Sam was reminded of her true self.

When her vulnerability passed, Levy would demonstrate, as they all would, innocence and warrior the same—poet warriors on the cross-country course who looked so right and powerful, one could ask . . . *perfect?* Levy used that term in looking back on the sweep of '14. "It seemed almost unreal," she said. "Completely perfect."

She thought back to her canvas of perfection. "Bill could be tough in practice, not giving in to our backing off in any way," said Levy. "But he also knew how to coach us outside of training. The whole enterprise was really personal. *That* was its power."

It was an opalescent and lasting power. Levy's grace and intellect eventually led her to Johns Hopkins University, where she would study political science, do research abroad, and run on the Blue Jays' NCAA Division 3 championship cross-country squad.

Since Levy's years at F-M, technology and its collateral damage in teens has gotten only worse, "diffusing their focus and energy," said Aris, and making it that much harder to enforce purity and suffering at Green Lakes. One recent season, he asked the girls' captains to give up social media in order to be good role models. They did. Another time, he asked the same of the varsity boys, all of them. Most acquiesced and, Aris said, "they found it liberating."

Never one to stand pat, Aris, prophetic enigma, has taken to daily reading of the Bible, both old and new testaments, as well as texts on Stoicism, for both a deeper understanding of himself and as a resource in which to cultivate an even richer erudition to meet the needs of kids today. He feels he travels on two parallel paths—secular from Cerutty, faith as a devout Christian—and that the two align with the same messages. "As a by-product," he said, "believe it or not,

I feel I'm a kinder, gentler person, less task oriented. Maybe that stems from wisdom, or getting older."

The teenage contradictions that will always confront Aris and Fayetteville-Manlius called to me in a disarming *New York Times Magazine* piece by Sam Anderson exploring the paradox of perfection. The article was based on the minute but paramount sculptural flaws in Michelangelo's *David*, on display at the Accademia in Florence. I had just come back from Florence with my wife. We'd gone to the *David*. To see the *David* was to witness something unfathomable, beyond the human. Anderson considered the work's newfound imperfections a metaphor for life and its scars.

What about the "perfect" runners from Fayetteville-Manlius? Was there some *David* in them? "Every one of our kids," said Aris, "was far from perfect. We accepted that. Could we become better together? You say to yourself, 'Is it perfection we're seeking?' Could it be that we achieved something beautiful despite our imperfections? Maybe that's a form of perfection."

I'd suggest that is what Annika Avery really meant when she said she was nervous at the start and nervous at the finish, waiting for the boys to "complete *it*." The team's *David* had to stand. Avery's "It" was more than the victory sweep but also affirmation that the runners' improbable quest to create something better was worth it. The kids had something of value, of wholeness and dignity, to try to protect and defend. And they did. At the same time they showed that they, girls and boys summoned from the unknown—that *they* were worthy of the effort, the *It*. They did not let themselves, or the idea, down.

"Is *it* worth it? Am *I* worth it?" Owen Kimple, one of the most heartfelt of Stotans, contemplated that idea as we sat on the dock of his family's summer cabin one day at Lake Bonaparte in the Adirondacks, where the F-M story was birthed. We talked before running some of the same trails his team did at camp in 2004. The lake was quiet except for the cries of loons. It was mating season.

Kimple said that while no one from his squad ever questioned the Aris mission, it had taken him years of reflection to understand how committed they all were to the same thing, and to each other. "It's still a huge part of our core," he told me. "All of us."

I reminded him of the day in October 2004, two months after camp when we sat together after the boys' breathtaking debut at Van Cortlandt Park: Owen, Jared Burdick, Bill, and me, on a bench near the finish line.

Then the boys spoke of love. Owen spoke of it now.

That's how they do it.

EPILOGUE I

HUMAN SACRIFICE
(2015)

D espite warnings from other runners that the Fayetteville girls trained too hard, Kaitlyn Neal, attending a high school an hour away from the Syracuse area, asked Bill Aris if she could join in F-M workouts over the summer. Aris agreed. Neal found she loved the team, the girls, the training, everything. With her father's job located in Syracuse, Kaitlyn and her family moved closer—right into the Fayetteville-Manlius school district, thus beginning a fateful union.

Neal, a senior, started winning race after race for the F-M team. She grew from a timid athlete to one with pride and confidence, on and off the racecourse. Before long, she was considered a state-championship contender and even a threat for nationals.

All along, there seemed to be a sisterly karma in how Neal wound up shining at F-M. At her old school, Neal was a good but not great runner. At F-M, embraced by empowered teammates, Neal's running was boundless. Among Neal's records was one for Stotan transformation. From her first summer strides she was hooked. "I never knew I was this strong," she told me, as though speaking for every F-M girl ever.

That strength was put to a test in midseason when on a morning run before school Neal was hit by a motorist and crashed to the ground. Several F-M hearts—notably that of a certain coach—stopped beating. But a hospital visit turned up only superficial bruises, and after a couple of days off, Neal was back running close to her old self.

At nationals, there was more talk than ever about challenges to the F-M girls' reign, again, by Great Oak of California, all the rage on social media. Some team supporters took to tweeting insults. The F-M camp said nothing.

Aris devised a race plan to subdue the challenge. He would have Neal race out too fast for her individual good, to try and draw out the California opposition, like a breakaway bike racer on a mountain pass. Neal welcomed the chance to offer this rose to her teammates for the welcome she'd received as a transfer. The plan worked. The California runners, going after Neal, fell back in exhaustion. Neal would fall back, too, but not until the last part of the race, placing fifteenth. When the scores were settled, Fayetteville girls won their ninth NXN championship in ten years by eighty-nine points. Great Oak took third, over one hundred points behind.

The F-M boys, with a revamped lineup after the senior-led 2014 triumph, struggled with the loss of their top runner, senior Peter Ryan, to injury. Ryan, who would go on to Yale, took on the role of an assistant coach with glee. In one dressing down of the boys, he ripped into them for a lackadaisical attitude and training in basketball shorts. Another time, in disgust, Ryan threw his watch on the ground and told the boys to do the same. "They thought I was psycho," said Ryan, "but it drew everyone together and made them more like 'men.'"

Inspired, the team of young talent ran perhaps its most heartfelt race ever at regionals, qualifying for nationals by a mere two points. Without their top gun and nothing left but pride, the F-M boys were in over their heads at NXN and finished well down in the field. Great Oak made up for its girls' disappointment with a boys-team championship by forty-nine points.

This fall season, Papa Bisson was missing from the Fayetteville lineup. He had died of cancer the prior spring. After Bisson had taken ill, the boys team would visit him at home and treat him to breakfast at Dave's Diner. One day, they presented him with a gift, an F-M racing singlet. Papa was a Stotan for eternity.

EPILOGUE II

EVERYONE ACCOUNTABLE
(2016)

After a tough practice, Rebecca Walters, a junior, took the wheel of the family car. Her sister, Claire, a freshman, would hop in. Their brother Joe, a senior, would make it three. And the Walters' kids, the latest of the pivotal Fayetteville-Manlius families, would moan and groan and delight in foxhole humor on the ride home. Every bump would bring a collective "o-o-o-o-h" as spent muscles would rebel with sibling unity. "We all shared in the same pain," said Claire. "I didn't have to go through it alone."

From her first strides as an eighth grader on the varsity the previous year, Claire showed that innocence could be leavened with maturity. Remarkably, she'd won the 2015 state championship over a who's who of future national headliners—Jessica Lawson, Kelsey Chmiel, and Katelyn Tuohy—and in F-M's ninth national-championship run placed twenty-fourth as the team's second scorer in Portland with a valuable low stick of eight team points.

Embracing team values, Claire welcomed being treated as "varsity," being held accountable and having to work for every inch of growth. "Once in high school, I felt so ready," she said of her freshman season in 2016. "I grew up fast and made big changes."

Claire's heady apprenticeship put her in a leadership position that season. Not that she had much to do. The top girls were solid from the outset. Bill Aris made sure they knew the stakes. The first five were unimpeachable, but after that a performance drop-off made the team vulnerable. A bad day here and there from any one girl could cause Stotan authority to crumble. "No bad days," Aris told them, in what became another team mantra. "Everyone accountable."

The girls were close like birds in flight as they mastered the long, arduous Campground Hill at Green Lakes, reaching the park's pinnacle, with the spectrum of central New York spread out before them. "It felt good to push through," said Claire. "It made us feel strong."

Claire led the team to victory in the Manhattan Eastern States at Van Cortlandt Park. Fayetteville placed 5-7-8-9-12 to triumph by over one hundred points. Claire placed fourth in a national-caliber state meet race as Fayetteville won with a scintillating 18:10 scoring average at Chenango Valley State Park. Then, in her best race of the fall, Claire ran third in the New York Regional in 17:59 at Bowdoin Park. Fayetteville romped to victory by seventy points as the team finished its preparation for Nike Cross Nationals.

The squad's mandate had not changed. Fayetteville's sixth runner at regionals was a full minute behind its fifth. There could be no lapses in Portland. At the California state meet, Great Oak had run better than ever with a 17:54 average time in capturing its fifth-straight title. The Wolfpack had an enviable thirty-six-second compression. They also had experience with four seniors in their top five.

Claire and Becca, along with freshman Phoebe White and juniors Palmer Madsen and Sophie Ryan, closed ranks as the NXN race shot out at Glendoveer Golf Course. All five ran toward the front of the pack, and at the one-mile checkpoint, Fayetteville led a stunned Great Oak by over one hundred points. Claire held position with the leaders—actually the lead chasers behind arm-churning Brie Oakley of Colorado, who amassed a commanding lead after two miles.

Oakley went on to win by twenty-eight seconds as all but three of the first thirty finishers were "individual" runners. Two of those three team scorers were Claire and Sophie. Among the next dozen team runners were Phoebe, Palmer, and Becca. Great Oak's first girl placed fifty-sixth for eighteen team points. The F-M girls had done the unthinkable: they *swept* Great Oak by placing all five scorers ahead of Great Oak's first; and Fayetteville outran the Californians by thirty-six seconds per girl and 144 points. The scores: Fayetteville 41, Davis of California, from the San Jose area, second with 181, and Great Oak third with 185.

It was an impressive day for the west. Bozeman (Montana) was boys champion, and Casey Clinger of runner-up American Fork (Utah) joined Oakley in a southwest regional individual sweep. Fayetteville boys, New York region winners by thirty-one points, could muster little Stotan gravitas and placed nineteenth.

The F-M girls had won their tenth national championship in eleven years. All five scorers would return for 2017. Becca: keep the motor running.

THEIR FINEST HOUR
(2017)

By the time the Fayetteville-Manlius girls arrived in Portland for the fourteenth Nike Cross Nationals, they had everything nip and tuck. They'd won another Manhattan Eastern States Championship with a record-low twenty-two points and record average time of 14:25.28 after an unprecedented 1-2-3 individual finish led by victorious Claire Walters. They'd won their twelfth-straight state title, by fifty-five points, with its top-four girls placing third, fourth, fifth, and sixth within eleven seconds. They'd won the New York Regional with the same 3-4-5-6 front-loaded rush. All the polls had Fayetteville in a national runaway.

Then, after lights out at the hotel on Thursday night, less than forty-eight hours before race time, Sophie Ryan, now in her senior year, got up, rushed to the bathroom, and "puked a ton." She started shivering and threw up six times. Claire Walters, sharing a bed with her, thought she would be next. Actually, her sister Becca would be next. The same night, Becca came down with strep throat. On Friday morning, on the bus ride back from checking out the course conditions at Glendoveer, Sophie vomited all over Becca.

"This has got to be a joke," said Claire, so far healthy and unvomited upon. "This can't be happening."

The two ill girls attempted to contain the damage. Sophie, as yet, hid her condition from Bill Aris while letting her parents know. Becca, likewise, kept things quiet. Her parents, who'd made the trip, were able to obtain medication for her.

Once Aris found out, he looked sick himself. He joked to the girls that "You're only doing this to commemorate the tenth anniversary of my collapse." Who could forget *that?* Now, what could Aris do? He took out his emergency first-aid: Churchill quotes. "Finest hour . . ." The coach had to be a wartime consigliere.

On Friday night, while the team had dinner on the Nike campus, Sophie stayed in her hotel room. When her parents, Pat and Tim, came to the hotel, they found Sophie "white, crying, and rolled up in a ball in bed." She had not been taking in fluids. She was lightheaded and passing out. Mom and Dad decided to get their daughter to the hospital.

This was around seven o'clock. Sophie lay in a hospital bed with her parents and F-M assistant coach Kyle Braziel at her side. Bill was with the team getting periodic reports. Sophie had food poisoning, maybe some bad chicken she'd eaten. For the next several hours, Sophie was given three IVs: for fluid replenishment, nutrient replenishment, and to calm nausea. She left the hospital at one A.M. and tried to get some sleep. Her ER doctor, a runner, was supportive. "I never thought I wouldn't run," said Sophie.

Saturday morning. Sophie. Becca. IVs. Antibiotics. A 5k racecourse. Bill's philosophical cupboard was bare. He told them, "If you don't give up on it, I won't."

A mother worried. "Sophie was ghostly white, extremely skinny," said Pat Ryan. Sophie showed some levity, telling Bill, "This is the first time all season I'm at my appropriate running weight."

The boys ran first. Oh, right . . . *the boys.* After rejoining the team in mid-season following cross-training while his fibula stress fracture healed, Garrett Brennan won the New York Regional in 15:55 as Fayetteville triumphed by forty-eight points. Brennan, a junior, had moved to Manlius from Maryland a year before. As a sophomore, after his first few F-M practices, Brennan was unable to walk up, or down, stairs.

With a nothing-to-lose camaraderie as a young team no one picked for the podium, the boys "ran out of their minds," as Brennan said, to startle the nation with a second-place finish. The favorite, Loudon Valley of Virginia, came through first with eighty-nine points. Fayetteville beat everyone else, scoring 159. Could this be a good omen for the girls?

Final insurance at the girls' start: WD-40 sprayed on the soles of shoes to assure easy liftoff. At the gun, a nervous Sophie slipped and fell. She got up spouting f-bombs. "It cleared my head," she said. Further up, on the opening straightaway, Becca had to stop and throw up her breakfast. After, she raced on.

Meanwhile, unknowing Claire along with Phoebe White secured excellent position among the first team runners. The individual title was a foregone conclusion. The spectacular New Yorker, North Rockland sophomore Katelyn Tuohy, rocketed ahead en route to a 16:45 victory by forty-five seconds. The F-M pair, also sophs, poured on all they had to place fifth and fifteenth, for two and five team points. Palmer Madsen struggled in midpack, putting more pressure on Sophie and Becca. Were they still on their feet?

The two-mile split times had Fayetteville in front with eighty-one points and Naperville North of the Chicago area, way back at the mile, closing in with 120. Sophie and Becca, denying weakness, trudged home gallantly in the top fifty overall for sixteen and twenty team points, respectively. Their times were about forty seconds off what they would have run healthy. "I did the best I could," said Sophie.

Waiting for the results, fourteen years of Stotan emotion welled up in Aris and the team. Soon the announcement came: Battle Mountain of Colorado third with 162 . . . Naperville North second with 94 . . . *Fayetteville-Manlius, winner for an eleventh time, with 89.*

Sophie Ryan. Four years, her last cross-country race. This was the girl who as a freshman ran on a torn-up ankle in 2014, the year of the sweep. "You take some hits in life," she told me. "It's just how you deal with it."

At the Saturday-night awards ceremony, in line with Nike casual, most girls came up on stage in jeans. The Fayetteville girls wore dresses.

POSTSCRIPT

As *Amazing Racers* was going to press, Fayetteville-Manlius continued its streak of qualifying for Nike Cross Nationals every year (boys or girls the first four years, then both for the last eleven years) since the event began in 2004—the only school to do so. On December 1, 2018, in Portland, Oregon, the F-M boys placed fifth at NXN while the girls took fourth. Fayetteville was named the event's top program for the seventh time by achieving the best combined performance for boys and girls squads. In thirteen NXN appearances, the F-M boys have now earned eight top-five finishers—one victory, three 2nds, one 3rd, two 4ths, and one 5th—the most by any boys team. The F-M girls national domination now stands at eleven victories, one 2nd and one 4th in the last thirteen years.

In fall 2018, the F-M girls started competition rated the third-best team in New York. With steady progress, the Stotans—after placing second at state by one point and second at NXN regionals by two points—went on to run their best race of the season at nationals. The F-M boys won the state Class A championship on Long Island with a course-record-breaking team performance. The boys also won the NXN New York Regional to earn their nationals berth.

In Portland, the Fayetteville boys lined up with Garrett Brennan (senior), Sam Otis (junior), Matthew Tripp (senior), Peyton Geehrer (sophomore), Yakob Kelley (freshman), Nolan Chiles (senior), and Geoff Howles (junior). Brennan led F-M as the seventh team scorer in the nationals field. The top five boys teams: 1. Repeat champion Loudon Valley (VA) 77 points; 2. Great

Oak (CA) 114; 3. Dakota Ridge (CO) 115; 4. Bishop Hendricken (RI) 206; *5. Fayetteville–Manlius (NY) 209.*

The F-M girls ran with Claire Walters (junior), Phoebe White (junior), Grace Kaercher (sophomore), Hannah Kaercher (eighth grader), Chloe Bullough (senior), Lejla Borcilo (sophomore), and Emily Cook (senior). The top five girls teams: 1. Summit (OR) 120; 2. Naperville North (IL) 186; 3. Wayzata (MN) 207; *4. Fayetteville-Manlius (NY) 212*; 5. Niwot (CO) 219.

Walters placed fifth in the country and was the second team runner across the line, to lead Fayetteville. When Walters competed, she had the following message inscribed on her arm, expounded by coach Bill Aris in the team's predawn shake-out run on the morning of the race: Love the pain. Seek "The White Moment.'"

The Last Word

On April 25, 2019, almost five months after leading the F-M girls at Nike Cross Nationals, Claire Walters ran a sensational anchor 1600 meters at the 125th Penn Relays in Philadelphia to deliver a team victory in the Distance Medley Relay, the Carnival's signature high school event. After receiving the baton in eighth place, Walters rallied from 70 meters behind as Fayetteville-Manlius triumphed by 25 meters at Franklin Field. Walters's split time, 4:43.34, was one of the meet's fastest ever in the event. She was preceded by Phoebe White on the leadoff 1200 (3:40.27), Fiona Merjico in the 400 (60.41) and Susan Bansbach in the 800 (2:21.27). It was F-M's third Penn Relays distance medley victory in three attempts. The boys won in 2006; the girls won prior in 2011. Fayetteville is one of only two schools to win both boys and girls distance medley titles at Penn.

APPENDIX I

FAYETTEVILLE-MANLIUS AND NIKE CROSS NATIONALS

The F-M girls have won eleven of the last thirteen national championships.

Girls Team		Points Scored	Victory Margin	Time Margin
2004	did not qualify.		Winning Team: Saratoga Springs (NY)	
2005	did not qualify.		Winning Team: Hilton (NY)	
2006	1st	128	50 points	14 seconds per scorer
2007	1st	83	88 points	22 seconds per scorer
2008	1st	66	69 points	23 seconds per scorer
2009	1st	74	73 points	28 seconds per scorer
2010	1st	27	77 points	59 seconds per scorer
2011	1st	60	24 points	14 seconds per scorer
2012	1st	54	144 points	43 seconds per scorer
2013	2nd	120	*2nd by 12 points to Wayzata (MN)*	
2014	1st	70	79 points	12 seconds per scorer
2015	1st	55	89 points	28 seconds per scorer
2016	1st	41	140 points	36 seconds per scorer
2017	1st	89	5 points	2 seconds per scorer
2018	4th	212	*Bend (OR) wins with 120 points*	

The F-M boys have the most podium finishes of any school: five.

Boys Team		Points Scored	Winning Team
2004	2nd	127	York (IL) 92, by 35
2005	3rd*	134	Saratoga Springs (NY) 111, by 23
2006	did not qualify.		Coatesville (PA) 126, by 22
2007	did not qualify.		Neuqua Valley (IL) 125, by 2
2008	16th	314	North Central (WA) 134, by 17
2009	9th	270	Boerne (TX) 195, by 6
2010	2nd	135	Arcadia (CA) 92, by 43
2011	12th	304	Christian Brothers (NJ) 91, by 4
2012	16th	372	Arcadia (CA) 108, by 14
2013	4th	216	Gig Harbor (WA) 111, by 28
2014	1st	111	Fayetteville-Manlius (NY) 111, by 48
2015	21st	425	Great Oak (CA) 114, by 49
2016	19th	349	Bozeman (MT) 105, by 36
2017	2nd	159	Loudon Valley (VA) 89, by 70
2018	5th	209	Loudon Valley (VA), 77, by 37

Second in a tie, third on tiebreaker

APPENDIX II

WHERE THE STOTANS ARE NOW (AS OF OCTOBER 2018)

There have been eighty-three athletes who competed for Fayetteville-Manlius at Nike Cross Nationals from 2004 through 2017. They are listed with their NXN years, college information, and, for many, their current line of work.

Jonathan Abbott: 2014
In his senior year at Colgate University, running track and cross-country, an English major.

Meagan Anklin: 2008
Boston College '13 graduate, ran track and cross-country. Works in wealth management in the Boston area.

Annika Avery: 2011, 2012, 2013, 2014
In her senior year at University of California, Berkeley, ran briefly. Studying vector-borne diseases.

Kyle Barber: 2013, 2014
In his senior year at the University of Connecticut, running track and cross-country. Studying geoscience including global warming.

Mary Barger: 2012
In her senior year at Cornell, running track and cross-country. Studying in the college of arts and sciences.

Charlie Beeler: 2012
SUNY–Cortland '17 graduate, ran track and cross-country.

Andrew Bergé: 2013
University at Buffalo '18 graduate, ran track and cross-country. Doing a master's in accounting at Buffalo.

Eric Billinson: **2010**
SUNY–Albany '15 graduate, ran track and cross-country.

Garrett Brennan: **2017**
In his senior year at Fayetteville-Manlius.

Jack Boltman: **2015, 2016**
Attends St. Bonaventure University, running track and cross-country, political science major.

Katie Brislin: **2010, 2011, 2012**
Started college at Villanova, ran track and cross-country, transferred to Le Moyne College in Syracuse '18 graduate.

Kathryn Buchan: **2006, 2007, 2008**
Cornell University '13 graduate, ran track and cross-country, studied in the college of agriculture and life sciences, living and working in the Syracuse area.

Kristen Buchan: **2007**
Wake Forest '13 graduate, ran track and cross-country, living and working in the Syracuse area.

Jared Burdick: **2004**
Rochester Institute of Technology '09 graduate, ran track and cross-country. Electrical engineer living in central New York. Married, ultramarathoner who's run Western States 100-miler.

Eli Capri: **2016**
In his senior year at Fayetteville-Manlius.

Catie Caputo: **2006**
Georgetown University '11 graduate, played on the Hoyas' lacrosse team. Studied in school of foreign service, law degree from Emory University School of Law '18, MBA from Emory business school '18.

Mackenzie Carter: **2006, 2007, 2008, 2009**
SUNY–Albany '15 graduate, ran track and cross-country. Works in the creative field in central New York.

Alexandra Chapman: **2008**
Bucknell University '13 graduate, ran track and cross-country. Master's in education at Lehigh, currently pre-K teacher and administrator in Boulder.

Courtney Chapman: **2006, 2007, 2008, 2009, 2010**
Villanova '15 graduate, ran track and cross-country. Lives in Brooklyn, works in New York in finance.

John Cico: **2008**
Emerson College '13 graduate, ran cross-country (the school has no track program).

Matt Deyo: **2011**
Massachusetts Institute of Technology '16 graduate, ran track and cross-country. Master's in computer science from MIT. Working in aerospace engineering and vehicle autonomy engineering in California.

Michelle Duffy: **2012**
Syracuse University '18 graduate, ran track and cross-country, majored in biology.

Jack Duncanson: **2017**
Freshman at St. Bonaventure University, running track and cross-country.

Jillian Fanning: 2009, 2010, 2011, 2012
Providence College '17 graduate, ran track and cross-country. Doing a master's in school counseling at Providence.

Brendan Farrell: 2008, 2009
Iona College '14 graduate, ran track and cross-country, studied finance. Lives in Queens, works in New York in the technology field.

Connor Farrell: 2012
SUNY–Oneonta '17 graduate, ran track and cross-country, majored in human biology.

Jenna Farrell: 2011, 2012, 2013, 2014, 2015
Attends Columbia University, running track and cross-country.

Colin FitzGibbons: 2011, 2012
Michigan State '17 graduate, lives in Watertown, NY, works in demand forecasting for air freshener company.

Luke FitzGibbons: 2005
University of Rochester '11 graduate, ran one season, mechanical engineering degree, lives in Fayetteville, holds senior position at engineering firm in central New York.

Bryan Geehrer: 2015
Attends Edinboro University, running track and cross-country, sports and recreation administration major.

Peyton Geehrer: 2017
In his sophomore year at Fayetteville-Manlius.

Tommy Gruenewald: 2004, 2005
Brigham Young University '14 graduate, ran track and cross-country. Furnishing consultant for retail chain in the Syracuse area. Married with one child.

Joseph Hartnett: 2008, 2009
Fordham University '14 graduate, ran track and cross-country, biological sciences major. Studying to be a physician at SUNY–Upstate Medical University in Syracuse.

Alex Hatz: 2008
University of Wisconsin '15 graduate, ran track and cross-country. Lives in Austin, Texas, works in sales and marketing for a natural food company.

Jessica Hauser: 2006
Brigham Young University '11 graduate, ran track and cross-country. Lives in Utah, married with three children, has her own business.

John Heron: 2004, 2005
Coastal Carolina '11 graduate, ran track and cross-country. Manager with Dale Carnegie company in Jacksonville, Florida.

Hillary Hooley: 2006
Colgate University '11 graduate, ran track and cross-country. Lives in New York City, works in merchandising.

Jessica Howe: 2013, 2014
In her senior year at Marist College, running track and cross-country.

Geoff Howles: 2017
In his junior year at Fayetteville-Manlius.

Riley Hughes: 2012, 2013, 2014
Attends Marist College, running track and cross-country.

Adam Hunt: 2012, 2013, 2014
Attends University at Buffalo, running track and cross-country, history major, involved in ROTC.

Grace Kaercher: 2017
In her sophomore year at Fayetteville-Manlius.

Owen Kimple: 2004, 2005
Cornell '10 graduate, ran track and cross-country. Did a semester abroad in Australia. Lives in Brooklyn, works in real estate.

Geoff King: 2004, 2005
North Carolina State University '10 graduate, ran track and cross-country. Lives in Brooklyn, works in finance.

Samantha Levy: 2013, 2014, 2015
Attends Johns Hopkins University, runs track and cross-country, member of NCAA III championship cross-country team.

Hannah Luber: 2007, 2008, 2009
University of Iowa graduate '14. Did a semester abroad in Fiji. Teaching and coaching cross-country in Costa Rica after a teaching stint in Guatemala.

Palmer Madsen: 2015, 2016, 2017
In her freshman year at the University of Dayton, running track and cross-country.

Reilly Madsen: 2013, 2014, 2016
Attends University of Dayton, running track and cross-country, majoring in exercise science.

Molly Malone: 2006, 2007, 2008, 2009
Syracuse University '14 graduate, ran track and cross-country, studied design. Master's degree in fine arts from Boston University. Works in community and brand development at Tracksmith.

Michael Malone: 2011
Site manager at a landscaping firm in the Syracuse area.

Dan Marnell: 2004, 2005
Lehigh '10 graduate, earned a PhD in bioengineering from University of Rochester in 2018.

Heather Martin: 2009, 2010
Georgetown '16 graduate, ran track and cross-country. Doing graduate work in business at Georgetown.

Andrew McCann: 2004, 2005
University of Massachusetts–Amherst '10 graduate, ran track and cross-country. New Balance account manager based in Atlanta.

Emily McGurrin: **2010**
Brown University '16 graduate, ran track and cross-country. Works in technology field in New York City.

Mark McGurrin: **2009, 2010**
Brown University '15 graduate, ran track and cross-country. Studied brew mastery in England.

Megan Menz: **2013**
Attends Nazareth College, running track and cross-country, early-education major.

Paul Merriman: **2009**
University of Massachusetts–Amherst '14 graduate, ran track and cross-country, business major.

Bryce Millar: **2013, 2014, 2015**
Attends Indiana University Bloomington, running track and cross-country.

Kaitlyn Neal: **2015**
Attends the University of Washington, running track and cross-country.

Ben Otis: **2015, 2016, 2017**
Freshman at Manhattan College, running track and cross-country.

Sam Otis: **2017**
In his junior year at Fayetteville-Manlius.

Alana Pearl: **2012, 2013, 2014**
University of Connecticut '18 graduate, ran track and cross-country. Doing a master's in school counseling at University of Massachusetts–Boston.

Max Perry: **2015**
In his senior year at Fayetteville-Manlius.

Patrick Perry: **2013, 2015, 2016**
Attends Yale University, running track and cross-country.

Jocelyn Richards: **2007**
Brown University '12 graduate. Living in Syracuse area working as a journalist specializing in China after living in China for many years.

Andrew Roache: **2008, 2009, 2010**
Syracuse University '15 graduate, ran track and cross-country Has master's in history from SUNY–Binghamton and master's in library science from Syracuse. Works as a law librarian.

Christie Rutledge: **2010**
University of Miami '18 graduate, competing in triathlons. Working at University of Miami Hospital Physical Therapy Clinic while applying to medical school.

Nick Ryan: **2010, 2011, 2012**
Syracuse University '17 graduate, ran track and cross-country. Doing graduate work in education at Lewis & Clark College.

Olivia Ryan: **2014**
Started college at SUNY–Geneseo, ran track and cross-country, transferred to SUNY–Buffalo State, now in her senior year, running cross-country and majoring in fine arts.

Peter Ryan: 2013, 2014
Attends Yale University, running track and cross-country.

Sophie Ryan: 2014, 2015, 2016, 2017
Freshman at the University of Utah, running track and cross-country.

Katie Sischo: 2009, 2010, 2011
Providence College '16 graduate, ran track and cross-country. Works in development at MIT Sloan School of Management.

Hannah Smith: 2011
SUNY–Albany '16 graduate, ran track and cross-country. Lives in Bethesda, Maryland, working in commercial real estate.

Owen Strong: 2009
SUNY–Albany '15 graduate, ran track and cross-country, business major.

Ben Thomas: 2009, 2010, 2011
University of Massachusetts–Amherst '16 graduate, ran track and cross-country, psychology major.

Matthew Tripp: 2016, 2017
In his senior year at Fayetteville-Manlius.

Andrew Veilleux: 2008, 2010
University of Buffalo '15 graduate, ran one year, lives in Virginia, works as customer development manager.

Alex Villalba: 2016, 2017
Freshman at Fairfield University, running track and cross-country.

Claire Walters: 2015, 2016, 2017
In her junior year at Fayetteville-Manlius.

Joseph Walters: 2014, 2015, 2016
Worked for AmeriCorps in Flagstaff, Arizona, now works for a property-management firm in upstate New York.

Rebecca Walters: 2015, 2016, 2017
Freshman at Marist College, running track and cross-country.

Jules Wellner: 2010
SUNY–College of Environmental Science and Forestry '15, ran track and cross-country.

Phoebe White: 2016, 2017
In her junior year at Fayetteville-Manlius.

BIBLIOGRAPHY

Anderson, Bob, and Joe Henderson. *The Varied World of Cross Country*. Mountain View, California: Runner's World Publishing, 1971.

Anderson, Sam. "David's Ankles," *New York Times Magazine*, August 21, 2016.

Askwith, Richard. *Today We Die a Little: The Inimitable Emil Zátopek, The Greatest Olympic Runner of All Time*. New York: Nation Books, 2016.

Auster, Paul. *4 3 2 1: A Novel*. New York: Henry Holt & Company, 2017.

Badiou, Alain. *The True Life*. Malden, Massachusetts: Polity Press, 2017.

Barnum, Art. "Teens Who Burned Down $1M Home Sentenced," *Chicago Tribune*, September 8, 2006.

Barron, James. "Amateur Historian Says a City Park's Vast Expanse Is a Half-Acre Too Much," *New York Times*, May 29, 2018.

Batuman, Elif. "How to Be a Stoic," *The New Yorker*, December 19/26, 2016.

"Big and Little Stars of the Popular Cross Country Sport Now at Height of Its Season," *New York Times*, December 8, 1907.

Bloom, Marc. "Girls Cross Country Taking a Heavy Toll," *New York Times*, December 4, 1993.

Bloom, Marc. *God on the Starting Line*. Halcottsville, New York: Breakaway Books, 2004.

Bloom, Marc. *Cross Country Running*. Mountain View, California: World Publications, 1978.

Bloom, Marc. Marlboro, New Jersey: *Harrier Cross Country Magazine*, 1974–1978, 1989–2011.

Bloom, Marc. "In the Bronx, A Century of Mud, Sweat and Tears, *New York Times*, October 13, 2012.

Bloom, Marc. "Olympic Moment: Herb Elliott Obliterates the Competition in the 1500 Meters," *Runner's World*, August 2004.

Bloom, Marc. "Track and Field: Florida's Fashion Statement," *New York Times*, January 10, 1996.

Bloom, Marc. "High School Girls: Are Your Ferritin Levels Up to Speed?" *Running Times*, December 2013.

Bloom, Marc. "Why Are These Teens So Fast?" *Running Times*, May 2014.

Brown, Daniel James. *The Boys in the Boat: Nine Americans and Their Epic Quest for Gold at the 1936 Olympics*. New York: Viking Penguin, 2013.

Cerutty, Percy. *How to Become a Champion*. London: Stanley Paul and Company, 1960.

Collins, Jim C. *Good to Great: Why Some Companies Make the Leap . . . and Others Don't*. New York: Harper Collins, 2001.

Connery, Dan. "The Amazing Herb Elliott," *Sports Illustrated*, November 10, 1958.

Cousineau, Phil. *The Olympic Odyssey: Rekindling the Spirit of the Great Games*. Wheaton, Illinois: Quest Books, 2003.

Cousins, Norman. *Anatomy of an Illness*. New York: W. W. Norton and Company, 1979.

Chungliang, Al Huang, and Jerry Lynch. *Thinking Body, Dancing Mind: TaoSports for Extraordinary Performance in Athletics, Business, and Life*. New York: Bantam Books, 1992.

Cowley, Geoffrey, and Sharon Begley. "Fat for Life: Six Million Kids Are Seriously Overweight," *Newsweek*, July 3, 2000.

Damour, Lisa. *Untangled: Guiding Teenage Girls Through the Seven Transitions into Adulthood*. New York: Ballantine Books, 2016.

Dent, Jim. *The Junction Boys: How Ten Days in Hell with Bear Bryant Forged a Championship Team*. New York: St. Martin's Griffin, 2000.

Epstein, Robert. "Everything You Know About the Teen Brain Is Wrong," *Brandeis Magazine*, Summer 2015.

Eskenazi, Gerald. "Title IX Rules Issued for Equality in Sports," *New York Times*, June 3, 1972.

Fitzgerald, Matt. *How Bad Do You Want It? Mastering the Psychology of Mind Over Muscle*. Boulder, Colorado: Velo Press, 2015.

Fitzgerald, Matt. *Brain Training for Runners: A Revolutionary New Training System to Improve Endurance, Speed, Health, and Results*. New York: New American Library, 2007.

Frankl, Viktor E. *Man's Search for Meaning*. Boston: Beacon Press, 1959.

Friedman, Richard A. "Why Teenagers Act Crazy," *New York Times*, June 29, 2014.

Genzlinger, Neil. "Ira Berlin, 77, Historian Whose Books Upended Notions of Slavery, Dies," *New York Times*, June 9, 2018.

Gibbs, Nancy. "Being 13," *Time*, August 8, 2005.

Gopnik, Adam. "The Parenting Paradox," *The New Yorker*, January 29, 2018.

Grady, Denise. "Operation for Obesity Leaves Some in Misery," *New York Times*, May 4, 2004.

Greene, Robert. *Mastery*. New York: Viking, 2012.

Haikkola, Rolf, and Antero Raevuori. *Lasse Viren: Olympic Champion*. Portland, Oregon: Continental Publishing, 1978.

Hannus, Matti. *Finnish Running Secrets*. Mountain View, California: World Publications, 1973.

Highet, Gilbert. *The Art of Teaching*. New York: Random House, 1950.

Hilburn, Robert. *Paul Simon: The Life*. New York: Simon & Schuster, 2018.

Hillenbrand, Laura. *Unbroken: A World War II Story of Survival and Redemption*. New York: Random House, 2010.

Hutchinson, Alex. "What Is Fatigue?" *The New Yorker*, December 12, 2014.

Hutchinson, Alex. "How Trees Calm Us Down," *The New Yorker*, July 23, 2015.

Hutchinson, Andrew Boyd. *The Complete History of Cross Country Running: From the Nineteenth Century to the Present Day*. New York: Carrell Books, 2018.

Jensen, Frances E., MD, with Amy Ellis Nutt. *The Teenage Brain: A Neuroscientist's Survival Guide to Raising Adolescents and Young Adults*. New York: Harper Collins, 2015.

King, Perry. "The Starting Line: How One Meeting in Schenectady Changed XC Forever," Milesplit.com, July 6, 2015.

Kipling, Rudyard. *The Second Jungle Book*. New York: Macmillan Publishing, 1895.

Kirsch, Adam. "Tales of the Tribe," *The New Yorker*, March 26, 2018.

Knight, Phil. *Shoe Dog: A Memoir by the Creator of Nike*. New York: Scribner, 2016.

Kolbert, Elizabeth. "The Terrible Teens," *The New Yorker*, August 31, 2015.

Lane, Daniel. "Herb Elliott Motivated by Pursuit of Perfection Not Cash or Glory," *Sydney Morning Herald*, February 23, 2014.

Lenton, Brian. *Off the Record*. Canberra, Australia: Brian Lenton Publications, 1981.

Levine, Madeline. *The Price of Privilege: How Parental Pressure and Material Advantage Are Creating a Generation of Disconnected and Unhappy Kids*. New York: Harper, 2006.

Lydiard, Arthur, and Garth Gilmour. *Running the Lydiard Way*. Cleveland: World Publishing, 1978.

Marquez, Gábriel García. *Love in the Time of Cholera*. New York: Knopf, 1985.

Marquez, Gábriel García. *I'm Not Here to Give a Speech*. New York: Vintage International, 2019.

Merrill, Sam. "Zátopek: Then and Now," *The Runner*, December 1979.

Moriello, John. "Federation Cross Country Meet Cancelled Due to Weather," *New York State Sportswriters Association Newsletter*, November 16, 2018.

Nelson, Cordner, and Roberto Quercetani. *Runners and Racers: 1500 meters/Mile*. Los Altos, California: Tafnews Press, 1973.

Newton, Joe, and Karl Schindl. *The Long Green Line*. Oak Brook, Illinois: All American Publishing, 1969.

Noakes, Timothy. *Lore of Running*. Cape Town: Oxford University Press, 1985.

Parfit, Derek. *Reasons and Persons*. Oxford, England: Oxford University Press, 1984.

Pérez-Peña, Richard. "Obesity on Rise in New York Public Schools," *New York Times*, July 9, 2003.

Pigliucci, Massimo. *How to Be a Stoic: Ancient Wisdom for Modern Living*. New York: Basic Books, 2017.

Postman, Neil. *Amusing Ourselves to Death*. London: Methuen Publishing, 1985.

"Public Schools Athletic League of New York City High School Cross Country Championship," *New York Times*, December 5, 2008.

Putnam, Robert D. *Bowling Alone: The Collapse and Revival of American Community*. New York: Simon & Schuster, 2000.

Richards, Keith. *Life*. New York, Little, Brown & Co., 2010.

Ripley, Amanda. "Can Teenage Defiance Be Manipulated for Good," *New York Times*, September 13, 2016.

Robinson, Marilynne. *Gilead*. New York: Farrar, Strauss, Giroux, 2004.

Rosenblatt, Roger. "Time Is, Time Was," *New York Times Book Review*, February 25, 2018.

Salinger, J. D. *The Catcher in the Rye*. New York: Little, Brown & Co., 1951.

Segal, David. "After 38 Medals, Norway Feels Stress of Success," *New York Times*, February 25, 2018.

Sheehan, George, MD. *Running & Being: The Total Experience*. New York: Simon & Schuster, 1978.

Sillitoe, Alan. *The Loneliness of the Long-Distance Runner*. New York: Signet/New American Library, 1959.

Sims Graem. *Why Die? The Extraordinary Percy Cerutty, Maker of Champions*. Cambridge, Massachusetts: Star Bright Books, 2003.

Smith, Gary. "An Exclusive Club," *Sports Illustrated*, June 27, 1994.

Snell, Peter, and Garth Gilmour. *No Bugles, No Drums*. London: Minerva, 1965.

Squires, Bill, and Bruce Lehane. *Speed with Endurance*. Boston: Boston University Press, 2009.

Thoreau, Henry David. *Walden; Or, Life in the Woods*. Boston: Ticknor and Fields, 1854.

Tough, Paul. *How Children Succeed: Grit, Curiosity, and the Hidden Power of Character*. New York: Houghton Mifflin Harcourt, 2012.

Tucker, Jonathan B. "Pain: Why It Hurts," *The Runner*, February 1980.

Vecsey, George. "Lost Boy of Sudan Chases His American Dream," *New York Times*, May 31, 2007.

Vlasov, Yuri. *The White Moment*. 1972.

Walls, Laura Dassow. *Henry David Thoreau: A Life*. Chicago: University of Chicago Press, 2018.

Walker, Sam. *The Captain Class: The Hidden Force That Creates the World's Greatest Teams*. New York: Random House, 2017.

Weil, Elizabeth. "Growing Up Fast," *New York Times Magazine*, March 8, 2015.

Wilentz, Sean. *Bob Dylan in America*. New York: Doubleday, 2010.

Wood, James, and Karl Ove Knausgaard. "Writing *My Struggle*: An Exchange," *The Paris Review*, Winter, 2014.

Yalouris, Nicolaos. *The Eternal Olympics: The Art and History of Sport*. New Rochelle, New York: Caratzas Publishers, 1976.

York, Michelle. "12 Year Term Given to Man Who Tried to Seize Girl," *New York Times*, July 13, 2006.

York, Michelle. "High Schools Crack Down: Dance Nice or Not at All," *New York Times*, December 17, 2006.

FILM REFERENCES

300. Zack Snyder, director. Paramount, 2007.

A Bronx Tale. Robert DeNiro, director. TriBeCa Productions, 1993.

Ben-Hur. William Wyler, director. MGM, 1959.

Cast Away. Robert Zemeckis, director. 20th Century Fox, 2000.

Chariots of Fire. Hugh Hudson, director. Warner Bros., 1981.

Dead Poets Society. Peter Weir, director. Touchstone Pictures, 1989.

Deliverance. John Boorman, director. Warner Bros., 1972.

Godfather II. Francis Ford Coppola, director. Paramount, 1974.

Goodfellas. Martin Scorsese, director. Warner Bros., 1990.

In the Heat of the Night. Norman Jewison, director. United Artists, 1967.

Miracle on Ice. Gavin O'Connor, director. Walt Disney Pictures, 2004.

Rocky III. Sylvester Stallone, director. United Artists, 1982.

Seinfeld. Season 4, Episode 16, "The Shoes," 1993.

The French Connection. William Friedkin, director. 20th Century Fox, 1971.

The Fugitive. Andrew Davis, director. Warner Bros., 1993.

ACKNOWLEDGMENTS

I am indebted to the collaboration of Bill Aris, the Fayetteville-Manlius coach, who opened his heart and mind for more than fifty hours of conversation about his team, the athletes, and his attempt at profound change in teenage running. We spoke at his training sites in the Syracuse area, at track and cross-country meets, and by phone.

Bill's abundant strengths came through, and, as with anyone, his vulnerabilities too. Rarely have I engaged with anyone whose breadth of knowledge spanned everything from psychology and philosophy to history and art, not to mention all things running and especially the runner's full immersion in pain and how to embrace it. As Bill would say, leaning on the operatic nuggets of a certain favorite film, "We took care of all family business."

Bill's ability to weave the finer threads of a youngster's development, while never losing sight of the big picture, was passed on to his son, John, who helped to burnish key passages in his capacity as an assistant coach for six years and, of course, as his father's confidant. John could have been a head coach at any program.

So, too, am I thankful to the dozens of former F-M athletes (and a few still on the team at the time) who shared their experiences with me. When we spoke (sometimes in person, other times by phone or via email) most of the young men and women were out in the world working, and a few were married with children. Many were in college. Their voices—perceptive, insightful, rich with emotion and weight—at times made me shudder. It was bracing to find how deeply they could go in their understanding, with the distance of time, of the wonder in what they encountered and the impenitent complexities of growing up; to this day, these young people cherish what was bequeathed to them.

I spoke with many athletes more than once, a few even four or five times.

These are the young people who entrusted their stories to me: Meagan Anklin, Annika Avery, Kyle Barber, Andrew Bergé, Garrett Brennan, Katie Brislin, Jared Burdick, Mackenzie Carter, Courtney Chapman, Matt Deyo, Brendan Farrell, Jillian Fanning, Jenna Farrell, Tommy Gruenewald, Alex Hatz, Jessica (Hauser) Eraso, John Heron, Hilary Hooley, Riley Hughes, Adam Hunt, Owen Kimple, Geoff King, Samantha Levy, Hannah Luber, Molly Malone, Dan Marnell, Heather Martin, Andrew McCann, Mark McGurrin, Bryce Millar, Kaitlyn Neal, Alana Pearl, Christie Rutledge, Nick Ryan, Olivia Ryan, Peter Ryan, Sophie Ryan, Katie Sischo, Kristin (Taylor) Beilein, Ben Thomas, and Claire Walters. *(Bryce Millar and Olivia Ryan's comments were from earlier interviews for magazine stories.)*

Special thanks to Christie Rutledge for her courage in attempting to help others with a frank discussion of her eating issues in chapters 17 and 18. And, as well, to Owen Kimple, whose delightful account of his semester abroad in Australia grew into its own chapter, 14. Owen wore many hats for this project. He was also my tour guide and running partner at his family's cottage in the Adirondacks where the "Amazing Racers" story began.

Another multi-hat collaborator was Marnie Carter: team parent (of Mackenzie), assistant coach for a number of years, and team photographer whose work graces the front and back covers and inside photo section. Marnie's contributions were invaluable.

On the coaching side, Dave Davis, a longtime F-M assistant, helped unearth some long lost stories important to the narrative. On the photo side, inside section shots by John Nepolitan, Don Rich and Victor Sailer add historical recognition. My younger daughter, Jamie, a professional photographer in her own right, deserves a big hug for making me look good on the back flap. Hugs, too, to older daughter Allison (whose running ranges from the Colgate Women's Games to the New York City Marathon) and all family for their love, laughter, and devilish pokes at my alleged idiocyncracies.

Among team parents, Molly Malone's father, Peter, and Patricia Ryan, whose four youngsters (Nick, Olivia, Peter, Sophie) all ran for the team, provided insights and anecdotes. Many thanks as well to Owen Kimple's parents, Jim and Emily, for their hospitality at idyllic Lake Bonaparte when my wife,

Andrea, and I came up to visit. *(Earlier conversations for magazine purposes with Courtney Chapman's and Christie Rutledge's moms were also included in the story.)*

Appreciation to these former or current high school coaches who provided pertinent ideas and recollections: Dan Dougherty of Pearl River (New York), Dave Emmons of Wayzata (Minnesota), Tom Heath of Christian Brothers Academy (New Jersey), Mark Lacianca of Unionville (Pennsylvania), Justin Leonard of Southlake Carroll (Texas), Stan Morgan of Midlothian (VA), Rene Paragas of Saugus (California), Mike Sczcepanik of Hilton (New York), and Corbin Talley of Davis (Utah). Also: Martin Keino of Kenya, a coach, businessman, former world-class runner, and son of Kip Keino.

Gratitude to these experts in their fields who helped elucidate essential concepts: Dr. Kate Berg, a physician specializing in the care of young, female athletes; Lisa Damour, PhD, a psychologist and author who counsels teenage girls; Jerry Lynch, PhD, a sports psychologist and author who has advised numerous athletes and teams; and the exercise physiologist and coach Jeffrey I. Messer, PhD, of Arizona, who chairs the Mesa Community College Exercise Science Department.

Many former high school stars who competed against Fayetteville gave generously of their time: Eric Dettman of York (Illinois), now a high school coach in Portland, Oregon; Serviceman Chris Horel of Christian Brothers Academy (New Jersey); Rachel Johnson of Plano (Texas), now a professional; Greg Kiley of Saratoga Springs (New York); Nick Kuczwara of York (Illinois), Sean McNamara of York (Illinois), and Steve Murdock of Saratoga Springs and Shenendehowa (New York). I am also grateful to Ashley Higginson of Colts Neck (New Jersey) and Princeton University—and then the professional ranks—who shared her experience. Higginson is practicing law in New Jersey.

Key personnel from various periods of service with Nike Cross Nationals shared recollections: NXN co-founder Josh Rowe, now at Tracksmith; National Scholastic Athletics Foundation CEO Jim Spier; original course designer Paul Limmer of the NSAF; and current course manager Ryan Canning.

I would like to cite Tullyrunners.com and its chief, Bill Meylan, for indispensable archival results from New York and beyond. Other support was provided by ultra-marathoner Chris Raulli, webmaster and photo editor of amazingracersbook.com, and F-M uber-fan Bruce Laidlaw of Syracuse, whose humanitarian spirit is infectious.

My agent, Laurie Fox of the Linda Chesler Literary Agency, was fervently taken in by the Fayetteville-Manlius tale and provided wise counsel throughout.

Jessica Case, deputy publisher of Pegasus Books, brought the story to fruition with a gentle touch and her own athletic sensibilities. Both have been delightful to work with.

Also in the book's corner from the beginning were the running pioneer Kathy Mills Parker and her husband, Mark Parker, the Nike CEO. Bill Aris and I have shared many good times with the Parkers on NXN weekend in Portland.

Seeking to experience as much as I could of the F-M training landscape, I tried to run with the girls' team one day at Green Lakes (that was pretty funny) and, another day, tackled the notorious Gulf Road hill, 1.5 miles straight up (not as funny), with Bill at my side in the "sag wagon." Inspired by the Stotan footprints of runners past, I managed to make it to the top in one piece.

I probably would never have made it to Syracuse without my wife Andrea's guidance during GPS malfunctions. And I probably would never have gotten this book done without her. Andi, while in peak shape for a woman of a certain age, admits to being no great cross-country fan. But with Andi on my arm through thick and thin, fifty years and counting, great things happen.

Marc Bloom
Princeton, New Jersey
May, 2019